DOCUMENTS OF AMERICAN THEATER HISTORY

DOCUMENTS OF AMERICAN THEATER HISTORY

Volume 2

Famous American Playhouses

1900-1971

William C. Young

American Library Association, Chicago 1973

Library of Congress Cataloging in Publication Data

Young, William C   1928–
  Famous American playhouses, 1900–1971.

  (His Documents of American theater history, v. 2)
  Bibliography: p.
  1. Theaters—United States—History. 2. Theater—
United States—History. I. Title.
NA6830.Y68   792′.0973   73–657
ISBN 0–8389–0137–9

International Standard Book Number 0–8389–0137–9 (1973)

Library of Congress Catalog Card Number 73–657

  Printed in the United States of America

Contents

Illustrations

facing page

facing page

facing page

Famous American Playhouses
1900-1971

Chapter 1

New York Playhouses

The new century brought a boom in theater building that reached its peak between 1911 and 1928. During this period so many new playhouses were built that the critics were constantly warning against overexpansion. The Chanin and Shubert brothers built dozens of theaters, most of which could not make a profit and soon closed their doors or were converted into motion picture theaters. There were periods of several months' duration when new playhouses were opening almost at the rate of one a week.

The competition between theater managers was very spirited, for each man was literally fighting for survival. The advent of various unions covering most aspects of the theatrical business caused a spiraling of costs for theatrical productions—costs that were passed on to the spectators through the rising price of tickets. The increase in ticket prices caused a change in the kind of audience attending legitimate theater productions. People in a lower income group were finding diversion in the increasingly popular form of entertainment known as vaudeville or, later, in the rapidly expanding motion picture medium. The theater during the first seventy years of the twentieth century faced the ever-growing danger of pricing itself out of an audience.

The development of the Little Theater movement throughout the country, and the invasion of New York City by such groups as the Provincetown Players and the Washington Square Players, affected theater architecture. A number of playhouses were built to give a feeling of intimacy. Some seated less than three hundred persons, and with the rising cost of production, such theaters could not survive. In 1970 union wage scales for small playhouses and off-Broadway theaters were adjusted in a move to help houses with limited financial potential.

The coming of age of the motion picture, particularly once sound had been added, proved to be a mortal enemy of the legitimate theater, since it provided entertainment for the masses at a fraction of the cost of a ticket to a play. Many playhouses were converted into motion picture houses or, later on, into television studios.

By 1928 construction of new playhouses in New York City had virtually come to a halt, and no new ones were to be built until the 1960s. The rapidly escalating cost of land in

Manhattan, high taxes, and the exceedingly high cost of construction in the city were largely to blame.

The majority of legitimate theaters in New York in 1971 were well over forty years old. Most of them had been refurbished and redecorated but were still basically the same as when they were first built. The architectural innovations that had been taking place in regional and university theaters had scarcely touched New York.

Undoubtedly one of the greatest events in New York theater history during the second half of the twentieth century occurred in 1964 with the opening of the temporary quarters of the Repertory Company of the new Lincoln Center for the Performing Arts. This was the first new playhouse erected in the city in more than thirty-six years, and although it was used by the company only until the new Vivian Beaumont Theatre at Lincoln Center was completed, the playhouse caused much excitement in theatrical circles. New concepts in theatrical design were applied, the proscenium arch was not used, and a new type of fluid staging was employed.

The opening of Lincoln Center signaled a new interest in building playhouses in New York, and several important projects went into the planning and construction stages.

1. REPUBLIC THEATRE
New York City
Opened September 27, 1900

Certainly the busiest theatrical manager in New York between 1890 and 1910 must have been Oscar Hammerstein, who, with the opening of the Republic Theatre in 1900, had built seven major theaters in the metropolitan area. His greatest enterprise, the Olympia, had been lost because of financial troubles, but Hammerstein was undefeated and became engrossed in plans for his new playhouse, the Republic. This he built on Forty-second Street just west of Seventh Avenue, adjoining the Victoria Theatre, another of his buildings, which had been opened in 1899.

The New York *Dramatic Mirror* carried pictures of the theater in addition to an elaborate description.

1:1   THE THEATRE REPUBLIC

To-morrow (Wednesday) evening will witness the opening of this city's newest playhouse, Oscar Hammerstein's Theatre Republic, with James A. Herne in the first New York presentation of Sag Harbor as the attraction. The Republic is the seventh place of amusement that Mr. Hammerstein has built in New York, and he considers it the handsomest and most perfectly appointed of the seven. An inspection of the house last week made the indefatigable builder's opinion credible.

The theatre is located on the north side of Forty-second Street, just west of Seventh Avenue, and adjoins the Victoria, that Mr. Hammerstein also built and manages. It has a frontage of seventy feet and the height to the cornice is one hundred feet. The front wall is of brownstone and dark gray brick, surmounted by a row of Doric columns, in the centre of which is a carved stone medallion bearing the words "Theatre Republic." From the street a broad double stairway leads to the piazza, where the entrance to the second balcony is located. The stairway and piazza are ornamented with wrought iron lamps of artistic design. The second balcony has its own box-office and is entirely independent of the lower part of the theatre.

Directly beneath the piazza, and level with the street, is the main entrance, with three doors through which one passes into the lobby. Here are found the box-office and coat room. Doorways communicate with the orchestra floor, that has a spacious foyer, whence marble stairways rise to the first balcony.

The seating capacity of the Republic is 1,100, though it is said that the house could accommodate 1,500 chairs had less

1:1. New York *Dramatic Mirror*, Sept. 19, 1900.

thought been given of the comfort of the audience. The seats are large and richly upholstered, and the spaces between the rows are wide. The construction of the theatre is such that every seat commands a full and unobstructed view of the stage. The furnishings of the orchestra and the two balconies are exactly alike.

Besides the six proscenium boxes, the theatre has a number of other boxes set in the side walls, a novelty in theatre construction that adds greatly to the beauty of the house. The proscenium arch is thirty-five feet high, and is decorated elaborately with allegorical figures and classic designs in relief. Above the arch are life-sized figures representing Harmony and Melody, and behind these figures is a balcony where the musicians will be located.

The color scheme in the decorations of the interior is green, ivory and old gold. The most beautiful and striking feature of the theatre is the great gilded dome that covers the entire auditorium. It is illuminated by cardinal lights concealed behind its rim. A large chandelier, with a myriad of pale green lights, hangs from the centre of the dome.

On the stage there is the same completeness of equipment as is found in the auditorium. The stage itself is thirty-five feet wide, thirty-two feet deep and seventy-five feet to the gridiron. There are no sheaves, pulleys and counterweights, as in the ordinary stage, all the scenery, as well as the curtain, being operated by an electric motor controlled by one man from a switchboard on the stage. The dressing-rooms, fitted with all conveniences, are off the stage and communicate with the exit alleys. Both hot and cold air, as occasion requires, can be circulated to all parts of the auditorium through ducts running under the asphalt floors, there being no disfiguring radiators nor crackling steam pipes. The theatre is as fireproof as it is possible to make a building. There is absolutely nothing combustible in the house except the upholstery and the plank sheathing for the floors. There are exits from the front and from alleys on either side, and from iron outside stairways all around as well as from the great front stairway. Mr. Hammerstein has never had a plan of one of his houses questioned by the building or fire departments.

Regarding the policy of the house, Mr. Hammerstein announces that he will devote the Republic to all that is best in dramatic and lyric art. All the time for this season is held by Liebler and Company. James A. Herne's engagement will be followed by Viola Allen in In the Palace of the King and other attractions of an equally high standing.

The drama critic of the New York *Times* had some interesting comments about Mr. Hammerstein in the review of the opening night proceedings.

1:2 Mr. Herne, in his long speech between the acts of "Sag Harbor" in the new Theatre Republic night before last, spoke of the big place of amusement on Longacre Square* as the "finest building in New York" (a somewhat exaggerated phrase, by the way, for a blunt realist,) and declared that Mr. Hammerstein's ability to recover from the effect of losing such a structure was the best proof of his wonderful vitality. But it is likely that the loss of the Olympia was one of the luckiest things that ever happened to Oscar Hammerstein. The detached theatre in the south end now pays off well, and doubtless the roof garden is profitable in Winter. But the difficulty of finding a suitable attraction for the big music hall, which occupies the larger part of the block front, seems to be enormous. So far the performances offered there have ranged from out-and-out variety to spectacular "religious" melodrama, without establish-

1:2. New York *Times*, Sept. 29, 1900.
*Hammerstein's Olympia

ing the house in the public mind as one in which entertainment is reasonably sure to be found. The cost of running the music hall is large, and it seems that shows there must be of an expensive kind or they will not draw at all. . . .

It is certain, though, that Mr. Hammerstein's newest playhouse, the Theatre Republic, will be no white elephant. It is not quite, in relation to the other first-class theatres in Manhattan, what the adjoining Victoria is to the other music halls. For there is no other music hall quite as cheerful-looking, comfortable and handsome as the Victoria, while there are theatres as comfortable and cheerful as this new house, and some that may fairly be called handsome, according to one's taste. But the Theatre Republic will easily hold its own as a resort of refined playgoers if the right kind of plays are performed there. The Venetian facade is attractive, and the interior, if richly, even gorgeously, decorated, is still tasteful and positively handsome. . . .

2. NEW AMSTERDAM THEATRE
New York City
Opened October 13, 1903

The New Amsterdam Theatre, for more than forty years to be the home of outstanding productions, including the Ziegfeld Follies, opened its doors October 13, 1903. The theater was under the management of Klaw and Erlanger, who were part of the Theatre Syndicate, which was controlling theatrical productions throughout the country. For their first production at the New Amsterdam they presented Nat Goodwin in a spectacular *Midsummer Night's Dream.*

2:1   NEW AMSTERDAM OPENED

———————

A GORGEOUS THEATRE AND A DAZZLING
SHAKESPEAREAN PRODUCTION

———————

2:1. New York *Times*, Oct. 27, 1903.

Mr. N. C. Goodwin in "A Midsummer Night's Dream—Mendelssohn's Music and Additions

———————

At the opening of the New Amsterdam Theatre last evening a vision of gorgeousness was disclosed to the New York theatregoers, inured to sights of that description, that may well have caused the most experienced of them to wonder and admire. The playhouse itself, one of the most elaborate in design and one of the most thoroughgoing and consistent in its embodiment of the "New Art," through the labors of architects, sculptors, decorative painters, and designers, came first in its insistent appeal to the eye with all that plastic art, sinuous line, and the blended harmonies of form and color could jointly accomplish.

The setting was no more elaborate than the dramatic show that was exhibited upon the stage. It was "A Midsummer Night's Dream" in which the scene painter, costumer, electric engineer and mechanic of stage effects had done all in their power to realize the possibilities that the fairy comedy of Shakespeare offers ingenious handicraftsmen, who worked with all that skill and all that profusion of resource and money could give them. There was, furthermore, Mendelssohn's music composed for the drama, with many additional pieces arranged and fitted to the performance with great skill by Mr. Victor Herbert. The chief actor was Mr. N. C. Goodwin, who took the part of Bottom, and there was a company of considerable merit.

The stage was thronged with fairies beautiful in face and figure, beautiful in the richness and daintiness of their costumes; with diminutive spirits and elves of all sorts. Fairies soared through the air. Puck made a brilliant entrance from the upper regions with precision and grace. Electric bulbs twinkled in endless profusion among the flowers, and the woodland glade and Titania's bower were symphonies of soft light and subdued color.

The ass's head became Bottom as though he had been born with it, and was full of all that asinine graces and expressiveness as to eyes, ears and mouth. There was, in fact, an unceasing showing of the things that mechanical skill could accomplish.

The result was a representation that in many ways charmed and delighted the senses of the listeners; though it sometimes seemed almost as if it overburdened and wearied them, nothing was left undone; nothing was omitted that could be exhibited to the eye; the ear was continually delighted with the witchery of Mendelssohn's fairy music. Yet it seemed as if the imagination were not always touched in the highest sense by this lavish and opulent display, and that Shakespeare's own poetry and exuberant fancy were somehow buried beneath it. The audience was very large, and gave frequent manifestations of pleasure and amusement, more frequent ones, perhaps, of its amazement. . . .

Mr. Goodwin at the close of the third act came before the curtain and made a brief speech, in which he said that he thought the occasion warranted his violation of the principle he held that an actor ought not to come before his audience during a performance in propria persona. He thanked his audience warmly for the interest they had shown in the performance. People had been saying that there was need of a typically American theatre in New York: he thought they had it in the New Amsterdam. The proprietors of that theatre had been spoken of as speculators; but, he said, all honor to them if such a theatre as that was the result of their speculation. To which the audience assented with a polite tribute of applause.

The New Amsterdam Theatre is presented as being the first complete carrying out of the idea of the "Art Nouveau" throughout a whole building. The aim had been in the interior to produce a "pastel effect," in which vines and flowers are the chief motives. Each of the boxes, for instance, with its draperies, represents a flower—a heliotrope, a buttercup, &c., and the same idea is carried out on the curtain. The color scheme is of green, relieved by mother of pearl and mauve.

The decorations include a large composition over the proscenium arch by the late Robert Blum and A. B. Wenzell, typifying the drama. There has been a lavish use of sculptured decoration in the lobby, friezes on the two side walls representing scenes respectively from Shakespeare's plays and from Wagner's "Nibelung" dramas. On the end are panels typifying Greek drama and "Faust." The foyer contains bas reliefs on the side walls representing the old and new cities of New Amsterdam with vivid realism; also is a panel depicting "Progress."

In the promenade foyer masses of vines and flowers, with animals, are modeled into the balustrades, and here, too, is another panel and sylvan subject. The general reception room shows a rich green effect, with two large decorative lunettes, "Inspiration" and "Creation," and an uncommonly elaborate fireplace of Caen stone and Irish marble. Smoking and retiring rooms are ample in size, and show the same consistency in carrying out the scheme of decoration.

3. HUDSON THEATRE
New York City
Opened October 19, 1903

Ethel Barrymore opened the Hudson Theatre in 1903 with *Cousin Kate,* a play that did not present her to her greatest advantage as an actress, but was mildly successful. This playhouse has had a long and interesting history, and, at the writing of this volume, is still standing on Forty-fourth Street, west of Sixth Avenue. During its history it has been used as a television theater and for radio broadcasting, as well as for commercial theater productions. At the time it was built it was praised for its beauty and practicality.

3:1

MISS ETHEL BARRYMORE IN
"COUSIN KATE"

A Teacup and Saucer Romeo and
Juliet Play by H. H. Davies.

A Pleasantly Successful Opening of the
Beautiful New Hudson Theatre.

"There certainly are compensations in being old!" exclaimed Miss Ethel Barrymore as Cousin Kate last night at the beautiful new Hudson Theatre. Her hair was braided in a coronet about the top of her head, in a way that was positively middle-aged, though she was only meant to be twenty-nine, but the spirit of girlish well-being was so flush and obvious in her that that shamelessly and admirably friendly first-night audience did nothing but laugh and applaud, and ended by quite breaking up the dialogue, just as they had done at the first night of "Her Own Way," (Miss Barrymore assisting,) when Georgie Lawrence, combing out Miss Maxine Elliott's hair, paid her that pretty compliment about her particular good looks.

It was pretty and cheerful as could be, but when the green and orange and old ivory curtain rang down on the play the saying came back to mind with a new connotation. There certainly are compensations in being old, and when Miss Barrymore has come into them she will give a fuller, more rounded, and far deeper interpretation to such roles as Cousin Kate. And let us hope—indeed, we know!—she will only be more beautiful. . . .

It is impossible to close without a word of rapture on the new playhouse. Its verd-antique, in Graeco-Roman marble, silk plush and metal trimmings, harmonizes admirably with the dull old ivory of the proscenium arch, tricked out with the tridescence of fevrile glass. The masked

lights in the golden house coffers and the moons of opulescent luminaries of the foyer ceiling, the constellations of dull incandescence in the ceiling of the auditorium; all combined to suffuse the house with a rich brilliancy never to be forgotten. No richer and more tasteful auditorium is to be found short of the splendid Hofburg Theater in Vienna, with its old crimson, ivory and gold.

The New York *Tribune* devoted an entire article to a description of the playhouse.

3:2

NEW HUDSON THEATRE

Henry B. Harris's Hudson Theatre, the latest addition to New-York's handsome playhouses, will be opened to-morrow night with Miss Ethel Barrymore in "Cousin Kate." The main entrance of the Hudson Theatre is on the north side of Forty-fourth-st., between Broadway and Sixth-ave., the theatre proper extending to Forty-fifth-st., with the stage entrance in that street. The facade of the Forty-fourth-st. building, which is four stories in height, is simply treated in the Renaissance style; the design of the Forty-fifth-st. facade is carried out on severely classic lines.

Simplicity is the architectural keynote of the new theatre. Its special feature is an exceptionally spacious lobby and foyer, a hundred feet in depth and thirty feet wide, the largest of any theatre in the city. Four entrance portals lead to the tiled vestibule, thirty-six feet wide and sixteen feet deep, with a wainscoting of Verde antique marble, twelve feet in height. A frieze in tones of green rises to a domed ceiling illuminated by a unique scheme of concealed electric lights that is introduced in all parts of the theatre. This system was designed by the late Luther B. Steiringer, who devised and executed the illumination of the Pan-American Exposition in Buffalo.

The lobby, access to which is gained through four sets of massive double

3:1. New York *Times*, Oct. 20, 1903.

3:2. New York *Tribune*, Oct. 18, 1903.

2. Main entrance, New Amsterdam Theatre, New York, 1906. Courtesy of the Museum of the City of New York.

2. Interior, New Amsterdam Theatre, New York, ca. 1910. Photograph by Hall. Courtesy of the Museum of the City of New York.

3. Hudson Theatre, New York, ca. 1906. Photograph by Byron. Courtesy of the Byron Collection, Museum of the City of New York.

doors, is Graeco-Roman in its architectural lines. Its walls are treated with a wainscoating of Verde antique marble similar to that of the vestibule. A low relief frieze in green and old bronze colorings is surmounted by a coffered ceiling of stucco elaborately modelled after a design suggested by the wall surfaces in the Baths of Titus at Rome. The ceiling gives forth a flood of light, for in each of the 264 coffers is an electric bulb of sixteen candle power, the frame work being ingeniously arranged so as to give the maximum of reflection. The brilliancy of this exposed lighting is designed as a contrast to the concealed illumination that prevails elsewhere throughout the building.

The box office at the right of the lobby is notable. The marble wall surface formed by the wainscoting is divided into three panels bearing bronze tablets. Supporting a classic entablature are four bronze headed Hermae, the figures simplified to shafts, a motif frequently introduced in Greek temples and early classic buildings.

The foyer, which is divided from the lobby by massive doors of bronze and brass, is more markedly Roman in character and more elaborate in treatment. A low wainscoting of wood forms pedestals for ornate pilasters that support the entablature and domed ceiling, all designed and colored in mellow combinations of old ivory, green and orange, after the manner of Perlnezi, one of the first to discover the architectural value of old buildings and tombs of early Roman days and to apply them to the palaces of his period. There are six archways between the pilasters, one forming the entrance to the balcony stairway. These arches are treated with subdivided mirrors in the style of the salon of glass at Versailles. Midway in the left wall is a carved mantle bearing bronze antiques and flanked at either side with torcheres of carved wood and bronze. An effect of airiness and height is gained by a triple domed ceiling of Tiffany glass and bronze framed by conventional ivy leafed bands.

The first impression gained on entering the theatre proper is of the absence of pillars—the balconies being supported by cantilevers. The elliptical formation of the auditorium and the manner in which the boxes are arranged gives an unobstructed view of the stage from any seat in the theatre. Every part of the stage, including the top of the proscenium arch, can be seen from the rear of the auditorium. There are four boxes on each side, the facings of the lower tier being formed by a continuation of the Verde antique marble surbases. They form a part of the proscenium vault, which rests on Roman columns and is laid out in low relief panels copied from the Golden House of Nero. Its coloring is subdued, to serve as a mellow reflecting surface for the concealed lighting. The proscenium arch, or stage frame, is of an unconventional architectural pattern, composed of relief frets, bay leaf bands and mosaic panels studded with iridescent glass. The ceiling is worked out in flowing lines, direct lights being sunk in the stucco to emphasize the design. The coloring, although in a lighter tone, is uniform with that of the mural surfaces of the auditorium. A vivid note in the color scheme is furnished by the use of Tiffany glass mosaics in the fronts of the balconies and upper boxes. The drop curtain is of silk velours, similar to that used in the upholstery of the theatre, with ornamentations in green and yellow.

In addition to the main doorways there are twenty-eight exits, a number so unusual as to be worthy of note. This not only guarantees the safety of the patrons of the Hudson Theatre, but provides for their speedy egress at the close of a performance.

4. NEW LYCEUM THEATRE
New York City
Opened November 2, 1903

The "old" Lyceum Theatre had been

built by Steele MacKaye in 1885 and was on Fourth Avenue. When MacKaye's management proved unsuccessful, the theater was taken over by Daniel Frohman, who managed it successfully until it was demolished in 1903. The New Lyceum, also under Frohman's management, was built uptown in the new theater area on Forty-fifth Street just east of Broadway. Before the opening the New York *Tribune* reminisced about the past and commented on the new playhouse bearing that distinguished name.

4:1 NEW LYCEUM OPENS TO-MORROW NIGHT

E. H. Sothern the First Attraction—Some of the Successes of the Old Lyceum

To-morrow night another of the numerous new theatres in this city will be opened, the New Lyceum in West Forty-fifth-st., near Long Acre Square. Daniel Frohman will be the manager, and E. H. Sothern in "The Proud Prince" will furnish the first attraction. The new Lyceum Theatre, unlike most of the other new houses, is intimately connected with the past, replacing, as it does, the old Lyceum in Fourth-ave., which was torn down two years ago, and about which for many years had clustered the pleasantest of recollections, and where some of the best dramatic offerings of past seasons had been served. The intimate connection, too, of Mr. Sothern, both with the old and the new theatre, and with Daniel Frohman, the manager of both houses, adds interest to the opening to-morrow.

In the early winter of 1886 Sothern was playing under the management of Helen Dauvray at the Lyceum in "One of Our Girls," and as the season ended in May he was available for any manager for the summer months. One day he spoke to Daniel Frohman about his father's famous "trunk full of plays," and thought that one called "Trade" would go. Mr. Froh-

man changed the name to "The Highest Bidder," and presented Mr. Sothern at the Lyceum in the leading part in June. The play went so well that the manager tried to secure for the actor a release from his road tour with Miss Dauvray the next season, but she demanded $3,000. This Mr. Frohman would not pay, but Mr. Sothern, against the advice of friends, paid it himself. Thus he began the next season in the Lyceum, under the management of Mr. Frohman, in "The Highest Bidder," supported by Rowland Buckstone and Mr. Le Moyne. It was a time of doubt and importance both to his fortunes and those of his manager. The two men used to stroll over to Second-ave. and back to the theatre two or three times of an afternoon, watching the box office sales. The sales were all to the good, however, and a road tour was planned and carried out, and Mr. Sothern was established as a successful star.

Messrs. Belasco and De Mille were then set to work on the contents of the trunk of plays, and "Lord Chumley" was the first result. In that play Mr. Sothern, who had been trained for an artist, not for the stage, by his father, began to show his skill as a stage manager and shaper of stage pictures. He took the stage management into his own hands, and made a success of the leading part as well. In this play Miss Anglin and Miss Adams made their first New-York appearance.

"The Maister of Woodbarrow" by Jerome was the next Lyceum production made for Mr. Sothern. In this play Miss Harned, now Mrs. Sothern, made her first appearance as a member of his company. Mr. Frohman found her down in Fourteenth-st. playing in a second-rate company, and brought her up to his theatre for the new production. Miss Harned, of course, was partly responsible for the next production, "The Dancing Girl." Mr. Sothern shifted from his former vein of light comedy into a more serious style of character, and he awaited with great

4:1. New York *Tribune*, Nov. 1, 1903.

anxiety the public verdict. It was favorable, and from the verdict the romantic and heroic characters Mr. Sothern has since portrayed were made possible.

Another Lyceum play which brought into public notice that charming child actress, Miss Elsie Leslie, was "Editha's Burglar," in which Mr. Sothern played the burglar. Then came "Captain Lettarblair," which, as Mr. Sothern says, illustrated the truth of Boucicault's statement that "plays are not written, but rewritten." Mr. Sothern modelled the character largely after that of an uncle of his, Hugh Lytton. The business in the play, when Miss Harned leaves the room after the row with her lover, was accidentally suggested at a rehearsal, when he [her] dress caught in the door as she was going off the stage. In "Lord Chumley," too, there was a bit of such accidental business. At a rehearsal Meg had left her feather duster sticking up in a chair, and the actor, when he sank into the chair at the end of the act, felt the tickle of a feather in his neck and started up nervously. This business was incorporated in the play. . . .

The ultimate policy of the Lyceum is not yet clearly outlined by Mr. Frohman, but after eighteen months, for which length of time bookings have already been made, at least a semblance of a stock company will be organized, and productions will be regularly made at the new house. The old style stock company, Mr. Frohman says, is impossible in the present state of commercial theatrical enterprise, but he hopes to assemble good actors for a production, and out of each new effort develop some one actor or actress who can be sent out on tour at the head of a company. Thus there will always be a producing company at the Lyceum if its personnel does change.

The New Lyceum is situated in Forty-fifth-st., a little east of Broadway. There is not only a theatre, but in the rear, connected with the stage, a ten-story building. The main building, in Forty-fifth st., contains the auditorium, foyers, the stage and its appurtenances, the rehearsal and dressing rooms, the offices of the management, and the heating, lighting and ventilating apparatus. The annex includes carpenter shop, studios for scene painting, additional dressing rooms and the scene dock, a large extension to the stage. In this way are brought together within a single compact structure every department and every detail of the modern playhouse complete from the theatre proper down to the most minute requirements.

In the general arrangement and decorative treatment the architects, Herts & Tallant have developed a building fitted to become the home of the drama. The gray limestone facade, with its composite order, its enriched window openings, its statues and its marble panels and bronze cheneau, recalls in its style and amplitude Roman art, and strikes the keynote of dignity and richness. Three vestibules give access to the main entrance foyer. Here are the ticket offices and portals opening to the main auditorium, and marble staircases lead to the balcony foyer and to the smoking rooms. From the foyer special staircases and elevator service lead to the business offices of Mr. Frohman, which occupy the entire upper portion of the Forty-fifth-st. front. Mr. Frohman's library has been decorated in Chippendale style, and the furniture and decorations of the room are a reproduction of the library of David Garrick. In order that the stage rehearsals may be superintended directly from this headquarters, a window has been concealed in the ceiling of the main auditorium in such a way as to command a complete view of the entire stage, while telephone communication allows direct instructions to be given to the stage manager.

On entering the auditorium from the foyer, the first noticeable feature is the great width of the house as compared with its depth. In this way the seats are all brought forward near the stage. At the

9

same time the seating capacity is maintained, for although there are fewer rows of seats than in the ordinary theatre, this is more than offset by the greater length of the rows, and at the same time the sight lines are greatly improved. The total absence of all posts, the rods or other structural encumbrances also greatly facilitates the view of the stage, and, finally, the comfort of each patron has been sought by the ample dimensions of the seats, which are 22 inches wide and 24 inches high from the seat to the top of the back. They are covered with dark yellow Cordovan leather.

The stage is 89 feet wide and 37 feet deep, with an extra addition of 40 feet, so that a scenic production with a depth of 71 feet having direct entrance and exit from the street may be arranged and horses and vehicles of all kinds can be brought in on the stage if necessary. The proscenium opening is 35 feet in width and 30 feet in height.

The stage proper is built of a series of elevators with a drop of 30 feet to the bottom of the sink, so that an entire scene can be dropped below the stage instantly and the auxiliary stage slipped over it. These bridges can be raised or lowered and set at any angle required, so that, by the manipulation of the mechanical appliances, terraces, cliffs or lakes can be produced.

At the rear of the stage in the Forty-sixth-st. branch of the building are dressing rooms for two hundred people, two large rooms for supernumeraries, storage rooms for scenery, and a complete scenery warehouse. There is a mechanical plant, with a carpenter shop, where twenty-five stage carpenters can be put to work; and a large studio with north light and scene room for painting scenery of all kinds. The studio is sufficiently large to paint four back drops simultaneously. There is a studio for scale models for stages and also a large costume room,

where fifty seamstresses and a number of cutters and costume makers may work.

The entire control of the color scheme and decorations were placed in the hands of the architects, to produce harmony throughout. At the same time the architects were able to collaborate in this work with James Wall Finn, the artist who painted the ceiling of Sherry's ballroom, the house of Stanford White, the residence of Miss Anna Gould and the St. Regis Hotel. From his brush are the two lunettes in the entrance foyer. One of these contains the portrait of Mrs. Siddons, the other David Garrick in the smiling pose indicative of his famous words, "Tragedy is easy enough; but comedy is serious business." It was also Mr. Finn who tinted the three figures over the proscenium, representing Pallas Athene, the Goddess of Wisdom, accompanied by Music and Drama.

The color scheme approximates tones of autumn foliage, running from deep yellow to warm red and brown. It is maintained throughout by special selection of all the materials constituting the interior finish of the building. The house is fireproof, and also provided with numerous exits and a special water service.

5. THE HIPPODROME
New York City
Opened April 12, 1905

The largest theater in America, the Hippodrome, on Sixth Avenue between Forty-third and Forty-fourth streets, opened in 1905 with the greatest spectacle that New Yorkers had ever seen on the stage. More than five thousand people attended the opening-night performance, according to the report in the New York *Tribune* the day following the opening, and reveled in the fact that New York now had a theater that was "the biggest in the world."

The New York *Times* critic also waxed enthusiastic over the new playhouse and the spectacular performance:

HIPPODROME'S OPENING SEEN

BY THOUSANDS

Novel Programme That Includes Circus,
War, and Ballet.

PASSES OFF WITHOUT HITCH

Crowds Applaud Performers and the
Promptness with Which Every Detail
Is Carried Out.

The biggest amusement enterprise this
city has ever known, The Hippodrome,
was opened to the public last evening with
an audience such as only New York can
turn out, and the crowds saw a series of
stage performances that seldom have been
equaled. This is true of every detail, from
the opening scene depicting a circus about
to give a show to the climax, depicting the
Battle of Rocky Ford Bridge, with its lack
of water and plunging horses.

Not the least marvellous thing to relate
is that from curtain rise to curtain fall,
there was not one hitch in the performance
or in the handling of the acres of scenery
and the army of employees. Every number
on the long programme, that began shortly
after 8 o'clock and lasted until midnight,
was given in its exact order.

What the rehearsals for such a succession of stage pictures must have been can
only be guessed from seeing the finished
product. It is doubtful if the most san-
guine of Thompson & Dundy's supporters,
or even the managers themselves, looked
for such a flawless premier, for it must
be understood that in that programme
was a comic opera, a circus, a spectacular
drama, and a ballet of marvelous beauty.

When the immense drop curtain arose
on the first act, the exterior of a circus,
the scene in the body of the house was one
of surprising beauty. Every seat in the

5:1. New York *Times*, Apr. 13, 1905.

great auditorium, from pit to last row in
the high gallery, was taken.

The lights gleaming on the jewels and
the brilliant costumes of the women and
the faultlessness of detail in the arrangements all contributed to a scene nothing
short of remarkable.

It looked as if the Metropolitan Opera
House had suddenly been transpalnted
over to Forty-third Street and Sixth Avenue, and in addition, as if Madison Square
Garden had emptied one of its mighty
throngs into the same space.

Along the great corridors were ranged
a great array of flower pieces sent by the
friends of the management, and ranging
from a modest wreath to an elephant six
feet high and a great horseshoe bearing
within it a horse's head. . . .

BIGGEST IN THE WORLD

FEATURES OF THE HIPPODROME
THAT EXCEL ALL OTHERS

"I never seed nothin' as big as this out
Walla Walla ways," remarked one visitor
to the Hippodrome last night. He was
right. Larger communities of art and culture than the one he mentioned would be
surprised at the size of this new amusement resort, which Thompson & Dundy
have provided.

Some idea of the size of the Hippodrome may be obtained by a comparison
with other theatres. Its seating capacity is
5,200, as compared with 3,400 for the
Metropolitan Opera House, 3,000 for the
Academy of Music, 1,800 for the Broadway Theatre, and 1,782 for the New
Amsterdam. The area of the Hippodrome
balconies is said to be larger than the
total area of the largest theatre in this
city and to equal in seating capacity that
of almost any two other theatres.

To illuminate the building 40,000 electric lights are required, as compared with
6,000, the most so far as is known, in
use in any other house, and whereas the

back drop curtain in most theatres averages about 24 by 50 feet, the one in the Hippodrome is 85 by 200 feet.

In the Alexander Opera House, St. Petersburg, they have what is generally considered the largest asbestos curtain in the world. That great sheet of curtaining is 40 feet shorter than the one that will be rolled up nightly in the new theatre, the exact dimensions of which are 114 by 48 feet.

That portion of the stage which extends from what is ordinarily the curtain line is known technically as the "apron." It is the part of the stage upon which the actors in an ordinary play do not appear, though the vaudeville monologist uses it when he walks down to the footlights to get in close touch with his audience. The "apron" of the Hippodrome stage is just 28 feet larger than that of La Scala, the famous Opera House in Milan. With the exception of that of the Pantheon, in Rome, the Hippodrome's dome, covering almost an acre in itself, is the largest in the world. The ground floor promenade, 16 feet wide and 200 feet long, is as great in area as the body of other New York theatres.

A large amount of interest in the Hippodrome centres in the stage and the entirely novel mechanical arrangement for operating the moving platforms, filling and emptying the tank, raising and lowering the stage, and handling the scenery. The stage may be divided for the purposes of description into two portions, that which is behind and that which is in front of the proscenium arch. This arch is the biggest ever built in a theatre. It has a total width of 96 feet and a clear height of forty feet.

The depth of the stage from the extreme front to the back wall is 110 feet, or 50 feet from the back wall to the proscenium opening, and 60 feet from the arch to the front of the stage. The main stage at the rear of the arch measures 50 feet in depth by 200 feet in width between side walls. Of this area the central portion immediately back of the arch is carried on four twelve-inch hydraulic rams, and is capable of a vertical movement of eight feet.

The use of large quantities of water necessitates an extensive hydraulic plant. The main tank is served by three centrifugal pumps of a combined capacity of 8,000 gallons per minute. Around the back of the stage, at a height of 14 feet, a twelve-inch pipe extends for a distance of 180 feet. From this pipe, by means of flexible connections leading to a cataract and fountains, a fine cascade with a fall of 14 feet is formed, with the full capacity of the three centrifugal pumps to maintain it in constant flow. There is also an eight-inch pipe placed just inside the runway, by means of which a considerable flow of water is produced across the surface of the tank, giving the effect of a river. Flowing water in volume is also used in the Andersonville battle scene, where a considerable mountain torrent is shown rushing under a bridge of thirty-foot span, and flowing with a slower current across the whole length of the tank in the foreground.

The total height of the stage to the gridiron is eighty feet, and the great height well matches the other proportions of the stage. It is here, in connection with the handling of the scenery, that this stage presents some of its most original and striking features. The scenery, in place of being dropped and lifted, is carried, by means of traveling electric hoists, on four separate lines of overhead tracks, which are attached to the gridiron, and curve in concentric semi-circles above the stage, and extend into deep side wings known as scene pockets, each of which is of sufficient depth to enable the whole of the one-half of the scenery to be moved within it, clear of the stage.

The cost of the building was $1,500,-000.

4. New Lyceum Theatre, New York, ca. 1905. Courtesy of The New-York Historical Society, New York City.

5. Hippodrome, New York, 1905. Courtesy of the Museum of the City of New York.

6. Stuyvesant Theatre, New York, ca. 1907. A cigar card, "Between the Acts." Courtesy of The Hoblitzelle Theatre Arts Library, The Humanities Research Center, The University of Texas at Austin.

6. STUYVESANT THEATRE
New York City
Opened October 16, 1907

The Stuyvesant Theatre was built by David Belasco. In 1910, when the Republic Theatre, which had assumed his name, reverted to its original title, the Stuyvesant became known as the Belasco. The new playhouse opened with the popular actor David Warfield in a new play, *A Grand Army Man,* by Belasco, Pauline Phelps, and Marion Short. The play and the playhouse were an immediate success.

The theater was beautifully designed, and it was here that Belasco lived, worked, and presented his dramas until his death in 1931.

6:1   STUYVESANT FINISHED

New Temple of Dramatic Art To Be Dedicated Wednesday Night.

Mr. Belasco's new playhouse on West 44th street is finished. Yesterday afternoon the architects formally turned over the Stuyvesant Theatre—that is its name —to the representatives of the manager-playwright. Mr. Belasco is a happy man. He himself says so. He says the Stuyvesant as it stands today represents his ideas of what a temple devoted to dramatic art should be. It cost $750,000, and is, without a doubt, a structure in which New York will take pride. Wednesday night next this playhouse will be dedicated with the first performance here of "A Grand Army Man," with Mr. David Warfield impersonating the chief character. An American play opening an American playhouse! Such an occasion happens only at intervals, and this time the occasion becomes the theatrical event of the week. But to the Stuyvesant:

A three story structure of the simple but graceful lines of the Colonial period, it is built on a site fronting 116 feet on 44th street, with a total depth of 210

6:1. New York *Tribune*, Oct. 13, 1907.

feet. It has a seating capacity of 1,000, 450 seats being arranged in the orchestra, with four boxes, each arranged for six persons. The moment you enter the vestibule the genius of Belasco is apparent in every nook and corner of the interior. Here and there you are confronted by the arms of celebrated dramatists and of Stuyvesant, in whose honor the playhouse was named. The ceiling has twenty-two stained glass panels, each decorated with two shields and heraldic mantling. The panel next to the stage has in the dexter shield the arms of Stuyvesant, in the sinister the arms of Goethe. The panel to the right has in the dexter shield the arms of Greece and in the sinister the arms of Shakespeare. The audience will have an unobstructed view of the stage, there being no pillars visible. The balconies have been built on the cantilever principle, guaranteed to increase in resistance in proportion to the weight they support. The stage proper is equipped with all the appliances that modern ingenuity has devised to lessen the labor of the employees and at the same time shorten the time between the acts. This includes a huge elevator in the centre, with the aid of which the stage may be quickly cleared of portable properties.

The plans for lighting the house and stage were arranged by Mr. Belasco and his assistants and executed by the Tiffany Studios.

The footlights differ from those of every other theatre by their division into seven sections, under complete control of the electrician, each one being on separate resistance, so that any part of the actor can be illuminated and another's left in shadow, as desired. There are five border lights, with 270 lamps in each, eighty-eight plugging pockets in the fly galleries and stage, to be used in the various electric calcium lights employed by Mr. Belasco in his productions, and sixty-five "dimmers" on the switchboard, which is said to be the largest in use at any theatre in the city. There are 500 lights in the dressing rooms alone and 4,500 electric lights distributed over the stage.

There are ten exits on the main floor— one to every forty-five seat holders or, counting the double doors as two, one exit to every twenty-two persons. So complete are the provisions for emptying the house in case of fire that the total ratio of exits to the seating capacity is as 1 to 16. There are in all 135 doors in the theatre, including four large double doors opening directly on the sidewalk.

7. MAXINE ELLIOTT THEATRE
New York City
Opened December 30, 1908

Maxine Elliott was an actress of considerable charm and ability. In 1908 she decided to enter into the management of her own theater. She opened her new playhouse, in partnership with the Shuberts, on December 30, 1908, with a very successful play, Marion Fairfax's *The Chaperon*. The playhouse was on Thirty-ninth Street east of Broadway, and perhaps its location was the cause of its basic difficulty in later years, as the theater district moved farther uptown. The house did have numerous successes before it was torn down in 1960.

The New York *Tribune* commented on the new addition to the theater scene:

7:1   MAXINE ELLIOTT'S THEATRE
TO BE OPENED ON WEDNESDAY EVE.

The most important theatrical event of the week will occur on Wednesday night when a new playhouse, built by the Shuberts and named for Maxine Elliott, will be formally opened. Miss Elliott herself will dedicate the structure, appearing in a new comedy entitled "The Chaperon," made for her by Miss Marion Fairfax. The new playhouse is situated in West 39th street, between Sixth avenue and Broadway. It will be built for Miss Elliott,

7:1. New York *Tribune*, Dec. 27, 1908.

and as may be seen from the accompanying picture, its official name is

MAXINE ELLIOTT'S THEATRE.

That actress is associated with the Messrs. Shubert in the enterprise, and will be her own manager. It is her purpose to appear there once every season in some novelty. It was designed to be a woman's theatre, the permanent stage home of Miss Elliott and other actresses under the direction of the Shuberts. Julia Marlowe, Nazimova and Mary Mannering will appear there from time to time. During the regular season new comedies by Clyde Fitch are to be produced at that playhouse.

This new temple of the drama was constructed in conformity with the latest laws of the city governing the building of places of amusement. It is a building by itself, externally imposing and rich in its simplicity. It is a low edifice, as it appears facing the street, reaching no higher than the third story of an ordinary city residence. It is fireproof and built of marble, steel and concrete. The floors of the auditorium, the cellar and the balconies are of steel and concrete, as are also the stairways, which are topped with marble. Wood has been used only in panelling the reception room, for the windows, the swinging doors leading to the balcony from the stairways and in the framework for the theatre seats. Swinging glass doors are used in the front of the theatre, but all other exits are closed by steel doors. The only wood used behind the proscenium opening is the stage proper.

All the modern devices for public safety have been introduced. The heating plant is outside the building, cut off entirely from any connection with the theatre save by the connecting pipes. Two systems for heating and ventilating are employed. They are known as the direct and indirect systems. Fresh air is drawn in from outside, heated and forced by powerful blowers into the auditorium, and by a system of suction all foul air is exhausted through the roof. In this way those sitting in the second balcony are not distressed by the heat rising from below, which is so often found to be the case in other theatres.

THE SEATING CAPACITY

The seating capacity of the theatre is about nine hundred. All the chairs are the same, the seats in the second balcony being as comfortable as those on the ground floor. Each seat is twenty-two inches wide. This measurement is several inches wider than the average theatre seat. On the ground floor there are only twelve rows of seats. The balconies have only a few rows each. The first balcony is so low that it might be called a mezzanine, whereas the second balcony is only slightly higher than the regular first balcony in any other theatre. Spectators, therefore, seated in any part of the house are near the stage.

The cost of the theatre, including the value of the site it occupies, is estimated to be $750,000.

The decorating was supervised by Miss Elliott. There is an harmonious blending of colors in silks, velvets and satins, and the expensive quality of the materials employed to carry out the effective scheme of interior embellishment is indicative of the actress's fine taste. It was she who suggested a marble facade for the theatre, and Le Petit Trianon, at Versailles, was her model for the general design of the interior of the theatre, with adaptations necessary to modern ideas. It is said to be the only theatre in the city having a front of pure marble. The finest quality of Dorset marble was employed. Excepting four Corinthian columns and a balustrade running along the entire top of the front, the aspect of the theatre from the street is severely plain. The four columns support the cornice, into which was chiseled the name of the theatre. Surmounting the cornice is the marble balustrade. Nothing will be placed on the marble front to announce the attraction, nor will any part of the structure be defaced with advertising matter.

There is a foyer in the rear of the auditorium and separated from it by curtains. On the left side of the foyer are stairs of white Italian marble leading to the balconies. The second balcony is reached by a separate entrance on the outside. To the left of the foyer are stairs leading to the women's reception and cloak rooms. The lounging room for men is on the right side of the foyer. There are no columns to obstruct the view from any part of the theatre. The columns which support the balcony are placed behind the last row of the orchestra seats and forms part of the partition which separates the foyer.

INTERIOR DECORATIONS

The interior decorations are in old ivory, old gold and mouse colors. The walls on all sides of the auditorium and in the foyer are panelled in gold silk damask. A marble base runs around the foyer. The foyer ceiling is in panels of ornamental relief in old ivory. Velvet curtains separate the foyer from the auditorium. The dome, ceiling, balcony fronts and fronts of the boxes are of plaster in rose garlands, colors in old ivory color. The entire decorative scheme is in keeping with the period of Louis XVI, the pattern being copied from an old French palace.

A feature that attracts the eye is the proscenium arch, supported on each side by two fine columns of golden grained Skyros marble. The columns cost $2,500 each. The curtain is of silk velvet.

Above the proscenium and extending one-third into the auditorium is a vaulted ceiling with a cornice of rose garlands, the same as the cornice extending around the entire ceiling. Back of the vaulted ceiling is a flat dome. The ceiling and dome are colored in old ivory. Suspended from the centre of the dome is a large chandelier of French glass. All the electrical fixtures are of old gold. On each side of the auditorium on the orchestra floor is a large double box separated from the rest of the house by a balustrade of Skyros marble. This arrangement gives four boxes on the lower floor. On each side of the balcony is a single box, the front of each in old ivory, with garlands of flowers in the decoration. The furniture for the boxes is carried out in Louis XV style. The chairs have old ivory frames with seat coverings of silk broche in floral design. In each of the lower boxes are six chairs, and the upper boxes have eight chairs each.

The floor of the entire house is covered with a rich mouse colored velvet carpet, the tone harmonizing with the general color scheme. The orchestra seats and those in the two balconies have frames in old ivory effect, and are covered with silk velvet in the same tone as the velvet drapings. All of the drapings, carpets and silk panellings are fireproofed. Three curtains are used. The asbestos fireproof curtain is in the same tone as the velvet drapings and the drop curtain. The drop curtain will be used after each act, but a third curtain, made of yellow silk damask, of the same material as the side panellings on the walls, will be lowered first at the end of each act. The dressing rooms are large and have windows opening on the passageway on the east side of the theatre. Miss Elliott's dressing room is directly off the stage. Marshall & Fox, of Chicago, were the architects.

8. NEW THEATRE
New York City
Opened November 6, 1909

"The most beautiful, stately and complete theatre in America, one of the most beautiful and nearly perfect theatres in the world, . . ." heralded the New York *Tribune* of November 9, 1909. This playhouse, which received more favorable publicity from the major New York newspapers than any other theater of its day, had difficulties from its inception and was never able to fulfill the high goals set for it by its founders and financial backers. It was to be the home of repertory in an age when repertory was too expensive to maintain in New York. It had been financed by a number of very wealthy New Yorkers, many of whom cared little or nothing about drama; and it was designed for aristocrats, with the great number of private boxes found in European playhouses of the nineteenth century.

The venture did not succeed, and after two years the playhouse was closed and reopened under the name Century Theatre. The following articles give a brief idea of the rise and fall of the New Theatre.

8:1   THE NEW THEATRE

TO BE OPENED TO THE PUBLIC ON
MONDAY NIGHT, NOV. 8.

Antony and Cleopatra the Opening
Drama—The Seat and Box Lists Show
That It Will Be A Great Civic and
Fashionable Event—A Description of
the Magnificent Building

The New Theatre will inaugurate its first season Monday night, Nov. 8, with a revival of Shakespeare's Antony and Cleopatra. The seat and box lists prove that the premiere will be a most notable civic and fashionable event. This magnificent structure, the most completely appointed playhouse in the English-speaking world, was erected by thirty citizens in the interest of dramatic art. It is intended to take the place of a National Theatre, such as the Comedie Francaise of Paris and the Hofburg of Vienna. As the theatre is not a commercial venture, considerable latitude was allowed the architects in its construction. Before drawing the plans the architects visited and studied the representative theatre abroad and took from each the best points. They paid par-

8:1. New York *Dramatic Mirror*, Oct. 23, 1909.

ticular attention to sight-lines, with the result that every seat in the house commands an excellent view of the stage. The acoustics were also carefully considered. The building is provided with a commodious foyer, two grand staircases, retiring and smoking rooms, a tea room, restaurant, buffet, offices for the directorate and staff, a Founders' room, greenroom and library.

From the approaches along Central Park West the structure is both dignified and imposing. It is of clear gray Indiana limestone, occupying the entire block frontage between Sixty-second and Sixty-third streets. Although the theatre is modern it is somewhat in the spirit of the Italian Renaissance of the late sixteenth century. The front entrances are on the park side. The carriage entrances are on Sixty-second and Sixty-third streets. By this arrangement there will be no crowding or confusion. The house is exceedingly simple and so planned that the auditorium and countless rooms can be emptied in three minutes. More than fifty stairways lead to the streets or lobbies. The stage and dressing-rooms above can be flooded instantly by automatic sprinklers. The ground floor embodies the main auditorium, which is in the shape of half an egg with the proscenium arch in the center of the straight line. Along the curved line are the Founders' boxes, the foyer stalls, and first and second balconies in a receding field of driftwood gray and dull Roman gold. The floor pitches at a moderate angle towards the stage, so it has not been necessary to raise the boxes much. They are but four feet above the level of the orchestra floor, making it possible for one to chat with the occupants from the floor during intermission. The twenty-three boxes correspond to the "Golden Horseshoe" at the Metropolitan Opera House, but instead of a second tier above them there are six rows of foyer stalls. Each box accommodates six persons, and is divided by tapestries from the tiny parlors in the rear. These parlors open into a private hall from which short flights of stone steps lead either to the main foyer, or to the corridor on the ground floor. The hangings of boxes and parlors are of a rich cerise. The foyer stalls are also done in cerise. Above the stalls is the first balcony, and over that the second balcony. The chairs are placed on a pitch sufficient to insure every playgoer seeing the entire stage without interference in front of him.

The color scheme of driftwood gray and gold is quiet and suggests dignified simplicity. The relief has been studied to interpret the architectural design, so that the gray is sometimes seen on a heavy gold background, and again the gold predominates on a background of gray. The carpets are in cerise. The proscenium arch is framed in greenish-tinged Conemara marble. Over the arch is the theatre's crest, two masks with a looking-glass in the center bearing the motto, "To hold as 'twere the mirror up to nature." Conemara tablets along the walls and under the dome are inscribed with the names of fourteen great dramatists.

The auditorium is surrounded on each floor by a broad corridor, which forms a circulation to be used between acts as well as in entering and leaving the playhouse. On the ground floor access is obtained to this through many vestibules and entrances, some of which lead directly to the corridor, and others to the boxes, stairways and balconies. At the corners are two monumental spiral staircases. Each is double, one flight being directly over the other, so that the ascent is made without meeting.

The boxes are reached from the main corridor by ascending a half flight of stone steps. This brings one to the private hall, which in turn leads to the small parlor in the rear of the box. From the top of this half flight of steps the main foyer is reached by ascending another flight of equal length. It is this foyer which will contain the majority of the art works to be exhibited from time to time. The foyer is constructed of rich Sienna marble and gold and has at either end an orchestra platform cut off by arches which will be used by the orchestra during the intermissions of dramatic performances.

At one end of the circulation on the same floor as the foyer is a tea room. Here tea will be served during the entre-actes for those who desire it. The windows on this floor front on Central Park West. The circulation[s] in the rear of the first and second balconies are intended to be used as promenades during intermissions. On one floor is the Founder's room, and on the other the library. The former has been furnished by the Founders themselves. The library for the players, which adjoins the dressing-rooms, has oak bookcases rising from the floor to the ceiling. The books will include standard works on the drama, books of reference, and volumes devoted to art. Many have been given the institution and others have been purchased.

The top floor of the theatre in the front is devoted to a roof-garden, which at the present time is used for rehearsals. This garden sets back a bit from the terrace overlooking Central Park and is partly roofed with glass. The doors, all of glass, lead to the walled terrace. In all probability a stage will be erected here for concerts or performances.

Back of the garden are similar rehearsal rooms, comfortably furnished rooms for chorus-men and women, and model make-up rooms for supernumeraries. They are all airy and illuminated during the daytime by skylights. They have every appearance of modern studios and could be used as such. This floor, like others, is reached by elevators. The green-room, in disuse since the late Augustin Daly, has been revived. It is located on the ground floor just off the stage on the Sixty-third Street side and is adjacent to two extra dressing-rooms to be occupied only when quick changes are necessary. The room will be used by the players for social intercourse. It will never be open to the public. The dressing-rooms rise from the stage floor on the side of the theatre. Each is fitted with a double wardrobe, containing interior electric lights, a marble-topped make-up table with vari-colored lights that the effects of paints, powder and wigs may be determined, comfortable lounging chairs and hot and cold water. On each floor are tub and shower baths and many other luxuries and conveniences for the use of the players. The offices of the directorate and executive staff are on the third, fourth and fifth floors. The house is fitted with the latest appliances for quick communication.

The opening, although a great social success, was not an artistic triumph. E. H. Sothern and Julia Marlowe performed Shakespeare's *Antony and Cleopatra* and received very mixed reviews. Although the public seemed delighted with the new playhouse, they did complain about the acoustics. Perhaps the most interesting innovations were not seen in the house itself, but in equipment backstage.

8:2   STAGE OF THE NEW THEATRE
The Machinery Cost More Than a Quarter of a Million Dollars and Contains More Than One Million Pounds of Steel

The revolving stage at The New Theatre is said to be the most intricate and yet, in its operation, the most simple device of its kind in the world. It is sixty-four feet in diameter and revolves in one minute. It is made up of eight transverse sections and four segments, weighing altogether 56,000 pounds. There are more than one million pounds of steel in the stage machinery alone and it requires 700 horsepower to put it in full operation. The cost of the stage machinery alone was over $250,000. The device was the invention of Claude L. Hagen, technical director of The New Theatre.

8:2. New York *Tribune*, Jan. 6, 1910.

In describing the stage for Tribune readers Mr. Hagen said:

"The first revolving stage was in use during the sixteenth century by the Japanese. It was merely a round turntable. Since then various modifications have been devised. The stage of The New Theatre is a distinct type, inasmuch as it revolves, moves backward and forward, or transversely and up and down, as a whole or in parts. It also permits sections of the transverse stage to be dropped, and the rest of the sections to be opened so as to form sinks or cuts through which to lower whole sections.

"The main or underlying stage consists of eight members, each 7 by 48 feet. Each one of these members is operated by a vertical screw at each end so arranged as to engage with or be disengaged from a trackway on each side of the stage. Each one of these members is supplied with its own motor power, pneumatic drops, switches and telltales, for the purpose of safety and registering their positions. On the top of the transverse sections are 360 radial rollers, and pointing to the exact centre of the revolving stage floor.

"The revolving stage floor consists of eight sections, 7 by 48 feet each. These sections, when not used as a revolving floor, form the top floor of the transverse sections. At each side of the square formed by these eight sections is the segment, which, when locked together with the eight transverse sections, forms a circular slab 64 feet in diameter and 4½ inches in thickness. Two scenes may be built upon this stage—one facing the audience and one facing the back wall. When the first scene is through, the stage can then be revolved, bringing the second scene to face the audience, after which the first scene can then be taken from its place and the third scene set.

WAITS ALMOST ELIMINATED

"This stage enables us to reduce to a minimum the time between scenes. In so far as we are concerned, we could produce the scenes one after another without an appreciable wait—that is, when all the scenes are set beforehand. The only thing we have to do in such cases is to put in a new backing or a drop to make each scene complete. In 'Antony and Cleopatra' the palace scene was so large that we could not revolve the stage. . . ."

One of the most remarkable devices connected with the stage is the counterweight system for the raising and lowering of scenery. Instead of relying for this purpose on electric motors, which are notoriously unsafe in time of fire and unwieldy at all times, Mr. Hagen has invented an ingenious device, in which he uses small shot to balance the weight of the "drops" or scenery. . . .

The failure of the New Theatre is perhaps best explained by a critic, Walter Eaton.

8:3   A YEAR AT THE NEW THEATRE—
SUMMARY

The New Theatre has seemed to many observers not unlike the New Thought—somewhat vague and not particularly new. Just what artistic advance the theatre intends to further by its choice of plays is not much clearer at the conclusion of the first season than it was at the beginning; just what the theatre stands for in the dramatic world is not yet definitely outlined. And, in its physical proportions, the New Theatre is a reversion to the auditorium of a half-century and more ago—it is at least fifty years behind the times; while in its scheme of highly privileged support, its utterly undemocratic horseshoe of founders' boxes around which the auditorium has in reality been built, it is a directing product, almost a copy, of conditions pertaining to that fashionable and exotic pastime of the very well-to-do,

8:3. Walter Prichard Eaton, *At the New Theatre and Others* (Boston: Small, Maynard & Co., 1910), pp. 13–19.

—grand opera. In these important respects, there is nothing new about it.

In the New York *Evening World* of
March 28, 1908, was published an interview with the late Heinrich Conried, then
director of the Metropolitan Opera House.
In the course of this interview he said, "I
have been chosen to plan the New Theatre
in every detail. The architects made their
plans in accordance with my suggestions,
and I now have in preparation the plans
for the stage, the mechanical arrangements
necessary for the proper production of
plays." And he further stated that the
New Theatre, though it was not supported
by the government, would be a truly
"national" theatre, an "educational" institution. Unfortunately, his first statement
was correct—unfortunately, because Mr.
Conried's entire dramatic experience in
America had been confined to his German
playhouse, and later to the Metropolitan
Opera House. His own training as an
actor had been gained in the old-fashioned
Teutonic plays of long ago. He was igno-
rant of many obvious conditions on the
modern stage, especially the English-
speaking stage, and, furthermore, he was
ambitious to continue his operatic management, so profitable to him in many
ways. Mr. Conried died, and when the
group of some thirty wealthy men whom
he had gathered together as founders of
the New Theatre, each subscribing at the
start $35,000, summoned Granville Bar-
ker from England to consider the post of
director, Mr. Barker found an auditorium,
already nearing completion, which was
so vast and so badly constructed for the
performance of modern drama that he
took one look and went back to London.

The auditorium was designed by the
architects on its present scale not only to
meet the needs of opera (since opera
cannot be profitably presented without
large audiences), but also to make prominent display of a horseshoe of twenty-
three founders' boxes. The founders of
the New Theatre are chiefly men finan-

cially interested in the Metropolitan
Opera House and pillars of its social
prestige. Their idea, and presumably the
idea of their wives,—whose influence cannot be left out of the reckoning,—was to
duplicate at the New Theatre operatic
conditions, "to dramatize the diamond
horseshoe," as Henry Miller puts it. Now,
quite aside from the utterly undemocratic
nature of such a social display in a playhouse loftily announced as "national" in
scope and "educational" in intention, this
horseshoe of boxes, ranged at the rear of
the orchestra-chairs, threw the whole
scheme of the auditorium out of scale for
a theatre. In order to make the occupants
of the boxes prominently visible, the
balconies could not be swung forward
over the orchestra floor. The first row of
the balconies is no nearer the stage than
this row of boxes, and the last row of the
third, and highest, balcony is thus distant
from the stage almost double the depth of
of the large orchestra pit, besides being
raised an enormous distance in air. Over
this orchestra pit yawns a mighty void,
wherein the voices of the actors wander
tentative and dim. From the balcony not
only is it a strain to hear, but the stage is
so far off that it seems to be viewed
through the wrong end of an opera-glass.
Any intimacy with the play and players
is utterly out of the question. Thus, as a
result of the double blunder in the original
scheme of the New Theatre, the plan to
mix drama and opera in the same house
and the plan to make of it a social diversion for the wealthy founders, the
theatre has started on its career under a
well-nigh insurmountable handicap.

It would seem that the founders and
their families, if we may judge by the infre-
quency of their use of the boxes, recognize
this fact. The truth is that the dramatic
performances at the New Theatre do
not interest them; and a potent cause is
the lack of intimacy in the auditorium,
for which they themselves are to blame.
It should require no argument to convince

anyone at all familiar with the stage that the modern intimate auditorium is an integral part of the modern intimate drama and acting; that we can no more go back with pleasure and profit to the old vasty spaces where Forrest thundered than we can go back to the old plays which gave him ammunition. And it should require no argument to convince any thoughtful observer that men, however wealthy, prominent, and philanthropic, when they announce that they are going to build a playhouse for the public good and the uplift of the drama, and then, for the exotic pastime of grand opera and the prominent display of their own persons, erect an auditorium utterly destructive of dramatic illusion, especially in those regions where the poorer classes must sit, need not be surprised if the public does not hail them unreservedly as benefactors nor flock to their theatre. There is a distinct taint of insincerity and and snobbishness in the New Theatre which has perverted its physical design and threatens its usefulness. To deny this, or to try to disguise it, would be, to put it mildly, a waste of time.

The crying need of the New Theatre before another season begins, then, is a radical alteration of the auititorium, which of course means, first, the abolition of the incongruous grand opera. Fortunately, the abolition of opera is certain, and some consequent changes will be made in the auditorium, looking toward a reduction of its size. The founders of the theatre, who are its absolute owners and who will bear the heavy deficit, have a right to their boxes, and neither critic nor public has any voice in the matter. But possibly a lessening of the deficit might atone to some extent for the loss of the boxes, and possibly, too, the greater usefulness of the theatre to the public, the greater vividness and interest of its productions, might act as compensation, if the founders are sincere in their expressed desire to serve the stage in America. By alternate occupancy

a lesser number of boxes ranged (no less prominently!) to right and left of the proscenium, as in an ordinary theatre, might conceivably suffice. Then the balconies could be swung forward, the top balcony —at present a pocket to catch and deaden sound—eliminated, and the too-high ceiling lowered. If some of the overload of ostentatious decoration were lost in the process, so much the better. Thus arranged for greater intimacy, the house would hold enough people—say sixteen hundred—for probably profitable operation, with eight performances a week, if it was kept reasonably full. As originally constructed it seats twenty-three hundred people, at least half of them farther from the stage than the rear of the orchestra pit. Certainly the gain in intimacy, vividness, and enjoyment of the play would be incalculable. Until something of the sort is done the New Theatre will remain an opulent semi-failure, be the company never so fine and the plays presented never so worthy. . . .

9. GLOBE THEATRE
New York City
Opened January 10, 1910

Named for the famous Globe Theatre in Southwark, London, with which Shakespeare was associated, this playhouse was opened by Charles Dillingham in 1910 and played legitimate theater productions until 1932, when it was converted into a motion picture theater. In 1958, however, the playhouse was completely remodeled and reopened as the Lunt-Fontanne Theatre, to become one of the most popular playhouses in New York.

The opening performance at the theater was a musical play, *The Old Town* by George Ade. The New York *Dramatic Mirror* described the house as follows:

9:1   Mr. Charles Dillingham opened his new theatre on Monday evening, Jan-

9:1 New York *Dramatic Mirror*, Jan. 22, 1910.

uary 10, under the most gratifying auspices with Montgomery and Stone in The Old Town, an attraction that provided a thoroughly enjoyable entertainment and promises to rank high in popular favor for months to come.

Named for the old playhouse at Bankside in which Shakespeare produced his plays, the new house is one of the most comfortable theatres on Broadway, with a large stage and a compact auditorium designed after the architecture of the Italian Renaissance, with draperies of Rose du Barry and the walls of an old gold and blue and ivory white. The theatre has its main entrance on Broadway, just above Forty-sixth Street, flanked on either side by Ionic pilasters with simple panels between. The principal facade, in handsome design, is on Forty-sixth Street. A foyer on level with the first balcony, affords admittance through large windows to an exterior balcony on Forty-sixth Street, and provides, the weather permitting, an entr'acte al fresco balcony promenade. The Forty-sixth Street entrances include a vestibule for carriage patrons, decorated in character with the rest of the interior. A large oval panel of the ceiling may be opened when desired, the audience being then permitted to contemplate an open sky from the auditorium, a complete novelty in American theatrical architecture, by which the theatre may be transformed into practically an open-air theatre. . . .

Following the transformation of the playhouse into the Lunt-Fontanne Theatre, an article in *Theatre Arts* pointed to a few new decorative and architectural features.

9:2   The Globe, one of New York's most celebrated playhouses, with prestige comparable to that of the Empire and the

9:2. Ward Morehouse, "Famous American Theatres," *Theatre Arts*, May 1958, pp. 64–65; by special permission of Jovanna Ceccarelli, Publisher.

Lyceum, was recently renovated and renamed the Lunt-Fontanne, after the noted acting team. It has been turned into a dazzling theatre, and it is now quite as beautiful as any house given over to the legitimate stage in all of America. It has begun a career all over again after being lost to the stage for twenty-six years. The job of renovation has been truly spectacular. Of the old Globe, only a shell remains. The stone facade maintains the Italian Renaissance style of the original. But the new marquee has the look of antique silver, and during the winter months there will be heat in the ceiling of it, thus keeping the sidewalk warm and dry. And in the summertime that adaptable marquee will be air-cooled, and you'll know it if you walk under it. The entire theatre is air-conditioned at all times and furnished with what Robert Dowling calls "clear mountain air." The new interior is one of soft powder-blue walls, crystal chandeliers and a "three dimensional" blue curtain. "The theatre is one place," remarked Mr. Dowling, "in which everyone is looking at the same wall, meaning the curtain, so we decided to have a curtain that is really beautiful. . . ."

. . . The mezzanine promenade, in yellow and silver, features a lounge, eighteen by eighty-eight feet, which is accessible directly from the aisles, rather than from a single entrance. The two balconies of the old structure have been replaced by a single mezzanine seating 750 persons. The mezzanine can be reached from the foyer by climbing one short flight.

The impressive interior of the Lunt-Fontanne is in rococo style, and the dominant color is soft blue. The orchestra section seats 800 and its first eight rows comprise upholstered armchairs. Under each seat of the 1,550-seat house are a pillow (for use of short persons) and a footstool (for those with short legs). Opera glasses are also provided.

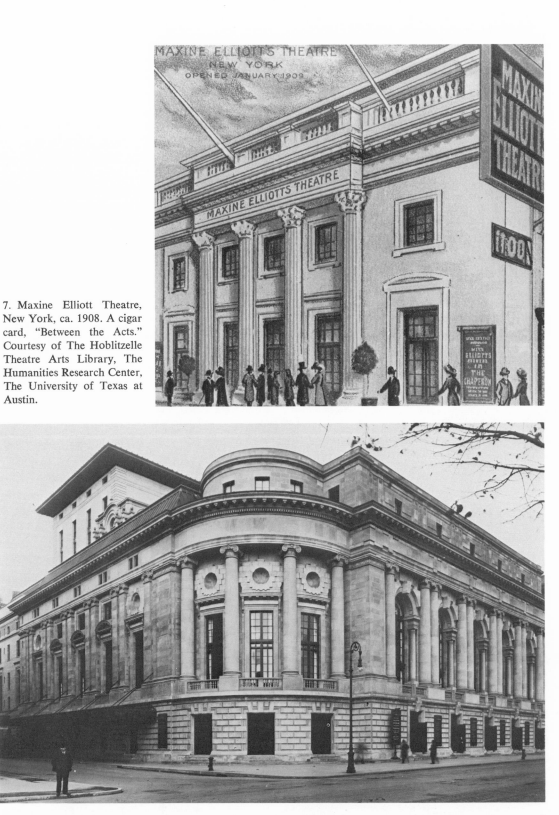

7. Maxine Elliott Theatre, New York, ca. 1908. A cigar card, "Between the Acts." Courtesy of The Hoblitzelle Theatre Arts Library, The Humanities Research Center, The University of Texas at Austin.

8. The New Theatre (later the Century), New York, 1909. Photograph by Geo. P. Hall and Son. Courtesy of The New-York Historical Society, New York City.

9. Globe Theatre, New York, ca. 1910. Courtesy of The Hoblitzelle Theatre Arts Library, The Humanities Research Center, The University of Texas at Austin.

10. Winter Garden, New York, ca. 1911. Courtesy of the Museum of the City of New York.

10. Interior, Winter Garden, New York, ca. 1911. Photograph by Hall. Courtesy of The Hoblitzelle Theatre Arts Library, The Humanities Research Center, The University of Texas at Austin.

10. WINTER GARDEN
New York City
Opened March 20, 1911

One of the most popular playhouses in New York has been the Winter Garden, which opened in 1911 at Broadway and Fiftieth Street. It was originally built by the Shuberts and through the years was famous for the musical productions presented there.

The review in the New York *Tribune* tells of the performance and describes the theatre as it appeared to the first-night audience.

10:1   WINTER GARDEN OPEN
Continental Variete at 50th Street
and Broadway.

The new Winter Garden, at 50th street and Broadway, opened last night. The novelty and interest of the performance repaid the public for submitting patiently to several postponements. Such a combination of talent as was exhibited last night is not to be seen usually except at some benefit performance where the best artists of all types contribute their services. The quality of the music, the beauty of the costumes, the daring brilliancy of the color schemes, the skill of the players and the variety of the acts so pleased the large audience that it found the usual methods of applause inadequate and expressed its appreciation by cheers. To the critical eye and ear the artistry of the performers was a delight. It was a brilliant opening, long to be remembered in the annals of New York amusement. . . .

The new place of amusement will doubtless prove popular in all seasons, for architecturally it is adapted to the roof garden type of entertainment in the summer and to the variété in the winter.

The Winter Garden occupies the plot of ground extending through Broadway to Seventh avenue, just above 50th street. The main entrances are on the Broadway front with the stage entrance and numer-

ous exits from the orchestra and balcony on the Seventh avenue side. Five mahogany doors, separated by pilasters, open directly from the sidewalk into the spacious marble lobby.

The interior decorations are of old ivory and gold. The walls are finished in lattice work done in plaster. The ceiling is also latticed, and through the interstices is visible an artificial "sky." The auditorium is lighted by electric lamps concealed above the latticed ceiling.

A pleasing feature of the Winter Garden is the liberal allowance of promenade space. On the orchestra floor the aisle behind the rear row of seats is sixteen feet wide; in the balcony the promenade is even wider. During the intermissions last night the spectacle was a lively one. A large smoking room, with service room and bar adjoining, is on the ground floor. Here liquors are dispensed at New Theatre prices. A dutch refreshment room, finished in Delft blue, is on the balcony level at the Broadway side.

The orchestra seats a thousand people and the balcony seats eight hundred more, but the front of the balcony is given exclusively to a horseshoe of twenty-nine boxes, flanked at either end by two additional stage boxes. . . .

11. THE PLAYHOUSE
New York City
Opened April 15, 1911

William A. Brady, an actor and theatrical manager, opened the Playhouse on Forty-eighth Street on April 15, 1911, with a production of *Sauce for the Goose,* starring his wife, Grace George. The theater saw some very successful productions from its inception; one of the most popular was Tennessee Williams's *The Glass Menagerie.*

11:1   THE PLAYHOUSE.

11:1. New York *Dramatic Mirror,* Apr. 19, 1911.

10:1. New York *Tribune,* Mar. 21, 1911.

William A. Brady's New Theatre on
Forty-eighth Street Described
and Pictured.

The Playhouse, William A. Brady's new
theatre, has opened its doors. The formal
opening and dedication took place Saturday night, when Grace George gave
two performances of Sauce for the Goose,
her new comedy, by Geraldine Bonner
and Hutcheson Boyd. Overnight opened
Monday evening, April 17, for a run,
moving from the Hackett Theatre.

The Playhouse is New York's newest
theatre. Its location on Forty-eighth Street,
just east of Broadway, brings it within
easy reach of lines of travel centering in
the uptown theatre district. The building
is constructed of brick, with stone facing,
and is a combination of the French and
Colonial styles of architecture. The front
of the building is imposing and almost
severe, but this severity is relieved by
stone carvings of comedy and tragedy, set
in the wall, marble window medallions,
a flowered frieze, and other ornaments of
trimmed stone, and also by the novel
beauty of the entrance.

The main entrance is under a handsome
canopy of steel and glass, and leads
through oaken doors, set with diamond
glass, into the lobby, which is inclosed in
white marble. The main entrance, as well
as the entrances leading to the gallery and
studios, are flanked by brick posts, surmounted with stone urns, and joined by
a novel grilled iron fence. The effect is
quaintly effective.

The interior of the house gives the impression of cosy compactness. All parts
of the house, including the balcony and
gallery, are brought very near to the stage,
so that audience and players will be in
close sympathy. The loss of depth in obtaining the result is compensated for by
the extreme width of the auditorium. The
boxes are set back, although they are
large and roomy, and there is no interference with the line of vision.

The decorations are in deep red, gold,
and brown, with brown carpets and blue
draperies. The chairs are wide, and sufficient space is left between the rows for
easy ingress and egress. The heating and
ventilation are up-to-date, and the arrangements for the comfort of patrons are
unusually complete.

The stage of The Playhouse is large,
and fitted with every appliance known to
modern stagecraft. It can be utilized for
the simple stage settings of a parlor comedy or the intricate stage paraphanalia of
a spectacle. Mr. Brady has given particular attention to the stage of The Playhouse, because it is here that all his important new attractions will be staged and
rehearsed. Especial attention has also
been given to the dressing-rooms for the
players. They are cosy and comfortable,
steam-heated and well ventilated, and furnished with every convenience. The star
dressing-rooms have bathrooms attached.
The lighting arrangements are especially
complete, and the curtain and all other
lifting work will be controlled by electricity.

The Playhouse is declared to be absolutely fireproof. There is not a stick of
wood in the construction of the building,
and the oak trimmings are all imbedded
in cement. The platforms and parapets
are all cement, and the seats are fastened
to a solid cement flooring. Fire escapes
of the most improved pattern with wide
platforms and steps afford a ready and
expeditious means of emptying the upper
part of the house. A ten-foot alley, in
each side of the house, with doors opening outward from the audience, will make
it possible to empty the main part of the
auditorium in one minute. The alley extends around the rear of the building, so
that the theatre is completely isolated from
other buildings.

Mr. Brady's entire theatrical business
will centre at The Playhouse. All the
theatrical organizations under his control

will be managed from his general offices in the building, which he has recently occupied. These offices occupy the entire floor immediately over the theatre, and are large, roomy, and light. The offices surround a large reception room, and comprise a suite of offices for Mr. Brady, the office of the general manager, the booking office, the financial office, the press room, and other departments. The top floor of The Playhouse Building is devoted to studios. The Playhouse Company is the lessee of the building, and William A. Brady is the sole manager.

12. FULTON THEATRE
New York City
Opened October 30, 1911

This playhouse originally opened on April 26, 1911, as a restaurant-theater, something completely new to the New York theater scene. It was named the Folies Bergere, after the famed cabaret theater in Paris, but it did not prove successful and soon closed. After some slight remodeling it was reopened on October 30 as the Fulton Theatre and has been a successful playhouse. In 1955 it was again renamed, this time the Helen Hayes Theatre in honor of the famous actress.

A description of the structure, before it opened as the Folies Bergere, appeared in the New York *Dramatic Mirror*.

12:1   THE FOLIES BERGERE
A Novel Entertainment Structure Added to New York's Amusement Places.

The scaffolding was removed last week from the front of the new Folies Bergere in Forty-sixth Street west of Broadway revealing the colored-tile front and the mural painting, "Comedy," the work of artist William de L. Dodge. The facade drew interested crowds, and it was re-

12:1. New York *Dramatic Mirror*, Apr. 12, 1911.

marked that the Folies Bergere is the most original theatre structure in New York.

Henry B. Harris and Jesse L. Lasky announce the opening late in April. The place will be a restaurant-music hall. More than $1,000,000, it is said, is being invested in the theatre and its companies. The house is an architectural exotic with a front of glazed tiles set in Louis Seize designs and inset with the mural painting depicting the origin and development of comedy. This outside will be lit at night by blazing gas torches softened with steam.

The Folies Bergere aims to be the smartest restaurant and the smartest music hall in the world. The orchestra de luxe of the Folies Bergere will have no seats as in the ordinary theatre. Instead the entire space will be taken up by movable tables and chairs. By a patented arrangement all chairs and tables face the stage, and tables can instantly be set in units for parties of any size. There are boxes with chairs and tables in the box circle and behind them more restaurant room. There are theatre seats in the balcony and grand circle. The kitchens, wine cellars and storerooms are cut out of solid rock beneath the street and alleys. The space directly beneath the auditorium is given over to two Louis Seize dressing-rooms, bathrooms, barber shop, manicures, valets and other comforts of a club or hotel. The Folies Bergere will open for dinner at 6 p.m. During dinner mandolin and guitar players, violinists, singers and dancers will go from table to table giving tabloid shows full of verve and sensation. At 8:15 when the diners have reached their coffee and cigarettes the curtain will go up on a revue which will be followed by a ballet and then by another revue. At 11 p.m. the first show of the evening will be over, and at 11:15 there will begin supper and the cabaret show made up of sensational novelties from Europe. This will run until

1 a.m. The second, or cabaret show has nothing to do with the first entertainment and to see both it will be necessary to purchase two sets of coupons. Prices will range from $1 to $2.50 at the early show, and $1 to $1.50 at the second. One may buy for either one or both. Smoking will be permitted all over the house.

The Folies Bergere will have a broad promenade, bars on every floor and a big gold champagne bar for the promenaders. There will be a luxurious greenroom, flower shops, information bureau, forty telephone stations, special taxicabs, girl pages in costume and novelties in every feature of the house, the entertainment and the policy. . . .

The New York *Times,* reviewing the opening of the Fulton, called it a cosy little playhouse.

12:2   The Fulton, minus its tables, is a comfortable, a cosy, and attractive little house. It should be popular with audiences when it has just the right play. . . .

13. LITTLE THEATRE
New York City
Opened March 12, 1912

Winthrop Ames was one of that group of producers and artists who revolted against the commercialism of the Broadway theater and tried to bring new playwrights, designers, and actors to the people who were interested in seeing experimental theater. His Little Theater movement had been gaining momentum for several years and would later result in the organizing of the Provincetown Players and the Washington Square Players.

In order to present the new plays, which he felt would not have a large audience in New York, he built an intimate little playhouse with only 299 seats and named it The Little Theatre. It was built on the south side of Forty-fourth Street between Broadway and Eighth Avenue.

12:2 New York *Times,* Oct. 31, 1911.

13:1   PLAYHOUSE DECORATIONS

Lobby in White in Colonial Style and Auditorium in Walnut.

The audience of Winthrop Ames's Little Theatre last night found almost as much interest in the arrangement and decorations of the playhouse as they did in the production of the play. The red-brick, green-shuttered exterior, with white entrance doors, attracted first attention, and then the lobby came in for inspection. This is done in white, in Colonial style, with a fireplace at one end, opposite the entrance. A stairway leads down to the smoking room and the tearoom. The only relief to the white walls is a large piece of Italian brocade velvet of the eighteenth century, that still holds its brilliant colors.

The auditorium itself has only 299 seats, and is without a balcony or boxes. The seats are arranged on a steep incline, so that a full view of the stage can be had from every chair. The decorations, which follow the elliptical form of the hall, consist of high paneling in walnut effect, topped by tapestry hangings. This tapestry is a copy of a design by Jacques Tessier of the gobelin works, made about 1766–71, with central medallions from designs by Boucher.

The ceiling of the auditorium is in white, bordered with old ivory, with panels in low relief. The lighting is by two ceiling candelabra and several groups of electric candles around the walls. The curtains are of blue and silver brocade, with tapestry borders, and the drop curtain is of gobelin blue. The carpet is mouse gray, and the seats, of walnut effect, are upholstered in brown leather.

The ladies' parlor, which opens from the lobby, has white woodwork and walls and is furnished in mahogany. Downstairs the smoking room has woodwork in walnut effect, with a red tiled floor and red leather upholstery on the wall benches.

13:1. New York *Times,* Dec. 13, 1912.

A number of old English prints of actors hang on the walls.

The tea room, which is half as big as the auditorium, has white woodwork, and also has a big fireplace at one end. The furniture is of oak, of the period of William and Mary. The other rooms of the building follow closely the Adam period of colonial design. In the tea room there is a large service table and a number of small tables. Here tea and coffee are served free during the intermissions. . . .

Artistically the Little Theatre was a success, but financially it was impossible to support such a program with a seating capacity of only 299. Edith Isaacs, in her book *Architecture for the New Theatre,* stated: "Perhaps the main fault with New York's Little Theatre is that it was built in New York. Where rents are exorbitant and land assessments high, a theatre of small audience capacity is severely handicapped as a business project."*

An announcement in the New York *Times* bore out this contention.

13:2   MAY LOSE LITTLE THEATRE
_____

Ames Plans to Remodel House to Increase Its Capacity to 1,000.

If contemplated plans carry, New York will lose her first and most luxurious intimate theatre before next season. Winthrop Ames is considering entirely remodeling his Little Theatre and making it into a playhouse of regulation size, seating upward of a thousand people. Plans have been drawn up, and whether or not the change is made will depend on the practicality of remodeling the present building.

The contemplated changes will necessitate a complete remodeling of the building. A balcony will be added, the auditorium greatly enlarged, and probably a new stage built. The work will be done in the Summer to allow the theatre to reopen next Fall.

The playhouse was bought and enlarged by the Shuberts and later was used as a radio broadcasting studio and as a television theater. It reverted to theatrical productions again in 1963 and a year later was renamed the Winthrop Ames in honor of the builder.

14. CORT THEATRE
New York City
Opened December 20, 1912

Forty-eighth Street received a new playhouse in 1912 when the Cort Theatre opened with Laurette Taylor in *Peg o' My Heart,* one of her most popular successes. The theater was a relatively small one, seating less than 1,000 persons, but it was admirably suited to the presentation of intimate dramas.

The following description of the playhouse is from the New York *Tribune:*

14:1   CORT THEATRE OPENS TO-NIGHT
_____

Laurette Taylor, in "Peg o' My Heart," by J. Hartley Manners Will Be First Attraction to Appear at New Playhouse.

New York's newest playhouse will be thrown open to the public to-night when the lights go up in the Cort Theatre, in West 48th street. Laurette Taylor in "Peg o' My Heart," a new play by J. Hartley Manners, under a comparatively new manager, Oliver Morosco, will have the honor of dedicating this latest temple of the stage art. It is the first of three theatres to be erected in the East by John Cort, himself a new factor in local theatricals.

The new theatre is the work of Edward B. Corey, who has drawn upon the architecture of the time of Louis XVI of France for his inspiration. Its facade is of marble, with four Corinthian columns as its most distinctive feature.

In its interior the Louis Seize type is also maintained. The lobby of the theatre

*Edith J. R. Isaacs, *Architecture for the New Theatre* (New York: Theatre Arts Books, 1935), p. 43. Copyright 1934, 1935 by Theatre Arts, Inc.

13:2. New York *Times,* Mar. 11, 1915.

14:1. New York *Tribune,* Dec. 20, 1912.

is of Pavanozza marble with panels of Marie Antoinette plaster work, the metal work of the box office being bronze with gold leaf and enamel relief. The design and execution have been in the hands of the Tiffany Studios.

The auditorium has been arranged in a general color scheme of old rose and gold against a background of plaster work in tones of champagne and sienna. The theatre has a seating capacity of 999, with an orchestra floor, balcony and gallery. There are 424 seats in the orchestra, 244 in the balcony and 259 in the gallery, while an arrangement of twelve boxes, seating six, completes the seating plan of the house.

A distinctive feature of the interior is the proscenium arch, which is of perforated plaster work against a background of art glass capable of illumination during the performance. The sounding board has been decorated with a painting of a minuet during the period made famous in Watteau's drawings of French court life at Versailles.

There will be no orchestra in the theatre, its place being taken by the installation of the Wurlitzer Hope-Jones unit orchestra, an electrical instrument capable of operation by one musician.

15. SHUBERT THEATRE
New York City
Opened October 2, 1913

The Shubert Theatre, officially The Sam S. Shubert Memorial Theatre, was built as a memorial to the Shubert brother who knew the most about the theater, started his brothers in the theatrical business, and died as the result of a railroad accident when he was only twenty-nine. It was also built to house the widespread Shubert theater empire, and here the brothers kept their offices until they died. Lee lived in his office suite.

The playhouse had an impressive beginning, presenting the great British actor Johnston

Forbes-Robertson in his farewell performances as Hamlet.

15:1   NEW SHUBERT THEATRE

Description of Playhouse to Open with Forbes-Robertson.

The Shubert Theatre, named in commemoration of the achievements of the late Sam S. Shubert, will open its doors to the public for the first time on Thursday evening, Oct. 2, when its dedication will be marked by the appearance of Forbes-Robertson in his farewell engagement. The management feels that using the stage for such a purpose as this at the very beginning will establish a dramatic precedent of the highest order. The Shubert Theatre is situated on the north side of 44th street, west of Broadway, and under the same roof as the new Booth Theatre, opening under the management of Winthrop Ames, in the near future. It is, however, an entirely distinct building, not only in its internal separation from the other structure, but also in its style of decoration and many other particulars. The seating capacity is just about 1,400—624 orchestra seats, 413 balcony seats and 363 gallery seats and four boxes. The style of the building might be described as Venetian Renaissance, with certain modern adaptations. The most striking feature of the exterior is the use of hand-carved agrafitto for decorating purposes. Henry B. Harris, architect for the new Shubert Theatre, is the first man to have used agrafitto for this purpose.

The interior of the theatre has been elaborately and tastefully decorated by O. H. Bauer with mural paintings by Lichtenauer. The stage, which is large enough for the "heaviest" productions, is most completely equipped, and the dressing rooms are in a wing of the building completely isolated by fire walls and fire doors. The theatre building also contains

15:1. New York *Tribune*, Sept. 28, 1913.

two floors of studios, which are to be used for administrative purposes.

16. BOOTH THEATRE
New York City
Opened October 16, 1913

The first theater to bear this illustrious name was built in 1869 by Edwin Booth, the great tragic actor. That playhouse was acclaimed as one of the most innovative of its day, but it had a short life—it was torn down in 1883 to make way for a department store.

The new Booth Theatre was built by Winthrop Ames, one of the more active producers of the day, who had managed the New Theatre and the Little Theatre. He opened the Booth with *The Great Adventure,* a play by Arnold Bennett, based on his novel *Buried Alive.* Both the play and the theater were warmly received by the public, and the Booth Theatre in the early 1970s was still one of the more popular playhouses in New York.

The New York *Tribune* first described it on October 5.

16:1   NEW BOOTH THEATRE
    WINTHROP AMES'S NEW PLAYHOUSE
        OPENS NEXT WEEK.

Winthrop Ames's new Booth Theatre, in 45th street, west of Broadway, is to be opened on Thursday evening, Oct. 16, with the first American production of "The Great Adventure." The theatre is back to back and connected with the new Shubert Theatre, in 44th street, although [the] buildings are not in direct communication. It is built in the same style of architecture as the Shubert; that is, it is a development of the early Italian Renaissance, with designs in agrafitto in brown and ivory, colors which harmonize with the exterior of the theatre, which is yellow brick and ivory terra cotta. The interior of the Booth, however, is its more remarkable feature. The auditorium is large and spacious, and there are ample facilities for foyers and reception rooms. Several

16:1. New York *Tribune,* Oct. 5, 1913.

novel features of theatrical architecture will be seen for the first time, notably a wall which partitions off the entrance from the body of the house, preventing outside sounds and drafts from coming directly to the auditorium. The reception room is a further development of Mr. Ames's idea of a French foyer.

This new theatre has been called the Booth to commemorate the interest which Mr. Ames's father had in the old Booth Theatre, which was situated on 23rd street and Sixth avenue, as well as to pay tribute to America's greatest actor. The theatre contains many souvenirs of Booth, such as the armchair which Booth had in his greenroom at the old Booth Theatre and in which he used to sit between acts. A statue of Booth, the only copy of the famous one at the Players' Club, is in the promenade foyer, and the walls are hung with bills announcing Booth's appearance at various American theatres. . . .

The following Sunday the New York *Tribune* continued its description with a picture of the interior.

16:2   THE BOOTH THEATRE
    ――――――――――

Some Notes on the Decoration of
Mr. Ames's Playhouse.

The new Booth Theatre, to open on Thursday with "The Great Adventure," has for the color scheme of its interior decoration a combination selected by Mr. Ames of neutral tints of driftwood gray for the woodwork and walls, enlivened by draperies and upholstery of mulberry velvet—the only shade of red which harmonizes with practically every other color used. Incidentally the decorations of the theatre, like those of French playhouses, will set off and harmonize with a gown of any color. The carpet, of a lighter and darker shade of mulberry, was especially manufactured for the theatre.

As the interior of the Booth Theatre is

16:2. New York *Tribune,* Oct. 17, 1913.

an adaptation of the Georgian style, the chandeliers and appliques along the walls give the impression of candle lights. The real lighting of the house, however, comes from a softened reflection of the light from the alabaster bowls which support the bronze candlesticks forming the chandeliers. The curtain of the Booth Theatre is of the same rich shade of mulberry velvet as the decorations of the house, but painted and embroidered in a glowing mosaic of colors shading from the rich varieties of peacock blues and greens to brilliant orange and topaz.

The Booth Theatre has a relatively small seating capacity. There are 638 seats in the house, 445 in the orchestra and 223 in the balcony. There are no orchestra boxes, but there are four in the upper tier. Altogether the Booth Theatre is a fitting monument to the memory of the great actor whose name it bears.

17. BANDBOX THEATRE
New York City
Opened December 22, 1914

Originally opened in 1912 as the Adolph Phillipps Theatre for a German theater group, the playhouse in 1914 was taken over by the New York Play Actors, Inc., and renamed the Bandbox Theatre. It was a small, intimate playhouse, well suited for the type of experimental drama in which the group was interested. Later, in 1915, the Washington Square Players performed in this theater until they moved into larger quarters in the Comedy Theatre in 1917. The Bandbox was at 205 East Fifty-seventh Street.

The formal announcement of the new playhouse in the New York *Times* explained the aims of the performing group.

17:1   PLANS FOR THE BANDBOX
_____

Douglas Wood to Open New Theatre
Before Christmas.

Announcement of the final plans for

17:1. New York *Times*, Nov. 29, 1914.

the opening of the season of the New York Play Actors, Inc., in the Bandbox Theatre, 205 East Fifty-seventh Street, formerly the Adolph Philip [Phillipps] Theatre, call for the formal opening Tuesday night, Dec. 22, when "Poor Little Thing," a new comedy by Jerome K. Jerome, will be presented for the first time. The story is an adaptation from the French play of the same name by Jules Lemaitre which Guitry presented in Paris for a run last Winter. Rehearsals are now in progress. The first performance on any stage will be an invitational dress rehearsal on Monday night, Dec. 21.

The theatre will be under the managing directorship of Douglas J. Wood. Edward Elsner has been engaged as the technical stage director. Associated with Mr. Wood in the management of the new enterprise are Harry Doel Parker, Miss Marie Keickhoefer, and Theodore Mitchell. A company of professional players has been gathered into the roster of the organization. There will be no stars, and each member will be assigned whatever role it is thought will serve to give a complete and perfect production. A new play will be presented each month. For the current season five plays have been selected by the director and an advisory committee of associate members, who head the subscription lists for the new company. In the event of one of the plays proving suitable for a longer run in any of the larger commercial theatres of the regular district, the play will be given later under these conditions.

The aim is to make the theatre a permanent home for a thoroughly equipped company where new plays and occasional classical revivals will be the rule. The management will also have the cooperation of the Rehearsal Club, the Three Arts Club, and the Music League, and the theatre will be at the disposal of these companies when it is not devoted to the six nightly and two matinee performances of the permanent organization.

11. The Playhouse, New York, 1911. Photograph by White. Courtesy of The Hoblitzelle Theatre Arts Library, The Humanities Research Center, The University of Texas at Austin.

13. The Little Theatre, New York, 1912. Photograph partially retouched. Courtesy of The Hoblitzelle Theatre Arts Library, The Humanities Research Center, The University of Texas at Austin.

14. Cort Theatre (under construction), New York, 1912. Photograph by White. Courtesy of The Hoblitzelle Theatre Arts Library, The Humanities Research Center, The University of Texas at Austin.

15. Shubert Theatre, New York, 1913. Courtesy of The Hoblitzelle Theatre Arts Library, The Humanities Research Center, The University of Texas at Austin.

17. Bandbox Theatre, New York, 1914. Courtesy of The Hoblitzelle Theatre Arts Library, The Humanities Research Center, The University of Texas at Austin.

The theatre is to be supported by a subscription clientele. It will be cooperative to the extent that 50 per cent of the revenue is to be devoted to a sinking fund to assure the permanency of the organization and to provide pensions for those of the company who make it a permanent institution. Ten per cent of the profits will be monthly given to the Actors' Fund.

The New York *Tribune* commented on the physical aspects of the theater.

17:2 . . . It is a small house, the capacity being limited to 299 seats on the lower floor. . . . The Bandbox Theatre has been made into a cosey and yet entirely practical theatre for the presentation of most any play the company shall decide upon producing. It has been refurnished throughout, and while it has not been elaborately decorated, there is the intimacy maintained between the theatre and the stage which fits in with the purposes of the new organization. . . .

18. NEIGHBORHOOD PLAYHOUSE
New York City
Opened February 12, 1915

The attempt by two women, Alice and Irene Lewisohn, to bring cultural opportunities to the deprived people living on the Lower East Side of New York resulted in the building of The Neighborhood Playhouse at 466 Grand Street. These two philanthropic lovers of the drama were the daughters of Leonard Lewisohn, a copper magnate. In the afternoon plays and motion pictures were presented for the children of the ghetto area, while the evening performances were devoted to the adults. The Lewisohn sisters had been active in the Henry Street Settlement house and had performed in plays there. Their productions in the new playhouse were of very high caliber.

Alice Lewisohn (Crowley) wrote a history of the Neighborhood Playhouse with the sub-

17:2. New York *Tribune*, Dec. 20, 1914.

title, "Leaves from a Theatre Scrapbook." The following excerpts tell of the building of the theater:

18:1   PLANNING A HOME

Those early years, we had been schooled in the ways of the wandering players, perpetual poachers. Our rehearsal preserve was the dining room of the Henry Street Settlement after dinner hours; our theatre was where we found it, the gymnasium, the improvised stage at Clinton Hall, the neighborhood streets. So the thought of a home of our own had grown to more than a wistful dream. Although the idea of a new building was to carry further the work of the festivals and plays, its possible scope and value extended beyond our own productions. In fact, we thought of it first as a center for the creative expression of artist, craftsman, and student, not limited strictly to the neighborhood. Even as image, it anticipated the opportunity for the old and the young, the initiated and the potentially gifted in the arts, to contribute their part to an individual adventure in theatre.

The building was planned for utmost simplicity. Decorative values were indicated merely through architectural proportions, the use of materials, and the play of light and shade produced by a special system of indirect lighting. Not only were hangings and upholstery eliminated but the same frugality was observed in relation to the stage lighting equipment, and so forth, so that ingenuity and imagination might be the directing forces in all departments. The building was also planned for the running of motion picture shows, projected as an experimental venture.

Months were required to study the complex needs of the building: adequate rehearsal and classroom space, dressing

18:1. From *The Neighborhood Playhouse* by Alice Lewisohn Crowley, pp. 35–41. © 1959 by Alice Lewisohn Crowley. Reprinted by permission of the publishers, Theatre Arts Books, New York.

rooms, workshop for making costumes and properties, scene dock, greenroom, lunchroom, and office. Children's classes had also to be considered, besides the more obvious problems of stage and auditorium. The preparation and execution of the plans absorbed two years, largely because many city departments had to be consulted about peculiar problems the Playhouse presented. These included the unprecedented plan to operate for both motion pictures and plays. Also, we sought permission to operate Sundays, for the Neighborhood Players and the Festival Dancers were to alternate in presenting weekend programs, while the motion pictures were planned for nightly midweek performances.

The city officials, however courteous, maintained a justified doubt. Was it a theatre or not a theatre? In each situation, the influence and rapport of Lillian Wald with the city departments paved the way to the cooperation of the department chiefs in the building of this wholly untraditional enterprise.

In the spring of 1914, after each brick, hinge, and nail had been chosen, Irene and I went abroad to make contacts with the foreign theatre and to see the new technique in stage lighting in Germany. We were amazed at the extravagance with which whole lighting systems were introduced today and discarded tomorrow. The elaborate mechanism of revolving stages and huge plaster cycloramas of the German theatre did not always add the promised glamour to the performances. *A Midsummer Night's Dream* at the Reinhardt theatre suffered a total eclipse under the maneuvers of the revolving stage. Moreover, the effect of the German interpretation of Shakespeare, with the substitution of burlesque for comedy and farce for fantasy, was not a happy innovation. On the other hand, there was rare beauty in the intimate theatre of Germany. The subtlety of direction and the quality of

playing in Reinhardt's production of Wedekind's *Frühlings Erwachen* remains one of the great experiences of theatre.

The Dalcroze School was an important experiment in dance at that time, so we went to Hellerau to observe its work. There was an atmosphere of the Greek gymnasia about the school. The students, men and women, moved about freely in their dance costumes, which were one-piece bathing suits in effect, over which they wore, when not in class, a brightly colored mantle cut doctor-of-law fashion.

The auditorium, an immense room devoid of decoration, was lighted by an indirect system, again screened to afford the play of light and shade. The stage consisted of a mass of steps designed for proportion and line. Accuracy and precision, the relation of movement to musical notation, were the foundation of the system. As Dalcroze himself said, it was a system and not an art form. Later we studied and adapted the method in combination with other techniques for our own group training.

One day, while we watched the classes, Pavlowa was also present as visitor. I still recall her quick perception and her pleasure in the work. Years later, when we met again at the Neighborhood Playhouse where she had come to attend a performance of *An Arab Fantasia*, she was still as alert and responsive as a bird perched for flight.

The Dalcroze visit was early in the fateful summer of 1914, and much that we saw and felt in the air of Germany was to be explained in August. We were haunted by the sense of crass, obvious sensualism, a proficient efficiency rather than skill, indeed a dynamo of objective power. In Germany, theatre, music, audience, workers, the simple and the great, seemed pressed into a military mold.

In England, the stormy battle between Parliament and the suffragettes was raging. Hunger strikes! The figure of

Sylvia Pankhurst waiting on the Prime Minister's doorstep entreating an opportunity to present a petition of East-End working women. A scuffle with the police, then Sylvia Pankhurst shoved back into prison, threatening a hunger strike which might end in death. Meanwhile, suave and decorous Parliament lords and ladies, cabinet ministers, politicians, sipping tea on the terrace, with an air of "all's well with the world." Delegations, marches, and bands, festivities and trooping of the colors for his Majesty's birthday, turbulent meetings of non-enfranchised women laborers. All this curious mélange and color interspersed with the serenity of Oxford, and visits to quiet hillsides and bleak moors. And then suddenly, that night of horror, August 2, 1914. Mobs waiting outside Parliament for the deciding vote. Finally it comes; awed silence, as if a realization of the consequences has dawned for a moment. And then, the long, long night of marching steps, rumbling gun carriages, muffled drums, and farewells!

Returning to America was like stepping upon another planet. The guns, the ominous treading, the partings, were still as gripping to us as when we had been in their midst five thousand miles away, but only the slightest reverberation seemed as yet to have reached the United States. After a moment of wavering between the collective problems and our own, we plunged with furious zeal into the work of completing the new building. Each nail hammered, each brick laid, now became a challenge to liberate values of the spirit, in opposition to negative and destructive forces elsewhere in command, forces directed to crush the impulse of life. But even such a challenge did not anticipate the dynamo of creative energy that a decade of working, struggling, loving, suffering for an image might release.

In February 1915 the completed Playhouse building finally emerged. Its red brick Georgian design, its apple green shutters and front door were modestly in keeping with the character of the neighborhood's early nineteenth-century architecture. There it stood, on the corner of Grand and Pitt streets, and beside it the familiar landmark of the drugstore with its perennial exhibit of trusses in the window. The white signboard, swinging from the building like those of the old inns, carried the insignia in simple lettering:

THE NEIGHBORHOOD PLAYHOUSE

From the time we knew that we were to have the dignity of a home, we had been haunted by the problem of the kind of production that should initiate it. Neither research nor travel revealed the desired drama. Apparently the opening would have to be a homegrown product fashioned in the tradition of the festivals.

Finally a theme drawn from the Book of Judges was selected. Jephthah, a Gileadite chief, hired by the Israelites to protect them from invasion, vowed that if the Lord would grant him success, whatever object he should first perceive on his return would be a sacrifice to the Lord: "an behold, his daughter came out to meet him with timbrels and with dances." This was the nucleus of the drama around which chorus, mime, and dance were woven.

Heretofore the musical themes for the Biblical festivals had been taken from old Hebraic chants, and classical themes were used for the dance motives, a necessary compromise because the composer of that day was unfamiliar with the dance as an independent form. Lilia Mackay Cantell, a young American pianist and composer, grasped the experimental work necessary for our requirements. She had written a score for *The Shadow Garden,* a children's production, and was now eager to produce one for *Jephthah's Daughter.*

Soon *Jephthah's Daughter* was assembling in every available corner of the Settlement and in every crevice of the new building that could be wrested from the builder's hands. It was like the occupation of territory by a friendly enemy; every few days we attacked a new frontier of scaffolding. The vicissitudes of a home-made production had to be faced, not least the opening date, February 12, 1915.

To this day, the production of *Jephthah's Daughter* remains a kind of nightmare. I can no longer recall its actual beginnings or its end, only that there were weeks of agony, with a kind of tenacity and faith that nothing could destroy or deflect. At last, the dreaded moment of opening the doors. The audience assembled terribly on time. Irene and I, both playing in this dance drama, were in the dressing room "making up" when the manager reported in dismay that the seats were still being fastened in and that the setting was unfinished. There was only one answer—the audience must wait until Helen Arthur, not yet manager, was corralled to beguile the waiting group with her inexhaustible fund of anecdotes. This saved the face of the Playhouse and introduced the audience to the homelife of theatre.

Jephthah's Daughter bore much criticism. Our orthodox Jewish neighbors were scandalized at the free interpretation of the Bible text. Caricatures of us appeared in the Yiddish press showing "Miss Neighborhood Playhouse" slamming the door in the face of the Yiddish playwright. The radically inclined were disappointed that the Old Testament was used as source, rather than Andreyev or Gorky, and the conventionally minded were shocked at the bare feet of the dancers. Still another chorus raised its voice in behalf of strictly American culture, protesting that only poor material and no good could come from this East-Side venture. Notwithstanding the criticism and the production's many imperfections, *Jephthah's Daughter* concluded its scheduled run. Whatever it lacked in finish was compensated by its fervor and originality. . . .

18:2   COMMUNITY THEATRE OPENS

The Neighborhood Offers "Jephthah's Daughter," a Biblical Festival

The Neighborhood Playhouse, which is to be run as an adjunct of the Henry Street Settlement, was formally opened last night with a Biblical festival entitled "Jephthah's Daughter." The Playhouse is at 466 Grand Street, near the intersection of that street with Pitt, and if you intend visiting this interesting community theatre unless you can go in a motor car take a crosstown car from subway or "L," for Manhattan Island is astonishingly wide at this point.

For several years some of those most interested in the work of the Henry Street Settlement have been developing the dramatic talents of the young people of the district. This work has been conducted through dramatic classes, and it was to provide a centre for the activities of these classes that the Playhouse was built. It is a handsomely appointed theatre of the intimate type. It is not unlike Winthrop Ames's Little Theatre, both as to the Colonial architecture of its facade and the size and shape of its auditorium.

The many excellencies disclosed by the opening entertainment seemed to justify the generosity of those who made possible the project. The performance did not depart from the amateur sphere, but in the methods employed in producing its several scenes as well as in the skill of some of the players and the smoothness with which the performance progressed it became immediately apparent that interesting things are to be done in this little theatre on the east side.

The disciples of the new art of the stage are to be followed, if one may judge

18:2. New York *Times*, Feb. 13, 1915.

from the first offering. By the simplest methods very effective scenes were composed. The use of the back wall of the stage, the white surface bathed in blue light, made a wrinkleless sky far superior to scores of skies professional stages of Broadway have shown.

Against this background set pieces representing conventionalized trees, a wall, a gate, or tree tops at the horizon line to indicate a hilltop, were used tellingly. There were mistakes in lighting and composition, but the general results should encourage this band of amateurs to depart further from the conventions of fishnets and undeceptive drops. . . .

The costumes and properties were designed by Miss Esther Peck and Miss Dorothy Rich and were made by members of the costume class and clubs of the settlement. The producing staff of the Playhouse consists of Miss Alice Lewisohn, Miss Irene Lewisohn, Mrs. Sarah Cowell Le Moyne, Miss Helen Arthur, and Miss Agnes B. Morgan. The Misses Lewisohn, who are largely responsible for the new institution, took part in the festival, Miss Alice playing the title role.

19. PROVINCETOWN PLAYHOUSE
New York City
Opened December 1, 1916

The Provincetown Players were organized by George Cram Cook, a novelist and playwright, and his wife, Susan Glaspell. The Cooks and some of their friends started presenting one-act plays in a fish-house on a wharf in Provincetown, Massachusetts. By the end of the second summer, in 1916, the Provincetown Players had been organized. The Wharf Theatre is described elsewhere in this volume.

The group journeyed to New York and took a ground floor at 139 Macdougal Street in Greenwich Village. Here they began the presentations that were to help shape modern American drama. The New York *Times* announced their new project.

19:1   NEW GROUP TO STAGE PLAYS

The Provincetown Players to Put on Ten of Their Own Here.

The Provincetown Players, a group of actors and playwrights, who, for the last two Summers, have produced their plays at the Wharf Theatre in Provincetown, Mass., will open their first season in New York at their theatre at 139 Macdougal Street on Nov. 8. The organization plans a twenty-week season, under the personal direction of the authors, a new bill to be staged each two weeks.

The productions will be simple in stage settings, and, except for two salaried officers, who will devote their entire time to the work, the members will receive no financial return, either for their plays or their services. Two of the plays to be given at the Macdougal Street theatre were among eleven which were produced at the Wharf Theatre during the Summer of 1916.

Among the active members are George Cram Cook, Susan Glaspell, Mary Heaton Vorse, Hutchins Hapgood, Neith Boyce, Edna Kenton, Edwin Davies Schoonmacher, William Zorach, Frederick L. Burt, John Reed, Max Eastman, Ida Rauh, Floyd Dell, Eugene O'Neil [O'Neill], Charles Demuth, Wilbur Daniel Steele, Marguerite Zorach, Edward A. Ballantine, and B. J. Norfeldt.

The Survey magazine also announced the the coming of the group.

19:2   ON THE ROAD FROM CAPE COD
TO BROADWAY

The Provincetown Players, newest of experimenters in drama, begin their first New York season early in November at 139 MacDougal street. There are about thirty of them—journalists, novelists, short-story writers, painters, sculptors,

19:1. New York *Times*, Oct. 28, 1916.
19:2. "On the Road from Cape Cod to Broadway," *Survey*, Oct. 28, 1916, pp. 78–79.

socialists, social students, labor agitators, rebels, revolutionists, suffragists and reformers, and some with all these qualities combined.

For several summers they have been collecting on Cape Cod. Since 1915 they have been turning to drama as a means of expressing their ideas. First someone wrote a one-act play, which was given on the balcony of a private house overlooking the sea. Then original plays, all in one act, followed in rapid succession. Then, still in Provincetown, a picturesque little theater, originally a fish-house on an old wharf, was fitted up simply and the enterprise was launched.

Now they have come to New York for one more experiment in cooperation. All the plays are written by members of the group; all the plays are judged by members of the group; all the plays are staged and acted by members of the group; and —which is carrying community drama one step further—all the plays are watched by members of the group. They guard this togetherness with special care. Hutchins Hapgood, who is one of them, says:

"It is up to the members of the Provincetown Players to prevent the gradual usurping of the selection of plays by any person or 'committee' within the group. If such a usurpation takes place, the players will have no special social or artistic meaning, though of course some good plays may be produced."

"This Provincetown impulse," he goes on, "is an expression of what is stirring in many other fields today. . . . The community center movement, demanding the building of social forms from within, is an analogous phenomenon. One might call it an aristocratic democracy. Not so big that a boss must usurp the power in order to be at all effective; not so small as to become sterilized by the mental habits, prejudices, and interests of one or two or three active and executively gifted individuals. . . . All the problems of democracy and of art, at the points where they

touch, are latent in this little spontaneous and hopeful group."

According to Mr. Hapgood, the players are holding as far aloof from professionalism as possible. They lay weight neither upon elaborate stage settings nor acting efficiency,—"not even upon the technique of a play except as a means to an end." That end is not propaganda of any sort, they say, but seems to be "to express a certain modern spirit." Their plays will be "in the moment of time, vital and spontaneous." They will be given four times, running for a fortnight, Friday and Saturday evenings.

Susan Glaspell wrote of the beginnings of this venture and of the Macdougal Street Playhouse.

19:3   I was appalled the day Jig [George Cram Cook] said, "When we go to New York for the winter, we will take our theatre with us." That, I thought, was a very different thing. I was afraid for him. I knew how it had been through the summer. Many had been interested, and some of them had worked hard, but after all the others worked when they wanted to. "What is Jig going to do about this?" they would say when a real difficulty presented itself. There were people who would be animated when they were with him, and then next day—"But really, I haven't time for it, you know," and they would have to be captured anew, or let go, and someone else captured. He was the centre; for the most part, he made the others want to do it, as well as persuaded them it could be done. I felt the energy must go into keeping that fire of enthusiasm, of belief, from which all drew. It was hard to see Jig hurt—he always seemed so surprised it should be like that. He had so much trust, valuing people by the finest moment they showed him—sometimes largely a radiation from his own glow. And I was

19:3. Susan Glaspell, *The Road to the Temple* (London: Ernest Benn Ltd., 1926), pp. 198–205.

afraid people would laugh at him, starting a theatre in New York—new playwrights, amateur acting, somewhere in an old house or a stable. He himself never thought of this, too concentrated on the thing to be done.

I said I did not think we were ready to go to New York; I feared we couldn't make it go. "Jack Reed thinks we can make it go," he said.

Those two were the first to believe—adventurers both, men of faith. "Impractical."

One of Jig's notes: "The deep and original creative feeling that is found in some American men." I do not know of whom he was thinking when he put that down, but as I look at it now, I think of Moscow, I think of Delphi.

"Where will we get the money?" I asked.

"Our associate members will subscribe for the New York season. That will be our nucleus."

It was one of Jig's warmest satisfactions that members of our audience that summer of Nineteen-sixteen were members every year thereafter. That was our strength, he said; we did not need to take money that would threaten what we were; our audience was part of us.

We were going to call ourselves the Provincetown Players, but Gene proposed we be also the Playwrights' Theatre.

Two hundred and forty-five dollars in his pocket, in the glow of vision, energetic with belief, Jig boarded the train to look for a place for the Provincetown Players in New York. He stood alone on the back platform, waving to me. "Don't worry!" he called, as the train was starting. Then something I couldn't hear, and I went running after him. He cupped his mouth with his hands to call back: "Write—another—play!"

FIRE FROM HEAVEN

"Writers, critics, adventurers, painters, having in common a feeling that it would

be better to be destroyed than not to create one's own beauty." Jig said this of the group from which the Provincetown Players came.

You have the police to reckon with in creating your own beauty in New York; you have small boys who kick tin cans down Macdougal Street while the curtain is up, people upstairs who put their garbage in front of the theatre just as the audience is arriving, the phonograph next door.

A little disheartening, when finally he found a ground-floor at 139 Macdougal Street, to learn that two hundred of the two hundred and forty-five dollars, capital from Provincetown, must be paid for putting in a steel girder, or the partition which would give the stage couldn't be torn out.

When I arrived in New York, having dutifully written "The People," my first glimpse of Jig was standing amid shavings, lumber and bags of cement explaining the Provincetown Players to a policeman and an impersonal-looking person from the building department. "Now here is Susan Glaspell," he said, as if I had entered for just this. "She is writing plays. And there is a young Irishman, O'Neill"—turning to the Irish policeman. We all went downstairs to have a drink and talk it over. Broadway. That wasn't what we wanted to do. In fact, we weren't doing this for money at all. "My salary is fifteen dollars a week," said Jig. The person from the building department looked a little less impersonal as Jig talked to him of plays out of American life, quite as if this were one of the man's warm interests. The Irish policeman remained a friend to the last, more than once telling us what to do when we would have blundered.

I have heard Jig explain the Provincetown Players to firemen, electricians, women tenement inspectors, garbage collectors, judges. Our Italian landlady, our real estate agent, our banker, were drawn into the adventure. "We are doing it for fun," Jig said to a judge, when the question of our playing Sunday nights was up. "Oh, of course, profound fun. The fun of death, for instance—the profound amusement of imagined death, followed swiftly enough, your honour, by the real moment."

The judge gave him a swift keen look. The look held between them.

"But what shall the sergeant do?" said the gentleman from the police, "if they play again Sunday night?"

"Oh, tell him to do something else," said his honour, and subscribed to the Provincetown Players.

It didn't always come out so charmingly. Many nights Jig would sleep a couple of hours, then figure in his little book—how to prevent a theatened disaster. We had no theatre licence; often we did not know whether we would play once more, or be closed that night.

Hard, too, to create one's own beauty without dressing-rooms, without space for shifting scenery. Even knowing we did it, I am disposed to say what we did that first year couldn't be done. I can see Jig, say, an afternoon of dress rehearsal, coat off, sleeves up, perspiring as any other labourer perspires, lifting, pounding, working to help finish a set; wrestling with a stage-manager who says a certain thing can't be done, checking up on props—himself going over to Sixth Avenue for some of them—yes, sweeping the theatre, if the woman who should have done it failed to come. "You must have your lunch," I say. He shakes his head. I go out and get a bottle of milk, and he works through till performance time—works as if it were death which waits if the thing is not done.

He believed that the gifted amateur had possibilities which the professional may have lost. It was with an amateur group he worked in those early years; with no money, the only hold he had on them was through making them want to do it. It was his intensity held the thing together.

They would cut rehearsals, be late—things professionals would not dream of doing. He would reorganize a whole scene-shift, rehearse it, himself drive it through to save three minutes, only to have the gifted amateur actress hold the curtain while she finished her make-up. There are people who are not equal to the intensity of the theatre; they are there to thwart your own intensity, and from their superior calm look with amazement upon your righteous fury. "I sweat blood for that three minutes, and she threw it away powdering her nose!"

And the thing it was all for? The beauty created? Judging that first year by itself alone, it was not worth the struggle of making it possible. Bad acting and producing plays there seemed little reason for giving. Sometimes it would be almost impossible to cast a play. Why then did his faith hold?

Because beneath fatigue and disappointment, he believed in the thing as a whole. In a theatre for experiment you may do things which in themselves are not worth doing. Yet he would feel something in that play—a thing that was on its way to something else. Why not give this boy a chance to see it in action, see how he can improve it in rehearsal? Let him know that here is a stage for the better play he can write.

In those years there were no tickets for critics. If they wanted to come and pay for a seat, they were as welcome as anyone else. We were not doing it for them any more than for other members of the audience. "We knew the joy of the theatre last year in Macdougal Street," he writes at the beginning of our second season, "and that joy, strangely uncommon in our great play-giving, play-going world is, like beauty, its own excuse for being. There ought, moreover, to be one theatre for American writers to play with—one where, if the spirit move them, they can give plays which are not likely to be produced elsewhere. We mean to go on giving artists of the theatre a chance to work out their ideas in freedom."

"We have no ambition to go up-town and become 'a real theatre.' We have a theatre because we want to do our own thing in our own way. We believe that hard work done in the play spirit has a freshness not found in the theatre which has become a business.

"There are rich backgrounds behind the people of this group. They were accustomed to deal imaginatively with life before they came together and began to focus their creative impulse upon their untrammelled little stage. There are more interesting things latent in their minds than they have yet written or acted. Their hope is greater than it was in the beginning.

"We are still not afraid to fail in things worth trying. This season, too, shall be adventure. We will let this theatre die before we let it become another voice of mediocrity. If any writers in this country are capable of bringing down fire from heaven to the stage, we are here to receive and help."

A beautiful thing had happened. That "fire from heaven"—had it been withheld? The scenery might totter at times, the waits were long, the ventilation bad and the seats uncushioned, but that audience is already an historic one. For one after another they were seeing those dramas of the sea written by Eugene O'Neill. No one else was producing him then, and I leave you the story of the unfolding of his career, of his growth in power upon that tiny experimental stage, as justification of the idea of this man George Cram Cook.

Yet because of his integrity of idea, that conspicuous success never made him see as less important the work of those who had not yet succeeded, who might never, in the usual sense of the word, succeed. If certain things we did reached the larger public, then perhaps our intensity should more and more go into the work which also had meaning, but which might be harder to project. The things that others would do were not so particularly our individual job. To *cause* better American plays to be written—that is what he kept saying.

As when he was teacher at Iowa City, he would give of himself to whomsoever wanted him. There was perhaps one of his faults as a director. He did not hoard himself. He had none of the usual exclusions. Though busy or tired, he would talk half an hour to a person if some one thing intrigued his mind, if there was chance for the serious things of life to take form as play. Once in a deeply serious talk, Jig asked me quite simply why people undervalued him. And I spoke as truly as I could when I said, 'Because you are so generous. Because you are not afraid.' Most people hold back—cautious, that they may seem impressive. But with Jig, the idea, whatever might be the imaginative content of the moment, was a thing in itself, so important that it must have its way, not limited or shaped by the kind of impression he himself might make. This is more than courage. It is purity. And it was a growth; an achievement in personality, for in the early years, as we have seen, he had good measure of self-consciousness and vanity. He reacted from the dangerous self-abnegation of those days at the Cabin, when he followed God's orders, yet the man who came back to the good old dimensions had a new sense of what life is worth. Life is worth play. I have seen poor-souled people hug their reticence that it might pass as superiority before Jig's experimental fooling—that rich, sunny unashamed play, which honoured the most serious things of life by including them. When he found one who could play with him—nothing else was so important. A solemn business appointment waited while he and Joe O'Brien and Hutchins Hapgood "recreated religion" at the bar of the Brevoort. We cannot measure him without reckoning with those radiant moments he called into being; and those, we know, cannot be measured. They are perhaps of that All to which he spread his arms in the silence of noon in the Iowa City Library. No specific achievement could so secure one.

After a first night there would be a party in our club-room over the theatre. We were very poor at times, but never so poor we couldn't have wine for these parties. It was important we drink together, for thus were wounds healed, and we became one again, impulse and courage as if they had never been threatened. We had said hard things to one another in the drive of the last rehearsals, the strain of opening night. Now I might see Jig's arm around a neck he had threatened to wring. "Jig, you are getting drunk," some one would say. "It is for the good of the Provincetown Players," he would explain. "I am always ready to sacrifice myself to a cause." When the wine began to show the bottom of the bowl, "Give it all to me," Jig would propose, "and I guarantee to intoxicate all the rest of you." He glowed at these parties. Things which years before had lain lonely in his mind flowed into a happy convival hour, and dawn might find him eloquently espousing the cause of the elephant as over the lion, perhaps closing with a blaze of prophecy of a world in which men did not tear each other as lions tore, but where the strongest was he who did not feed upon his brother. . . .

20. MOROSCO THEATRE
New York City
Opened February 5, 1917

Oliver Morosco was a successful West Coast producer and theater owner who booked some of his shows into New York playhouses. Because of some difficulties in obtaining the theaters he felt he needed for certain plays, he and the Shuberts built a new playhouse, which was appropriately named the Morosco, and

opened it in 1917 with a new musical by Morosco, *Canary Cottage*.

It was quite an upsetting time for Morosco because of marital difficulties with his first wife, Annie, and their bitter quarrels affected him throughout the period of building and opening the theater. This is evident in a letter of his that appeared in his biography, *The Oracle of Broadway*, written by his second wife, Helen, and Leonard Paul Dugger:

20:1 . . . My experience with Davis's play, together with other somewhat similar grievances, started me thinking of securing a permanent house for my Broadway productions. The Shubert brothers had asked me several times to utilize a plot of ground they owned on Forty-fifth Street, opposite the Astor Hotel. The location was ideal, and since I booked Shubert houses almost exclusively anyway, the plan seemed feasible.

I called the Shuberts and arranged to have lunch with them at the Astor.

Before we finished eating, I had posted with them a fifty-thousand-dollar bond, and the germ of the new Morosco Theatre began to develop. We agreed to have Edward Margolies, the most skilled man in New York at theater building, to do the work. I reserved the right to supervise the interior decoration. . . .

Between designing the interior of my new theater, caring for my ever-increasing business, reading the new scripts that poured into my office from the ends of the earth, and exercising a constant effort to find the ideal actor or actress for each and every one of my creations, I was kept delightfully busy during the remainder of my stay in New York.

Peg O' My Heart was still touring this country and Canada with eight companies; *The Bird of Paradise* was still on the road and going strong; *Up Stairs and*

20:1. Helen Morosco and Leonard Paul Dugger, *The Oracle of Broadway* (Caldwell, Idaho: The Caxton Printers, Ltd., 1944), pp. 284–95.

Down and *The Unchastened Woman* were packing them in on Broadway; *So Long Letty* continued to be the laugh riot of the day; my six Los Angeles theaters, with the splendid plays I was sending them from New York, were all doing a good business; and my picture holdings were all but minting money.

I was beginning to be hailed on the Great White Way as "The Oracle of Broadway." Whereas if a producer can average one hit out of every three plays he stages, he will do a flourishing business, I had never had an out-and-out failure, had never even lost money on one of my productions, and with but two exceptions, every play I had taken to New York had been phenomenal successes. . . .

The morning after my return [from Los Angeles] I breakfasted alone on my upstairs porch, then called my chauffeur and went to the Morosco.

. . . Elmer Harris, who had been waiting in the outer office, came running in, grabbed my hand, patted me on the back, and, after a few hurried preliminary remarks, said, "Ollie, I've got an idea. How about us writing another musical play?"

"About what?" I asked.

"I have a sort of idea," he announced jubilantly, "and a great title."

I was tempted to say, "You contributed that much to our last collaboration." Instead, I merely said, "A good title helps."

"You know that old restaurant down the road a bit, the one with such a shady reputation? Reports say murders and robberies have been committed there—"

"Wait a minute," I interrupted. "You are not trying to tempt me to write a melodrama?"

"No," he said in all earnestness, "I'm only talking about the title."

"Oh," I laughed. "I failed to see the connection. What is your title?"

"Canary Cottage," he pridefully announced.

I liked the title, and, after hearing something of what he had in mind for the musical, I became as jubilant as he was. Things began to crowd into my mind. Forgetting all about my already over-crowded schedule, I joined Harris in plotting out our new brain child.

That night I wrote the scenario. The next day he started work on the dialogue. I wired for Earl Carroll to come to Los Angeles at once and bring his pianist.

While waiting for him to arrive, Harris and I wrote and rewrote. We did not get along so well, however, and, when Earl Carroll arrived, we had nothing but a rough draft of the first act ready. He had lost none of his enthusiasm, and Elmer Harris being on this occasion just as wholeheartedly with me, we worked like maniacs for the next few weeks. The dawning of one day often found us still at the day-before's work.

Between work periods on *Canary Cottage* I rehearsed the three plays I had brought with me from New York. . . .

. . . In the meantime Harris, Carroll, and I set about casting it. Almost every character in it was unique, and each one was vital to the entire play. Charlie Ruggles was a natural for the boy. I extracted a character woman from the Kolb and Dill regime to play the comedy old woman, and sent to New York for Trixie Friganza to play a fat cook, a major part in the show. My brother, Leslie, sent me Herbert Corthell, a comedian I knew and liked, from New York.

That left only one important role unfilled, and in the whole theatrical world I did not know of an actor suitable for it. The part was that of an effeminate "coon," a character never before portrayed on the American stage. Carroll wrote some great "cheese" music and lyrics for the part, and we went the rounds of Los Angeles vaudeville houses looking for him. Luckily for us, for him, and for the whole amusement world, we found what we were looking for, found him doing an act at the Orpheum. He was as new to the stage as was our effeminate "coon." He spoke little in his act, but his antics were unprecedented.

After the show Carroll went backstage to talk with him, and the next day he came to my office. I told him the nature of the character I wanted him to portray and asked him if he would do it. He grinned, rolled his enormous eyes, and with a native Jewish gesture, said, "Mr. Morosco, I'd play my grandmother to get a start."

I signed him up so quickly he gasped.

That "coon" chauffeur nearly walked off with *Canary Cottage* the opening night, and the newspapers hailed him as a new find of no meager importance. They were right. He was Eddie Cantor.

Throughout the play the character played by Herbert Corthell had delirium tremens, and was possessed with miniature demons, the Orgotti twins. No one else in the play saw them, but of course the audience did. Throughout the entire performance, two Lilliputians followed him about. The results were side splitting.

I had twenty-four beautiful girls in the chorus and sixteen men singers.

I opened *Canary Cottage* in San Diego where it got a wholehearted response. Satisfied with it, I took it to Los Angeles. My audience there received it with loud and jubilant approval. *Canary Cottage* was an unqualified success. "I Never Knew" and "Canary Cottage," two of its songs, were played by every orchestra and whistled by almost every boy from coast to coast.

I was in seventh heaven. I gloried in a vision of opening my own Broadway theater with a production I had produced and coauthored!

But before the New York *première,* I felt the show should have an additional tryout, a tryout before an audience that was wholly new and unprejudiced in its favor. So I sent it to San Francisco to the Cort Theatre. It was so well received by the conservative San Franciscans that it closed to "Standing Room Only" and jumped to New York.

Just before I left for San Francisco with *Canary Cottage,* a young man called at my office seeking a part in *Somebody's Luggage,* the next week's attraction at the Morosco. He had a winning smile and a pleasant manner, so I sent him backstage to talk to my director Fred Butler.

The following week while I was in San Francisco I picked up a Los Angeles paper and was pleasantly surprised to learn that a youngster, Harold Lloyd by name, was proving so riotously funny in the role of a seasick passenger in *Somebody's Luggage* that it was being prophesied he would find a permanent position under the Morosco banner.

Wanting to be on hand to put the finishing touches on my new Broadway theater, . . . I went on to New York, leaving *Canary Cottage* under the able management of Mike Yack. . . .

To give my theater the homeyness and warmth I desired I chose my drapes with care. I worked with the artists to get just the shade of French gray and lavender which would go best on walls and ceiling. My object was to make simplicity of coloring and design mark the whole interior with aristocracy and gentility.

Those were happy and exultant days. My ecstasy and expectancy increased with each completed job upon my new theater. I was free in spirit . . . and I watched the culmination of my dream of having a New York theater, with the mingled emotions of a child viewing his first Christmas tree. . . . My theater was to open the following night, and I was determined not to let anything prevent my being in fit condition to attend to business.

I was at the theater early the following morning and, forgetful of dinner, stayed with the workmen until four o'clock getting everything in good shape. I wanted every detail cared for before the opening. Knowing that any one of a myriad seemingly inconsequential things might disrupt the harmony of such a momentous occasion, I looked to everything from the toilets to the auditorium—saw that the dressing rooms were completely stocked, the fire apparatus in order, the sprinkling system practical, the box office wholly equipped, the carpets securely fastened down, the ushers thoroughly rehearsed and properly costumed, the ladies' and men's parlors as thoughtfully and commodiously arranged as possible, the orchestra rehearsed, the scenes all in readiness, and the cast correctly and neatly wardrobed.

About four o'clock Annie [Morosco's first wife] rushed into the theater, her eyes blazing anger, and demanded that I return with her to the hotel.

I tried to reason with her, pointing out the many things which must be done before the curtain went up that evening, but she was too infuriated even to hear my voice.

"If you don't come with me at once," she fairly screeched, "I will create such a scene, you'll wish a thousand times you had come."

"I cannot go now, Annie," I said, my face burning with embarrassment, for the theater was full of people—members of the orchestra, the cast, the ushers, the carpenters, and a few friends.

"You will come now," she shrieked. "What is this opening in comparison with me, your wife? You neglect me for your old theaters, for everything. I'll not have it. Come!"

So humiliated that my skin was fairly crawling, I took her by the arm and left the theater.

At the Claridge I had to listen to her hysterical denunciations and accusations until, dressing nervously in my evening clothes, I left to witness the opening of the new Morosco. I tried to persuade Annie to accompany me, but my entreaties fell on deaf ears.

It was like stepping from a Christian's hell into a Mohammedan's heaven when I rounded the corner at Broadway and Forty-fifth Street and saw a virgin edifice with blazing lights flashing to the world its designation, "The Morosco Theatre."

By eight o'clock the house was packed with the elite of New York. The curtain went up. My company, with the spirit I have always admired in a cast, plunged into *Canary Cottage*, one of my fairest brain children.

The audience entered into the gala spirit of Earl Carroll's songs, and when the chorus, each with a great basket of golden fruit on his arm, sang "It's Orange Time in California," and the comedians began to pelt the audience with soft paper and wool citrus, gay pandemonium broke loose. For fully ten minutes the audience and the company threw artificial oranges at each other while the blossoming orange trees on the stage filled the auditorium with the fragrance of rich distilled perfume.

Verily, the Morosco opened in a blaze of glory and a peal of laughter.

I was like a caged squirrel. My nerves goaded me on, backstage, up to the balcony, outside on the walk, inside to the lobby, downstairs in the smoking room, and out to the box office. I couldn't stop. I think I traversed a good ten miles that night before I finally stepped aside to watch the audience file out.

At the Claridge after the show I gave a brilliant party for the cast. Everyone was radiant. My success was theirs, and I have never been in a more wholeheartedly happy group. . . .

In its review of *Canary Cottage,* the New York *Times* briefly describes the new house.

20:2   . . . "Canary Cottage" is a rather low form of entertainment, but it has the elements of popular success, and perhaps that is all Mr. Morosco asks in this vale of tears. With such entertainment, at least, he was willing to dedicate the handsome new theatre which bears his name.

That theatre stands in Forty-fifth Street

20:2. New York *Times*, Feb. 5, 1917.

opposite the Booth. It is none of your little theatres, but a spacious one that has seats for 905 and standing room for many more. It is comfortable and an attractive color scheme of gray and purple greeted the first audience after they had passed through the lobby. . . .

21. BIJOU THEATRE
New York City
Opened April 12, 1917

This was the smallest playhouse built in the Times Square area, and its very size spelled trouble, since it could not produce enough revenue. It had some great successes, however, and in 1971 was still an attractive little house.

Beginning in 1938, as expenses rose, it was used for long periods as a motion picture theater, although periodically it returned to stage shows.

The Sunday preceding the opening the New York *Times* told of the new playhouse.

21:1   The second of the new theaters just across Forty-fifth street from the Booth erected by the Shuberts during the season has been named the Bijou. It is an intimate playhouse with a seating capacity of 650, of which 236 are in the single balcony. The interior is in the style of the period of Louis XVI, the prevailing colors being blue, ivory, and gold. The theatre was originally intended to be the home of the local French theatre. . . .

In 1957 a move was made to return the Bijou to a playhouse once again. Two young producers, Carmen Capalbo and Stanley Chase, felt there was need for such a theater in the Times Square area and made plans to present outstanding plays there.

21:2   A playhouse in the heart of New York's theatrical district that will be in the com-

21:1. New York *Times*, Apr. 8, 1917.
21:2. Ward Morehouse, "Small House, Big Plans," *Theatre Arts*, Mar. 1957, pp. 22–23; by special permission of Jovanna Ceccarelli, Publisher.

plete control of the men who are producing its plays, that will have a definite identity of its own, just as the Princess Theatre did during the triumphant regime of Bolton, Wodehouse and Kern, and that will give Broadway from four to six productions every season—such is the objective of Carmen Capalbo and Stanley Chase, the two young men who have taken over the Bijou in New York's West 45th Street.

The Messrs. Capalbo and Chase have long-range plans. They have a lease on their playhouse for a year, options for other years. They feel that the well-located Bijou is ideal for their operations. Having moved uptown from the tiny Theatre de Lys in Greenwich Village, they find the 603-seat Bijou fairly enormous. "We like the fact that it's the smallest house in the Broadway area," they tell you. "It's compact, it's wieldy, and a house of its size is definitely an asset to certain plays of quality. We have such works in mind. If we can play to capacity we will gross $20,400 on the week. Nobody will be getting rich on that, but we'll have fun and we'll be doing what we want to do in the thing we love best, the living theatre."

The Bijou, a playhouse built in 1917 (and in which Tallulah Bankhead made her Broadway debut in *The Squab Farm*), the home of such memorable offerings as Guthrie McClintic's production of *The Dover Road,* Owen Davis' *The Detour* and Helen Hayes's revival of *What Every Woman Knows,* is owned by the City Investing Company, of which Robert Dowling is the alert and theatre-loving president. It was turned over to Capalbo and Chase by Dowling, who believes in their talents and who was impressed, as was everybody else, by the spectacular success of their *Threepenny Opera* production at the downtown Theatre de Lys, which seats 199. The new surge of activity at the Bijou began with the late-January presentation of Graham Greene's *The Potting Shed,* starring Sybil Thorndike. The second play will be Eugene O'Neill's *A Moon for the Misbegotten,* with Wendy Hiller in the role of the oversized Josie, which arrives in late April, and the third may be a musical piece. Or Bernard Shaw's *Heartbreak House,* to which Capalbo and Chase hold the rights.

Anyway, the forty-year-old Bijou is starting life all over again, and its emphatic return to the legitimate fold is to be heartily welcomed. Perhaps this development will give some imaginative showman the idea of wandering around into 39th Street and seeing what's going on at the beautiful Maxine Elliott Theatre, which has been lost to the living stage for years.

Just who are the young men behind the revitalization of the Bijou? Well, Carmen Capalbo, of Italian parentage and born in Harrisburg, Pennsylvania, studied at the Yale Drama School. He began writing for radio in his early years and he has had considerable television experience. One of the pioneers in New York's off-Broadway movement, he founded The Spur, a repertory company which operated at the Cherry Lane Theatre and gave its clientele such productions as *Juno and the Paycock, Awake and Sing! Dear Brutus* and *Shadow and Substance.* Stanley Chase, graduated from New York University in 1949, and a writer and producer for television, was born in Brooklyn. He and Capalbo met in 1953, liked each other's ideas, and by 1954 they found themselves coproducers of *The Threepenny Opera.* They both now insist that they're in the theatre to stay.

Capalbo can be eruptive, and he is generally articulate when he gets to talking of the theatre and of the plans of Capalbo and Chase: "We're hoping to have the Bijou open for fifty-two weeks in the year. It's equipped with fine air-conditioning facilities, and we'll have no problems in the summertime. It will be our plan to change the bill from time to time; if we're lucky enough to get a big

hit, there'll be no trouble in finding another house for it. Our seats will be sold at a $5.25 top during the week and at $5.75 for week ends, beginning Fridays. We'll go along with union scales generally, but we'll have to get concessions from individuals, as in the case of Dame Sybil Thorndike; and it will be the same with Wendy Hiller. We could never pay such people their regular salaries.

"One of the great problems in production today is that producers don't operate the theatres in which their plays are being presented. But the Bijou will be ours— ours. Robert Dowling has been wonderful; he gave us the theatre for a song. We thought of trying to play at popular prices, but that's impossible under present conditions. Even at the price scale we've decided upon, it will be necessary for our stars to work for less than half of their normal salaries.

"We want to go in for modern plays, anything from 1900 up, and once we get established we hope to try a lot of variety. Perhaps there are some of the American plays of the early century that might be worth trying. We'll be looking into the matter of the Clyde Fitch plays. He wrote from fifty to sixty, and certainly it would seem that two or three of them are deserving of revival."

The Messrs. Capalbo and Chase became fascinated with O'Neill's *A Moon for the Misbegotten* upon the first reading of it, began negotiations with the playwright's widow, and finally obtained the production rights. "Casting was a problem," Capalbo admitted, "but we solved it when we got Wendy Hiller to sign a contract to play Josie, who is supposed to be earthy and have a maternal look. Wendy should be great in the part."

So if the Bijou, seating a mere 603, can turn out to be a success in this era of frightening costs and a trend (in thinking, at least) to big houses, it will put showmen to wondering, and may even get somebody to investigate the possibility to bringing back the one-time Punch and Judy, later called the Charles Hopkins Theatre, in 49th Street. That attractive bandbox seated only about 300, but Hopkins went along with it for years, putting on imaginative plays and having a great time.

22. PLYMOUTH THEATRE
New York City
Opened October 10, 1917

The number of theaters on Forty-fourth and Forty-fifth streets west of Broadway continued to grow at a rather amazing rate, and in the New York *Times* the opening of the new Plymouth Theatre was announced.

22:1   THIS WEEK'S HAPPENINGS

It is a dull week when no new theatre opens, and Arthur Hopkins will supply the event this week by opening his new house, the Plymouth, on Wednesday night. The Plymouth is one of the four theatres which now stand en bloc between Forty-fourth and Forty-fifth Streets, being the house immediately west of the Booth. Clare Kummer's comedy of last year, "A Successful Calamity," will have the honor of opening the new house. Mr. Gillette, of course, is still the star, and the company, as a whole, is practically the same as that which supported him last season.

The actual opening of the theater received very little notice, but then this was to be the case with many of the theaters opened between 1917 and 1928. Perhaps there were so many new playhouses opening that the novelty wore off for the readers of magazines and newspapers. The review in the New York *Times* was quite brief.

22:2   PLYMOUTH THEATRE OPENS
HOPKINS' NEW HOUSE IN 45TH STREET
BEGINS WITH
'A SUCCESSFUL CALAMITY.'
The Plymouth Theatre, Arthur Hopkins's contribution to New York's rapidly

growing list of playhouses, opened its doors last night with Clare Kummer's comedy, "A Successful Calamity," as its attraction. The new house is immediately west of the Booth, in Forty-fifth Street, being of the group which includes the Booth, the Broadhurst and the Shubert. Its completion makes this section one of the city's most important theatrical centres, with eight playhouses within a radius of a few hundred feet.

The new theatre was built by the Shuberts, and has been leased for a number of years by Mr. Hopkins. It follows the prevailing mode in theatre building in that it is simple in design, and is finished in brown, blue, and gold. The seating capacity is about 1,000, there being only one balcony.

Miss Kummer's polite comedy is acted for the most part by the same cast which appeared in it during its great success at the Booth in the Spring. William Gillette, of course, continues in the leading role.

23. HENRY MILLER THEATRE
New York City
Opened April 1, 1918

"At the opening of Henry Miller's Theatre last night good taste was lapped in luxury as seldom before. Every detail of the new house is studied with intelligent regard to comfort of the body and repose of the eye." So stated the New York *Times* critic in his review of the opening night of this handsome new playhouse.

Henry Miller was a very popular actor-manager who in 1917 decided to build his own theater, designing it for the comfort of the spectators as well as for the best and most innovative techniques of staging. Arthur Edwin Krows, critic for the New York *Times*, described the theater in his column in the Sunday *Times*.

23:1   HENRY MILLER BUILDS A THEATRE
To a large portion of the amusement-loving public the news that the Henry

22:1. New York *Times*, Oct. 7, 1917.
22:2. New York *Times*, Oct. 11, 1917.

23:1. New York *Times*, Mar. 3, 1918.

Miller Theatre is soon to open means that just another playhouse is to be added to the amazing number already standing in and about Times Square. To the smaller group that watches things dramatic with understanding and sympathy it means that one of the sturdiest figures in the history of the American stage has founded an institution of his own.

Like most stars, Henry Miller long has had in his mind an ideal theatre. On more than one occasion he has mentioned its larger points of superiority, notably at those times when his opinion was sought on so-called "national" temples of drama. He described it in detail some two years before the former New Theatre was built. This vision he defined as "a real American theatre for the real American people conducted on real American principles." Its prices were to range from 50 cents down to 10—but, of course, that was long before the mailed fist of the Kaiser had lifted the high cost of living.

He was to have three companies and in time at least three theatres in New York, so perhaps this new house is but one of a series. Each company would specialize in a broad kind of drama—one in tragedy, one in comedy and lighter pieces, and the third in naturalistic plays of contemporary life. No hard-and-fast line was to be drawn, and the players of one company might now and then be called upon to supplement those of another.

It is not the purpose here to recall the many other interesting things in the Miller scheme, because doubtless he has modified many of them with passing seasons. If his present theatre demonstrates that he has reconstructed certain ideas, such as that about the private box which he once stigmatized as "artistically criminal," it is the more of a tribute to him in proving that, with all of his temptations to become didactic, he has remained open to conviction.

The Henry Miller Theatre in fact is not a radical from the structural standpoint. Going through the house with Bertram Harrison, Mr. Miller's righthand man, and himself a producer of considerable reputation, I was impressed with the fact that everything in the place had been tried and tested. All the devices that had been admitted were those that had proved their worth elsewhere. Many of them were new in the sense of not having been in common use, but they were not exactly original for all of that, for the aforesaid very good reason that the presiding genius wanted mainly a theatre that would work smoothly with no question about the efficiency of its parts.

As a whole, the Henry Miller Theatre is an "intimate" theatre, which is to say, one of size so moderate that every seat is within easy visual and auditory range. By an "intimate" theatre one usually has come to think of a house seating 300 to 800 persons—which makes all the more surprising the fact that this has a capacity in the neighborhood of 1,000. This is surprising because the auditorium just doesn't look it.

The secret is that it has a gallery, or "second balcony" as they call it in polite managerial circles, something rarely attempted in so small a theatre. A really intimate house with three tiers of spectators is a circumstance worthy of notice in itself. How these three tiers have been worked in here is, to a certain extent, an architectural feat; but it has been done apparently with no sacrifice either of convenience or comfort.

As is the ceiling, that has to be quite lofty to admit of two balconies intervening between it and the orchestra floor; but the great height does not seem by any means disproportionate. Doubtless the gallery is one means of providing a cheaper division of seats, for Mr. Miller remains a believer that theatre chairs should be kept within reach of small incomes. It not only is easier to supply cheaper seats above rather than on the orchestra floor because of the high real estate values per square foot in New York, but it also gives the occupants great advantages of seeing and hearing them closer to the stage.

In form, the auditorium follows the semi-circle of the ancient Greek theatre rather than the rectangle of the Elizabethan inn yard or the French tennis court of the sixteenth century. This perference is to be expected of an actor-manager, because actors of experience frequently are heard decrying the box-shaped auditorium as disconcerting and injurious even to the most careful enunciation. They like to feel that the audience is around them. And with the gentle curves here that intimacy is one thing that the players of Henry Miller's home company will enjoy.

Boxes are not dispensed with despite the old Miller apathy. Whether or not there should be boxes in theatres is a debatable subject, with the balance in favor of having them. There are two boxes here, one at each side, on a level with the first balcony and commanding an excellent view of the stage.

Sight lines seem splendid. The chairs had not yet been installed when the visit was made, but it seemed likely then that patrons would be able to see well from every seat in the house. With none of the fixtures in place, it was also impossible to determine acoustical values accurately; but the flattened side walls where the auditorium joined the stage, the absence of depression and raised panels in the ceiling, and the careful contour of the orchestra floor were decidedly hopeful signs. The sharp pitch of the balcony ceiling, due to the necessary slope of the gallery, may lessen the force of sound waves at that point, but the shallowness of the auditorium from front to back doubtless will make any defect there negligible.

The orchestra pit is concealed by a curved double screen, the outer part of which is removable in sections to make room for extra musicians when required. The pit itself is made of wood for greater resonance. Importance of using as much wood as possible in construction of a theatre was recognized as a sound principle as long as 2,000 years ago. Vitruvius, the ancient architect, relates that Alexander the Great once projected a stage built of bronze, but had to give up the plan because the metal impaired the acoustical effect.

The lobby of the Henry Miller Theatre is both commodious and beautiful. It is designed as a graceful oval, and has full facilities for handling crowds. But the foyer back of the seats is narrow, because, instead of a promenade, there is provided a tearoom downstairs, where patrons may refresh themselves during the longest entr'acte.

As to the stage itself, it seems a good working space properly without a square foot of waste. The relative location of an auditorium has much to do with construction of a stage. The proscenium opening must meet the auditorium at dead centre, irrespective of space available for the wings. It automatically determines which side of the stage shall have the most room. And the side with the greater space naturally shall be used for the "working side," or place where the chiefs of the stage crew discharge their more important duties. This also is where the prompter or stage manager is supposed to have his table, that he may give his instructions first-hand to the men.

It is advisable for the working side also to be convenient to the dressing rooms, so that players readily may be called to their positions on cue. Unfortunately, the working side here is at left and the dressing rooms are at right, so there will be occasions when the stage manager will have to take for granted the fact that actors over the way are in place.

It may be remarked in passing that the dressing rooms are all roomy, light, and airy and well equipped. Rooms of principals are within easy reach of the stage. Minor persons will have to ascend several flights of stairs. There is no elevator.

The stage proper is a bit narrow from front to back, although probably adequate for all demands likely to be made upon it. However, there is an added space of perhaps fifteen feet with a comparatively low ceiling back of that, so stage vistas of some distance are possible, provided only that the entire scene is not intended to be outdoors where this ceiling would show. A recess of this kind in the back stage wall may be very valuable. An instance is the opening in the wall of the Lyceum Theatre, New York, which was used with great effect several seasons ago for the disappearing street in "The Dawn of a Tomorrow."

As the Miller Theatre neared completion there seeped to Broadway the rumor that its stage boasted the most marvellous counterweight system in the city. A counterweight system, for the benefit of those not "in the know," is a method of counterbalancing objects to be raised from the stage into the flies, or overhead region, so that a single stage hand may "work" any given set of lines unaided. The system here is complete and compact, but with some questions to be answered about weights liable to break loose on high and not easy to adjust between moving ropes. It is by no means new, and for sheer novelty cannot compare with the ingenious system at the Century [New] Theatre, which is one of the most remarkable in the world. But it is a system which, like all other things in the new Miller Theatre, has been tried and proved efficient.

The gridiron, or succession of transverse metal bars almost touching the stage, from which the drops are suspended, is very high. This height is a marked advantage, for it is possible thereby to swing the drops so far up when they are not wanted that no part of them may be seen by the audience, even from the front row of the orchestra. It permits an exterior setting to continue upward into an apparently boundless sky, with

no canvass strips necessary to mark the top of the scene.

Over the prompter's head is the little balcony holding the switchboard. This is fully outfitted with interlocking switches and dimmers, and doubtless will operate the usual combination of colored lamps, red, amber, blue, and white. It is snug against the wall of the proscenium arch, so that the electrician in charge may view lights on the scene, in the wings, and in the flies above, just by turning his head. The advantage of keeping in close personal touch with operating parts is rather well recognized in modern theatres; stage workers do not use relay signaling save as a last resort.

Footlights are included on the Miller stage. Mr. Miller does not believe in their abolition unless their advantages may be matched by some more convenient device. Still, the system he uses at this point is not elaborate. The greater part of the lighting will come from above and at the sides.

On the whole, the Henry Miller Theatre is a thoroughly workable institution. Mr. Miller quite obviously wants all his experimentation in his productions. In the theatre itself he wants no dubious values.

The building was beautifully decorated by the time it opened, and rated comment in the *Architectural Record.*

23:2   THE HENRY MILLER THEATRE
NEW YORK CITY
Paul R. Allen & H. Creighton Ingalls
Associated Architects
by
Charles Over Cornelius

The opening, early in April, of Mr. Henry Miller's Theatre in West Forty-third street, is an event of importance, not only to the theatrical world and the theatre-going

23:2. Charles Over Cornelius, "The Henry Miller Theatre," *Architectural Record* 44:112–24 (Aug. 1918).

public, but in an equal degree marks a point of high interest to all who are impressed by an accomplishment of distinction in the art of building beautifully. The man whose cultivation has developed from an education of essential soundness towers above the dead level of human mediocrity by reason of his ability to revivify in his imagination important epochs of history and to relate accurately to them the present in which he lives. In much the same manner this latest addition to the list of New York theatres stands out from the writhing and contorted mass of its commercially designed confreres, recreating as it does in the busy midst of the twentieth century all the charm and polish of that mid-eighteenth century whose life and manners bore so great a similarity to our own.

The art of the drama in England made itself manifest in the very early days of that country's history, and its continuous development and elaboration from the simplest form of miracle and morality plays reached a definite stage in their evolution with the playwrights of the Elizabethan era. Here began the sturdy growth of the English drama as it exists today, yet there is a far cry from the crude productions of the Globe theatre to the perfect finish which a twentieth century audience demands. By the middle of the eighteenth century a form of play construction and a manner of theatrical production had developed, which is so closely akin to the demands of our own taste that the theatrical links are close-forged between that day and this. On the stage of the Theatre Royal in Drury Lane, David Garrick and Peg Woffington defied tradition by their interpretation of the plays of Shakespeare, Sheridan and lesser lights, rousing to enthusiasm a critical public by a finished presentation whose appeal is as valid today as it was in the days of George the Third.

Enough of the inspiration of Drury Lane has been breathed into Henry Miller's theatre to mark it as a lineal descendant in English tradition. The exterior has preserved largely the Georgian character in warm brick and lucent white marble, the scale tending toward the domestic rather than the monumental, and the while reminiscent of the Adam work contemporary with the Adelphi development and their remodeling of the theatre in Drury Lane. In general one might say that the Adam influence has confined itself to the larger aspects of the facade, the use and treatment of the pedimented end motifs, the proportioning of the main order, the slight reveal and the restraint of the decoration. In other respects and details the spirit is of slightly earlier type, the central doorway and the arched windows recalling the earlier English Georgian architecture which formed the point of departure for much of our American colonial work.

As the first theatre in the Broadway district erected under the new zoning and theatre laws of New York, the building shows an economical untilization of the spaces at either side of the lot which it was formerly required to leave open for the full depth. This gain in space has made possible a lengthening of the facade and its occupation of the entire frontage. The bays at either end mark the space of these courts, with their broad low arches giving access to the open areas behind. The group of three entrances in the centre admits to the box-office lobby, flanked at right and left by doorways, the first serving as an exit from the lobby, the latter as entrance and exit for the gallery. These two doorways also afford direct access from the street to Mr. Miller's private office and the offices of his staff, respectively. The facade is peculiarly successful in its expression of the interior immediately behind it, the levels of office floor and balcony recalled by the windows appropriately proportioned. The interest of detail is consistent throughout and extends even to the quaint playbill boards with their broken pediments and nicely spaced lettering.

The plan of the building behind this frank facade is thoroughly in keeping with its external expression. The central doors admit directly to the box-office lobby, which, with its oval form and nice proportions, serves as an appetizer for the feast of delicacy spread tastefully within. Three doorways from this lobby give into a shallow foyer that runs across the rear of the orchestra. At either end of this foyer stairs descend to the lounge and at the right ascend to the balcony. The main room of the theatre is entered directly from the foyer, from which it is separated by a wall which replaces the usual draughty opening behind the last row of seats. The remainder of this floor, given over to the stage and its necessarily adjacent service, is planned with an elimination of unnecessary complexity.

That part of the floor below which is designed for the comfort of the public is arranged with much nicety. The stairs leading down from the foyer approach from both sides to the lounge—a spacious room which serves as a meeting place for both men and women. The descent of both stairways is broken near the basement level by roomy landings, from which open the ladies' retiring room and gentlemen's smoking room, each with adjoining toilets and lavatories. The orchestra, which is screened from the view of the audience above, is placed in such a position that its music carries to both lounge and auditorium; while the organ chimes which announce the curtain-rising are similarly arranged.

The plan of the balcony floor requires no especial explanation; nor does that of the gallery.

If, in the plan, the hand of an experienced master is visible in the solution of so special a problem, no less is it seen in the execution of the plan in the third dimension. That part of the building which is designed for its effect upon the public has been carried out with such a consistency of good taste and an imagination so creative of individual atmosphere, that one instinctively feels a faith in all that one has heard of the positive psychological effect of really good architecture upon its beholder. The accompanying photographs by no means do justice to the building as it is, so much of its charm depending upon the color; but a passing description of the interior taken in conjunction with the photographs may present a facsimile of the building for those who have not seen it.

The decorations of the box-office lobby have been kept very simple, the painted walls being treated with molding and plaster cornice, and relieved by the well-placed wall lights. The floor is of black and white marble bounded by the black of the lower member of the base-board, and the ceiling of molded plaster is tinted a creamy tone. The only decoration of the trim occurs over the central door. The metal work of the grilles and the fixtures is finished in dull gilt and a grayish black, and the wall color is a warm cream with a mauve glaze, while the doors are the shade of old ivory.

The color chosen for the walls of the foyer is a bright blue, and this has been carried through all of that part of the building which may in general be called the circulation. The blue walls of the foyer are repeated in the stairway which leads from it to the balcony, as well as in those which decend to the lounge. In the lounge itself the color is a bright English green, of much the same value as the blue of the foyer and stairs. This consistency in the main wall color has a unifying effect without any monotony, for much of variety is obtained in the different parts of this circulation group by the use of different types of lighting fixtures and different drapery materials. In the lounge, the silk hangings of alternating rose and yellow stripes are brocaded with small flowers, while the over-door draperies in the foyer are heavily brocaded silk in deep blue, with a suggestion of chinoiserie in the design. The lighting fixtures, too, differ in each case: in the lounge the side lights have small oval mirror inserts in what might be considered a larger triangle of blue glass, while in the foyer the larger mirrors are surrounded by a gilded frame set with the same blue glass. All of the lights are softly shaded in parchment-colored silk. The carpeting is the same throughout, black with a small-scale design in greens and rose, whose colors will no doubt be softened by a few years' wear. The use of solid color for the walls, enlivened by the contrasting tones of the drapery, is consistent with the period style in which the theatre is carried out, as are the colors themselves—mauve, blue and green, rose, amber and blue.

The low-ceiled lounge is an unusually attractive feature and its atmosphere is that of a quiet English drawing-room. The inglenook in the centre is a little gem, of which the details in the marble mantelpiece, the brasses of fender, grate, fire irons and tools are brilliant facets. The candelabra here are particularly beautiful, being of onyx and crystal and gilt bronze set with Wedgwood medallions. The wall treatment utilizes arches with very slight reveal, and the plaster cornice—all in the same green—presents typical Adam ornament and the elimination of the architrave. The furniture at present in the room has not been chosen for the place and will eventually be changed for other pieces of greater appropriateness.

The *raison d'etre* of any theatre must perforce be its main auditorium, and in Henry Miller's theatre this room exhibits a number of features which will mark it as of a new *genre*. In the first place, the tradition has been followed which keeps consciously before it the development of the English theatre from the interior courts of buildings in contradistinction from that of the Latin theatre whose origins lie in the theatres and amphitheatres of Greece and Rome. Of late years this idea has been attenuated with its result in the little theatre movement where the theatre becomes practically a magnified drawing-room. In the theatre under discussion the architects have succeeded in keeping the little theatre atmosphere of intimacy and individuality, while at the same time incorporating into their scheme one of the demands of their client upon which he has stood firm—the presence of a comfortable gallery. Mr. Miller feels that the occupants of this tier have not altogether "gone over" to the moving pictures; for, as in the days of old much of the success of a production came from its reception in the pit, the presence of an enthusiastic gallery means much in the success or failure of a present-day play. Mr. Miller also is averse to the use of first floor boxes, and this has made possible the extremely pleasing form which the second floor boxes have assumed that of comparatively shallow balconies, whose paneled and decorative fronts carry out the line of the main balcony and tie it strongly into the side walls. It has meant, too, a considerable addition to the seating capacity of the parquet, the number of seats on this floor (404) being out of all proportion to that in the usual theatre of similar size, and this in spite of the sacrifice of an extra row at the rear by reason of the oval form of the lobby. Hence this room is a monument to the intelligent and appreciative co-operation between client and architect, each willing to give something here to gain a little there for the benefit of the whole.

The first impression of this room is made by the color harmony. The predominating tones are the warm, soft, putty color of the walls and the rich amber of the brocade hangings. The seats of tapestry in very small scale design blend more with the grays of the walls, while the darkest note is struck in the carpet, which is similar to that in the foyer and lounge. The decoration, in the Adam mode, is carried out in the painted panels in grisaille, with accents of bright color in medallions and swags, and in modeled plaster in the architectural members of capitals, cornice and ceiling. In the fans above the boxes the painted decoration has for a background a warm cream, which deepens toward the outer edge to a tone approaching that of the drapery and breaks what would otherwise be a hard line where the amber brocade cuts across its face. One particular detail, which will no doubt form a happy precedent for decorators, is the decoration of the kalamein doors of the exits, whose homely metal surfaces have here been turned into things of beauty and, from the nature of the material, let us hope joys forever.

The desire to create an impression of age has led to the use of glazes upon all of the trim and decoration, so that the whole has been antiqued with a great gain to the interest of texture. Many a good housewife might object to the dusky corners and moldings; but if ever the legitimacy of deliberate "antiqueing" has been justified, it has been in this building.

The use of the lighting fixtures in the room is worthy of note, the main source of light being the great crystal chandeliers hung from the ceiling, aided by the side-lights placed for their decorative value beneath the boxes.

So far we have turned our backs to the stage, which fills the full thirty-three foot space between the boxes. The curtain is of the same amber brocade, with its restrained decoration supporting a medallion portraying "Comedy" and "Tragedy" in a new guise after Mr. Miller's interpretation—the theatre, as an Alma Mater, touching with affection her two children, one of whom, Comedy, strives to draw her to play; the other, Tragedy, turns from her in tears. By an effect of lighting the color of the curtain seems to differ from the other drapery and takes on at times, particularly when the footlights are up, a tone that is not altogether pleasing.

The orchestra is entirely screened from the audience, the music reaching them through louvered openings in the top of the screen.

With the rising of the curtain a further display of the architect's versatility is revealed. The stage sets for the two plays which so far have been produced have been designed under Mr. Allen's and Mr. Ingalls' supervision, with the result of a tasteful and correct interior in each case suitable to its purpose, and the added consideration of an atmosphere which, seeming to pervade both sides of the footlights, gives to each member of the audience the feeling of actual presence in the room on the stage—a consideration of much interest when we consider the disparity between the average theatre and such a stage set as this of "The Fountain of Youth."

Behind the scenes there is much to interest the specialist, but which has little place in so general a description as this. The restriction of the building law forced the shape of the stage house as shown by the section; but by the use of the most-up-to-date counterweight system, the obstacles presented were overcome and the resulting ease of manipulation has simplified, too, the question of manual labor in setting the stage. The dressing rooms for the players have been given thoughtful consideration, and by the tasteful use of chintz and paint these rooms have been made charming and restful, unlike many of their ilk.

At the inception of the project Mr. Allen associated himself with Mr. Ingalls and Mr. Hoffman, architects of the Little Theatre and Neighborhood Playhouse, for the designing and execution of this particular building. At Mr. Hoffman's entrance into the government sevice at the very beginning of the work, the onus fell entirely upon Mr. Allen and Mr. Ingalls, and their competent cooperation has given to New York a theatre whose peer is scarce to be found except in the children of their own brains.

The theatre as a whole stands as a monument, first, to the debt which we owe to our mother country for her traditions in the arts; second, to the public whose appreciation in general has risen to such a plane that a theatre of so subtle an atmosphere should rise to meet its demand; and last, but by no means least, to the architects whose authoritative handling of so difficult a problem has served to unite artistically and esthetically two remote periods in the history of an art which may have reached another milestone with its present incarnation at the end of one world epoch and at the beginning of a new.

24. NATIONAL THEATRE
New York City
Opened September 1, 1921

A production of Sidney Howard's first play, *Swords*, proved to be an unsuccessful beginning for this playhouse. The productions that followed had more popular appeal, however, and included a number of long-run hits. In 1959 the name of the house was changed to the Billy Rose Theatre in honor of the Broadway producer and show-business personality.

An architectural description of the National Theatre appeared in the New York *Times*.

24:1 NATIONAL THEATRE LATEST ADDITION TO
TIMES SQUARE PLAYHOUSES

Many Novelties of Construction in Walter C. Jordan's House on West Forty-first Street, Built at a Cost of $950,000, to Open Monday, August 29.

Walter C. Jordan's National Theatre, the latest and the most unique of recent additions to the list of Broadway playhouses, is now nearing completion in Forty-first Street, just west of Seventh Avenue, It will be opened to the public Aug. 29.

24:1. New York *Times*, Aug. 21, 1921.

This new National Theatre, the plans of which were designed and executed by the well-known architect, William Neil Smith, is the first venture of Walter C. Jordan as owner and operator of a metropolitan house, although for the best part of a busy lifetime he has been the head and active factor in a large and most successful institution for the handling and exploitation of the plays and players of Europe and America.

The National Theatre is both a capacious and an intimate house. It contains 1,200 seats, and yet every seat is near the stage. The balcony contains half the seating capacity, offering the singular effect of an upward sloping ceiling to those in the parquet or orchestra.

Instead of the downward, awning-like effect, the ceiling under the National's balcony slants at a goodly angle toward the peak of the proscenium, the result being an enlarged radius of vision, with an added sense of spaciousness and freedom to those seated under the balcony projection.

The interior of the National is done in burnished Italian walnut wood, with gold delineations. The style is early Renaissance and the carved figures are of lyric and epic subjects, unobtrusive but attractive, and emerging in the half-round from the wood like Flemish carvings. The entire interior structure is of concrete, without any "stony visibility."

The lighting plan for the auditorium is developed by eighteen roof lights, from which the entire house can be flooded with amber, white, green, blue, yellow or rose colored radiance.

All of the textiles used, whether for the draperies, rugs or aisle strips, are of hues of mulberry or mauve, gently contributory to the color comeliness and easy beauty of the woodwork of the entire interior.

The stage opening is 40 feet, with a stage width of 86 feet in the clear and 100 feet from floor to gridiron, and can easily accommodate shows of any size or scope.

18. The Neighborhood Playhouse, New York, 1915. Courtesy of The Hoblitzelle Theatre Arts Library, The Humanities Research Center, The University of Texas at Austin.

19. Provincetown Playhouse, New York, ca. 1923. Courtesy of the Museum of the City of New York.

21. Bijou Theatre, New York, 1917. Photograph by Apeda. Courtesy of The Hoblitzelle Theatre Arts Library, The Humanities Research Center, The University of Texas at Austin.

23. Henry Miller Theatre, New York, 1918. Courtesy of The Hoblitzelle Theatre Arts Library, The Humanities Research Center, The University of Texas at Austin.

The dressing rooms, with their baths, outdoor windows, casements to the street and perfect equipments and luxuries, speak well for Mr. Jordan's consideration for the players.

The last word in utility and luxury has also been applied to the withdrawing rooms for men and women—for women especially. For the beauty of the smoking rooms and lavatories, the cloak booths and lounges are fully in keeping with the ornate and utilitarian features of the entire theatre.

The whole structure is of steel and concrete with a minimum of combustible material even in its woodwork and draperies. It is further safeguarded with the most elaborate and scientific equipment of automatic stage skylights, water tanks and hydraulic pumps for the prevention of fire.

The National Theatre covers a frontage of 110 feet on Forty-first Street and is to be conducted as a regular legitimate house for first-class dramatic and musical productions, although in equipping it with very modern devices a motion-picture booth has been installed.

The offices of the theatre are on the second floor, under the balcony, with direct stairway to Forty-first Street. The box office will be opened tomorrow morning.

25. MUSIC BOX THEATRE
New York City
Opened September 22, 1921

From its opening in 1921, the Music Box Theatre remained one of the most consistently successful houses in New York. The property was bought and the theatre erected by Sam H. Harris and Irving Berlin. The playhouse opened on September 22, 1921, with Berlin's *Music Box Revue*. An announcement of the new venture appeared in the New York *Times* on March 15.

25:1   STILL ANOTHER THEATRE.

25:1. New York *Times*, Mar. 15, 1921.

TIMES SQUARE SECTION TO HAVE A
BEAUTIFUL "MUSIC BOX."

The property at 239 to 247 West Forty-fifth Street, it was announced yesterday, has been bought by Sam H. Harris and Irving Berlin, who will take possession on May 1 and immediately begin the construction of a theatre. The house will be known as the Music Box, and its first attraction will be a revue by Mr. Berlin. It is planned to make the theatre one of the most beautiful in the city.

The site, which is west of Broadway and on the northern side of Forty-fifth Street, was bought at the Astor realty auction last week by L. and A. Pincus and Mr. L. Goldstone, who resold it to Messrs. Harris and Berlin.

The opening proved very sucessful, and the audience praised both the show and the theater highly. Alexander Woollcott reviewed the opening for the New York *Times*.

25:2   THE MUSIC BOX BEGINS TO PLAY

The Music Box was opened last evening before a palpitant audience and proved to be a treasure chest out of which the conjurers pulled all manner of gay tunes and brilliant trappings and funny clowns and nimble dancers. Its bewildering contents confirmed the dark suspicion that Sam H. Harris and Irving Berlin have gone quite mad. Manager and composer they have builded them a playhouse in West Forty-fifth Street that is a thing of beauty in itself, and then crowded its stage with such a sumptuous and bespangled revue as cannot possibly earn them anything more substantial than the heartwarming satisfaction of having produced it at all.

The Music Box began to play last night and a houseful of wide-eyed, open-mouthed onlookers gave every evidence of wondering if it would ever begin to pay. By the time the final curtain fell on the edge of midnight, everyone was cheer-

25:2. New York *Times*, Sept. 23, 1921.

ing loudly. . . . And there's this odd thing about the theatre itself. It is not only cosy, but beautiful.

26. AMBASSADOR THEATRE
New York City
Opened September 29, 1921

The Shuberts opened this theater in September 1921 with one of their all-time hits, *Blossom Time*, a musical that J. J. Shubert particularly loved, which produced a great deal of money for the Shubert coffers. The New York *Times* of November 18, 1920, announced the plans for the theater. The architect, Herbert J. Krapp, was to design a large number of the theaters erected in this period.

26:1   AMBASSADOR IS ITS NAME
First of Six New Shubert Theatres to Be
Opened in January

The first of six new theatres which the Shuberts are building in Forty-eighth Street, will be called the Ambassador, and will be opened in January. This will be a theatre seating 1,200 persons, and is being built upon the site at 215 to 225 West Forty-ninth Street, just west of Broadway.

The Ambassador offers a novelty in construction, in that it runs diagonally upon the plot, so as to gain the benefit of additional space. Herbert J. Krapp is the architect and Edward Margolies is the builder.

Four of the new Shubert theatres will be on Forty-ninth Street and two on Forty-eighth. One of the latter, immediately across from the Longacre, is now in the course of construction. Another Shubert house is in process of construction on Seventh Avenue, immediately below Fifty-ninth Street, and still other Shubert houses are planned for Eighth Avenue and Fifty-fourth Street and Broadway and Sixty-eighth Street.

26:1. New York *Times*, Nov. 18, 1920.

27. EARL CARROLL THEATRE
New York City
Opened February 27, 1922

Earl Carroll was a successful song writer, director, and producer who, in 1922, opened his own New York playhouse, where for the next two decades he produced a series of musical revues that he titled *Earl Carroll's Vanities*. His playhouse and its decorations and stage machinery earned major articles in *Scientific American* and *Arts and Decoration*, three of which are reproduced here.

27:1   The theatre's the thing! At least so believes the ambitious and idealistic Earl Carroll, who opened his new playhouse with a play of his own last month. "A playwright creates for the theatre that is at his disposal. If the stage and the equipment is limited, his work will be limited. . . . .Before the play can be the thing, the theatre must be the thing." Certainly, if this premise is true, this new Earl Carroll Theatre must prove an inspiration to the American author and the American actor. Here are some of the advantages it offers to the actors and actresses fortunate enough to find themselves ensconced in this new theatre: a greenroom, commodious and beautiful, with a cheerful fireplace, rows of inviting books and even a goddess of Good Luck—a graceful concession to the actor's picturesque superstition; in his Greenroom, the actor can meet his friends, study his lines, talk of his work and establish within himself the mood that is necessary to the play: dressing rooms but one flight above the stage— an arrangement which saves the actor the customary, laborious stair climbing; dressing rooms that are cozy places, attractively furnished, properly ventilated and lighted, each with a private shower bath, com-

27:1. "Earl Carroll Opens the Theatre of His Dreams," *Arts and Decoration*, Apr. 1922, p. 433.

fortable divans and long, accessible mirrors. (In addition, the star's suites have miniature reception rooms where they may meet their friends.) Such consideration as this for the actor is, of course, unprecedented, but it is only in accordance with the principle that dominates the entire theatre: The actor is an artist. He must have every consideration that an artist requires.

The technical features of the stage are also unusual. There is, for instance, a horizant, a great, concrete, concave wall which will furnish a comprehensive sky background having a vibrancy and depth impossible to the painted drop. For the orchestra, a disappearing platform has been built which will rise to the level of the stage during the intermissions and sink from view during the acts. Special importance is attached to this arrangement, for it makes an apron stage possible; and just now the apron stage is about to become an intrinsic part of the modern commercial theatre.

Believing that the curtain call is destructive to the stage illusion, Mr. Carroll has designed duplicate stage platforms which take the place of boxes. Here the actors can appear at the conclusion of each act, their appearance being a personal one, entirely separate from the stage picture which will never be disturbed after the curtain once falls.

Unique is the arrangement of the electrical apparatus which will be controlled by a master pilot wheel. In the past it has been almost impossible to make the lights synchronize perfectly with the action. When, during the action of the play, the maid walked to the mantle to turn on the lights, an awkward pause would always follow the moment when she first touched the button and the moment when the lights really went on.

The general style of the interior is Italian Renaissance. The mural color scheme is a wonderful, luminous, turquois blue, not previously adapted for theatre interiors, here enriched with low relief ornamentation finished in antique burnished gold.

The triple draperies of the proscenium arch are a very novel feature and produce a wonderful effect. The curtain nearest the audience extends out some sixteen feet into the auditorium, entirely concealing the orchestra when closed and when drawn back discloses the succeeding drop or act curtains. The outer curtain is made of an iridescent silk fabric, which hangs in rich folds or flutes disclosing radiations of rose, turquois blue, hyacinth and opalescent tones, and is beautifully ornamented.

27:2   Although it was generally believed that the limit of novelty in stage setting and scenery had been reached such has recently been proved not to be the case, for the third production at the Earl Carroll Theatre in New York City has witnessed the introduction by Mr. Carroll of an original and simplified method of building up scenes that bids fair to be of great usefulness, especially on rather small stages.

Heretofore, when raised platforms and steps were required, these were specially built. They invariably occupied a great deal of space, and could only be used on an extended scale in such places as the New York Hippodrome, where there was ample room to store them when not in use. Some of the most effective scenes at this giant playhouse were obtained by long and wide flights of stairs down which row upon row of girls marched out of sight beneath the waters of the tank.

In producing his latest offering, Mr. Earl Carroll determined to make use of these staircase effects if possible. Heretofore, staircases had been built up in two sections and separated for storage, while platforms were elaborate affairs (sections of the stage) that required hydraulic elevators to raise them into place. Needless to say, the expense and cumbersomeness would preclude their use in a small theatre, the latter particularly in a revue with many scenes. To get around the difficulty, Mr. Carroll invented a system of unit building block construction whereby he could build a long, wide flight of stairs in a limited space, as well as any number of raised platforms of any shapes which might be desired.

After working out his problem on a small scale with a tiny model, Mr. Carroll proceeded to construct the actual settings for the stage of his theater. In doing this he followed the model precisely to scale.

As will be noted in the accompanying view, large units are shown horizontally, with stairs leading up to them, and with other stairs leading up from each side to the apex. These stairs are all constructed in units of two steps each, assembled upon different sized blocks whose corners form intermediate steps. Any scene whatsoever can be quickly and easily built up by but four stage hands, since the different sized units consist of light frames covered with three-ply veneer. For transportation purposes all units except the smallest can be knocked down flat, while these non-collapsible two-step units can be placed in interlocked arrangement, forming a block. In order to get a long flight of steps in the limited space of about thirty feet, the steps were made with but a ten-inch tread. This is not exactly a sumptuous stair, but is sufficient for all purposes.

The tread and height of the steps play an important part in obtaining the proper lighting effects. In the present instance much thought has been put upon securing the lighting that will properly display the figures and costumes. On each side of a secondary proscenium is a vertical row of spotlights, while colored and white lights in the flies and in the "canopy" in front of the stage, as well as below the balcony railing (called "face" lights) properly light the actors and do away with shadows. There are also the usual spotlights in the cinematograph booth at the rear of the balcony. All these lights must be carefully calculated to meet the stair dimensions.

Mr. Earl Carroll's unit block system of ground stage scenery construction or setting, is adapted to many forms of scenery, as the blocks may be covered or masked with painted scenery wherever desired. The blocks are all painted a light blue and sprayed with silver. Italian blue was found by experiment to be the proper color to tint the back wall of the theater which represents the sky and forms a suitable background for any scene. The invention is a decidedly novel and useful one.

27:3 APPLYING THE LESSONS OF INDUSTRY TO THE THEATER

Ingenious Devices, Partly or Wholly New, Incorporated Into New York's Newest Play-House

Great improvement in theater building has been made in the past few years, largely with a view to the comfort and convenience of patrons. Methods and devices for handling scenery also have been improved and adopted by a few theaters, again with an eye to the patron, for these have been for securing clever stage effects or for shortening the wait between acts. Now comes a theater embodying all of these improvements, but designed also with the specific idea of making it easy for actors, electricians, stage hands, scene shifters and all others of the army of workers behind the footlights, to coordinate their efforts to produce a good play.

27:3. First published in *Scientific American* 124:228–29 (Apr. 1922). Reprinted with permission. Copyright © 1922 by Scientific American, Inc. All rights reserved.

Moreover, for the first time recognition is given by a theater to the fact that the quality of workmanship (in this case the play) may depend mightily upon the surroundings and environment of the workman.

The designing, especially of the stage and its equipment, has been gone about with precious little regard for precedent and tradition. Many of the old devices of the stage, which are present in nearly every stage in the country, are gone and in their stead is a collection of new devices which are so obviously good that we are forced to exclaim, "Why didn't someone think of that before?"

Our drawing shows the main features of the stage construction. The theater, from the rear of the house as far as the edge of the balcony, although elegantly appointed, does not differ appreciably from that in other new theaters. The first discrepancy we discover is the absence of the battery of spotlights usually located, with their operator, somewhere in the gallery. Instead there is a bank of floodlights so cleverly concealed in the decorations of the under rim of the balcony that the audience sees only their effect and never notes their presence.

The most striking innovation, perhaps, is the absence of boxes, which have long been a traditional feature of theaters, although a notoriously inconvenient and high-priced spot from which to view a play. In the space on either side of the stage usually occupied by the boxes there are two miniature stages, which communicate from the rear with the main stage. Their most important use is for the purpose of acknowledging applause. When the main curtain descends at the end of an act it remains down and the time usually devoted to raising and lowering it to acknowledge applause is saved. The actor or actors, meanwhile, step to the miniature side-stages into the illumination of spotlights concealed in the balcony decorations. These stages also may be used for

the presentation of a prologue, or in the cast of a large spectacular production may be easily connected to the main stage as "aprons," thus extending the available stage room across the entire width of the building.

Another feature which will be quite noticeable to the audience and quite as puzzling, will be the sudden appearance of the orchestra, apparently from nowhere. The explanation is that the orchestra pit is really a huge hydraulic elevator, which can be lowered out of sight or raised to suit the occasion. The orchestra enters through the basement, and when ready to play is suddenly lifted into view of the audience. The elevator takes the form of a crescent, supported on several hydraulic lifts. The orchestra pit can be raised even to the level of the stage and used as an extension.

The effect which seems next most remarkable to the audience, no doubt, is that in out-of-door scenes the sky, instead of being a wavering "drop" of blue cloth, seems real and quite as limitless as the heavens themselves. This is accomplished by the use of a "horizant," a device which originated in Europe, and which has been used in one or two of the small "art" theaters in this country, but never before in a commercial theater here. The back wall of the building is simply shaped of smooth cement with curved corners. It is a neutral gray, and the stage director, through his electrician, paints upon this background in light the effect he desires—be it the effect of night, of dawn, or the shimmering heat of the desert noon. A small trench is constructed just in front of the wall so that workmen and actors may pass across the stage unobserved during the progress of an act.

Mr. Earl Carroll, the designer of this theater, regards the adoption of the "horizant" as the greatest single step forward he has taken. "Playwrights have been very cautious," he said, "about writing out-of-doors scenes into their plays because of their unreality. I have experimented extensively with the horizant and I am convinced that this demonstration will cause it to be generally adopted. I think it will bring the out-of-door play, now almost entirely limited to the movies, to the speaking stage."

From the viewpoint of coordination of effort, an important change is in taking the electrician and stage manager from the "wings" and placing them at the very front and center of the stage in plain view of all of the players. They sit in a pit with their heads just above stage level, but are concealed from the audience because their heads are just below the line of vision from the topmost seats in the gallery over the footlight reflectors. From this point of vantage the director and electrician observe not only every light and every effect, as well as the actors, but through a telescopic peephole at their backs can see the entire audience and all of the house lights. Hitherto this was impossible because these two important men were located in the wings, where they had an imperfect and distorted view of the stage and no view at all of the audience and house.

The electrical arrangements alone for a large modern theater might well occupy a page of description here, but we shall have to note them briefly. The rheostats for "fading out" or "fading in" the footlights and floodlights are huge motor-driven affairs, while the great number of switches are of the remote control type and altogether occupy solidly a good-sized room. All are operated from a central control board by the chief electrician, who may have a number of assistants. In this new theater the electrician is provided with a master hand wheel to which his assistants "hook," electrically, the various apparatus he is using at a particular moment. For instance, if he is changing from the effect of dawn to daylight, the deep blue and red lights would be so connected that turning the wheel would slowly fade them out, while by the same movement the blue and white lights would fade in. Within reach of the electrician, also, are a great number of master levers by means of which he operates the switches in a room beneath the stage to secure his lighting effects, in much the same manner that the organist operates the stops on a pipe organ.

Another discarded inadequacy, small in itself but as old as the theater, is the peephole in the curtain. This has been replaced by a telescopic lens arrangement on either side of the stage, which gives an easy view of the entire audience.

The degree to which realism can be carried may be realized from the fact that the stage equipment includes a kitchen range with utensils and dishes for cooking and serving a full meal. When the lines of a play call for the serving of a meal it will be a real meal of real food, served piping hot from the kitchen in the wings.

The arrangement for handling scenery and drops also is noteworthy. The large pieces need no longer be pushed about by "main strength and awkwardness," but instead are whisked aloft by counterbalanced cables and secured there by a few men stationed on a platform some 60 feet above the stage. The counterbalances are buckets filled with buckshot, which may be emptied or filled to the proper weight. Thus a few men are able to perform the work that once required the services of a large number of scene-shifters. This system is coming into gradual use, but for the first time the theater designer has realized that it makes unnecessary the two wing balconies on each side of the stage, which the standard to theater construction. Once useful for raising and lowering drops by hand, these balconies lately have been not only useless but collectors of dust and junk.

One of the obvious improvements is a simple lift system for handling the trunks of performers with a minimum of effort. Of the scores of theaters in New York, it is said this is the only one where the moving of trunks does not involve back-breaking expedient of climbing stairs.

The arrangement of dressing rooms for the players also marks a distinct step away from tradition. It has long been the custom to have two or three dressing rooms on the same floor with the stage for the use of the stars. These sometimes were elegantly appointed. The rest of the cast, however, had to climb stairs to stuffy dressing rooms with little or no regard for comfort and convenience. The space on the stage level of any theater is always precious, and that which might have been given to the stars' dressing rooms has been given over to a "green room," for the use of the whole cast and their guests. The room is a cozy one, artistically decorated, and with a mammoth fireplace at one end. It is expected that this room will not only serve innumerable social purposes for the players, but will be the scene of gatherings of notables, the reading of plays, and the like.

From the green room, a marble staircase winds to the dressing rooms above. Something of the psychology of players has been taken into account in building the staircase, for half-way up one is confronted with a very cheerful "good-luck" statuette.

The theatrical world of New York never tires telling of the architect who, with his head in the clouds, undertook the construction of the ideal theater. All sorts of expensive and new-fangled things were introduced into the plans looking to the comfort of the audience and the better presentation of the play. But just in the nick of time, before actual work on the theater itself had begun, some practical-minded person got his eye on the plans and called the attention of the architect to the fact that he had omitted to provide a single dressing room of any description. Mr. Carroll has not repeated this error.

The players, in their dressing rooms, are given the same conveniences and service that they might expect in a great hotel. The rooms are fitted with shower baths and are elegantly outfitted and equipped. Excepting that the rooms for the stars are directly at the head of the stairs, there is no distinction between the treatment of star and chorus girl. The women's dressing rooms open into a common reception room, where they may receive guests, and which is fitted with an excellent library and lounging couches.

All of these improvements have involved the spending of thousands of dollars on the construction of the theater which might have been saved by ordinary construction. Many of them never are seen by the audience, and old-time theatrical men will contend, no doubt, that they contribute nothing to the value of a play, which after all marks it for success or failure.

Mr. Carroll has spent large sums on improvements of this nature with the idea that they will make it easier to coordinate all of the myriad activities back of the footlights; that this will contribute directly to the success of any theatrical production staged there and therefore to the financial success of the theater itself. "If this be idealism," says Mr. Carroll, "certainly it is a very practical sort."

Furthermore, the democratic treatment accorded the players is in direct line with a marked tendency in the theatrical world toward the labor conditions which obtain in industry. Most actors now belong to one of two organizations conducted along the lines of the labor unions. As a rule, conveniences for industrial workers in their leisure moments have not been carried to the extreme attempted in this theater, but similar methods applied to industry have paid definite profits. They enhance the interest of the worker in the enterprise and spur him or her to better effort at the machine—or before an audience.

"We are not dragging art," declared Mr. Carroll, "into the mire of industrialism. I do not think you will find a better appreciation of art in any other theater in the world. What we have done is simply to recognize established facts about human beings, and in applying them to the theater we have had to invent some new devices and discard many old ones, and have made the best use possible of those already at our disposal."

The theater, from the standpoint of seating capacity, is not a large one, having 1026 seats. This makes it possible so to arrange them that every seat is in direct line with the stage and there is hardly any choice, except as to distance from the stage, of any two seats in the house. Here is applied democracy for the audience, too.

28. IMPERIAL THEATRE
New York City
Opened December 24, 1923

The Shuberts continued their phenomenal building program by opening their fiftieth playhouse in the New York City area. Christened the Imperial, this huge theater housed many of New York's most successful musicals. It was still functioning in 1971. The New York *Times* heralded the playhouse:

28:1   THE IMPERIAL ITS NAME
New Shubert Theatre in 45th Street
to Open With "Mary Jane."

The Shuberts announced yesterday that the new theater now under construction for them on Forty-fifth Street, west of Broadway, and scheduled to open Christmas night with the production of Arthur Hammerstein's musical play "Mary Jane," will be known as the Imperial. The theatre, which is located on Forty-sixth Street but will have a Forty-fifth Street entrance, will have a seating capacity of 1,540, of which nearly 700 are on the orchestra floor, with the remainder in a single balcony.

Herbert J. Krapp is the architect, and the building operation is being done by the O'Day Construction Company. Work is being carried on day and night at pres-

ent, to have the theatre in readiness for the scheduled Christmas opening.

On December 21 there was a dedication ceremony for the new house.

28:2   THE IMPERIAL DEDICATED
New Shubert Theatre in 45th Street Has
Seating Capacity of 1,650.

The Imperial Theatre, the new house built by the Shuberts on Forty-fifth Street, was "dedicated" yesterday in the presence of a considerable crowd. May Hay, who will head the cast of "Mary Jane," broke a bottle of champagne over the theatre marquise.

The Imperial is the fiftieth playhouse to be built by the Shuberts in and around New York City. It has a seating capacity of 1,650.

29. MARTIN BECK THEATRE
New York City
Opened November 11, 1924

"In reporting the dual festivities in Forty-fifth Street last night it must first be set down that Martin Beck has presented the town with one of its handsomest playhouses." So began the review of the opening night by one New York critic. And this was the consensus in a time when a dozen new theaters were being opened in a year's time. An assessment of the new playhouse had appeared the previous Sunday in the real estate section of the New York *Times*.

29:1   NEW MARTIN BECK THEATRE TO OPEN
TUESDAY EVENING

The new Martin Beck Theatre, at Forty-fifth Street and Eighth Avenue, scheduled to open Tuesday evening, the only one in America in the Byzantine genre, was conceived by Mr. Beck, designed by G. Albert Alnsburgh, San Francisco architect, and had its art work done by Albert Herter, the mural painter.

28:1. New York *Times*, Dec. 5, 1923.

28:2. New York *Times*, Dec. 22, 1923.
29:1. New York *Times*, Nov. 9, 1924.

It seats 1,200, has dressing rooms for 200, an unusually large foyer and promenade after the Continental custom.

This is the ninth theatre to be erected in the short block of Forty-fifth Street from Broadway to Eighth Avenue, the other eight being the Astor, Bijou, Morosco, Booth, Plymouth, Music Box, Imperial and Klaw.

The opening performance was a "sumptuous production" of *Madame Pompadour,* a musical play.

30. GUILD THEATRE
New York City
Opened April 13, 1925

The Theatre Guild was founded in 1919 by Lawrence Langner and his wife, Armina Marshall. By 1925 it had become such an important producing organization that it built its own playhouse, the Guild Theatre, on Fifty-second Street west of Broadway. Outstanding productions were presented during the Theatre Guild's tenure there. One such was the opening drama, Shaw's *Caesar and Cleopatra,* starring Helen Hayes as the young queen of the Nile.

The name of the playhouse was changed in 1950 to the A.N.T.A. Theatre, and the house became the headquarters of the American National Theatre Association.

Stage designer Claude Bragdon discussed the new playhouse and its technical advantages in the *Architectural Record.*

30:1 The new home of the New York Theatre Guild, now being built on West Fifty-Second street, though a theatre building of the usual type, is somehow different from those monsters of the mere market which in the roaring Forties nuzzle up as close as they can to Broadway. Although like them the Guild theatre will depend

30:1. Claude Bragdon, "New York Theatre Guild's New Theatre," *Architectural Record* 58:508–16 (Dec. 1924).

for its sustenance on the amusement-loving public, there is a subtle difference, not unlike the difference between a transient and a family hotel. That is to say, the Guild's productions are paid for in advance, by the year, cash over the counter, by subscribers many of whom are stockholders. These people constitute a group which however lacking in cohesion or solidarity has nevertheless a distinct psychology of its own. It stands for something other than what "Broadway" stands for; its demands in the amusement line are not those of the tired business man— some would say that they are more nearly those of the tired business woman, since the cultural and aesthetic side of life is so largely, with us, a feminine engrossment, most intense with those who are most emancipated.

Be this as it may, there is a social and educational aspect of the Theatre Guild's activities, and this registers itself in an interesting way in the new building, which contains class-rooms, studios, a book shop, a library and club room, besides having a ground floor lounge almost as great in floor area as the auditorium itself. The stockholders, indeed, constitute a club, whose home is here. The club room occupies the middle of the front of the building at the balcony level, and is reached by an independent entrance and elevator directly from the street.

The large lounge beneath the auditorium was made possible through a special concession of the building department which permitted the Guild to establish the auditorium floor level of their theater considerably higher than the three low steps called for by the ordinance. The safety of the audience has been insured by making a wide exit direct to Fifty-Second street by means of two ramps and a flight of only five broad steps. This is entirely independent of the entrance to the auditorium, which is through the lounge and up a double stairway discharging at each end of a long foyer immediately back of the auditorium. Another double stairway leads to an upper foyer beneath the balcony.

The theatre has a seating capacity of 914; there is no second balcony and there are no boxes. The apron of the stage, which is lower than is usual, extends completely over the orchestra pit, thus eliminating that chasm which sometimes divides the audience from the actors. There is no proscenium arch, strictly speaking, for the walls and ceiling of the auditorium simply come to an end where the stage begins, but this omission of the picture frame does not constitute this, as some have supposed, a "prosceniumless theatre," which implies something altogether different, namely, that the stage is in the auditorium instead of behind it.

The stage presents no unusual features except that it is higher and deeper than most New York theatre stages built in recent years. The dressing rooms are arranged in the usual inconvenient fashion, in vertical tiers reached by iron stairs, the the number of such flights an actor has to climb to reach his dressing room accurately indicating his position in the company, for the higher he ascends towards the stars the farther he is from stardom. This vertical disposition of the dressing rooms is really imposed in a city like New York because of the high land values, which make lateral expansion prohibitive, and by the reason of the stringent fire regulations which forbid dressing rooms beneath the stage.

All of the scenery is handled from the stage floor by a counter-weight system, instead of from a fly gallery. The electrical switchboard possesses special features, being not only much smaller, but far more full and flexible than the old fashioned theatrical switchboard because equipped with interlocking and automatic devices whereby entire sequences of light changes ensue upon the operation of a single master switch. The dimmers are relegated to a fire and sound-proof vault in the basement.

These features, though not common, are not new: the real novelty in the matter of stage equipment is likely to be the cyclorama—that which in the theatre represents the sky. This is the *bête noir* of every art director, whose experience with stage firmaments is likely to give him a new respect for the architect of the universe, that he can keep the wrinkles out of his vast and seamless cyclorama in all weathers, never let it get in the way of the rest of the scenery, and can produce such a wide variety of subtly changing light and cloud effects. In the theatre the cyclorama is usually a great sheet of dirty linen, suspended from the gridiron in the form of an ellipse, slaty blue in color, as perishable as lingerie from a cheap shop, susceptible as a consumptive curate to every change of temperature which registers as wrinkles and as puckers in the seams, swayed by the slightest breeze, and always in the way of everything and everybody. To overcome all this the plaster cyclorama was invented, of which there are three in New York, but this has also its disadvantages, for if the one looks too much like cloth in certain lights, the other looks too much like plaster, and waves in the sky are just as disillusioning as wrinkles; dirt also has as great an affinity for the one as for the other.

When Mr. Lee Simonson—the Guild's art director—was in Europe he discovered in use in certain theatres a cyclorama of a new type, the invention of that Linnebach whose lantern for painting scenes on the back drop with light instead of pigment has been used in the Guild productions from time to time. This cyclorama was of linen, sewed in such a way that the seams did not appear, but its uniqueness consisted in the fact that it was rolled up when not in use—and therefore out of the way and well protected—on a kind of gigantic vertical shade roller, the cloth attached at the top in such a way that by the pressing of an electric button it rapidly unfurled itself along the line of an elliptical track high aloft, out of the way and out of sight. This is the type of cyclorama that will be used in the Guild theatre. It will be lighted by the Pevear system, which makes possible every conceivable color combination, and insures perfect diffusion, the lamps being placed at top and bottom, within four feet of the cloth. The lamps at the bottom will be sunk in a trough in the stage floor, so that ground rows—which conceal the floor lights from the view of the audience—can be dispensed with. The other lighting devices will be, in general, like those in use at the Garrick now, but there will be in addition concealed projectors for lighting the stage from the auditorium. All these matters of back-stage lighting, planning and equipment were Mr. Simonson's particular charge, one for which his experience as the Guild's art director makes him particularly well fitted.

The architects of the Guild Theatre are C. Howard Crane, Kenneth Franzheim, and Charles Hunter Bettis. Norman Bel Geddes was retained as consultant—the man who performed the miracle of the Miracle, the transformation of the interior of the Century theater into a church. In the early conferences between the Guild directors and their architects, Mr. Geddes submitted a solution of his own, embodying many of the features of his "theatre number six," described in the September, 1922, number of THE ARCHITECTURAL RECORD. But to carry this plan out would have presented grave difficulties, since it violated ordinances framed for theatres of an entirely different type, and it would have involved delays and additional expenses in the matter of rock excavations, etc. Therefore only a few of Mr. Geddes' suggestions were adopted, and his hand appears in the final result scarcely at all.

The Guild architects are specialists in theatre planning and construction, and from a study of the drawings it is apparent they have evolved a somewhat conventional and conservative, but wholly admirable solution of their problem, doing with it all that was possible under those most stern conditions governing theatre building in New York. Between the devil of land and building costs, and the deep sea of legal and operating requirements, ideal success being out of the question, they have escaped with such honor as may attend the designing of what is likely to prove the best theatre building of its class in New York. It would be unfair to institute a comparison of it with certain German theatres built by Professor Max Littmann, under so much more kind conditions and with a less restricted hand.

The style of the exterior appears to be that of the late Italian Renaissance—stucco wall surfaces, with heavily rusticated stone quoins and window trim, an overhanging decorated wood cornice and a tile roof. The facade is well composed, the intricate elements of the plan being transformed, in the fenestration, to order and some semblance of symmetry. It is truthful, in the main: these little windows show the offices and dressing rooms; here, where the large French windows and balconies occur, is the club room; the triply arched loggia while concealing, reveals the presence of the fire-tower exit; the long marquise and the battery of doors publish the fact that here is a theatre.

There has been no attempt to give aesthetic expression to the upper part of the stage enclosure, or to relate it to the facade in any way: it remains a crude, rude pile of brick. Though this is according to the usual practice, it is an opportunity missed. The rear of the Metropolitan Opera House is an object lesson of what may be made with a stage enclosure: there are few finer things, architecturally, in all New York, than the great grey buttressed wall and pediment.

Architecture is itself an art of *dramatization:* a building should be made eloquent of itself, expressive of its purpose. Now there are at least three things that might differentiate the exterior of a theatre from that of a hotel or a club for example. One of these is the towering stage enclosure above mentioned, and the others are the so necessary long marquise sheltering the numerous entrance and exit doors, and the quite indispensable electric sign which ballyhoos to Broadway the fact that here is pleasure to be purchased for a price. It would be interesting to see a theatre in which these two last-mentioned features were recognized as characteristic and dramatically important, and therefore designed with deliberate and distinguished art, instead of being left to the untender mercies of some maker of commercial electric signs. It is to be hoped that the Guild theatre will not be thus afflicted, but that the architects will extend their jurisdiction over every last gleaming letter of every latest glistering sign.

This theatre should be a temple of austere joy, of fresh and living beauty, and as such its custodians and ministers should fling their harlequin cloak wide enough to cover every outer confine and affiliated field of endeavor, of which there are a number, for the theatre touches life at many points. It is a matter of theatrical history that the Guild made an excellent start in this direction during the difficult early days of the organization; now that they are beginning anew in so admirable a theatre of their own, may they dedicate themselves anew to their great task.

The decorative aspects of the new playhouse received special attention in *Arts and Decoration*.

30:2 Into New York, which is the 20th Century, hard and crude and soaring, an uncut jewel sparkling prismatically in a malleable, impersonal sky, a nightmare dream city of tall stone and steel boxes striding inexorably into a retreating sky,

30:2. Louis Kalonyme, "Italian Architecture for the New Guild Theatre," *Arts and Decoration*, July 1925, pp. 30–31, 62.

evading parallel realisms, meeting toppling in the casual human eye, forming hard cubes and blazing angular cones, blinding the sun and overshadowing the moon, all fused in an inevitable, unimaginable, vibrant gray and black line—into this grating, exulting, striding city, a gracious facade, fresh and merry, of vellum white and vivacious green, has been introduced to remind us (and, perhaps, the Theatre Guild) of Florence, which was the 15th Century.

It is good to be reminded of 15th Century Florence, of her freshness and creative energy, the brilliance of her spirit and color, of Giotto and Leónardo, the rising and setting suns of her genius. But cities are not built by architects alone. Florence of the 15th Century sprang from the lusty life of the Trecento and the Quattrocento, from the sonnets of Petrarca and the magnificent threats of Dante, from the omniscience, cunning and honor of the enterprising Arti, the masters of all the arts and crafts, from the purple plots of magnificent Lorenzos and the crimson counterplots of Machiavellian Borgias, from the Tuscan soil made gracious by the brassy Arno, from coarse white bread and red Tuscan wine. The architects, Brunelleschi, Michelozzo, Ghiberti, and the early Bramante, were Florentine workers, masters of stone and wood and iron and glass.

A house was, to them, a poem, carefully and delicately molded as a sonnet, but somehow extemperaneous, an intuitive record, an unconscious commentary, living, an improvisation of the face, body and soul of the life, needs, desires, ideals and the sensibility of the day.

Consequently, at first glance, the Theatre Guild's villa-palazzo of a theatre on Fifty-second Street, west of Broadway, with its facade of small blue-green shutters and grilled balconies set in a pleasant rough white stucco, spacious, wide and low, lavender and pink at dawn, a dazzling yellow and white at noon, a crystallization of green and lavender and ivory during dusk and a soft, luminous pearl at night, is a very oasis among the paunched gray and brown lustreless facades of Broadway's bulky jocosities that serve, miserably, as theatres. It does not nudge its way into the febrile ensemble of Coffee Pots, chipped squat brownstone piles, and its intimate neighbor, mirroring a restless electric message of "Iceland" on its warm, flashy tiles. It is calm, in repose, separate, unentangled in the feverish life that swirls purposelessly around its doors.

But though the Guild Theatre is a refreshing structure, one is not exactly prostrate with admiration before it. One wonders a little, and speculates. It certainly it not New York. It does not really spring from the life of our huge mechanical toy city, so dark and ravishing, throbbing jarringly with the jerky rhythm of an immense unwinding toy and opposed by an impromptu counterpoint of a million untimed, complementary noises. It is a facet of 15th and 16th Century Florence, a polished jewel of Italy, though just a step off Broadway.

It does seem strange that the Guild, which appreciated the idiomatic design of John Lawson's "Processional," and itself born of an idea, also could not have created a building out of the American genius. Disregarding the utilitarian hymns to our breathless engineering feats, there is a line, a *design* in our soaring buildings that could have been broken up abstractly, as Louis H. Sullivan finds an ornament in a simple green leaf or awakens a pentagon.

But there always is the shadow of money, or rather the ominous shadow of its lack, to be considered. There are problems of 20th Century architectural compromise with real estate values, and so, perhaps, the Theatre Guild could not experiment. Perhaps it did not wish to experiment—its career of seven years without doing a play by our greatest dramatist Eugene O'Neill and painting the tweeded lily who is George Bernard Shaw, is a

possible evidence—perhaps, it wished to identify itself rather with the spirit of the Arti, the fertile guilds of Florence. There is indubitably something of that spirit in the Theatre Guild's enterprises, and its theatre is built rather splendidly in that spirit.

It is not a moving mass of architecture. No gray Florentine *rustica* frowns lurk in its facade. In fact, the rusticated stone so characteristic of the Cinquecento palaces is altogether missing. Only simple stone quoins knit the walls together. In place of this usual rusticated groundwork, and the brickwork above, as in the Davanzati Palazzo, a stucco facade, typical of the 15th and 16th Century Tuscan villas, has been substituted. And instead of the usual *putra serena*, a grayish brown sandstone, the floors and frames of the windows, doorways and balconies are of travertine, a stone even mined 2,000 years ago in the quarries at Tivoli, Italy, whitish with a thin black grain, has been used. A tiled roof slopes down and shades, like a heavy brow, the facade, set with a row of small square windows which are framed by charming blue green shutters, the *gelosie* of the Tuscan countryside, the grey and green countryside of Southern Europe. If one concentrates long enough on these slatted shutters, one can almost see cypresses, the entwined olive trees and the purple of the mulberry trees of Florence's hills. Underneath this row of small eye windows, in the very center of the facade, framed in stone, semi-penthouse-topped, opening on individual balconies, with delightfully wrought iron grille railings. Each grille has two brass knobs which flirt all the day with the sun and at night with the rays of "Iceland's" electric appeals. That old Florentine institution, the loggia, usually found at the top of the building under the roof or on the ground floor, has been introduced to the right of these balconied windows. At night it is rather melodramatic with the red light of the fire exit, but by day this triple arched loggia awakens vistas of Florence. In fine, it is a singularly inviting facade and makes one eager to enter.

One passes in under a hanging portico through square gates of glass with a frame of iron grille, of a quatrefoil design, characteristic of the iron and bronze work of the 14th, 15th and 16th centuries in Florence, into a vaulted lobby with walls of electric lighted plaster, down a series of shallow travertine steps, covered with a deep red carpet woven with a black grille pattern, past the doorman into the upper portion of a long wide lounge, bisected by another series of shallow steps, three in number, which lead through a simple arch of two series of stairs on either side. There is not time to examine this lounge as the girl, with a batik scarf uniform, which all the attendants wear, is announcing gleefully that the "curtain's up!" So one rushes up the travertine steps, becarpeted in the same deep red, enclosed by a wrought iron railing to the orchestra floor. One passes through swinging doors covered with a brownish leather and stencilled with a square border design of red, blue and gold into a comfortable chair—far more comfortable than Cinquecentro Florence ever boasted, and into the courtyard of Cleopatra's place on the Syrian border.

"The palace, an old, low, Syrian building of whitened mud, is not so ugly as Buckingham Palace," suggests Mr. Shaw, and Mr. Frederick Jones, the scene designer has here, as throughout the play, more or less obeyed the crochety old Irishman, imaginatively. His Sphinx is smaller, more genial than the one designed by Gordon Craig. Craig's design is overwhelming, his Sphinx is ominous and remote. Mr. Jones has made his Sphinx a smallish friendly cat with soft paws. His stars in this scene, however, are a little too pointed. In the end, of course, with all the lighting, one remembers nothing so much as Shaw. "Caesar and Cleopatra" is "better than Shakespeare" even

though Lionel Atwill and Helen Hayes are neither Caesar nor Cleopatra, and the acting generally, with the bright exception of Henry Travers, as Britannus, and the extremely decorative Schuyler Ladd, as Apollodorus, is inconsiderable. It is a commonplace to praise Shaw, but it also is a commonplace to perform his work, and Egypt in a Florentine setting is sometimes a trifle trying.

When the curtains of velvet close on the play for the various scenes one might be in a magnificent, somewhat modernized and melodramatic, palazzo. Gorgeous curtains of velvet blue green (it seemed in the mellow amber light) patterned with gold fleur de lys, and one of red orange with a black pattern set off the enormous but simple proscenium arch. The ceiling is of huge painted beams, crossed by a series of smaller beams, forming a rich though heavy design. This ceiling might have been taken out of the room that served as a grand salon in the Davanzati palazzo, in Florence, probably the source for many of the theatre's interiors.

The coffers are gilded with a border of red, gold, blue and green quadrilobe pattern, the favorite design of the period, especially the 14th Century. From this rich ceiling hang two simple chandeliers, of bronze and iron it would seem, with an almost primitive tier of candle yellow tulip shaped lights which soften and mellow the plaster of the walls into a warm amber. Only the four cartouches, mock coats of arms, are forced. The rest is magnificent. The orchestra floor, which is reached by the flight of stairs, previously noted—an ingenious innovation that, of building the orchestra floor on the mezzanine level—slopes down toward the stage, and over on either side to triple-arched street-level exits, where the boxes ordinarily perch.

As one leaves the orchestra for the lounges one's attention is attracted to the ceiling of the balcony which overhangs only a few rows of the orchestra seats, of encrusted milky green plaster, studded with gilt stars, and lighted indirectly by charming flat golden glazed discs. The walls under the balcony are panelled with a dull lustred wood the color of walnut. These panels are octagonal shaped and cover the whole space of the three walls topped by the balcony.

Leaving the orchestra floor one strolls down to the long wide lounge, previously rushed through. This is the threshold of the real lounge, reached by three descending steps under a triple arch, with two smaller openings spanned by wrought iron railings, separate the two lounges. The long wide lounge is covered with the same deep red carpet, already described, and leads past straight-backed 16th Century Florentine chairs and chests, and a small niche, with stencilled wooden doors, containing a bright vase, to a special men's lounge.

Descending, however, first into the main lounge, one is immediately made to feel comfortable. The whole spirit of this room is one of repose and friendliness. Perhaps it is the fireplace facing one as the steps are descended. Or the heavy red carpet, and the ceiling beamed and coffered. The ceiling, much lower than 15th Century Florentine rooms, slopes down from the triple arch to the fireplace, which, rather deep at the bottom, slopes typically, as do most of the fireplaces in the Davanzati palazzo, upward into the ceiling. It is a simple fireplace, without any decoration save a little stucco pattern of fruit, and the usual heraldic design painted on its sloping hood. The ceiling is of the same design as the one in the auditorium, but the straight-backed chairs with their little fringes of tapestry and softer, modern couches of crimson upholstery, make the room less formal, a tempting forum for even the most obvious compliments. It is Continental in this respect and is an imaginative improvement on barbarous custom in most New York theatres of standing huddled in an ugly narrow corridor and smoking your neighbor's cigarette. To the extreme left of this room is a small fountain, of little tiles, with an engaging old-fashioned faucet, artificed a parish green. To the extreme right is an opening to the women's rest room.

This room is long, low and narrow, with a vaulted ceiling of pale green plaster. The rim of the ceiling is edged with stout, natural colored hemp rope, which gives the impression of holding the border of travertine and the ceiling in place. The walls are a darker green, covered with a fleur de lys design which gives the walls an appearance of being covered with a cloth texture. There are two framed mirrors, and the chairs are softer than the austere straight-backed benches of Florence and closer to the amiabilities of a modern boudoir. The private lounge for men is more ornate, though of exactly the same length and design.

Ascending once more the steps to the orchestra floor and examining the vaulted hall both flights of steps open on, one is moved by the beautiful curved lines of the intersecting vaults. It is a long hall, of candle colored plaster. The wall brackets seem to throw out the angles of the vault ribs, and the old lanterns that hang from the center of each of the six vaults throw quiet counterpoints of circular light against the angles. At one end of the hall is another fountain "shrine."

In the center of this hall, there are three steps that lead under a slight wide arch to two further flights of steps to doorways on either side of the balcony. The hall on the balcony floor is similar to the one below with the one difference that at the extreme left of the upper hall there is a window of leaded glazed "bulls'-eyes," flanked by two small travertine window seats.

The balcony is as comfortable as the orchestra floor and reaches to the beamed ceiling. It has two ascending iron railings, and beginning half-way from the proscenium arch a frieze of six cartoons, three on each wall by Victor White, commemorating, in a slightly satirical manner, the past triumphs of the Theatre Guild, are painted under the ceiling. From the balcony one wanders into the Guild's clubroom. This room is the one with the long casement windows, and individual balconies, that open on West Fifty-second Street. It is of the same length as the two private lounges for men and women, and of the same design. The tone of the room is a heavy crayon green. Even the hood of the fireplace is painted green, and the marks of the plasterers' trowels are purposely visible. The only departure in the design of this room is a small fairly deep "tabernacle" in the wall with room enough for a writing table. Also, the square perforations, visible by the way throughout the building's interiors, hide the modern heating system admirably.

From this room one may pass to the business offices of the Guild, its studios and schoolrooms.

The stage, able to house an Egyptian palace, a Sphinx, a throne room, a quay, and a lighthouse, has a technical grandeur all its own. Though its lighting equipment and stage machinery are not epochal, or the equal, say, of the cone-shaped Grosses Schauspielhaus in Berlin, or our own domed Provincetown Theatre stage, it is nevertheless considerably in advance of most of New York's theatres. It is ninety feet high and fifty feet wide, and thus the fourth largest stage in New York. It has no wagon, sliding or revolving stages, yet all the stagehands need do is to push the heavier sets to the wall when they are not needed, making the stage adaptable for repertory. It has no Kuppel-horizont, or a plaster dome covering over the stage, but its huge canvas cyclorama is illuminated by an equipment, designed by Monroe Pevear, the distinguished lighting engineer of Boston, which has the variability of a spectrum. This equipment is less than four feet from the surface of the cyclorama. The acting of the stage is lighted

by flexible soft edgeless lens units which do away with the sharp lines thrown by the average spotlights.

The excellence of the whole building is so striking, beginning with the work of the architects, C. Howard Crane, Kenneth Franzheim, and Charles Hunter Bettis, that it is only gracious to list the names of their collaborators. Mr. Bettis supervised the work on the whole building, including the decorations, quite in the tradition of the Renaissance architects who were masters in fresco, iron and engineering, as well as painters, and what you will. He had as consultants, Lee Simonson, the Guild's scenic director, and Norman Bel-Geddes, the talented stage designer.

The furniture of rare beauty and appropriateness was assembled and arrayed by the Orsenigo Co. The lighting fixtures were provided by the Sterling Bronze Company. The wrought iron doors, grilles, and railings were furnished by the Parkhurst Forge. The cabinet work was manufactured by the Jacob Froelich Architectural Wood Workers. While the extremely modern plumbing equipment, quite an advance on the primitive austerities of the bright "dark ages" in Florence, was installed by the Savoy Plumbing Company.

All these craftsmen very obviously have worked in the enthusiastic spirit of the Arti of Florence. Their separate works have been fused by the spirit of the Theatre Guild into a noble building, and a real theatre.

31. FORREST THEATRE
New York City
Opened November 24, 1925

This new playhouse was named originally for Edwin Forrest, the great tragedian of the early American stage. In 1945 the theater was renamed the Coronet and still later, in 1959, was rechristened the Eugene O'Neill Theatre in honor of the great American playwright. The opening performance produced by the Shuberts was an innocuous musical show, *Mayflowers*.

A brief description of the Forrest Theatre appeared in the New York *Times*.

31:1 NEW FORREST THEATRE

Shubert Playhouse in West 49th Street to
Open Soon.

The Forrest Theatre, a new theatre named after Edwin Forrest, the actor, West Forty-ninth Street between Broadway and Eighth Avenue, will open in about two weeks, according to an announcement made yesterday by the Shuberts. The theatre has a capacity of 1,200 seats, most of which are on the ground floor. The stage will be large enough to accommodate musical productions.

Herbert J. Krapp, the architect, has designed the theatre according to the Georgian period, and the builder, M. J. Kramer, is also constructing a sixteen-story hotel adjacent to the theatre.

32. BILTMORE THEATRE
New York City
Opened December 7, 1925

The Chanin brothers opened their second playhouse, the Biltmore Theatre, in 1925. The house had only moderately successful productions until the 1960s, when there were such hits as *Take Her, She's Mine*, and *Barefoot in the Park*.

The first production was not a new one for New York but was moved from another house; therefore, the opening night reviews were fairly brief. The following critique is from the New York *Times*:

32:1 THE BILTMORE OPENS

New Theatre in West 47th Street the Second in Chanin Chain.

The Biltmore, a new theatre in West Forty-seventh Street, was opened last night with "Easy Come, Easy Go," as its first attraction. The play was transferred from the George M. Cohan Theatre.

The new house, which is the first to be built on Forty-seventh Street, is on the north side of the street, just east of Eighth Avenue. It is owned and controlled by the Chanin Theatres Corporation, which built the Forty-sixth Street Theatre, opened last year, and will open another house on Forty-seventh Street next month. The Biltmore, which was designed by Herbert J. Krapp, has a seating capacity of 1,000, with but a single balcony. The color scheme is cerise and brown.

In addition to these playhouses listed above, the Chanin Corporation plans the construction of three additional playhouses. Its first theatre, the Forty-sixth Street, is under lease to the Shuberts, but the others will be operated as independent houses.

33. MANSFIELD THEATRE
New York City
Opened February 15, 1926

Richard Mansfield was an American actor of great popularity during the latter part of the nineteenth century and until his death in 1907. It was appropriate, therefore, that a theater should bear his name, and one was built in 1927 that was to be called The Mansfield until 1960, when it was rechristened the Brooks Atkinson Theatre in honor of the distinguished drama critic of the New York *Times*.

Since the trend of the day was toward smaller, more intimate playhouses, the Mansfield Theatre gained this feeling of intimacy with an auditorium wider than is usual but not as deep. In this way maximum seating space was achieved while still giving the spectator the feeling of smallness.

The review of play and theater appeared in the New York *Times* on February 16.

33:1 "The Night Duel"
Opens the New Mansfield

31:1. New York *Times*, Nov. 9, 1925.
32:1. New York *Times*, Dec. 8, 1925.

33:1. New York *Times*, Feb. 16, 1926.

Marjorie Rambeau Plays Well in a Fair
Melodrama With a Bedroom Scene

A new and good-looking theatre called
the Mansfield in West Forty-seventh Street
was added last night to the extensive and
ever-growing list of New York playhouses.
Its first attraction is a fair-to-middling
melodrama called "The Night Duel," a
thoroughly routine piece that does not
quite justify the leaflet distributed with the
evening's program—a folder which, out-
lining the policy of the new corporation
that sponsors the production, sees "a new
era in America's art of the drama."

What really happened was the appearance of Marjorie Rambeau in a play written
first by Donald Rubin, a newcomer who
has been about to emerge upon Broadway for a year or more, and later, apparently, written over again by Edgar
MacGregor, who staged the play. At all
events, Mr. MacGregor is programmed
with Mr. MacGregor as co-author.

The play is concerned with a loyal wife
who finds that she can save her husband
from a prison sentence only at the sacrifice of her honor. This bald reduction of
the story to a line does not quite do the
play justice; it is a piece that gathers momentum as the evening progresses, and
which really gives a new slant to an old
situation at the finish.

The opening act is devoted to a somewhat laborious creation, piece by piece,
of the dilemma in which the playwrights
desire to plunge their heroine. Thereafter,
however, things moved a bit more naturally. A bedroom scene in the second act,
between Miss Rambeau and Felix
Krembs, had moments fully as embarrassing as the play's sponsors hoped they
would be, and the audience seemed
pleased. The play has been beautifully
mounted and is in the main well played,
particularly by Miss Rambeau and John
Marston.

To return to the new playhouse, it follows the prevailing mode in theatre construction, in that it contains but a single

balcony. Old rose and gold and something
resembling a light tan seemed to be the
predominating colors.

After a period in the 1950s when the
playhouse was used as a television studio, it
was reopened on September 8, 1960, as the
Brooks Atkinson Theatre, celebrating Atkinson's thirty-five years as a writer and critic and
his retirement as drama critic for the New York
Times.

34. ROYALE THEATRE
New York City
Opened January 11, 1927

The Royale was another in the series of
theaters built by the Chanin Company. The
choice of location, on Forty-fifth Street west of
Broadway, was excellent, and the house proved
successful over the years.

A brief description was included in the
opening-night review in the New York *Times.*

34:1   OPENING A NEW THEATRE

With the first performance of "Piggy"
last evening the sixth of the Chanin theatres was opened—the Royale on West
Forty-fifth Street, near Eighth Avenue.
Like most of the Chanin theatres this new
one is comfortable, with plenty of leg
room around the seats, and quite as osten-
tatiously attractive as the stage decorations for the play. The program is more
specific about these embellishments—

The Royale Theatre is modern Spanish
in character. Predominant in the interior
decorations are two murals, "Lovers of
Spain," by Willy Pogany, which are placed
high on the side walls. The general color
scheme is in cardinal red, orange and
gold. The curtain has cardinal red and
light orange as its principal colors and
harmonizes in design with carpets and
draperies. The lounge, located below the
auditorium level, is of English architecture
with an Elizabethan ceiling. . . .

34:1. New York *Times,* Jan. 13, 1927.

28. Imperial Theatre, New York, ca. 1924. Courtesy of the Museum of the City of New York.

28. Interior, Imperial Theatre, New York, ca. 1924. Courtesy of the Museum of the City of New York.

29. Martin Beck Theatre, New York, ca. 1924. Drawing by V. Hagopian. Courtesy of The Hoblitzelle Theatre Arts Library, The Humanities Research Center, The University of Texas at Austin.

30. Guild Theatre, New York, ca. 1924. Drawing by Charles H. Bettis, published in *Architectural Record* (Dec. 1924). Courtesy of The Hoblitzelle Theatre Arts Library, The Humanities Research Center, The University of Texas at Austin.

33. Mansfield Theatre, New York, ca. 1927. Drawing published in brochure on Chanin Theaters. Courtesy of The Hoblitzelle Theatre Arts Library, The Humanities Research Center, The University of Texas at Austin.

MANSFIELD
Forty-seventh Street
West of Broadway

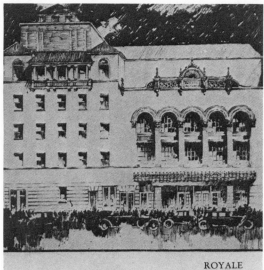

ROYALE
Forty-fifth Street
West of Broadway

34. Royale Theatre, New York, 1927. Drawing published in brochure on Chanin Theaters. Courtesy of The Hoblitzelle Theatre Arts Library, The Humanities Research Center, The University of Texas at Austin.

35. ZIEGFELD THEATRE
New York City
Opened February 2, 1927

Joseph Urban, the architect of the Ziegfeld Theatre at Sixth Avenue and Fifty-fourth Street, attempted to break with the usual practice of modeling playhouses after Italian or French chateaus and decorating them in the style of Louis XV or Moorish palaces. The exterior of the building was rather plain, while the interior depended on color and a huge mural for the principal decoration.

The playhouse was particularly well designed for large musical shows, and during its history housed some of the most successful musical comedies of the period.

The following comment was published in the *Architectural Forum* of May 1927, three months after the theater opened.

35:1   THE ZIEGFELD THEATRE, NEW YORK
Joseph Urban & Thomas W. Lamb, Architects

Editor's Note. Mr. Joseph Urban has long been so famous for his marvelous stage settings and for the bewildering productions which he has made at the Metropolitan Opera House that few have realized that he is an architect, and that it is as an architect he is chiefly known in Europe. In designing the Ziegfeld Theater he embraced an opportunity which afforded wide scope to his ability as an architect as well as to his skill as a decorator and designer, the opportunity made particularly attractive by reason of Mr. Ziegfeld's well known taste and his enthusiasm for what is best and most unusual in the theater and its architecture.

The building of the Ziegfeld Theater introduces a new note in theater planning and construction. Departing from the usual custom of erecting a theater without regard to the kind of form of amusement

which may be offered within its walls, the Ziegfeld Theater has been planned for a definite purpose, to house the lighter forms of dramatic entertainment, opera comique, musical comedies and revues. Consequently every effort has been made to create a wholly harmonius background for the productions contemplated. Considered from without, the playhouse is unlike any other in New York. The facade clearly expresses the purpose of the building. The auditorium is indicated by the bow on the avenue side, and the stage is represented by the ornamentation of the false proscenium. Two large masks, the conventional dramatic symbols of comedy and tragedy, are used at the sides of this proscenium opening. Thus the intent of the building is apparent to the passerby, marking the structure clearly as a temple devoted exclusively to the drama.

The widely used fan shape in theater planning is a section of a circle, and as such is only part of the perfect architectural form. It can never assume the aesthetic form of a room. The nearest approach to the form of the ancient theater which this building lot permitted was an elliptical ground plan. The ellipse was rigidly adhered to throughout in spite of all difficulties, and is only interrupted at the proscenium by a very slight opposing curve which projects over the orchestra. This curve allows a small forestage, or "apron," with doors at both sides through the proscenium arch. This arrangement permits of greater variation of scenic combinations, allowing encores or shallow scenes to be played on the apron in front of the drop curtain, while the main stage is being utilized for scene changes. With the proscenium doors for entrances and exits, the closed curtain not only accelerates the *tempo* of the production, but, what is more important, it puts the artist in intimate touch with his audience. He is no longer a dim figure, lost in the atmospheric background; he is in the same room with his listeners. This idea of the forestage, which of course has been adapted from the original Shakespearean stage, should be particularly emphasized for the presentation of drama. In this way actors may play intimate or dramatic scenes close to the spectators, the suggestion of a beautiful background helping to put the audience in the mood of the scene, yet with the actors so close that the background can only be a help and never detract from the dramatic values or the intimacy of the scene. Entire epilogues, prologues, small scenes and sometimes whole acts, especially as in French drama can be played here. The acoustic and optical advantages of this stage arrangement need not be dwelt upon, and the effect of the action upon the audience cannot be doubted. The two sides of the proscenium merge in soft curves from the elliptical auditorium into the proscenium opening, so that the stage and the auditorium melt into each other, bringing the stage picture into an unusually close, intimate relation with the auditorium.

The closer the contact between the players and the audience, the more festive the mood and the more the audience feels itself part of the whole occasion. Therefore the decoration of this particular theater is a part of the gay, colorful happenings on the stage, and not, as is usually the case, a stiff, architectonic affair which coldly and disdainfully withdraws from the stage picture. The auditorium should join the play; and when everything laughs and scintillates in the brilliance of the stage, the entire auditorium should share in the laughter, and with its own brilliance help carry the mood to its peak. For decoration reliance has been placed upon the blending of the tone of the carpet and chairs with the main decoration, the mural painting, which, by the way, is the largest oil painting in the world, the famous painting of the Sistine Chapel being nearest it in size. The mural was executed by Lillian Gaertner and the Urban Studios, at Yonkers. The general motif of the mural is the "Joy of Life." The painting of the auditorium has no tale to tell, no continuous action as its basis. Under a roof of flowers and foliage, among castles and hamlets, on meadows and in wood, hunting, laughing, running, leaping, music-making, singing, kissing, loving,—human beings in mad, happy medley,—no deep meaning, no serious thoughts of feelings,—only joy, happiness,—a veritable trance of color.

The foyer is designed to obviate the necessity of patrons' leaving the building during intermissions. Ascending wide stairways from the entrance to the theater, one enters the foyer which follows the bow on the Sixth Avenue side. Entrances lead off the foyer to the various coat rooms.

The stage equipment, while the most modern and complete in America, is designed to accommodate the many changes that will doubtless come with greater and more sumptuous productions. The stage has been designed with a flexibility that will permit of improvements from time to time as new methods are discovered and new accessories invented. There is a built cyclorama, 59 feet high, which will allow of unusual sky effects. There are only two or three of these plaster "domes" in the city, producers as a rule being content with "wrinkles" in their sky. The floor of the stage has been so arranged that traps can be fixed at a moment's notice at any point. The orchestra floor is constructed of a special wood, selected for its resonance. Few theaters anywhere in the world are as well equipped with electrical appliances. The switchboard is built on the principle of a pipe organ, where the operator of lights can play symphonies of light and color with all the deftness and finesse of an organist. There is also an automatic set of switches which may be set before the performance, fulfilling their function on mechanical cues. A new departure is in installing openings for lights at the right and left of the proscenium.

These will permit operators to throw lights from three levels.

36. THEATRE MASQUE
New York City
Opened February 24, 1927

The Chanin Corporation continued its challenge to the Shuberts by opening another new playhouse on Forty-fifth Street. The Masque was one of the smaller houses in the city's main theater district. In later years, as the John Golden Theatre, it catered to one- and two-man shows and dramas with small casts. The overhead operating expenses of such a small house make larger productions unprofitable.

The Theatre Masque opened with a play that had been translated from the Italian. It proved disastrous as a production and closed within a few days of the opening.

An announcement of the opening of the new playhouse appeared in the New York *Times* on February 14.

36:1   THEATRE MASQUE'S OPENING
Latest of Chanin Houses to Offer
"Puppets of Passion" on February 24.

The Theatre Masque, the latest of the Chanin houses, will open on Thursday evening, Feb. 24, with the first production made by the Chanins, "Puppets of Passion," as the attraction. The play has been adapted from the Italian of Rosso di San Secondo by Ernest Boyd and Edward Ciannelli and staged by David Burton. It will open in Stamford for two days on Feb. 21 before coming to New York.

The new theatre, in West Forty-fifth Street, adjoining the Royale, will be the fifth house which the Chanin brothers have opened in the Times Square district in a little more than two years. The Majestic, which is in the same development with the Theatre Masque and the Royale, will be completed in March.

36:1. New York *Times*, Feb. 14, 1927.

The Chanin Theatre Corporation, which became such a strong competitor of the Shuberts, put out a publicity brochure concerning their theaters and their philosophy of theater-building.

36:2   A few years ago, Irwin S. Chanin and Henry I. Chanin, engineers and builders, felt that theatre design failed to keep pace with the advance in the art of the drama and musical play. They decided that it was possible to incorporate into a theatre certain principles of engineering which in the past few years had so remarkably increased the usefulness and beauty of other modern structures. So they visualized theatres which, before the footlights, would be more worthy settings for the "jewel of the seven arts," and which, behind the footlights, would incorporate all of the newer facilities.

From their plans, a new type of theatre has come into being . . . the Chanin Theatre. Convention and tradition, which have shaped the history of the Stage through the centuries, now give way to a new order of things. Two years ago, there was only an idea. Today, an entirely new group of modern playhouses has taken a high place in New York theatredom.

. . . To those *behind* the footlights, a Chanin-built theatre means a marked advance in plan and equipment, new lighting methods, new ways of handling scenery, time and labor-saving innovations without number. Even such details as footlights show a distinct departure from the usual . . . a novel tilt which adds considerably to their effectiveness. An ingenious method of central control regulates the entire lighting system, both of house and stage. Fully-equipped booths for motion picture projection are installed and ready for movie engagements.

There is a new and unusual note in the back-stage atmosphere of a Chanin-built

36:2. "The Chanin Theatres: A Renaissance in Theatre Craft," publicity brochure (New York, 1927).

theatre. Dressing rooms are ample in size, light and airy, with carpets and comfortable furniture, sharply contrasting with the small, barren dressing rooms of other days. In addition to individual dressing rooms, each theatre has larger ones for the use of ensembles.

Back of all these details which contribute so richly to the ease and comfort of player, as well as playgoer, is that sense of the theatre . . . call it a sixth sense if you will . . . that not only recognizes, but anticipates, the varying responses of audiences to various types of plays. A chain is only as strong as its weakest link and it has been the aim of the Chanins to include in their chain, theatres for every type of legitimate presentation. The Biltmore and the Mansfield, located in West Forty-seventh Street, with 950 and 1097 seats respectively, are especially adapted to the presentation of drama and comedy, by virture of their size, their arrangement and decoration. The Theatre Masque in West Forty-fifth Street, with 800 seats, is intended to be the home of fine plays of the "artistic" or "intimate" type. The Royale, also located in West Forty-fifth Street, with 1200 seats, is a musical comedy theatre. The 1800-seat Majestic in West Forty-fourth Street, the largest legitimate theatre in the Times Square district, is expressly a house for revues and light operas. Thus there is an *entente cordiale* between players and audiences, even before the rise of the curtain, as each Chanin theatre is designed for a particular purpose. . . .

37. MAJESTIC THEATRE
New York City
Opened March 28, 1927

The Chanin company opened one of its most successful playhouses on March 28, 1927 —the Majestic Theatre. From its opening it was one of the most desirable playhouses in New York for the production of musicals. Its location on Forty-fourth Street between Broad-

way and Eighth Avenue has been particularly advantageous for producers who depend on the tourist trade for the greater part of their business.

The playhouse was described in the New York *Times* of March 28:

37:1 MAJESTIC THEATRE TO OPEN TONIGHT

Eighth of the New Chanin Playhouses to Offer "Le Maire's Affairs," a Revue.

BUILT IN STADIUM TYPE

Architecture and Decorations in Louis XV Style—Largest "Legitimate" Theatre in Times Sq. District.

The Chanins will open the third and last theatre of their development in West Forty-fourth and Forty-fifth Streets tonight when the Majestic, adjoining the Broadhurst on West Forty-fourth Street, will house the initial New York presentation of "Le Maire's Affairs," a review in which Charlotte Greenwood, Ted Lewis and Lester Allen are the principal players. Other playhouses in the development include the Royale and the Masque, while a thirty-story hotel, the Lincoln, facing Eighth Avenue, is now under construction.

The Majestic, with 1,800 seats, is said to be the largest "legitimate" theatre in the Times Square district. It is the fifth theatre built by the Chanin brothers within the last sixteen months for their own operation and the eighth which they have erected in Greater New York in the last two years.

The Majestic is the stadium type of theatre, like the first opened Chanin house in West Forty-fourth Street. Entrance to the theatre is through a foyer-promenade extending virtually the depth of the building from one side of which a grand staircase rises to the rear of the orchestra level. From the other side of the foyer two passages, one at each end, give entrance to

37:1. New York *Times*, Mar. 28, 1927.

holders of tickets for the first dozen rows of seats and for the boxes. The Majestic has a single balcony.

The architecture and decoration of the interior is in the Louis XV style, a general color scheme of gold and ivory being employed on the walls and ceilings and on the faces of the balcony. The house curtains, the valence, the box drapes and panels on the side walls are of gold and rose silk damask. A main lounge below the orchestra level is in the English style of architecture. As in other Chanin houses, the seats are said to be three inches wider than the ordinary theatre chair.

Among the back-stage innovations is a rigging loft which is said to be the largest in New York, with accommodations for 200 persons. The electric switchboard is said to be so arranged that the biggest musical productions can be handled directly from house installations without necessity for auxiliary switchboards.

38. ERLANGER THEATRE
New York City
Opened September 26, 1927

The Erlanger Theatre was named in honor of Abraham Erlanger, Broadway booking agent who became the leading member of the Theatrical Syndicate, formed in 1896, which created a monopoly over theaters throughout the country. The playhouse itself was a handsome structure on Forty-fourth Street between Broadway and Eighth Avenue. In later years the theater booked mostly musical shows and some of the greatest musical hits in modern theater history played there, including *Oklahoma!, The King and I,* and *Hello, Dolly!* The name of the playhouse was changed to the St. James in 1932.

The advent of the new theater was announced in the New York *Times* on July 16.

38:1 COHAN PLAY TO OPEN ERLANGER THEATRE

_____

38:1. New York *Times,* July 16, 1927.

'The Merry Malones,' Musical Comedy, Booked at New House on West 44th Street.

_____

The inaugural attraction at the new Erlanger Theatre in West Forty-fourth Street was definitely announced yesterday as "The Merry Malones," the new George M. Cohan musical play for which Mr. Cohan has provided the book, lyrics and music. The show will open in Atlantic City on Sept. 5 and will probably come to New York late that month.

The musical version of Edna Ferber's novel, "Show Boat," has also been reported to be a candidate for the honor of opening Erlanger's, but it was doubted that Florenz Ziegfeld could prepare the production in time, as he will be tied up until the middle of next month with the "Follies."

Erlanger's, which has been built at a cost of more than $1,500,000 exclusive of the land, has about the same seating capacity as the New Amsterdam. Booking of the Cohan show into this house is in line with Mr. Cohan's past affiliation with the Erlanger organization. Last Fall he also became associated with the Shuberts, for the first time in his career, when they purchased a half interest in the Four Cohans Theatre in Chicago. "Yellow," a Cohan production of last season, also was presented here at the National, a Shubert house, but at the time Mr. Cohan stated that, except for such attractions as played the Four Cohans, he would continue as a free agent and book wherever he got the best terms.

Following its review of the opening, the New York *Times* described the new theater.

38:2 NEW ERLANGER'S DESIGN IS GEORGIAN.

The new Erlanger's is probably the least ornate of all the theatres recently added to the Times Square district. Although the structure was erected at a cost

_____

38:2. New York *Times,* Sept. 27, 1927.

of $1,500,000, its entire effect, both on the exterior and interior, is one of simplicity. In the auditorium there has been a studied attempt to create an intimate rather than a theatrical atmosphere.

The interior design is Georgian, the color scheme coral and antique gold. All the materials used have been chosen to harmonize with these colors. Ornamentation, other than the proscenium boxes, has been done with painting rather than plaster decoration. Murals decorate the side walls and the proscenium arch.

Two large boxes on either side of the proscenium are known as the President's and the Governor's boxes, the latter having been occupied last night by Governor Smith and family.

The main entrance is through wide doors to a spacious marble lobby extending all the way across the building. The ladies' lounge, painted in antique green, is luxuriously furnished, as is a men's smoking room, done in the old English style. Back of the curtain line most of the devices known to up-to-date stagecraft have been installed.

The facade, stretching along West Forty-fourth Street, is of marble, stone and stucco on a granite base and is also said to be a representative example of Georgian architecture. Warren & Wetmore were the architects for the building and John Singraldi did the interior decorations.

39. ALVIN THEATRE
New York City
Opened November 22, 1927

Fred Astaire and his sister, Adele, opened this playhouse with their great hit, *Funny Face,* with music by George and Ira Gershwin. The production was outstanding and so was the playhouse, but the critics raved at such great length about the Astaires that there was little space left for the theater itself. The new playhouse, incidentally, received its name from its two owner-producers, Alex A. Aarons and

Vinton Freedley, who took the first letters of their names to form the name of the playhouse.

The opening-night review in the New York *Times* was by Brooks Atkinson.

39:1   ASTAIRES AND OTHERS

If there were not two or three good musical plays already in town one might be reckless enough to dub *"Funny Face,"* at the Alvin last evening, as the best of them all. With Fred and Adele Astaire, Victor Moore and William Kent in the cast, with music by George Gershwin and lyrics by his brother, Ira, and with excellent dancing throughout, "Funny Face" makes for uncommonly rollicking entertainment. It opens the new Alvin Theatre auspiciously. . . .

The new Alvin Theatre, set defiantly across the street from the scholarly Theatre Guild, seems to have all the best features of the modern playhouse—even an old English lounge where refreshments may be had. The auditorium is decorated with pastel shades of blue and gray, with ivory and gold decorations. The Alvin can serve 1,400 drama gluttons at one sitting. If "Funny Face" had been less engrossing the audience might have had more time to appreciate the new theatre.

A more detailed description of the new playhouse is found in a souvenir program:

39:2 New York's Newest and Finest Playhouse
THE ALVIN

Where brownstone fronts once flourished another impressive amusement edifice has arisen by the magic wand of building contractors, and on Tuesday evening, November 22nd, 1927, the Alvin Theatre advanced West Fifty-second street as a theatrical thoroughfare.

The new neighbor of the Theatre Guild presents an imposing facade in Colonial design, combining marble and terre

39:1. New York *Times*, Nov. 24, 1927.
39:2. "Alex A. Aarons and Vinton Freedley Present Musical Comedy Sensation 'Funny Face' with Fred and Adele Astaire" (New York, 1927).

[terra] cotta in an agreeable yet stately exterior. Erected expressly for the musical comedy productions of Alex A. Aarons and Vinton Freedley, who will be its managing directors, the playhouse has been planned with every facility, mechanical and otherwise, for the proper presentation of large musical entertainments, and for the comfort and convenience of its patrons.

The theatre proper occupies the entire frontage of 125 feet with three floors of offices atop the playhouse facing Fifty-second street. These are occupied by Aarons and Freedley and their staff.

A spacious lobby in black marble leads to an inner lobby of strikingly simple theme. The interior design is Adam and the decoration comprises a charming arrangement of pastel tones of blue, ivory and gray, blended with old gold and enhanced by mulberry hangings. A delicately tinted mural painting surmounts the proscenium arch.

While the Alvin has been designed and equipped for large musicals, a note of intimacy is dominant throughout, and the sight lines have been skillfully perfected to permit an unobstructed view of the stage from every vantage point. The capacity is 1400, of which 702 seats are on the lower floor, and 674 in the single balcony, access to which is gained by an ample stairway leading directly from the inner lobby instead of from the rear of the orchestra, thus minimizing disturbance from late arrivals on the upper tier.

The orchestra pit has been arranged to accommodate 48 musicians comfortably. The stage, measuring 35 by 100, is of sufficient size to afford adequate room for even the biggest of productions. The proscenium opening is forty feet wide and the height of the gridiron 68 feet.

Among the innovations of the new house is the Big Room, a strikingly large Old English lounge 35 by 100, done in ivory and carved oak, with a great fireplace as the central piece. Adjoining the Big Room are four separate retiring rooms with independent smoking rooms for men and women, as well as cosmetic quarters to please the most fastidious of feminine patrons.

Twenty large dressing rooms, two chorus rest rooms and a large rehearsal hall are outstanding features of the sanctified realm of behind-the-scenes. These facilities should prove exceedingly popular with Fred and Adele Astaire and their associates in "Funny Face," the Alvin's dedicatory attraction.

The Alvin was erected by the O'Day Construction Company under the direction of A. H. Pincus and M. L. Goldstone and from the plans of Herbert J. Krapp.

40. HAMMERSTEIN THEATRE
New York City
Opened November 30, 1927

Although Oscar Hammerstein built and managed numerous theaters in New York, no playhouse had been named in his honor. In 1927 his son Arthur undertook to remedy this situation by building a new theater at Broadway and Fifty-third Street, calling it Hammerstein's in memory of his father. Because of Oscar Hammerstein's love of music, the new house was equipped to handle musical shows and was noted as a "musical house."

The theater changed hands in 1931 and was renamed the Manhattan Theatre. The house was not a successful one, and although it was used as a playhouse occasionally after 1934, it was taken over for a broadcasting studio.

The Hammerstein Theatre had a dedication ceremony at the laying of the cornerstone on September 30, 1927, with the Mayor of New York, Jimmy Walker, as one of the principal speakers.

40:1 CORNERSTONE LAID AT HAMMERSTEIN'S

Late Producer Is Eulogized by

40:1. New York *Times*, Oct. 1, 1927.

Speakers in Ceremony at
New Broadway Theatre.

WALKER LAUDS HIS CAREER

Kahn Pays Tribute to Man Who Often
Opposed Him—Memorials Sealed
in Stone.

Broadway's past, present and future were encompassed yesterday afternoon by the ceremonies attending the laying of the cornerstone of the Hammerstein Theatre in Broadway, near Fifty-third Street. The theatre is dedicated to the memory of Oscar Hammerstein by his son, Arthur, and the speakers, after recalling memories of the father, congratulated the son.

Mayor Walker made the opening address.

"New York loves the name of Hammerstein," he said, "and the Mayor of New York belongs upon this platform to make acknowledgment of the fact. Oscar Hammerstein was a builder. He loved New York and did things for it. If you look at the artistic progress of New York and list those responsible for it, you must put his name at the head of the list.

"Great men seldom have great sons, but today we are foregathered to witness an exception to the rule. To Arthur Hammerstein I bring the congratulations and best wishes of his fellow-citizens."

KAHN PAYS TRIBUTE.

Otto H. Kahn likewise divided his tribute, and he earnestly praised Oscar Hammerstein, who in his lifetime, was frequently in the opposite camp from Mr. Kahn and the Metropolitan Opera House. Nevertheless, Mr. Kahn said:

"Arthur Hammerstein is a worthy son of a worthy father, the fighting son of a fighting father. How much of a fighter Oscar Hammerstein was I can testify, yet I wish to pay tribute to him as a builder and say that no man did as much for the cause of opera in New York."

As many people as could be packed into the main lobby of the unfinished theatre and on the sidewalk in front attended the ceremonies. Among them were leaders of the theatrical world and notables from other fields.

Those who spoke recalled the days of Hammerstein's Victoria Theatre, as well as the impresario's work in grand opera. There was Joe Weber, for instance, who said that Mr. Hammerstein had put the famous team of Weber and Fields on Broadway, in the Victoria, and Eddie Cantor said that he also had started in the old variety house that stood where the Rialto now stands.

Others who spoke were Lee J. Eastman, President of the Broadway Association, George Jessel, Maggie Cline and Arthur Hammerstein.

MEMORIALS PLACED IN STONE.

A box containing memorials of Oscar Hammerstein and the occasion was placed in the cornerstone by Mayor Walker and sealed during a benediction by the Rev. Dr. Nathan Krass.

The contents were: A silk hat worn by Oscar Hammerstein, a cigar made by him and given to Joseph Jarrow, a friend; the Legion of Honor button worn by him, the Golden Jubilee number of the United States Tobacco Journal, containing a biography of Oscar Hammerstein; a volume of the Memoirs of Weber and Fields dedicated to him, a program of the dinner to him given by the citizens of Philadelphia on the occasion of the opening of his opera house there, Feb. 10, 1909, and copies of yesterday's New York papers.

A description of the new playhouse appeared in the New York *Times* the day following the opening.

40:2 NEW HAMMERSTEIN THEATRE DEDICATED

Memorial to Oscar Hammerstein

40:2. New York *Times*, Dec. 1, 1927.

35. Ziegfeld Theatre, New York, ca. 1927. Drawing by Hugh Ferris, published in *Architectural Record* (May 1927). Courtesy of The Hoblitzelle Theatre Arts Library, The Humanities Research Center, The University of Texas at Austin.

37. Majestic Theatre, New York, ca. 1905. Courtesy of The New-York Historical Society, New York City.

THEATRE MASQUE
Forty-fifth Street
West of Broadway

36. Theatre Masque, New York, 1927. Drawing published in brochure on Chanin Theaters. Courtesy of The Hoblitzelle Theatre Arts Library, The Humanities Research Center, The University of Texas at Austin.

40. Hammerstein Theatre, New York, 1927. Drawing published in dedication program. Courtesy of the Museum of the City of New York.

43. Vivian Beaumont Theater, New York, 1965. In the foreground, a bronze sculpture by Henry Moore. © Lincoln Center for the Performing Arts, Inc. Photography by David Hirsch.

Has Interior Resembling Gothic
Cathedral

ART PANELS OF OPERAS

Life-Size Statue of Late Impresario in
Foyer—Notables at "Golden Dawn"
Premiere.

Eight years after the death of Oscar
Hammerstein, his son, Arthur, dedicated
the new Hammerstein Theatre last night
in honor of his father. The theatre, which
has a seating capacity of 1,265, is part of
an office building thirteen stories high,
and is in Broadway between Fifty-third
and Fifty-fourth Streets, with the main
entrance on Broadway. A life-size figure
of Oscar Hammerstein, the work of the
sculptor, Pompeo Coppini, stands in the
centre of the foyer and is the first thing
one sees on entering the theatre from the
lobby. Also in the lobby are eleven portraits of members of the "Golden Dawn"
cast painted by Joseph Cummings Chase.

The interior of the new theatre resembles a Gothic cathedral—it is done
throughout in a free variation of that type
of architecture, which, in its adaptation
to theatrical purposes, still retains its simplicity. On the left and right of the auditorium are ten large lettered glass windows
containing art panels illustrative of the
operas Oscar Hammerstein first produced.
A large dome, which forms the ceiling,
also forms the upper part of the side walls.
To relieve the severity of the auditorium's
stone work, the impanelling effects formed
by the ribs of stone are decorated with
mosiacs.

Thick carpets and Czecho-Slovakian
rugs cover the stairways from foyer to
balcony. The orchestra pit, which may be
raised or lowered, seats fifty musicians
and contains the console of a concert
organ.

An unusual feature of the theatre's
technical equipment is that there are no
footlights on the border of the stage. In
the basement is an elaborate ventilating
system, which purifies the air and regulates
the temperature in Summer and Winter.
Herbert J. Krapp designed the theatre,
which was erected by the O'Day Construction Company.

There was no formal dedication exercise
last night. Before the curtain rose, "Marguerite," a composition written by Oscar
Hammerstein in 1896, and "The Star
Spangled Banner" were played.

The first audience, while not without
its notables from all fields of endeavor,
was in a large part composed of theatrical
people. Many of Mr. Hammerstein's fellow managers and producers were present
to see his initial production in his handsome new playhouse. . . .

41. CRAIG THEATRE
New York City
Opened December 24, 1928

The Craig Theatre was singularly unsuccessful from the opening and, after several theatrical failures, stood empty for a long time before reopening in 1934 as the Adelphi Theatre.
A further name change took place in the early
1950s, when it was rechristened the Fifty-
fourth Street Theatre.

The following description of the playhouse is from the New York *Times:*

41:1   NEW CRAIG THEATRE IN W. 54TH ST.

OPENS

A Quiet Decorative Designed Playhouse
That Has a Seating Capacity of 1,435.

The new Craig Theatre, which opened
last night with an invitation performance
of "Potiphar's Wife," extends between
Fifty-third and Fifty-fourth Streets, just
east of Seventh Avenue. The entrance is
on Fifty-fourth Street. The house has a
seating capacity of 1,435, with 860 seats
in the orchestra.

41:1. New York *Times,* Dec. 24, 1928.

The lobby, from Fifty-fourth Street to the auditorium, extends through a remodeled building. A quiet decorative design has been maintained throughout the playhouse. The walls are of rough textured plaster, and are tinted, for the most part in Autumn brown. The lighting fixtures and decorations are simple and follow old English models. The ornamentation within the auditorium is concentrated on the boxes and proscenium and is of Tudor Gothic style. The proscenium itself is a Gothic arch, devoid of ornament except for a modeled frame about the opening.

The back of the house and the souffit of the balcony are finished textured plaster tinted in a suffuse of rose, buff and blue. The curtain is of mulberry velvet, with a wide green fringe. In the basement is a smoking room and there is a mezzanine foyer from which the balcony is entered.

Backstage the Craig is fully equipped for the handling of scenery and lighting effects and for the accommodation of a large number of players. The theatre's opening was first scheduled for Labor Day but was several times postponed.

42. A.N.T.A. WASHINGTON SQUARE THEATRE
New York City
Opened January 23, 1964

This playhouse was built as temporary accommodations for the repertory company that had been hired for the new Vivian Beaumont Theater of the Lincoln Center for the Performing Arts. It was built of necessity, since the center's completion date had not been met and seemed to be quite far off, yet the company had been hired and needed a theater. The Washington Square Theatre was the result. It was the first new playhouse to open in New York in thirty-six years, and the building received universal critical acclaim.

The comments on this theater, which appeared in *Progressive Architecture,* are typical of the praise given the building.

42:1 NEW YORK, N.Y. The opening of a new theater in New York is as scarce as the preservation of a notable building there, and the opening of a *good* theater even scarcer. There was cause for rejoicing, therefore, when the ANTA–Washington Square Theater made its debut last month with Arthur Miller's "After the Fall."

The theater was built as a temporary home for the Repertory Company of Lincoln Center when the Vivian Beaumont Repertory Theater fell considerably behind schedule. Site, budget, and time restrictions caused the designers (Eero Saarinen Associates and Jo Mielziner) to flaunt "many of the canons of good design as set forth by the Board of Standards and Planning for the Living Theater." Presumably this refers to the quite Spartan exterior and circulation areas, for the auditorium and stage provisions are most impressively accomplished within the range of the program.

The entrance to the auditorium, via the vomitories under the loge, is a dramatic experience in itself: the space is a pit dug 15 ft. into the earth, so that a theatergoer enters the orchestra at the top, perceives seating and stage spread out before him, and proceeds downward to his seat. The seating plan of the future Beaumont theater has been duplicated, with the exceptions that there the loge will be a five-row balcony and the designers will not be restricted to the thrust stage. In line with the policy of austerity, the seats are blue-fabric-recovered second-hand ones.

The stage consists basically of a central circular concrete platform bounded on three sides by seating, and backed up by a rectangular space that can be altered in many ways by use of screens. In addition to flexible use of screens, the platform can be placed at three different levels. All these various elements make for a stage

42:1. "ANTA Repertory Theatre Opens Temporary Quarters," *Progressive Architecture*, Mar. 1964, p. 55. Reproduced from PROGRESSIVE ARCHITECTURE.

alive with vitality and movement. Since there is no proscenium, all changes of scene, mood, as well as intermissions, are taken care of by the effective lighting system. Six fixtures per area are used in the thrust stage area (three in each of two colors), and four instruments per area (two in each of two colors) upstage of the end seats. There are also two groups of downlights, 60 "specials."

Although, as noted, this is a temporary facility, it can stand on its own as one of the finest new playhouse interiors around. It would be commendable if New York University, on whose land it stands, were to preserve it for future use.

The *Saturday Review* also told of the new playhouse and its facilities.

42:2 TEMPORARY THEATRE, PERMANENT EXAMPLE

by EDWARD F. KOOK, Vice-chairman of the Board of Standards and Planning for the Living Theatre and president of Century Lighting Inc.

"Sweet are the uses of economy." That's a dangerous sentiment for one whose activities include the manufacture of theatrical lighting equipment. But the impact of the new ANTA–Washington Square Theatre on future theatre structures in New York City must be examined. For here, at a time when the city has had no new legitimate theatre built in the past thirty-six years because no one could amortize an estimated building expense of at least $4,000,000 (exclusive of real estate cost), we have suddenly discovered that a theatre can be constructed for $525,000. Moreover, many consider it the most exciting theatre building yet erected in New York.

It is exciting even before the performance begins. From the moment you enter the top of the aisle and look down the

42:2. Edward F. Kook, "Temporary Theatre, Permanent Example," *Saturday Review*, Feb. 22, 1964, p. 30. Copyright 1964 Saturday Review, Inc.

steeply pitched bank of seats partly crowding around the open stage, there is an atmosphere of theatre. One feels that whatever is going to take place on the stage will be of central importance.

Since this room has no separation between performer and audience, there is immediate warmth and intimacy in the air. Furthermore, this type of seating arrangement strikes us instantly as more democratic than the conventional one. With more vertical dimension and good seeing angles from all seats, there is far less consciousness of any one seat being greatly superior or drastically inferior to any other. And with no balcony or boxes there is virtually no sense of "status" sought or felt.

But the real test of any theatre comes when the performance begins. And here, too, this theatre is surprising. Designer Jo Mielziner has colored his seats in shades of blue that are darker for those seats located near the sides than for those in the center. This not only helps make possible a greater auditorium darkness at performances when the house is not full, but minimizes the audience's awareness of any unglamorous emptiness.

There is a booth from which (for the first time in any large legitimate Manhattan theatre) the lighting cues are given by a man who can see the entire stage. Most amazing of all are the fine acoustics that have been achieved by the creation of irregularly-surfaced concave walls. Audibility is helped both by the bowl shape of the seating arrangement and the fact that there are no impediments like a proscenium arch or overhanging balcony. Such acoustics allow the 1,158 spectators (at capacity) to hear well without any electronic sound amplification.

The stage itself is equipped with an ingenious device of specially constructed screens made to slide across the stage floor to cut off sight of the area behind them. These are installed at three depths (25 feet, 32½ feet, and 40 feet) and when closed form graceful arcs. In this theatre, which could not afford to build a grid high above its stage, these screens do the job nicely.

There are, of course, certain drawbacks to the theatre building. The exterior of the building is not striking and might well be mistaken for a small industrial plant of some sort. The lobby is too small for the building's audience capacity. The thirty-two-inch space between rows is a bit tight; an extra inch would have been more comfortable, but would have cost a whole row of seats. The lack of forestage exit tunnels (like the ones at Stratford, Ontario) complicates the performers' task by forcing them to make long upstage departures from front and center stage positions. Furthermore, Mielziner's irregular step arrangements while they strongly reflect his own taste as an artist, have disadvantages.

Beautiful as these modeled steps and platforms are, the designers of subsequent productions must work with them, too. While each designer can rearrange these elements according to his own taste, he cannot reshape the elements themselves to express his own distinctive character as fully as he might like.

However these compromises and shortcomings all resulted from the necessity of meeting a very limited budget, and they should not lead one to underrate the total achievement of this remarkable theatre.

It would be wonderful if, when the Lincoln Center Repertory Company moves to its permanent Vivian Beaumont Theater in the fall of 1965, New York University, which so generously loaned the land, could find a way to leave this theatre standing and turn it over to someone like Joseph Papp and the New York Shakespeare Festival to use for winter seasons. However, even if NYU cannot do this, the beauty of this structure is that it can be readily dismantled and, except for its concrete bowl base, re-erected on some other public ground.

43. VIVIAN BEAUMONT THEATER OF THE LINCOLN CENTER FOR THE PERFORMING ARTS
New York City
Opened October 21, 1965

The importance of the theater complex developed in New York during the 1960s and known as the Lincoln Center for the Performing Arts can hardly be overemphasized. Although the early decades of the 1900s showed an amazing growth in the number of new playhouses built, there had not been a major new theater opened in New York for more than thirty-five years. During that period, however, there had been many innovations in theater architecture and staging methods, but these could not be seen in New York, the heart of America's theater world.

The opening of the Vivian Beaumont Theater, with its thrust-type stage, represented the beginning of a new period of theater-building in the metropolis. The theater was named for Vivian Beaumont Allen, whose interest in the theater and whose generosity helped make the new playhouse possible. In addition to the Vivian Beaumont, four other buildings comprise the complex: the Metropolitan Opera House, Philharmonic Hall, the New York State Theatre, and the New York Public Library and Museum of the Performing Arts.

A description of the Vivian Beaumont Theater was written by the staff of the playhouse and is reproduced here with a fact sheet concerning the backstage facilities.

43.1   ARCHITECTURAL DESCRIPTION
The Vivian Beaumont Theater and the Library & Museum of Performing Arts share the same building. Eero Saarinen & Associates and Skidmore, Owings & Merrill jointly designed the combined Theater and Library building. Eero Saarinen & Associates designed the interior of the Theater, with Jo Mielziner as collaborating designer.

Four major convictions guided Eero

43:1. "Vivian Beaumont Theater," publicity bulletin, mimeographed (New York, 1965).

43. Interior, Vivian Beaumont Theater, New York, 1965. Courtesy of Lincoln Center for the Performing Arts, Inc. Photograph by Ezra Stoller. © ESTO.

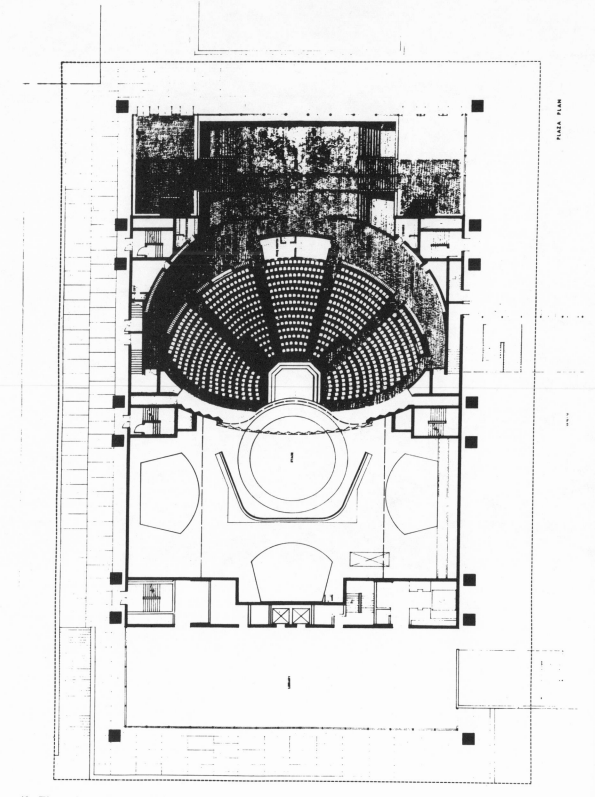

43. Floor plan, Vivian Beaumont Theater, New York, 1965. Courtesy of Lincoln Theater for the Performing Arts, Inc.

Saarinen & Associates and Mr. Mielziner in the design:

"One, that the special character of repertory theater required the simplicity, flexibility and variety of stage arrangements, without compromise to any system, lest an all-purpose theater become a no-purpose theater;

"Two, that the Theater should provide comfort and convenience, and should concentrate every element of design and mechanics on creating a unique and undisturbed intimacy between each member of the audience and the actors;

"Three, that in addition to offering flexibility, the Theater must mount and re-mount entire productions once or even twice a day;

"Four, that the architecture of the building should express the character of a theater and dramatize the sequence of excitements of theater-going."

Looking across Lincoln Center Plaza North, with its reflecting pool and Henry Moore sculpture therein, the Vivian Beaumont Theater is seen at its west facade. The building is a simple, forceful structure which proclaims its dual function as a theater and as a library-museum. Each has its own entrance and its own interior architectural identity.

The Theater entrance faces the Plaza. A structural box, housing a portion of the Library, forms a deep, solid roof over the Theater. It is supported by giant, square concrete columns, with a 150-foot span, which make a bold peristyle around the core of the Theater building itself. The large-scale concrete coffered ceiling, expressing the structure, continues, with similar lighting, under the powerful overhang into the lobby interior.

The Theater can be entered from both the Plaza and the Concourse vehicular access below, with the box office intermediate between the two. Similarly, rest rooms, telephones and other facilities and entrance into the "house" are on a tran-

sitional, split-level arrangement from the lobby.

The spacious yet intimate lobby was designed to facilitate functional transitions in and out; to provide a pleasant intermission space; and, with its handsome ceiling, walls and carpeting, to make a background for the pageant of incoming, outgoing and gathering audiences.

From the lobby, the audience goes down to the orchestra or up to the loge level, where there is a spacious balcony promenade. Both areas contain self-operating lockers for coats and packages—an innovation as a substitute for time-consuming checking.

In contrast to the light and sparkle of the lobby, everything within the auditorium is conceived as a subdued environment, a place which prepares the audience for the world of illusion, makes it feel enclosed within this world and forces it to focus upon the stage.

The environment has been achieved architecturally by bringing everything into one unified scheme. All the mechanical elements—acoustical, lighting, air conditioning—have been incorporated into a ribbed ceiling, which not only gives unity and scale to the whole auditorium but also emphasizes directional lines toward the stage. The edge of the loges and all the walls are coordinated into this theme. The consistent use of a dark color in the house reinforces the desired psychological environment and has the added advantage, once the stage is lit, of removing the usual distraction of reflected light within the house. All this, of course, increases the desired sense of intimacy between audience and actors.

Freed from the conventional facilities and use of the ordinary Broadway production, the architect and collaborating designer were also able to create a theater which allows a new approach to stage-craft.

The main theater can have either a proscenium stage or an open stage of extreme thrust. It may also be used as a combination of the two or in a number of variations. Two notable results have emerged from these arrangements: one, the flexibility has been worked out with a carefully designed framework of limitations, so that neither proscenium nor extreme thrust stage is comprised by the possibility of the other; and two, the possible arrangements have a look of architectural permanence. Unlike other "all-purpose" theaters, no mechanisms, no cables, no bleachers, no gadgets are visible; nothing given an improvsied or temporary look. When set up, each arrangement is inevitable, purposeful and permanent.

Intimacy between audience and actor was a prime goal in the design of the theater. "Each member of the audience must be able to see the expression in the eyes of a face as small as Julie Harris' " was the challenge.

To meet this challenge, architect and collaborating designer undertook a series of detailed studies (which included analysis of where the main action took place on the stage in more than 300 productions, and charts of the heights of human beings and the variations in their eye-levels when seated) and built full-sized mock-ups in an abandoned movie theater in Pontiac, Michigan.

A close audience-actor relationship was achieved in two major ways. One, the stage was pushed out into the auditorium to a possible depth of 28 feet in the extreme thrust and out to a curving apron 12 feet deep in the proscenium arrangement, thus allowing the audience to be wrapped around the stage; and two, the seats were carefully spaced and set at a rake so that the furthest seat is no more than 64 feet from the stage.

Within this requirement of intimacy also came the economical factor that the house had to seat at least 1100 persons and as many more as possible. The final solution is a house which seats 1140 (799 in the orchestra) with the proscenium stage and 1083 (722 in the orchestra) with the extreme thrust stage. There is seating for 361 in the five rows of the loge section. Only two rows of the loge overhang the orchestra, so that there is no disturbing balcony at its rear.

The audience portion of the Theater—lobbies, facilities, auditorium—occupies only about 25 percent of the Theater. In planning the other areas, thought was given to making each part realistically workable in terms of practical stage-craft and to allowing directors, actors and playwrights wide freedom within the controlled framework.

For the first time in the history of theater construction in New York, desirable traditional techniques of stage-craft can, by automation, be used with a new freedom. For example, the possible techniques of scenery include hanging scenery, traditional back to the fifteenth century, and a turntable, traditional to the sixteenth, but not motorized and large enough for an entire production. The turntable is 46 feet in diameter with an independently rotating outer ring, five feet wide.

Similarly, the lighting arrangements were conceived in terms of operational needs. "Saturation lighting" has been provided—that is, lights have been pre-angled to cover every square yard of either of the basic stage arrangements. This allows ease of operation, flexibility in production and a minimum need for special lights.

THE FORUM

The Forum, a second and smaller auditorium in the building, was born of the idea of creating an ideal rehearsal room. As it developed, the planners realized that it could be made into a place of public performance and so it was made large enough to seat 299 people.

In contrast to the main theater, with its flexibility and conveniences, The Forum is a simple, very economical, deliberately unelaborated chamber with all its structural "guts" exposed. It has a permanent thrust platform, which can be used with lighting and props but not with any formal scenery. The room is shaped essentially like a Greek amphitheater.

The Forum will be devoted to pilot projects, experimentation with new talents and forms and the interplay of the other arts with drama, and will function parallel to the larger theater. By engaging the imagination of painters, sculptors, musicians and poets, the Vivian Beaumont and The Forum will provide springboards to each others platforms.

Design and construction of the building were the joint of responsibility of the following firms and individuals:
Vivian Beaumont Theater
Eero Saarinen & Associates, architects
Jo Mielziner, collaborating designer
Library & Museum
Skidmore, Owings & Merrill, architects
Structural Engineers
Amman & Whitney
Mechanical Engineers
Syska & Hennessy, Inc.
General Contractor
Turner Construction Company
for Lincoln Center
Carl A. Morse, construction consultant
Col. William F. Powers,
vice president, engineering

BACKSTAGE FACILITIES

Stage: 138′ wall-to-wall (10,000 sq. ft.)*
75′6″ deep
89′8″ high

*As compared with the Martin Beck Theater, with 2,914 sq. ft., the next largest stage for legitimate plays in New York.

Surfaced with tempered masonite over wood; several traps; 46′ diameter turntable with annular ring; 49 counterweight fly sets
Proscenium: Opening adjustable by means of close-in panels; width variable from 26′ to 58′; height variable from 20′ to 36′
Thrust: 25′x15′6″ maximum, plus main stage apron. Platforms vary in size with production.

Seating: Flexible seating arrangement with elevator and rotation equipment in basement to change to either proscenium or thrust staging; possible to employ orchestra pit 11′x28′ wide and 8′6″ deep

Act Curtain: 61′6″ wide
43′ high
Travels up and down only and is constructed of alternating strips of reversible satin.

Sound: 4 channel stereo installation located in a booth at the back of the house above the balcony

Lighting: 180 dimmer-controlled circuits with unlimited pre-sets through the use of punch card control. The control booth is at the rear of the house on orchestra level.
565 spot lights
1 cyclorama
1 rear projection screen

Dressing Rooms: 20 rooms, 2 performers each
4 chorus rooms, 12 performers each

Rehearsal Rooms: 2 rooms: 42′x26′6″ and 12′6″x19′

Storage: Costumes, 2500 sq. ft.; Scenery, 6400 sq. ft. 27′x59′ storage and loading area on stage left

Chapter 2

Regional Playhouses

If the New York theater scene was particularly dreary during a great part of the twentieth century, the regional theater presented a much brighter picture. The regional theater movement developed slowly, but began gaining momentum in the '50s. By the early '70s, some of the most exciting new playhouses in the country were scattered throughout the United States.

The movement for community theater took drama from the hands of the professionals and placed it in the hands of the avocational theater lover and performer. The establishment of Le Petit Théâtre du Vieux Carré in New Orleans in 1919 was of particular importance, for the group still functioning in 1971, was the oldest major nonprofessional group in the United States. It acquired the St. Peter Street property in 1922, and led the way for other amateur organizations to build playhouses in other parts of the country. Such community groups as the Goodman Theatre in Chicago, the Pasadena Playhouse, and the Cleveland Play House were to be outstanding examples of regional theater at its best.

Following World War II a number of excellent theater groups were started, and in the years that followed many of these groups built new, experimental types of theaters. Breaking away from the usual proscenium "picture-book" staging, they acted in the round and on thrust stages of various shapes and sizes. The closeness of the audience to the players brought a sense of immediacy to performances that audiences had never experienced in proscenium staging. The Arena Stage in Washington, the Alley Theatre in Houston, the Dallas Theater Center in Dallas, the Guthrie Theater in Minneapolis, and the Mummers Theater in Oklahoma City are only a few examples of new playhouses built since 1950.

Two of these theaters in particular have been noted for their unusual architecture, both interior and exterior: The Dallas Theater Center, the only playhouse designed and built by the late Frank Lloyd Wright, and the Mummers Theatre, designed by John Johansen. Both playhouses offered the opportunity for flexibility of staging that seems to mark latter-day regional theaters.

A trend began developing in the 1960s toward a theater complex—that is, one major unit containing in its facility two or more theaters. Atlanta, Los Angeles, and Washington, D.C., all developed this type of complex, and a number of the other playhouses cited in this chapter have in their units at least two theaters. The major reason given for building such complexes is that they give greater flexibility in staging, but they also bring a basic problem, which is financial. Do the regional centers have the audience to make a multiple theater facility feasible and profitable? This problem seems to be increasingly critical, for many of the new regional theaters, in spite of their fine facilities, find themselves in serious financial difficulty, with no easy solution to the problems in sight.

44. PETIT THEATRE DU VIEUX CARRE
New Orleans, Louisiana
Opened November 20, 1922

The New Orleans *Item* of November 21, 1922, covered the opening of this new "little" theater in New Orleans: "Decorated with the Order of the Palm by the French Academy, the Petit Théâtre du Vieux Carré of New Orleans was dedicated Monday night to the Arts. Its new playhouse in St. Peter street, near Chartres—the largest Little Theatre in the country—is symbolical of this influence, for the Petit Théâtre is now one of the most cherished institutions of New Orleans. It becomes Tradition in the Making. . . ."

Le Petit Théâtre was the first of the important Little Theaters that would be built in the United States over the next fifteen years, and its influence was of the first magnitude in this important movement. The management of the playhouse published a brief history in 1940, which is excerpted here.

44:1   ORIGIN AND HISTORY

Le Petit Théâtre du Vieux Carré is the outgrowth of an organization called The Drawing Room Players which was launched in March, 1916, by a score of talented men and women of New Orleans who were desirous of expressing themselves through the medium of amateur theatricals. As their name implied, they found an outlet for their desires by staging plays in the drawing rooms of one [or] another of the membership. While

44:1. *Le Petit Théâtre du Vieux Carré* (New Orleans: The Theater, 1940), pp. 3–15.

they were aware of the crystalization of the Little Theatre movement in America at the time, they were neither activated nor stimulated by it in creating and carrying on their diversion. Their organization was independent and though its later growth was perhaps aided by a similar development in other parts of the country which became known as the Little Theatre Movement, for the first few years the activity of the Drawing Room Players was modeled after the best examples of professional stagecraft, the chief purpose being to present finer things than were offered elsewhere in the city, rather than to create or experiment.

Until the end of the war The Drawing Room Players gave plays intermittently in private homes. Their group was necessarily limited to a small number of persons by the size of the rooms used for auditoriums, yet so real was the need of the service they were rendering that outsiders soon began to request admittance.

By 1919 these requests grew to a demand whose sincerity could not be ignored, and The Drawing Room Players accordingly re-organized as Le Petit Théâtre du Vieux Carré with an initial membership of five hundred. Their first step was to lease apartments in the lower Pontalba building on Jackson Square, an ideal location in the heart of the old quarter. The outlook on the beautiful little park from their graceful second story balcony was enchanting. By their own labor they transformed the dingy hall into a charming little theatre with an auditorium seating 184 persons and a small but adequate stage. Every function, from ticket taking to direction, including the construction and decoration of scenery and the designing and making of costumes, was carried on by the members. There were no paid employees.

Despite the underlying fear that boredom would overtake and dissipate the membership, the demand for entrance grew and the limit was extended, first to six hundred and then to one thousand. An experiment with a waiting list resulted in 600 more persons promptly applying for that scant prerogative, and after three years Le Petit Théâtre found itself again compelled to seek larger quarters or to remain at a standstill.

In 1922 the present location at 616 St. Peter Street was purchased and the auditorium with a seating capacity of 410 was built. The membership limit was extended to 2,000 and still the demand grew and the membership was repeatedly increased until it had reached the absolute maximum the auditorium would hold in eight nights of performances.

The growing complexity of the organization and the desire for improvement led, late in 1919, to the employment of a professional director, technical director, a paid secretary and a mechanical staff. The spirit has remained amateur, however. All roles are taken by amateur members, many of whom have attained the poise and technique of professionals and some of whom have left to join the ranks of professional Thespians on Broadway or Hollywood. With these accomplished players the theatre might easily form a semi-stock company and be assured of uniformly competent performances, yet it seeks, rather, to induce more and more members to step forward into productions.

Practically the only requirements for membership are the desire to join and the deposit of the annual fee of ten dollars before the necessarily fixed limit of subscriptions is reached. This policy has resulted in attracting the culturally elite of the city, regardless of social or financial status. And the theatre is able to satisfy their desires for good plays because, owning its own building and equipment, it is financially, therefore artistically, independent.

Le Petit Théâtre du Vieux Carré is a corporation chartered under the laws of Louisiana. As provided in its constitution and by-laws it has two classes of members, active and sustaining members, from whose ranks the active workers are being constantly recruited. The latter usually number about 200, with an equal number on probation. Only fully accredited active members have the right to vote at elections.

The general management of the theatre is conducted by a board of governors, nine in number, three of whom are elected annually to replace three whose terms expire. At all elections and at all meetings of the corporation each active member is entitled to one vote, no proxies being permitted. One-fifth of the entire membership constitutes a quorum and the decision of a majority of those present governs.

From its own membership the board of governors annually elects a president, a chairman of the board, a treasurer, a recording secretary, a chairman of the play reading committee, a chairman of the production committee, a chairman of the house committee, and a chairman of the active membership committee.

It has the power also to name such other officers as it deems necessary, to employ any staff needed and to fix salaries. Customarily, it appoints a professional director each Spring to serve the following season.

The professional director devotes his attention entirely to casting, directing and producing seven plays before the entire membership each year. The season begins the last part of October and extends to the end of May.

The technical director supervises the making of sets, the painting of scenery, the lighting, the make-up, and the fashioning of whatever costumes and props are not otherwise economically procurable. He has the paid assistance of a stage carpenter and a seamstress, and the volunteer help of members who, by such work as well as by taking parts in plays, may become eligible for active membership. All administrative work is done by the administrative secretary and volunteer clerical workers are also eligible for active membership.

PROPERTY

The ground occupied by Le Petit Théâtre du Vieux Carré, measuring 90 feet on Chartres Street by 133 feet on St. Peter Street, lies in the heart of the original city, now known as the French Quarter. Half a square away are several sites of historic interest, including the Cabildo, the Pontalba buildings, the St. Louis Cathedral and the Place d'Armes. Clustered about are picturesque dwellings containing the studios and homes of artists, including those of several nationally known painters, writers and musicians.

When Le Petit Théâtre purchased this location in 1922, the corner portion of the ground was occupied by a two-story, stucco dwelling which in 1797 had been the residential palace of the seventh and last Spanish governor of Louisiana, Don Manuel Gayoso de Lemos.

The rest of the ground was littered by a collection of ramshackle sheds. From notarial records it is inferred the dwelling was built in 1794 by Jean Baptiste Orso, a wealthy citizen. Letters in the possession of a lineal descendant of Governor de Lemos indicate that haughty aristocrat improved the buildings and grounds in 1797 and personally supervised the planting of flowers and shrubs in the patio, to make a fitting setting for his beautiful young wife when she should join him from their former post in Natchez.

The records show the property was later transferred from one private owner to another and in the mid-nineteenth century became a rather exclusive bar called Le Veau Qui Tête (The Sucking Calf).

During the period when the French Quarter was neglected, this barroom degenerated into a rough dive and the property as a whole fell into decay.

The exterior and the patio never entirely lost their atmosphere of rich, gay old New Orleans, however, as was attested by their use by one motion picture company as a setting for Nazimova in "A Rose of a Thousand Years," and another for Theda Bara in "The Light."

What the motion picture producers saw in the Spanish colonial casa was also seen by the board of Le Petit Théâtre when it purchased the property and remodeled it into what often has since been described as the most picturesquely beautiful little theatre in America.

BUILDINGS

The buildings as they are seen now were not constructed at once but represent the gradual growth of the theatre since 1922. The stage and auditorium were first built, but did not adjoin the corner property. The theatre was later "tied-in" to the original corner building with a broad one-story loggia.

The Old Absinthe House at Bourbon and Bienville Streets was selected as the model for the street facade. In conformance with this model and with surrounding buildings, were constructed the broad doors with fan windows above, the solid shutters, the projecting iron balconies in front of the second-story windows and the small plaster cornice.

The theatre is entered by the loggia, whose doorway is an adaptation of the old carriage entrances to the courtyards of the Quarter. This loggia serves as a passageway between the old and the new building and also as an access to the courtyard or patio. The loggia floor is of flagstones taken from an adjoining building and the ceiling is of dark, stained pine such as may be found in any ancient town of Spain. There is a large crystal chandelier from one of the old houses in the Quarter. The walls are of plain plaster with replica tapestries and at one end is an old chest from Verona.

Next to the loggia and forming the Chartres Street corner is the coffee room in the governor's palace and later the famous cafe, Le Veau Qui Tête. The panelling is old and is an interesting adaptation of a French room. Back of this room are the men's dressing rooms, with entrances from the patio, and the stage.

The lobby of the theatre is off the opposite side of the loggia and acts as a buffer for the auditorium from the noise of the street, and as an exit. Two small iron stairways lead to the auditorium. This is a very simple room of tinted plaster walls, whose lines are broken on either side by door-ways, in front by the rectangular proscenium and in the rear by the iron rail of the balcony. The walls are hung with Cluny tapestry replicas and brocatelles. Four antique Italian chandeliers throw a soft amber light over the audience.

In the center of this elaborate setting is the gem of the ensemble, the courtyard. At night, when the audience overflows into it between acts from the foyer, loggia, and coffee room it becomes a glamorous garden in the blue flood moonlight which plays from a balustrade upon a sparkling fountain in the center, and spreads its soft glow unevenly over rich semi-tropical shrubbery, vines and flowers which grow profusely in all space not occupied by the flagstone walks leading to various departments of the theatre.

The site and form of the courtyard were suggested by the roof lines of the old building. This had been totally wrecked and the ground was covered by small sheds but enough remained to suggest on one side the brick arches of the arcade with spindled columns on the gallery above, such as may be seen in many preserved courtyards of the Quarter.

The climate is such that the patio also forms a practical means of circulation. The walls are covered with Rosa Montana, wisteria, star jasmine, begonia, blue morning glory and Cherokee roses, and the beds are filled with banana, myrtle, sweet olive, Japanese plum and Datura trees, azalea, camelia, Rose of Sharon, roses, and with spider lilies and other plants typical of Creole gardens. . . .

The opening of the playhouse was reported in the New Orleans *Item*:

44:2   PETITE THEATRE, N.O. SYMBOL
IS DEDICATED

Cherished Institution Decorated
With Order of the Palm;
3 Plays Given

by Thomas Ewing Dabney

Decorated with the Order of the Palm by the French Academy, the Petit Theatre du Vieux Carre of New Orleans was dedicated Monday night to the Arts. Its new playhouse in St. Peter street, near Chartres—the largest Little Theatre in the country—is symbolical of this influence, for the Petit Theatre is now one of the most cherished institutions of New Orleans. It becomes Tradition in the Making.

The dedicatory services were simple.

After the chimes had hushed the audience that packed parquette and balcony, Mrs. Oscar Nixon, Consul-General Barret of France, Harold Newman and Walter Keiffer filed out in front of the curtain, and began to speak in reverse order.

Mr. Keiffer, as chairman of the building committee, tendered the playhouse to the membership through Harold Newman, chairman of the Board of Governors, and gave credit to "Mr. Newman's strong vision and foresight for the success of the undertaking." He also paid tribute to the architects, Armstrong & Koch, and to the building contractor, Lionel Feyrot, who sacrificed part of his profits so that the structure might come within the budget.

DEDICATED TO ALL

Mr. Newman, in turn, declared that the Petit Theatre was dedicated to "every man, woman and child who loves New

44:2. New Orleans *Item*, Nov. 21, 1922.

Orleans!" "Every large city," he said, "is symbolized by some particular thing: New Orleans' symbol will be the Petit Theatre, for that in turn is symbolical of the artistic endeavor of New Orleans, and of the distinguishing charm that lies below Canal street—the soul of the city."

Then Consul-General Barret, referring to the deep relations between France and New Orleans, and sketching the artistic triumphs of the Petit Theatre, conferred upon the membership, represented by Mrs. Oscar Nixon, president of the organization, the palm of the French Academy.

Mrs. Nixon responded gracefully and gallantly in the idiom of Moliere, adding in well-earned English at the end that it was the first speech she had ever made in French.

Now for the play, which after all, is the thing!

Rhea Loeb Goldberg (in real life she's a Mrs. but this is dramatic criticism and the dramatic critic is nothing if not discreet) and Zillah Mendes Meyer were easily the stars of the evening, if it is necessary to single out any particular luminaries in the Milky Way. Oddly enough, their roles were diametrically opposite—the latter joyfully tragic, and the former tragically joyful.

SPLENDID CHARACTERIZATION

Zillah Mendes Meyer's interpretation of Praskovya in Calderon's "Little Stone House," the pathetic Russian drudge who achieves happiness supreme through idolizing her son, and then dies when she finds that her idol has feet of muck, was a splendid piece of work.

Rhea Loeb Goldberg in Sutro's "Man in the Stalls," played the part of Elizabeth Allen, an extremely friendly lady, remarkably free in her kisses, so free that she even gives her husband a few. It is an evident sacrifice, for a couple of minutes later, when she is snuggled in her lover's arms, she complains with sweet bitterness

that husbands don't shave their chins. Lovers do.

This caused a simultaneous movement of every male in the audience in the direction of his jaw, fearing lest his condition might lay him open to the epigram that husbands should be seen, not felt, or embarrassing imputations.

The morality of the play is interesting. Elizabeth Allen and Walter Cozens (he's the smooth-chinned chap) start out by being deliciously wicked. Lest there be any doubt of it, we are informed that the wickedness has been going on for two years. Then at the end of the play they get good. For, you remember, that there have been two years of it.

However, the playwright spoils it all by trying to churn up a little sympathy for the pair by suddenly remembering the Higher Life. Two years isn't enough motive: morals must be lugged in by the ears. The inescapable truth, however, is that no man and no woman ever went good for moral reasons, any more than a child stopped eating candy for worrying about his teeth. They just crave a change of diet.

EXCELLENT CAST

The third play, "The Falcon and the Lady" by Penney, is such a poor play that the excellent work of the cast can not be appreciated. The theme is that of a short story, not of a drama. Furthermore, there is not a sympathetic character in it. Once there was almost a dramatic situation.

That was when Count Mario went to kill his pet falcon so that the lady he thought he loved, despite her enervating virtue, might feast under the mistaken impression that it was a fat pullet.

But what happened? A couple of persons stood on the stage crying. The audience was tense, for it recognized that the death of that falcon represented the death of Mario's love for the said lady, he having fallen, with a satisfying thud, for the charms of another lady, who was a vegetarian, for purposes of weight-reduction. And the audience naturally expected the slaying to be done in a highly symbolical manner. But it waited in vain for the whunk! of the descending hatchet. The falcon simply went dead for no apparent physical reason.

However, two bulls-eyes out of three chances is good shooting. If the professional stage made as good a showing, it would perhaps not be necessary to organize Little Theatres to produce the best in drama. . . .

45. GOODMAN MEMORIAL THEATRE
Chicago, Illinois
Opened October 22, 1925

One of the leading professional institutions in the movement for a richer regional theater is the Goodman Memorial Theatre, which opened in 1925. The playhouse was a gift of the parents of Kenneth Sawyer Goodman, a young playwright, and was donated to the Art Institute of Chicago. The purpose of the theater from the beginning was to combine an actor's training program with a professional repertory company. The opening of the playhouse and its purposes were outlined in an article in the New York *Times*.

45:1   NOVEL REPERTORY THEATRE
            TO OPEN SOON IN CHICAGO

Presented to the Art Institute, Kenneth Sawyer Goodman Memorial Theatre Contains Newest Devices for Effective Producing—Student Performances, Too
by Donald Lawder

Cut into the stone over the entrance to the Kenneth Sawyer Goodman Memorial Theatre, now nearing completion in Chicago, are these words: "To restore the Old Visions and to win the New." With that as its motto Chicago's newest theatre hopes to win for the West something of

45:1. New York *Times*, Oct. 11, 1925.

the distinction that the East has long held in the field of first American productions.

The Goodman Memorial Theatre, one of the most completely equipped theatrical producing units in the country, is to inaugurate its first season on Oct. 22 with the American premiere of John Galsworthy's "The Forest," produced last year in London.

The theatre building, given to the Art Institute by William O. Goodman and his wife as a memorial to their son, Kenneth Sawyer Goodman, who died while stationed at the Great Lakes Naval Training Station during the war—is unusual in many respects.

While a "little theatre" as regards seating capacity, chairs being provided for only about 700 spectators, its proscenium and the stage are as large as may be found in the average Chicago theatre. The scene painting section, the carpenter shop, wardrobe, design and storage rooms are larger than in any other theatre in the city.

NOVEL INTERIOR PLANS

Possibly the most interesting feature from the playgoer's standpoint is the seating arrangement, for which Howard Shaw Van Doren is responsible. The European plan of spacing rows 42 inches apart instead of 34 has been adopted. There is no centre aisle, the rows of seats running from outer aisle to outer aisle.

The most modern of ideas in technical stage design have been incorporated in the construction of this theatre. Over the entire back wall of the stage extends a great curved shell of plaster. Along the base of this half-dome is a trench filled with lighting equipment designed to give the plaster surface the effect of a sky under varying effects of day or night, sunlight or storm. The sky will take the place of the usual painted sky in drop curtains, landscape effects being obtained by placing objects, horizons, trees, buildings, or the like against the lighted background. Thus many types of setting not usually available to the playwright may be realized.

The sky dome requires new methods for the rapid changing of interiors. It does not allow of the usual gridiron and fly gallery. Moveable floors, large enough to hold a complete interior set, are provided. These floors, or "wagon stages," are prepared at the sides and wheeled into place when the given scene is required, with the furniture and properties in place. As the floors of the wagon stages are somewhat higher than the regular stage floor, a section just back of the footlights is hinged and arranged to rise and meet the new elevation as it comes into place.

Such a play as Galsworthy's "The Forest" requires alternation of native hut interiors and scenes in a Central African jungle, worked out with lights and plastic material in the dome.

AFFILIATED WITH ART INSTITUTE

Still more intricate devices for changing scenic effects will enter into the production of Alexandre Dumas' old melodrama, "The Tower of Nesle," to be given during the first half of the present season. The sky dome will serve with a severely simple primitive architectural background for the studio's production of "Iphigenia in Taurus," and with an arrangement of complex and highly modern elements for the expressionistic "Gas," to be done under the direction of Marion Gering of the Meyerhold Theatre in Moscow.

While the theatre itself is not endowed, the membership list of the Art Institute is to be used as a basis for a supporting group of subscribers. The Theatre Guild of New York was similarly financed in the early stages.

Performances will be given by the repertory company on Thursday, Friday and Saturday evenings and at Friday matinees. The price of seats for the repertory performance will be $1 to the general public. All members of the Art Institute, however, will receive eight coupon tickets,

exchangeable for seats on payment of 50 cents. When the coupons are exhausted members may purchase tickets, without limit, at a 25 per cent discount.

In connection with a regular repertory company of professional players, the theatre will also be used as an experimental workshop for a school of the theatre, to be conducted under the auspices of the Art Institute. Thomas Wood Stevens, former director of the theatre at Carnegie Institute of Technology (the first comprehensive professional training school of its kind), will be director of both the school and the repertory company.

STUDENT ACTIVITIES

Performances given by the students of the drama department will be announced from time to time. The drama department of the institute has received hundreds of applications from prospective students in all sections of the country. To be accepted applicants must successfully pass competitive technical tests and possess credits for a typical university course, as it is expected that certain parts of the work will be carried on in cooperation with the University of Chicago.

Among the plays to be produced during the first season, after Galsworthy's "The Forest," will be Bernard Shaw's "Heartbreak House," Moliere's "Don Juan," Shakespeare's "A Midsummer Night's Dream" and George Kaiser's "Gas." A number of new American plays will also be performed.

Both companies, professional and studio, will execute every detail of their separate productions, including the designing of costumes, the painting of scenery and the planning of lighting effects. Students also will write most of the plays to be produced by themselves.

The director has explained his ideas, first of which is to afford the public an opportunity to see plays that would not in the usual course of a theatrical season be presented—just as, he points out, the passing art exhibitions of the Institute give the opportunity for the study and enjoyment of many pictures and pieces of sculpture not otherwise available.

PLAYS NOT GENERALLY SEEN

"As the theatre is constituted in America," said Mr. Stevens, "many excellent plays are given for brief engagements and revived only at long intervals. Some are produced in New York which never come to Chicago. Some are never presented to their audience as the authors intended they should be—by living actors in a theatre.

"Our repertory company intends to give each season as many good old plays as can be produced adequately, allowing time for the performances, as well, of an equal number of new plays, any one of which may disclose elements of lasting interest. The audiences of the Goodman Theatre may come upon a classic which has not seen the light of the stage for many years, or a play by one of the most important modern authors, accepted by the critics but unregarded in the commercial markets, or the audience may find itself assisting at the first public test of a play with a future. That is why the inscription, taken from a line in one of Kenneth Goodman's plays, was chosen for the stone over the entrance."

Thomas Wood Stevens, the director, enjoyed association with the late Kenneth Sawyer Goodman. He and young Goodman collaborated in the writing of a number of plays and masques.

While at Princeton, Mr. Goodman wrote verse, some of which has been published and won the Poetry Prize in 1904. After his graduation and return to Chicago, he took up playwriting. Twelve of his short plays have been published in two volumes, "Quick Curtains" and "More Quick Curtains." A number of one-act plays written in collaboration with Ben Hecht have recently been brought out in book form under the title "The Wonder Hat and Other Plays." In all, more than thirty plays, written wholly or in part by Mr. Goodman, have been produced by various little theatre organizations. Among the best known are "The Dust of the Road," "Barbara," "Ephraim and the Winged Bear," "Back of the Yards," "A Man Can Only Do His Best" and "The Game of Chess."

The latter was acted under the direction of B. Iden Payne at the Playhouse Theatre in Chicago during the season of 1912–13 with Walter Hampden and Whitford Kane in the cast. Prior to the formal public opening of the Goodman Theatre in October three of Mr. Goodman's one-act plays will be produced at an invitational performance by the professional players.

The advent of the Goodman Theatre received special notice in the *Theatre Arts Monthly.*

45:2   Like Browning's wise and weary cardinal who had known three and twenty leaders of revolts, and whose pulse refused to quicken over the twenty-fourth, the frequenter of our theatre is by this time more than usually calm when fresh trumpetings announce that the American repertory theatre is with us at last. We have heard the fanfare so often! The hope that the season about to open at the Kenneth Sawyer Goodman Memorial Theatre in Chicago may begin history of a different kind, therefore, may be partly based on the fact that it has a director who could never earn his salt or even his pepper with a trumpet; but it rests also on the nature of the experiment itself.

Most repertory theatres are commercial ventures. And when a commercial success comes in at the door, repertory flies out at the window. But the Goodman Memorial Theatre is not to be run for profit. Its beautiful playhouse is the munificent gift

45:2. Cora Jarrett, "The Goodman Memorial," *Theatre Arts Monthly* 9:609–12 (Sept. 1925).

to the Chicago Art Institute of Mr. and Mrs. William O. Goodman in memory of their son, Kenneth Sawyer Goodman, well loved and mourned as man and playwright. Its initiator and director, Thomas Wood Stevens, organizer and former head of the Department of Drama at the Carnegie Institute of Technology in Pittsburgh, works for a professor's salary for great love of his task, and has got together a company of co-workers who have a like spirit. This group functions like one of the ancient guilds: they act, they design and make costumes, they instruct the student actors and actresses who will graduate into the Repertory Company some day, they paint scenery, they do whatever comes to hand. They work incredible hours. Many of the company owe their ability to deal creatively with their art to previous training under Mr. Stevens in Carnegie Institute, learning to take a playhouse and play, and create theatre.

The Goodman Theatre's house and "works" are almost too good to be true. The building itself is mostly under ground. Because the Chicago Art Institute lies in Grant Park, between Michigan Boulevard and the lake, and an ordinance forbids any new building to project more than a few feet above the ground level, the earth was hollowed out for this playhouse, of which one sees only an austere stone parapet from the boulevard. This constraint in vertical space gives to the auditorium, to whose foyer one descends by a broad staircase, very beautiful proportions, widening its width, and cutting down its height. The same constraint has called for the greatest ingenuity in design from architect and director, in construction and arrangement of equipment, as there is almost no room overhead; and with sliding stages and specially designed machinery they have made this unique stage a technical miracle.

The plan of operation for the first season of the Goodman Memorial Theatre is as follows: The Repertory Company of professional actors and actresses will, from October to May, play not fewer than four performances a week. Their opening programme, not yet fully decided on, is expected to be a special performance of selected plays by Kenneth Sawyer Goodman, followed in October by the public opening of the subscription season. They will give important standard and contemporary plays not previously shown in Chicago, a small number of classical revivals, and some new plays of merit and experimental interest. In the arrangements for subscriptions and for the sale of seats, preference is given to the members of the Chicago Art Institute, under whose auspices the theatre is operated, and they will have special privileges given them in the theatre itself. A low scale of prices is tentatively fixed; only enough to provide for a part of the expense. The company includes Howard Southgate, Eula Guy, Hubbard Kirkpatrick, Walton Pyre, Mary Agnes Doyle, Russell Spindler, Ellen Lowe, Helen Forrest, Josef Lararovici, Neal Caldwell, Bess Catheryn Johnson, Arvid Crandall, and others.

Cooperating with the Repertory Company, and subordinate to it, will be the Studio Company, a group of students, not above forty in number, who come for a three years' professional training in the theatre arts under Mr. Stevens and Mr. Howard Southgate. They, too, will give a series of public performances in the theatre, and will be given opportunity to work with the Repertory Company as required. Close contact with the large and important school of the Art Institute should produce an unusual and interesting development in scene and costume design. A projected cooperative arrangement with Chicago University will add certain literary courses to the requirements, and candidates must comply with the university entrance rules before going into the tryout competition for admission to the Studio. Conditions so exacting ought to sift the applicants down to a group of real promise; and three years of work under Mr. Stevens' lash and in close daily touch with a stock company of a sort that is unique in our theatrical history should take them very far. The donors, the director, and the well-wishers of this new type of art theatre school and laboratory are joined in the hope of realizing the spirit of the building's inscription, taken from one of the eloquent poetic masques of Kenneth Sawyer Goodman: "To restore the old visions, and to win the new."

The Goodman Theatre was described architecturally in the *Architectural Record*, with special mention for the innovative features of the new playhouse.

45:3 Howard Van Doren Shaw faced serious problems when he undertook to design the Kenneth Sawyer Goodman Memorial Theatre, an addition to Chicago's Art Institute. The success of the achievement is noteworthy. Representing, as it does, one of the last works of the eminent Chicago architect, this unique theatre, symbolic in the simplicity and elegance of Mr. Shaw's style, is a fitting climax to an illustrious career.

Grant Park, where the theatre is located, is all made land. Comparatively few years ago, it was part of Lake Michigan, and little excavating is required to strike water. Thus there was a drainage problem to begin with; a problem which was aggravated by the existence of a city ordinance restricting the height of buildings in that section of Grant Park to within 15 feet of natural ground level. Hence the architect had to build down instead of up. Except for the entrance the theatre is practically under ground. A simple, ten-foot wall of Indiana limestone and a comparatively small entrance motif of the same material, built in simple, classic style, are all that one sees from the street.

45:3. Anne Lee, "The Kenneth Sawyer Goodman Memorial Theatre, Chicago," *Architectural Record* 61:13–22 (Jan. 1927).

The height demanded in theatre construction for the preferred vertical operation of curtains and scenery was not available on account of the imposed building restrictions. The architect had to work within the limitations of two dead-lines, which absolutely precluded a loft and necessitated the horizontal operation of stage appurtenances. At that, it was necessary to build to a depth of 26 feet below ground level. Inasmuch as the architect could not have height to work with, he had to have breadth. The low, horizontal lines which add to the charm of the theatre were a necessity and resulted in an unusually large backstage with an expanse of 165 feet behind the curtain line. Thus there is ample provision for the horizontal operation of curtains and scenery and wagon-stages. For the fire curtain, a rolling asbestos curtain on a steel drum was substituted for the type in general use in this country.

Mr. Shaw was permitted to digress somewhat from the Chicago ordinances by reason of the fact that Grant Park is under the direct jurisdiction of the South Park Board and does not, strictly speaking, come under the City of Chicago building requirements. Such digressions as were found necessary were made with precautions equivalent to those required by the city. Regarding the exit facilities, for instance, experiments with a full auditorium have shown that the theatre can be emptied in a minute and a half; this in spite of the fact that there are continuous rows of seats, with no front-to-back aisles. The chief advantage in building under the South Park Board jurisdiction in this instance lay in the fact that the City ordinances prohibit the building of public halls below street level.

Ordinary problems, the problems which are usually the chief concern of a theatre architect, such as lighting, heating, ventilation, acoustics and the muffling of outside noises (in this case, the noise of the Illinois Central Railroad whose tracks run directly behind the theatre), became of secondary importance in designing the Goodman Theatre because of the more vital issues involved, foremost among which was that of drainage.

Waterproofing the main portion of the theatre, which is 18 feet below ground level and gradually slopes down to 20½ feet, was accomplished by first laying a six-inch thickness of cinders. On top of this concrete was poured in two four-inch layers, between which was placed a waterproofing membrane of cotton cloth covered with asphalt. Wooden piles were driven close together into the earth to act as a support for the concrete grillage in which steel beams were erected. That portion of the building which reaches the greatest depth, 26 feet, and which provides for the orchestra pit, stage traps and lighting pit between stage and cyclorama, has a two-foot thickness of concrete for walls as well as base. Extra heavy waterproofing was placed between the two twelve-inch layers of concrete.

The Goodman Memorial Theatre, presented to the Art Institute by Mr. and Mrs. William O. Goodman of Chicago in memory of their son, Kenneth Sawyer Goodman, is a most appropriate memorial inasmuch as it carries out the ideas and ideals of the young poet and playwright whose untimely death, while serving as a Naval Lieutenant during the war, brought to a close the career of that promising young man. The theatre represents the young dramatist's ideas of what a theatre should be. He was interested in every phase of stagecraft; in producing plays as well as writing them; and, as an active member of the Art Institute, he had for some time prior to his death favored the expansion of the Institute's school to include a department for the teaching of dramatic art in all its branches.

That is just what the Goodman Memorial Theatre is,—a school to teach dramatic art; the laboratory of the Art Institute's Drama Department, of which Thomas Wood Stevens is the head. Mr. Stevens, by the way, as an associate of young Mr. Goodman's and as collaborator, with him, in the writing of several plays, is thoroughly conversant and in sympathy with the late playwright's ideas. A professional repertory company is provided in addition to the student company. Plays, old and new, are produced for whatever artistic and dramatic merits they possess, rather than because of any box office attraction. The students write plays and produce them. They design, make and paint their scenery. They create their costumes, doing their own designing, dyeing and sewing.

In lighting and stage accoutrements, the theatre probably is surpassed by none in the country. It is one of the few theatres in existence equipped with a permanent cyclorama. The limited height of the auditorium and backstage (in addition to its desirability in many other respects) caused the use of the cyclorama for effects of height and distance.

Built on a steel frame, lathed and plastered, this cyclorama, or sky dome, is 80 feet in width and curves over the stage at a height of 25 feet. It is elliptical in plan, and has a continuous lighting trough 5 feet deep and 5 feet wide, with an opening in the stage 3 feet wide. The curve of the cyclorama, vertically, for outdoor effects, entirely overcomes the feeling of lowness. An effect of a 50 or 60 foot height is obtained inasmuch as it is impossible to determine where the vertical surface ends and the horizontal begins. An enormous proscenium opening 37 feet wide and 19 feet high, enhances this effect.

The cyclorama is lighted entirely from below in three main sections,—right, left and center,—and the effects can be varied from side to side. Various atmospheric effects, effects of distance and great expanse are provided by the pit lights which are entirely controlled from the stage switchboard. The architect considered the cyclorama one of the most successful features of the theatre. Aside from its primary advantages, it has eliminated many back-drops. Concealed in the ceiling are five sets of lines which may be lowered for drops. The use of two 32-foot movable platforms or wagon-stages also offsets the disadvantages of not having a loft. Entire sets may be arranged on the platforms, which can be wheeled into place instantly.

Two floors of property room space, a large carpenter shop, ample scene racks and paint frames and a green room, which is tucked into the space at the side of the auditorium usually used for a lower box, are backstage features. Space over the side corridors provides exceptional dressing room facilities where the comfort of the players was given first consideration in spacious arrangement, good lighting and ample sanitary provisions.

There are no windows in the theatre. Except for the auditorium, which is illuminated entirely by concealed lights, and for the backstage region, most of the rooms in the building depend on large skylights for daylight. Heat is derived from the central heating plant of the Art Institute. An extensive exhaust fan system, operated from the fanroom under the entrance stairway, ventilates the building.

Traveling, now, 208 feet on Monroe Street from the extreme backstage on the north side of the theatre to the entrance on South Parkway, one passes through doors flanked by Doric columns to enter the stone vestibule with vaulted ceiling and through a second set of doors into the ticket lobby, also of stone. Going down the flight of shallow marble steps, one is immediately aware of an atmosphere of dignity and elegance; of a beauty of interior that is different.

Instead of the usual lobby, a Memorial Gallery, measuring 20 x 100 ft., stretches out at the foot of the stairs, covering the full width of the theatre. Walls of stone support a vaulted plaster ceiling, down the full length of which runs a metal sub-skylight. Heroic bronzes silhouette their figures against the light stone walls which are hung with three large tapestries and several portraits of theatrical celebrities. Notable among the small sculptures shown is a bronze bust of Howard Van Doren Shaw. Polished, black terrazzo flooring contrasts with the light walls. Looking up, one is aware of an unusal moulding which recalls the architect's love for detail and keen interest in untried ornamentations. Altogether, the effect of the Memorial Gallery is one of a great charm seldom achieved.

The Gallery gives access to the reception and smoking rooms, the office, rehearsal and class-rooms and to the studio where the costumes are created. This model workroom is equipped with sewing machines and with dyeing, washing and ironing facilities. Ample checkroom space is provided under the small balcony which covers the full width of the auditorium.

The Gallery gives access, too, to the 12-foot corridors which parallel both sides of the auditorium and are built on a slope to correspond with the auditorium. Five doorways lead from each corridor to the interior which has a seating capacity of 750. One liberty the architect took was the arrangement of the seats in continuous rows from side to side, with no front-to-back aisles, following the European plan (particularly that used in many modern German theatres and to some extent, in London). There are 37 seats in a row with a distance of 3 feet 6 inches back to back, which allows ample foot room and room for passing. This distance is somewhat greater than that used in most of the German theatres.

The interior of the auditorium is built entirely of quarter-sawed white oak, fumed and waxed, panelled in a style inspired by the Georgian Period. Here again the effect is one of charming simplicity. A chaste dignity and beauty of proportion and design have been achieved by the varied and interesting used of wood. Random-width oak boards, with knots and other imperfections, were used above the large panels to form the background for niches where the busts of noted dramatists are seen. Boxes have been eliminated. Instead, occupying the spaces generally devoted to upper boxes, there is a small balcony on either side of the stage. On occasion, these balconies are used in conjunction with the stage.

Contrasting with the soft brown tones of the oak, are the light plaster ornamental ceiling, the plaster busts, crystal chandeliers, the linen curtains (block-printed in red), and the rose-colored velvet hangings on the corridor-side. These curtains open and disappear into the doorways through which one glimpses colorful prints and paintings hung on the rough plaster corridor walls.

The Kenneth Sawyer Goodman Memorial Theatre, which is so significant a monument to the young playwright, is none the less a monument, too, to the architect who conceived and brought into being, in spite of serious obstacles, a theatre of charm and beauty as expressive of his own ideals in design as of the dramatist's ideals in stagecraft; blending his own personality in the exquisite handling of detail (for which Mr. Shaw was known), with the spirit of Kenneth Sawyer Goodman, whom the architect immortalized by the use of quotations from the young playwright's works, such as: "You yourselves must set flame to the fagots which you have brought," carved in wood over the proscenium arch, and another, inscribed in the stone lintel over the street entrance, which reads: "To restore the old visions and to win the new."

Thus is the purpose of the theatre explained; thus, the ideal of the young dramatist set forth in perfect harmony with the design of the architect.

46. PASADENA PLAYHOUSE
Pasadena, California
Opened May 18, 1925

Among the leaders of the community theater movement was the Pasadena Playhouse,

under the direction of Gilmore Brown. For nearly fifty years this playhouse stood for excellence in regional theater. Since it was founded in a community that had huge talent resources, the Playhouse has over the years fostered many outstanding stars and contributed greatly to the community theater movement and to professional theater throughout the United States.

The Playhouse was closed in 1970 because of financial difficulties, but the directors of the Playhouse hoped to reopen it once again.

The following historical account of the theater and its founders was published the year following the opening of the playhouse on May 18, 1925.

46:1   In the fall of 1916, Mr. Gilmore Brown brought his company of professional players to the Savoy Theatre—the old Community Playhouse—and many groups of people interested in the drama assisted and encouraged his attempt to keep alive the spoken drama, which, due to the war and the advent of the movies, was threatened with destruction.

The following summer the Community Players was organized around this group under an Advisory Committee and a program of play production with this nucleus of paid professionals assisted by amateurs was adopted, Mr. Brown assuming all financial responsibility. At the end of the first season, the financial condition becoming desperate, it was found to continue the services of these faithful professionals who had remained steadfast through two trying years.

After much hard, discouraging work the Advisory Committee, late in the summer of 1918, took the plunge and organized the Pasadena Community Playhouse Association, a legally incorporated nonprofit organization with a Board of Directors that assumed all financial responsi-

46:1. Clinton C. Clarke, "Playhouse History," *Pasadena Community Playhouse Association Year Book, 1925–26* (Pasadena: The Playhouse, 1926), pp. 10, 16.

bility and management, reconstructed the players on a purely amateur basis, and engaged Mr. Brown as manager and director. In November, 1918, production was started in the Shakespeare Clubhouse, three nights a week, the highest seat price 50 cents. However, this arrangement proving unsatisfactory both financially and in arousing public interest, the players soon returned to the Savoy, which was rented outright and renamed the Community Playhouse.

Attendance and interest increasing and the quality of the productions showing great improvement, the directors, by employing a trained publicity expert, put on an extensive campaign of selling the idea to the general public. Three years passed before definite results were obtained. While these foundations were being built the Association survived two serious financial crises—the two years of the influenza epidemic when attendance fell off markedly and the theatre was closed for long periods during the winter months. It was a question whether the organization could survive these blows, but through the financial assistance of interested friends the work continued.

During these formative years three attempts were made to obtain a suitable, convenient building through co-operation with commercial projects. Unfortunately the permanence of the playhouse not being sufficiently established, the money could not be found and failure resulted.

One project almost won through when the Association encountered its severest test and passed the most critical period of its career. The coming to Pasadena of a professional stock company, which, encouraged by the success of the Community Players, put on good plays in a new modern theatre near the old, poorly ventilated and heated, dilapidated Playhouse, brought competition almost too great to overcome.

At once all hope of a new theatre was gone, and the very existence of the movement threatened. This challenge only stim-

ulated the players and their friends to greater efforts to prove that they had at last become a necessary, a vital factor in the community life of the city. That the average theatre goer should flock to this new toy was to be expected; the first year of this unanticipated competition demanded unswerving loyalty and devotion. Again a large financial loss was incurred. However, the following winter the players by raising their work to a high standard of acting and production, won back their audience, and the value of permanence of the organization was universally acknowledged.

Thus encouraged a serious businesslike campaign was started to build a suitable theatre for the exclusive use of the players. The public generously supported the project, a lot was purchased, plans drawn, and money donated. At the end of two years of steady advancement, the building was finished. The players and their friends, 3000 strong, moved triumphantly into their new home, eight years after a building committee appointed far back in 1917, to "obtain a suitable building" reported "progress."

In the same publication as the previous article was another, "Facts and Figures," by Robert O. Foote, one of the active members of the Playhouse.

46:2   The present Playhouse was opened May 18, 1925, after nearly nine years of operations in a little old ex-burlesque house on North Fair Oaks Avenue.

The Playhouse seats 820 persons, 608 on the main floor and 212 in the balcony. Depth of auditorium is 69 feet, 2 inches; height, 33 feet, 1 inch; width, 63 feet, 11 inches. It is built upon a lot 110 by 195 feet.

The dimensions of the stage are: Height of proscenium, 20 feet; width of

46:2. Robert O. Foote, "Facts and Figures," *Pasadena Community Playhouse Association Year Book, 1925–26,* (Pasadena: The Playhouse, 1926), pp. 11, 16.

stage opening, 31 feet, 6 inches; depth of stage from curtain line to rear wall, 30 feet, 11 inches; width of stage from wall to wall, 80 feet; height of fly loft from stage level, 67 feet; forty-five sets of rope lines; twenty-one sets of counter weight work lines; 116 dimmers on switchboard; four light boarders; approximate number of lights in auditorium, 974.

Seating capacity of the Recital Hall, 300. The Recital Hall is 26 feet, 10 inches wide and 78 feet long; stage, width 19 feet, 8 inches; depth, 10 feet, 3 inches; height, 9 feet, 4 inches.

There are 11 exits off the auditorium and the amount of time necessary to empty capacity houses is three minutes.

There are 1000 costumes in the wardrobe, of an approximate value of $7,000.

Twenty-eight regular plays have been given in the new Playhouse, with 275 performances. Approximately 700 persons have participated in the plays and about 500 people have worked on the production and costume committees.

The acoustic perfection of the auditorium is assured by the scientific treatment of the ceiling which is covered with two inches of felt and open-meshed cloth.

The heating and ventilating system provides for a great volume of water-washed and moistened air, circulating downward from openings beneath the ceiling and out by openings under the seats, in such quantity as to be wholly without drafts and regulated or heated to the proper temperature by means of numerous thermostats.

The switchboard cost $15,000 and weighs 6 tons. Through it all the lighting units are controlled by one man. The lighting plant, in addition to the usual stage lights, has disappearing foot-lights, electricians gallery, concealed spot lights in the false boxes in front of the stage, an anti[ante]-proscenium gallery for lighting in front of the regular stage opening, and a disappearing foot-light in rear of stage. For handling the scenery are six

miles of rope and three miles of steel cable. The "grid" from which hangs all the scenery equipment weighs 27 tons, and is suspended from the roof 67 feet above the floor. Light in four colors is used throughout the theatre—white, California gold and two new shades of red and blue, never before seen in a theatre.

The Green Room beneath the stage is the home of the actors. Around this and leading from it are ten dressing rooms, two chorus rooms, make-up room, costume room, musicians' room, ushers' room, toilets and showers, and kitchen. Cast dinners and other social affairs are held in the Green Room.

The stone pavement in the court is made of petrified sea plants and ferns. It was found 200 miles from the sea in Nevada at an elevation of 5,000 feet.

There are 18 inter-phones and 8 outside phones.

The total value of the entire plant is over $400,000.

There are 66 rooms of all kinds in the building.

Each play is rehearsed an average of eighteen times.

Over 100,000 pieces of mailing matter were sent out last year from the office. Over $130,000 is handled each year through the business office. Practically all printed material used by the Playhouse with the exception of the Playhouse News and the tickets is done in the Playhouse. All financial details involved in the operation and maintenance of the building are handled through the Playhouse office.

In 1943 an article brought the history up to that date.

46:3   On May 18, 1925, with paint still tempting to the inquisitive finger and concrete not completely set, the curtain went up in the new Playhouse on Victor Mapes' *The Amethyst.*

46:3. "And Then . . . May 18, 1925," *And Then . . . the Pasadena Playhouse* (Pasadena: The Playhouse, 1943).

There seldom has been so proud an audience. And with good cause. Its members had built a far better theater than the ambitious dreams of most had dared conceive. In so doing they proved to the most sceptical critics that real drama was very much alive and enthusiastically supported 3000 miles from the canyons of Manhattan.

Just as far removed from the New York idea of a theatre was the Playhouse building itself. It was designed to hide its modern efficiency behind the leisurely effect of soft adobe and red tile, of curving staircases, playing fountains and fronded palms. From the patio to the stage, the Playhouse is architecturally a lovely reminder of California's heritage from the days of the dons and the mission padres.

However, even the most rabid of streamlined modern architects will admit that the Playhouse stands as a model of what an efficient play-producing plant should be. Its success as a functional unit has been proved repeatedly in the years since its curtain had its first proud rising.

The first years in the new building brought expansion in every department of Playhouse affairs. They brought satisfaction, to be sure; yet, on the other side of the ledger was a bonded debt of approximately $200,000. Interest and principal payments haunted the management with visions of bankruptcy should unforeseen events suddenly throw akilter the delicate balance of income and outgo. Several factors, however, served considerably to brighten this picture.

The never to be forgotten part Mrs. Fannie Morrison played in strengthening and extending the Playhouse at this time and later is a simple but greatly significant chapter in its history. In May, 1930, this quiet lady inquired at the Playhouse box office as to how she might help the Association. Told of the heavy mortgage which was preventing the organization from making any definitely great strides forward, she sent the Association a check for $180,000 to lift this bonded debt.

Again, in 1936, Mrs. Morrison donated $160,000 for the acquisition of property adjoining the Playhouse and for the erection of the new six-story annex, which for the first time made it possible to house all the various departments under one roof.

Second important factor was the reorganization of the Playhouse into two major departments . . . production and business. Gilmore Brown became Supervising Director and assumed charge of production; Charles Prickett, retaining his position as head of the business department, became General Manager. In this way, a synchronization of the various sub-departments, in both production and business was achieved. This eliminated waste and friction, kept red ink to a minimum during depression years.

Physical expansion, moreover, increased Playhouse problems other than of a financial nature. The dangers of professionalism, of separation of Playhouse and community, of a gradual decline in cultural and artistic integrity might have become real had not a system of organization capable of preventing them been evolved.

In the fore of that system is the loyal audience built up over the years—an intelligent, critical audience which can be said to be almost permanent.

With a high dramatic goal in view, plays for the winter season are selected during the summer by Gilmore Brown, who works out a schedule of dates for each production. From this point organization steps are as follows:

Six to ten weeks before an opening date, casting committee, director, and assistants meet to read and discuss the play. From a card index of some 1000 volunteer actors a cast is selected and tryouts are held. Weeks of intensive rehearsal follow.

Meanwhile, sets are designed and made up in model form. Details are worked out

44. Le Petit Théâtre du Vieux Carré, New Orleans, 1923. Courtesy of Louisiana Landmarks Society Collection, Special Collections Division, Tulane University Library.

44. Courtyard, Le Petit Théâtre du Vieux Carré, New Orleans, 1923. Color photography by Grant L. Robertson.

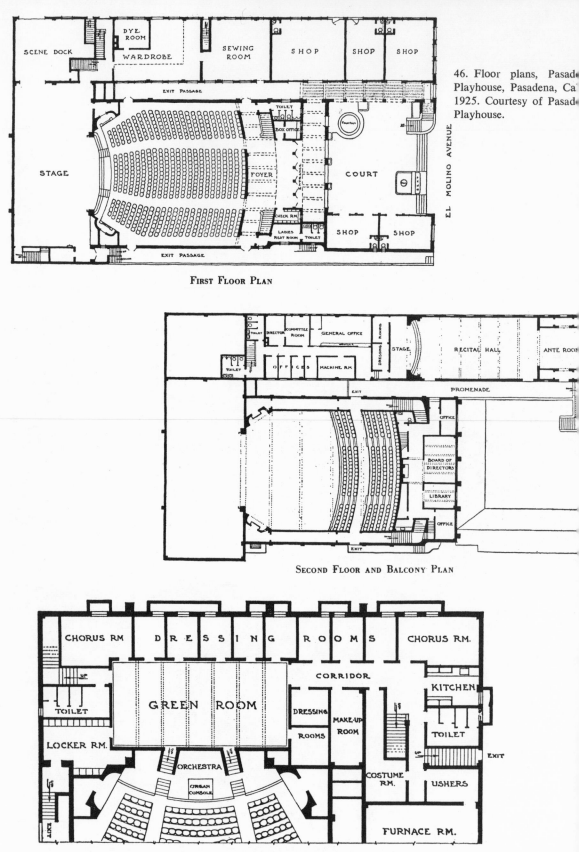

FIRST FLOOR PLAN

46. Floor plans, Pasad...
Playhouse, Pasadena, Ca...
1925. Courtesy of Pasad...
Playhouse.

SECOND FLOOR AND BALCONY PLAN

BASEMENT PLAN

with the Stage Manager and his assistants. Building, painting, and decorating of sets is done in the Playhouse workshop. The Costume Committee makes costumes or selects them from the Playhouse Wardrobe, which contains 10,000 costumes valued at $40,000. The Production Committee assembles the properties from the huge Playhouse property room or obtains loans of furniture and needed accessories from stores and friends.

During this preparation, the Business Office sees that tickets are sold, programs made up, publicity and advertising effectively circulated.

Finally opening night arrives. In the audience, as the footlights go up, are the familiar faces of many who have long been Playhouse "first nighters" and who form the backbone of the patronage that has kept the Playhouse alive these many years. Almost invariably there will be visitors from afar, for the reputation of the Playhouse has spread over the world and it has become a sort of mecca for those who love good drama. Then, too, there will be super-critical patrons who visit the Playhouse in their professional capacities in search of new material, both plays and players, so frequently found on the Playhouse stages. For the Playhouse is widely recognized as the most fertile source of new faces in the dramatic arts. Those whom its stages have helped include some of the most famous names in lights today, as well as many who, though still obscure, are aided in their struggle toward professional recognition by the impetus of their work at the Playhouse.

47. CLEVELAND PLAY HOUSE
Cleveland, Ohio
Opened April 9, 1927

47:1   The Cleveland Play House is an out-

47:1. Edith J. R. Isaacs, *Architecture for the New Theatre* (New York: Theatre Arts Books, 1935), pp. 46–47. Copyright 1934, 1935 by Theatre Arts, Inc.

standing example of a city theatre built to meet the needs of an organized permanent company carrying on a heavy production program in a main auditorium, and experimental work on a smaller stage in the same building.

Red brick with red sandstone trim and graduated slate roofs. Mass composition good. Stage tower an effective expression of a difficult element. Excellent auditorium completely panelled in knotty pine, good acoustically and in color. Balcony rather low. Portals beside proscenium do not improve acoustics. Seating rows spaced too closely. Horizontal sightlines very good. Stage quite high above auditorium floor. Reasonable area for circulation. One end of lounge used as smoking room. Small court included in lounging space in good weather. Interesting double use of areas for large and small auditoriums. Fine arrangement of two stages for joint use of shops, docks, and dressing rooms. Main stage a good working size, completely trapped. No cross-over on stage when plastered back wall is used as cyclorama. Riggings worked from fly gallery stage left. Spot booth and ceiling beam outlets. Removable steps over orchestra pit. Dressing room with exterior balcony over lobby. Ample workshops and dock, paint frame and well. small property room, storage on loft over dock and under stage. Wardrobe area small, supplemented by attic spaces. Completely equipped laboratory theatre seating 154. Traps, switchboard, gridiron, good depth on stage, front-of-house lighting, no footlights. Rehearsal or ballet room on upper floor with large open-air deck. Lunch room next to kitchen on third floor. Library, staff reading room, study room, anteroom between dressing room corridor and stage. Two telephone booths. Office.

So Edith Isaacs described the Cleveland Play House in 1935. This remarkable organization had its beginnings back in 1915, and in the early 1970s was still a vigorous project, using three different theater buildings for its productions.

A brief history of the Cleveland Play House written in 1963 by Ruth Fischer describes the organization and growth of the Play House from its inception.

47:2   "To be fully alive to ideas and beauty, every large city needs its own theatre as it needs its own library, musical center, forums and art museums." This statement was made some time ago by Brooks Atkinson, distinguished drama writer for the New York Times.

Many years earlier a group of Clevelanders with remarkable insight into the city's cultural needs launched the Cleveland Play House—thus giving expression to Mr. Atkinson's wise counsel long before he had enunciated it. Today, almost half a century later, the Play House is a professional resident theatre which stands second to none in the nation for the quality of its productions and for its educational service to the community.

It was during the years from 1915 to 1920 that a group of non-professional theatre enthusiasts gathered together to create a theatre for themselves—in protest against and in relief from the stereotype conventional commercial theatre then current. They met in attics, living rooms and coach houses to read and discuss new plays and new ideas of the "art of the theatre" which were then beginning to filter through from Europe. From this beginning the Cleveland Play House was founded.

The group was on a decidedly amateur level, as indeed were many similar groups throughout the country during the era of World War I. In 1917 an old church was converted into a theatre building and for a few seasons a number of plays were presented, many of them provocative and beautiful. Some members of the group had dreams of professional careers in the theatre, but they were otherwise engaged in their own occupations. In 1920 the organization disintegrated and ceased to function except in a casual and desultory way.

Frederic McConnell was engaged in 1921 to take over professional direction of the Play House. He was given a free hand and a clear field, a policy which has prevailed ever since: the trustees appoint a director; he in turn engages a staff and is responsible for the management of the theatre within the limits of a budget prepared by him and approved by the theatre.

Two professional assistants were engaged, K. Elmo Lowe as associate director and the late Max Eisenstadt as co-worker. This was a milestone in the development of professionalism within the framework of the American amateur community theatre. During the next five years nine additional staff engagements were made. Today this number has grown to seventy-five.

In 1927 the present building on East 86th Street was erected on land donated by Mr. and Mrs. Francis E. Drury. The structure is of Romanesque design and contains two theatres, parallel to each other and sharing shop facilities, dressing rooms and administrative office.

The larger of the theatres was named for Mr. Drury. It seats 530 and today, more than three decades after its opening, it still occupies a unique place in contemporary style. The companion small theatre, under the same roof and adjacent to the Drury, was named after Charles S. Brooks, first president of the Play House. The Brooks seats 160 in its intimate, brick-lined interior.

In the middle forties, realizing a need for a third theatre, the Play House acquired a former church building a few blocks away at Euclid and East 77th Street and, after extensive remodeling, the Euclid–77th Theatre became a reality in 1949. It has 560 seats and its general

47:2. Ruth Fischer, *The Cleveland Play House* (Cleveland: The Play House, 1963), pp. 1–5.

plan, conceived by Frederic McConnell, represents a radical departure from conventional design. The audience is seated in a high-banked, fan-shaped auditorium. There is no proscenium arch and the open, semicircular stage projects out into the seating area. Its style, derived from classic Greek, Roman and Elizabethan theatres initiated a new trend in theatre design and pioneered the development of the modern stage. Architect for the Play House buildings was Francis K. Droz.

In 1958 K. Elmo Lowe became executive director of the Play House following the retirement of Frederic McConnell, who continued to serve in the capacity of consulting director until he left Cleveland in 1963. Writing on the occasion of his retirement, Mr. McConnell said:

"It is the human structure that counts most. Daily at the Play House scores of paid actors, designers, directors, technicians and administrative personnel are busy on a strenuous program of performing and preparing a series of plays. In an average day there is a public performance in each of the three theatres, three other plays are in rehearsal and scenic preparation, and there is the usual quota of meetings, conferences, auditions, study, planning, script reading and research with —thrown in as a fillip—rumor and gossip, laughter and tears."

As a non-profit organization, how has the Cleveland Play House been supported during the decades of its phenomenal growth? Acquisition and construction of the buildings were financed by community contributions, a mortgage, and help from the Rockefeller Foundation. Box office receipts (including season ticket sales) cover 90% of operating costs. The Play House Fund, made up of contributions from individuals, foundations and other organizations, supplies the necessary financial aid for maintenance and operations. Since the Play House has no endowment or income other than that derived from operations, the annual acti-

vation of the Play House Fund is necessary for its survival.

Ticket prices are modest so that living theatre may be available to members of all income groups. Students are eligible for special rates to all productions; the price of a student ticket to the Play House is comparable to the cost of attending a movie. Members of the armed forces are admitted free.

During its slow but steady transition to professionalism, the Play House has weathered depressions, wars, sound pictures, the radio and TV. But despite fluctuations in its fortunes, the Play House has continued to present the finest plays of all time. A list of nearly 800 productions discloses an extraordinary number of exceptional dramas covering the wide span from Greek classics to outstanding contemporary works. It is the stated policy of the Play House to leave show business as such to the commercial profit-making enterprises already set up for that purpose and to keep the routine entertainment piece to a minimum.

With such a policy, the Play House makes an inestimable contribution to the Cleveland Community and to the theatre world. . . .

Director of the Play House until 1963, McConnell wrote about the new Euclid–77th Street Theatre acquired by the Cleveland Play House as an additional theater, giving the group more flexibility.

47:3 AN OPEN STAGE AND A RETURN TO STYLE:
AIMS OF THE TRANSITIONAL THEATRE

Play House in Cleveland Wins 10-Year
Freedom From Proscenium

by Frederic McConnell
Cleveland

Interest in the open stage has been

47:3. Reprinted by permission from *The Christian Science Monitor*, Sept. 3, 1960. © 1960 The Christian Science Publishing Society. All rights reserved.

heightened by recent events. The new Dallas Theater Center, conceived by Paul Baker and designed by Frank Lloyd Wright, has completed its first season. Plans of the Lincoln Center for the Performing Arts call for a repertory theater with a flexible stage, making possible the presenting of plays in free rein in front of the proscenium.

Meanwhile the Cleveland Play House, which has been a pioneer in the field of the open stage, has just concluded a revealing ten-year demonstration of its practicality. Some 75 plays of all types have been acted in the Euclid–77th amphitheater designed by the writer, with Francis K. Droz as architect, and built in 1949. A continuing audience of 400,000 people has been witness to the event.

The Euclid–77th embraces the basic principles evolved in the Greek, Roman, and Elizabethan theaters—a shelf for acting and a shell for lighting. The stage is 65 feet wide and 33 feet deep. A forestage extends 12 feet into the auditorium from shallow wings at the side, tapering to a width of 30 feet as it makes contact with the auditorium which follows a natural elliptical curve around the stage on three sides. This allows for an oblique view of the action, but does not force the audience to stare at itself across the stage and past the profile of the actors.

The whole thing, when the lights are down and the play is on, can be magic. "In fact," Brooks Atkinson once wrote, "the relationship of audience to stage is so normal that a playgoer hardly has time to realize that it is novel and revolutionary."

We determined at the outset against the doctrinaire idea that this stage would serve only the classics, for which such a stage was the norm. We were prepared to produce most of the plays which were likely to be in our future repertory, particularly works of realism.

Some authorities have persistently maintained that the realistic drama has no place on the open stage because realism requires elements of scenic illusion which can only be accommodated by the conventional proscenium and curtain. By providing some room and enclosure at the rear of our stage area, we have been able to install necessary scenic elements. These have been required, however, to conform to an esthetic and organic domain.

ACTOR MUST CRASH OUT

Here, indeed, Appia's corporeal actor must assert his sovereignty, burst through the fourth wall, leaving the proscenium and tons of scenery behind, and no longer heed the frantic cry of the director out front, "stay back there, you're out of the picture."

While there may be precedent for the open stage to be bare, there is none for it to be barren. Recorded in every chapter of theater history are examples of illusionistic embellishment and efforts toward contemporary connotation and a satisfaction of the eye's demand for artistic harmony. It would seem from the record that there never was an open stage which deprived the contemporary beholder of what was to him a picture.

So far as the illusionistic picture is concerned, there is of course a great difference between movable, photographic scenery and the fixed plastic form. We have found that many plays which apparently demanded realistic settings can be justly served on the curtainless, no-proscenium stage by indigenous, nondefinitive, architectural treatment. Such treatment enhances and objectifies the line of story and character.

CONCORDANT ILLUSION

By applying discretion and selectivity, by using such ancient devices as unit and multiple sets, we segregate the scene in space. Scenic elements and the whole composition are tapered, phrased, and blended in this space, just as a building is sculptured against the background of an open sky. Formalization and esthetic unity contribute a concordant illusion which transcends material and external garnish.

Of course, we cannot do "Uncle Tom's Cabin" or "Ben-Hur" or such contemporary genre as "Fair Game" or "The World of Susie Wong." But we have gained satisfaction and success with other plays, such as, for example, "The Crucible," "Darkness at Noon," "The Cocktail Party," "A Streetcar Named Desire," "Come Back Little Sheba," "Pygmalion," "Desire Under the Elms," "The Diary of Anne Frank," and "Rashomon."

All of these plays were written for the conventional theater. When staged afresh in the environment of the open stage and with new but age-old techniques, they not only retained their life and liveliness but took on new bite, magnificence, and urgency.

The stage in exercising its function to translate the author's thought and word must do it in terms of itself, if full expression is to be realized. That fullness seems realized eloquently on the open stage. The playwright gains new freedom and a welcome release from the conventional stage which provides almost the only market for his wares. For the playwright, the open stage, because of its very structure, illuminates communication and conveys more fully to the audience the play's inner spirit. This is an attribute which, if not expressly evinced by the audience, is nonetheless profoundly felt by it.

Whatever realities may be in the playwright's mind, they are best communicated to the audience by means of suggestion and imagination, through feeling the unconscious realization. "A View From the Bridge" does not need all of Brooklyn Bridge spread across a cyclorama; better, two or three actors, emerging from an eloquent emptiness into the ambience of a pool of light. This freedom of mutable space presents no impediment to the flow of action, no enclosure to imprison the imagination, and no convention to hamstring the director, actor and playwright. The designer for such a stage must be an architect, a creator of space, as well as a painter.

NOSTALGIA FOR PEEPS

Some ancients among us may suffer nostalgia for the peephole and the fourth wall, largely because they grew up with them. But we must remember that the proscenium frame never was in fact a constituent and organic part of the theater whole. Nor was it installed from any demand or need of the actor or playwright.

It was, rather, primarily a device to provide a showcase wherein the Renaissance dilettante might play with paint, perspective, and machines, as well as opera and spectacle.

Today, the proscenium—especially for those of us interested in serious theater—is for the most part artificial, ostentatious, anomalous, and in the way. There is little which the open stage cannot do better, with less obtrusion and more truth.

Why should now the playwright, producer, actor and designer be enslaved in and to a structure never intended for them, nor they for it, but to which they have been battened for generations, through the force of tradition and the inability of architects and entrepreneurs otherwise to comprehend? Meanwhile, although other media have preempted the theater of its tricks, none of them has as yet given us the actor on a podium out front.

The Cleveland Play House, as of 10 years ago, and others since, in America and England, now point the way toward endowing the open stage with other than theoretical use as the true practicable stage for the production of drama now and in future. In its organic wholeness and dynamic propulsion the theater of the open stage is not only the historical but natural forum in which to display what the theater has best to say.

A veteran of the United States professional theater outside New York, Mr. McConnell was engaged in 1921 as the first director of the Cleveland Play House and was the founder of the policy of operating the theater on a professional basis. He is now Consulting Director.

The *Architectural Record* had a detailed report by McConnell on the Play House.

47:4 The New Cleveland Playhouse is designed to accommodate the needs of a thorough-going and active repertory theatre where emphasis is put upon creative work in all branches of theatre art, where not only a season of important and significant plays can be produced with adequate and modern stage facilities by a permanent company, but also where the most important of these productions may be kept in the repertory of the theatre and saved intact both as to equipment and personnel for reproduction through a given season or in successive seasons. For the past five years the Playhouse has been conducting an experiment in building up the repertory theatre idea and the success of that venture in the rather small building in which it has been housed has justified the carrying on of the experiment in larger quarters and with more adequate facilities. The repertory principle seems to be a basic part of the new independent theatres that gradually are claiming attention throughout America, particularly outside of New York City. A revival of interest in good plays and original and interesting stage production on the part of many local communities is tending to give strength and importance to the efforts of these independent local theatres and is giving them an importance in the community equal to that of the art museum, the orchestra and other artistic institutions.

The new Playhouse is unique in that it will house two theatres, one seating five

47:4. Frederic McConnell, "The Cleveland Playhouse," *Architectural Record* 62:81–94 (Aug. 1927).

hundred persons, and the other two hundred persons. In the first theatre will be maintained the present policy of independent repertory, producing by means of a permanent direction, a more or less permanent production and acting ensemble; of a constantly increasing regular and, for the most part, permanent and built-up audience; of a program of plays of unusual interest and distinction, and plays which cannot, generally speaking, meet the commercial quotient of the regular commerical theatre.

In the smaller theatre which is to be known as the "studio" theatre the Play House will develop a major program of three parts:

(1) To provide leisurely and thorough experimentation in the arts of stage production and in the technic of play-writing, affording opportunity for try-outs of manuscript material and the development of composition through the stages of rehearsal and practice.

(2) To make possible, in connection with, and supplementary to, the program of the main theatre, the presentation of classics in dramatic literature and other plays of especial literary quality and distinctive novelty or newness, which in the first instance need not depend upon immediate or general popularity. Standing by itself such a theatre would have to depend upon some form of private endowment. But as an integral part of the entire Playhouse Program the highly specialized work of the "studio" theatre will be "carried" by the budget of the main plant.

(3) To provide a laboratory where student members of the Playhouse organization as well as young men and women of talent within the community or within the reach of the community may undergo explicit

training in the arts of the theatre by virtue of contact with definite theatre production. Besides training people who attach themselves to the theatre specifically for that purpose, the Playhouse hopes throughout the intimate contacts of this laboratory theatre to discover fresh talent and to interest and assure its development.

The "studio" theatre is a significant step in theatre planning because of its relationship to the main theatre with which it will share the most important element in the development of the artist, immediate contact with his public. The repertory and personnel of the two stages will interchange freely, and as a practical matter the spirit of experimentation set afoot in the "studio" theatre will, because of the close relationship between the two theatres, be quickly absorbed by and reflected in the work of the main producing theatre. Interchangeably between the two theatres emphasis will be constantly divided between building up and maintaining on the one hand a definite public taste for fine theatre values, and on the other hand, of training a personnel to interpret adequately the type of play expected by this public.

Quite the most important feature of any theatre is the audience from which it derives its support. A repertory theatre like the Playhouse is supported in a large measure by subscribers who purchase in advance a season ticket to the year's program of from twelve to twenty productions. This audience, therefore, is in constant attendance and is, in fact, as great a part of the permanent structure of the theatre as is the personnel itself. The interest of this audience is stimulated not only by the entertainment afforded by attending the plays but also from the friendly and intimate atmosphere provided in that part of the building which it is its privilege to frequent.

Artistic economy requires that a production be made from the ground up and on the premises. Furthermore, after the initial run of the play is over in a repertory theatre it is necessary that the production be kept for later repetition and revival, even though in the meantime other productions have to be completed and presented. Repertory does not eschew a successful run. Like any other theatre the repertory theatre thrives and prospers on the success of its stage presentations, but it must first preserve the continuity of its program, and the succession of a series of plays must not be disrupted by a single successful long run. Space and facilities have been provided, therefore, to adequately keep in storage a number of productions which later are to be replaced in the repertory, either during the season current or in years that follow. At the Playhouse, for example, a number of productions have been given in revival for five years and these plays are as much a part of the tradition of the theatre as some of the personalities that in time have grown up with the theatre. A permanent staff ensemble and production staff must attach to a theatre of this character and in the new plan facilities have been provided for their accommodation, study, rehearsal and recreation.

The heart of this enterprise is in the dual theatre plan above discussed. The architects, Philip Lindsley Small and Charles Bacon Rowley of Cleveland, have had from the start a special problem. First the usual problem of confining the building within a given space, and second of providing rooms for the rather special artistic and social purposes of the building, of necessity placed so as to be equally accessible to both theatres.

On the main floor is a large shop area set between the two large stages and serving as a production center for the entire theatre. In this area are the carpenter shop with work bench and shop machinery, two scene docks for storage of scenery, a paint room and movable paint frame, special rooms for the storage of furniture and properties, and numerous closets for electrical equipment and miscellaneous paraphernalia, and an office for the technical director. The costume section on the third floor consists of a sewing room facing upon a light court, a dyeing and drying room, and a vault for wardrobe storage. In the basement there is an auxiliary wardrobe room and another tier of dressing rooms. For further storage of scenery and properties, ample space underneath the large stage is provided. The large stage is sixty feet wide, forty feet deep and seventy feet to the grid and the proscenium is thirty feet wide and twenty-eight feet high. The space between the chairs in the large auditorium and the sight lines are of more than average proportion. The stage merges gracefully into the auditorium by means of a proscenium of utmost simplicity flanked by two portals that extend the full height of the room. A series of curved steps leading from the stage to the auditorium floor, complete the suggestion of intimacy between the stage and the audience. The chairs, of course, have been placed inside the range of the proscenium and from all parts of the room an equitable vision of the stage action is allowed for. A balcony is hung low in the rear and a feature of it is a row of six enclosed loges or boxes, each having its own entrance to the rear aisle. These are placed a little higher than the tiers of four rows in front and afford, of course, an excellent vantage point. The balcony, being hung low, is within comfortable range of the higher part of the stage. With the proscenium open to its height the spectator sitting in the balcony can see to a distance of forty-seven feet from the stage floor. The audience room will be finished entirely in wood and it is designed along simple plastic lines.

The second floor contains a library; an attractive greenroom which can be used for teas, receptions and concerts; a staff room which will be used for round table discussion and writing of plays, for staff meetings and an office for members of the staff; an atelier which is to be used for a scene-designers' studio and general production office.

The third floor plan shows a large rehearsal room which is to be used for rehearsal purposes when the two stages are occupied and which will also be used for classes in dancing, gymnastics and fencing. This room faces upon a flat roof set up against the wall of the small stage house. Later on the flat roof will be made into a hand-ball court. A lunch room and kitchen are also on this floor.

The building is on the corner of East 86th Street and Drury Lane, and, as will be seen from the plans and illustrations, a covered entrance is provided from either street, the main entrance on Drury Lane leading to an open vestibule and a loggia with groined ceiling leading from this to 86th Street. The lobby is a simple brick room with slate floor and very flat barrel vaulted ceiling, about twenty-five feet square, with a box office for both theatres and leads directly to the three important units of the entire plant: first, the public stairs to the green room, library and the corridors which give access to the offices, staff room and atelier and then on to the dressing rooms, and the various other working portions of the establishment which connect the two stages; second, through the lounge to the main auditorium; third, to the auditorium of the studio theatre. Both theatres may operate at the same time without the intermingling of the two audiences.

For the "long pause," the audience of the larger theatre has available the lounge and its adjoining smoking room, and in mild weather they may pass from this to the court where coffee will be served. Service for this court as well as for the greenroom, staff room and lunch room, is taken care of by a dumb-waiter which is available to each floor of the building.

The essence of the plan lies in so placing the two theatres that the public is served with one box office in a foyer which connects both of them and gives access to the other public space and the working space beyond which lies in the center of the building around a central court, and also that the shop area and dressing room units both connect the two stages. This will be clear from the plans.

The exterior of the building is in brick with red sandstone trim and graduated slate roof, a simple plastic expression of the various units enclosed. It is almost entirely free from ornament and is an admirable example of the dignity, character and beauty obtained by well studied mass, line, texture, color and silhouette without use of embellishment.

48. BARTER THEATRE
Abingdon, Virginia
Opened June 10, 1933

Certainly one of the most unusual theaters in American theatrical history is the Barter Theatre, designated in 1946 as the official theater of the State of Virginia. Born during the depression era, when acting jobs were almost nonexistent and potential audiences without money, the Barter Theatre opened its doors on a "barter" system. Each spectator brought some farm or food product in lieu of money. In this way the actors had food and the people had entertainment.

The story of the Barter Theatre appeared in *Virginia Cavalcade*.

48:1   Cocoanut cream pie has never meant slapstick at Abingdon, but the price of admission to the Barter Theatre. Looking back, barter sounds like the logical answer to the depression's lack of dollars and it

48:1. Reprinted from Ulrich Troubetzkoy's "From Sophocles to Arthur Miller: The Barter Theatre of Virginia," *Virginia Cavalcade*, vol. 10, no. 1 (Summer, 1960), 4–10, by permission of *Virginia Cavalcade* magazine. Copyright 1960 by the Virginia State Library.

seems natural to have a theatre at Abingdon, in the hills of Washington County. But twenty-eight years ago it took the pioneering spirit of Daniel Boone, plus the skills and experience of Broadway and a depression-born courage, even to think of opening a theatre in the "Bible Belt" 600 miles from Columbus Circle.

Of course, as founder Bob Porterfield would point out, it isn't so far "off Broadway" after all, but actually at a very convenient midway point between New York and New Orleans on U.S. Route 11. He could remind us that theatre-going is a very old Virginia tradition, for the first play, *Ye Beare & ye Cubb* was given at Accomac, on the Eastern Shore, in 1665, and, in August 1952, the Barter players celebrated with their own Shakespeare company the two hundredth anniversary of the Hallams' performance of *The Merchant of Venice* in the theatre on Waller Street in Williamsburg. Nevertheless, an estimated ninety percent of all Virginians had never seen "live theatre" before Barter went on its first tour.

In the lean of summer of 1932, when many an actor's only producing line was, "Brother, can you spare a dime?," Porterfield was on tour with Walter Hampden in *Cyrano de Bergerac*. With a farmer's eye and an actor's stomach, he surveyed thriving fields of crops which would go unsold for lack of dollars. Pondering how to get hungry actors and the farmers' surpluses together, Porterfield came up with the idea for a theatre for which admission would be paid in produce.

"Why don't we trade what we have —entertainment—for what they have? Let's let people barter their admission with eggs and corn, barley and ham . . ."

"Most of it would come across the footlights," exclaimed Hampden pessimistically.

Porterfield confided the brainstorm to another friend, the great actress, Jane Cowl, telling her of his father's farm, "Twin Oaks," and the old unused theatre at Abingdon. She too shook her head. "Actors in your back country? Impossible!" But she gave him a tiny inch-high statuette.

"This is Saint Rita, patron saint of the impossible. Carry it with you. And if by chance you succeed, pass it along to someone else who is attempting the impossible."

When the tour ended, Porterfield was one of the many actors who found himself uncomfortably "at liberty." Theatres were closing and other actors were queuing up at bread lines. But he did have a place to go—albeit an unlikely one for an actor—and he had a plan, not just for himself, but for 22 other actors who needed roofs, over their heads and food to eat.

Thanks to the depression, some of the best actors, who would not ordinarily stray far from Broadway, were willing to take the gamble and make themselves available for a theatre in what must have seemed almost the wilderness of Daniel Boone who had named the Wolf Hills to which they were bound. Happily the quiet but appealing town of Abingdon turned out to be a backdrop far less wild than they anticipated with Porterfield's barter plan in action, they ate well that year even if they had little hard money to jingle in their jeans.

Porterfield and his patron saint arrived in a baggage car, guarding the flats he had wheedled from a road company of *Rose Marie*. The other twenty-two actors arrived as best they could—by jalopy, bicycle, foot, or by thumbing rides.

Since Revolutionary days, the "Twin Oaks" farm in Glade Spring, had been in Porterfield's family whose traditions were as conservative as those of the community. "Not one of my sons is going into that wicked profession!" had been his father's reaction when Robert talked of the theatre—and he had only partly relented.

The townspeople had similar misgivings. The only theatre, if any, they had encountered had been a few seedy vaudeville acts and fifth-rate touring companies. Por-

terfield, of course, was one of their own people and they gave him the benefit of any doubts in his favor they may have had. Porterfield knew them too, so on Sunday his company of actors trooped to the Presbyterian Church. When they all rose to sing "Rock of Ages" they were even more impressed by a baritone that boomed out from the back of the church. That was quality they could understand and appreciate.

Porterfield appreciated but he did not understand, for he had not thought of the old character actor as much of a churchgoer. Afterwards the baritone confided to Porterfield: "Certainly brought back memories. I learned that song years ago in a show."

It still took subtle diplomacy of which, fortunately, Porterfield had plenty, to get living quarters, for the colonial doors of the historic little town were not readily opened to, well, "strolling players." With his actors sheltered, there was still the problem of props which had to be begged, borrowed or created by ingenuity out of odds and ends. Fortunately, there was an old theatre which long ago had known Fay Templeton and the Booths upon its stage.

Posters were tacked up advertising admission for thirty-five cents or the equivalent in produce: "With vegetables you cannot sell, you can buy a good laugh." A few of the actors hammered out of a fallen-down barn enough nails to put scenery together. Friends donated furniture and dishes.

Finally, on June 10, 1933, the first night audience arrived, lugging country hams, baskets of eggs, home-made pickles and jams, a rooster, a squealing pig and a devil's food cake. The curtain went up on John Golden's *After Tomorrow* to a full house of farmers, mountaineers and a few tourists. Other plays in the ambitious repertoire that summer were *Monkey Hat, Salt Water, Caught Wet, East Lynne, Three Wise Fools* and *The Bobtailed Nag*.

The more plays, they reasoned, the more often the farmers would come with hams, chickens, watermelons and potatoes.

"Nine out of ten theatregoers paid their admissions in anything from beans to cottage cheese," Porterfield recalls. "We ate well and the 'culture-hungry' Virginians thrived on our entertainment."

Barter proved a good name and method. The audience liked it. Travelers talked about it. Critics wrote about it and the story preceded them as the Barter actors went out to play small towns, courthouses and high schools, many of which had never seen live theatre before. They went on tour as far as they could afford gasoline to carry their truck full of scenery. People began putting up extra preserves and planting extra rows of vegetables with the next Barter season in mind.

Fred Allen quipped that the only way Bob Porterfield could tell if he had had a successful season was to weigh his actors. At the end of the first one, there was a cash balance of $4.35, two barrels of jelly and the opening night piglet which had grown up to be the Barter sow. Porterfield did weigh his actors and found that they had gained 305 pounds. It had been, he could tell Fred Allen, a successful season.

The squealing pig bartered on opening night began one of the most celebrated lineages of ham in America and its descendents still live on Porterfield's rolling acres at "Twin Oaks" in Glade Spring. Porterfield made an arrangement with the Dramatists Guild in New York so that, instead of paying the usual royalties for the privilege of producing their plays, the playwrights agreed to accept a Virginia ham as payment in full. It began as a tongue-in-cheek arrangement, but when the Barter sow presented the Porterfields with eight little pigs, it proved the beginning of a line of pigs which would provide hams for most of the best-known playwrights working in England and America, among them Philip Barry, Noel Coward,

John van Druten, John Golden, George Kaufman, Howard Lindsay, Thornton Wilder and Tennessee Williams.

Only George Bernard Shaw objected. "Don't you know I am a vegetarian?" he complained. Porterfield sent him a crate of Virginia-grown spinach. Except for that vegetable, the Barter sow and her descendants have paid the royalties for most of some 300 plays which the Barter Theatre has presented in the last twenty-seven years.

As the depression waned, box office receipts became less edible and easier for accountants to add. Porterfield could no longer look at the receipts and have a pretty good idea who was inside the theatre. It was not quite so apropos for Fred Allen to joke about making change, asking if a man brought a turkey, did they give him back a rabbit and a bunch of carrots. The troupe was spared wholesale "acidosis in tomato season." People still told such stories as that about the farmer who drove his cow to the door and drew his pail of "admission," leaving his wife outside, saying, "Let her draw her own 35 cents." But they themselves paid more and more often in cash. Today's box office gross tops $400,000 a year and Barter has played to more than a million theatregoers in Abingdon alone. The first, and long the only, summer theatre south of Mason and Dixon's Line, it is now the oldest summer theatre under one management in the whole country, and Porterfield has produced more professional plays than any other producer now living in the United States, including 54 world premières. The Barter company hires more professional actors than any non-musical company outside New York.

By the late 1930s, Porterfield had graduated from the barter financing idea to that of making the Barter Theatre an institution partially supported by government funds. But it was not so clear to others then that a State Theatre of Virginia might bring such prestige to the Old

Dominion as the Comédie Française and the "Old Vic" did to Paris and London. He had a selling job to do.

Porterfield arrived at the 1940 session of the General Assembly with an overstuffed barracks bag in tow. He pointed out that, as its members were well aware, tourists were becoming big business in Virginia, but that scenery and historical associations were not enough. "You've got to have something to advertise," he reminded them and, holding the duffle bag high in the air snowed thousands of press clippings over the astonished delegates.

He got promises of state aid which materialized in 1946 with a grant of $10,000 administered by the Department of Conservation and Development. The story is perennially relished on "The Hill" of how Porterfield appeared before the Assembly with the warning that to hold onto tourist dollars, Virginia wasn't offering enough after-dark entertainment.

"Young man," asked a crusty old senator, "What do you mean by after-dark entertainment?"

"I mean, sir, that entertainment you can go home and talk about."

"Give that boy his money!" roars the senator year after year as the story is retold.

The state grant was in recognition of the part Barter was already playing to "assist the Commission in its work of advertising and promoting the educational, cultural and economic interests of the Commonwealth . . . in attracting and encouraging people from other states and countries to visit in the Commonwealth where so many shrines and historical sites of national and international interest are located . . ."

By the agreement made at that time, Barter, as the official State Theatre of Virginia, was to produce twelve plays during June, July and August, 1946 and then go on an extended tour throughout the state with a selected repertory of plays during the remaining nine months. It was to give at least six performances each week, with twenty-five or more professional players and technicians taking part. The number of communities to be visited during the winter season was to depend on the ability of the communities to supply adequate stages.

The state subsidy has continued and increased and, in recent years, has been supplemented by grants from the Old Dominion Foundation, Inc., and various private donors.

In return, Barter Theatre has drawn thousands of tourists to the state and has offered professional performances of hundreds of plays to visitors and residents. Trucks and trailers haul personnel, scenery and props for classic and modern plays to all Virginia's counties, many of which had never enjoyed live theatre before.

But recognition has come from far beyond Virginia. The appealing story of American ingenuity has been translated into many languages, including Russian, and a film of Barter in action has been sent far afield by the United States Information Service. In 1948, this best known stock company in America was invited by the King of Denmark to present its version of *Hamlet* at Kronberg Castle, Elsinore, the first American production ever presented in the historic castle setting of Shakespeare's play. Walter Abel, Aline McMahon, Robert Breen, Clarence Derwent, Ruth Ford, Ray Boyle and Frederick Warriner were members of the Barter cast which played there under auspices of the Department of State, the American National Theatre and Academy and UNESCO.

The Barter Theatre has done a lot for Virginia and the state has done a lot for Barter. What has Barter done for actors and the cause of drama in America?

The Barter Theatre has given valuable training to many young actors and actresses who have found in Abingdon the opportunity to play a variety of roles with regularity, the sort of training needed but often hard to receive today. The "largest stock company of actors outside of Broadway" is a mecca for young actors as well as tourists. Gregory Peck is one of many who looks back with gratitude on Barter's training in versatility. In one play, *Lee of Virginia*, Peck played John Brown in the first act, "Stonewall" Jackson in the second, and U. S. Grant in the third. In one week he appeared in six different plays.

Among other "big names" in the theatre which got a first shine at Barter are Hume Cronyn, Lisbeth Scott, Jeffrey Lynn, Charles Corwin, Larry Gates, Ernest Borgnine. Many Virginians receive their training at Barter, a select two each year on scholarships sponsored by the Virginia Speech and Drama Association for the man and woman displaying outstanding dramatic ability who become apprentices at Barter for the summer. The Ernest Borgnine trophy is given each year to the most promising actor or actress.

There is a dynamic combination of experienced professional actors and "young blood" each year at Barter. Margaret Wycherly, Conrad Nagel and Brock Pemberton are among the many established players who have appeared in Abingdon. When Dame Judith Anderson played in *Family Portrait*, the amphitheatre in Bristol had to be used to accommodate the large audience.

Training is year-'round at Barter. After the close of the summer season at Abingdon, repertory troupes begin their cross-country tours. Porterfield says there are more than 300 cities in which they can play, but he employs no advance booking agent. "I just call a theatre and say we're coming. If they can't accommodate us, we go somewhere else."

One of the most coveted awards in the American theatre is the Barter Theatre of Virginia Award which Porterfield inaugurated in 1939, for an outstanding performance by an American actor or actress during the current season. The recipient receives a trophy potentially more useful than an "Oscar"—an acre of land near Abingdon and a ham and a platter to eat it off of." Not to end completely with two prepositions, the award carries the privilege of nominating two young actors at New York auditions for jobs at the Barter Theatre.

This award has brought to the southwest Virginia hills some of the most distinguished landowners in America including Dorothy Stickney, who won her acre and ham for her performance in *Life with Father,* Ethel Barrymore (*The Corn is Green*), Louis Calhern (*The Magnificent Yankee*), Henry Fonda (*Mister Roberts*), Tallulah Bankhead (*Private Lives*), and Mary Martin (*Peter Pan*).

The Barter Theatre has become so integral a part of the American dramatic scene that records of its productions are now made for filing in the David Belasco New York Library Theatre collection under the direction of George Freedley. Barter is a member too of the International Theatre Liaison of community theatres in the United States which are willing to meet and serve as hosts to foreign drama students visiting this country. Mark Barron of the Associated Press reports that Barter sets the pace for the summer theatre season in America, as the largest active repertory theatre now operating, touring about thirty of the fifty states and grossing about $400,000 annually at the box office, "big money even for a Broadway hit."

For the Barter Theatre's twenty-fifth birthday in 1957, Porterfield invited back all the Barter alumni, from that first group play in the Barter spotlight when they literally lived off the country—Ruth Guiterman, Nell Harrison, Eric Hellberg, Marjorie Lutz, Agnes Ives, Eleanor Power, Marjorie Quigley, Emily Woodruff, Helen Wright, Prentis Abbott, Rickey Austin, Jack Fawcett, Bog Fogle, Storrs Haynes, Robert Hudson, Percy Hunt, H. C. McCollum, Hugh Millerd, Charles Powers, Munsey Slack, S. Slaughter, Arthur Stenning, Bob Stillman, Robert Thomson and Chester Travelstead.

Broadway had come to Abingdon with them in 1932. Today, internationally known Barter Theatre is one of the springboards to Broadway.

Theatre might have been enough, but Porterfield did not stop there. Twelve years ago he decided that Abingdon was ready to embrace all the arts in the Highlands Festival. For two weeks in August, Abingdon goes all out for art and crafts. Shop windows display original paintings. There are craft demonstrations, poetry readings, antique shows and musical programs of many kinds. But after dark, of course, everyone goes to the theatre furnished with the brass, crystal and brocades of the old Empire Theatre in New York. One of the few which still carries on a traditional repertory, tourists can see a number of plays during each week of the festival. This year's repertory includes such variety as Noel Coward's *Fallen Angels,* William Inge's *Dark at the Top of the Stairs* and *Regions of Noon*, whose première took place on June 27.

How did it all begin? "Chatauqua readings," says Porterfield, and the glamorous example of a cousin who ran away to become a wire-walker in the circus. Porterfield, in a bed-sheet toga, played Marc Antony in the Saltville High School and, after a year at Hampden-Sydney, went off to Broadway. Since then he has taken Broadway back to Saltville many times, as the producer of more plays than any man living in America.

49. OLD GLOBE THEATRE
San Diego, California
Opened May 2, 1935

The Old Globe Theatre was originally conceived by Thomas Wood Stevens, director of the Goodman Memorial Theatre in Chicago, for Chicago's Century of Progress in 1933; it was finally constructed in San Diego, California, and opened in conjunction with the California

Pacific International Exposition in 1935. When the Exposition closed, a group of San Diego citizens provided the money to purchase the building for use as a community theater.

The following account appeared in a 1970 souvenir program commemorating the theater's anniversary:

49:1   The thirty-five year history of the Old Globe Theatre, home of the San Diego National Shakespeare Festival, reads like a melodrama scenario, complete with "foreclosure," a war, and the traditional happy ending.

A re-creation of the renowned Globe Theatre of Shakespeare's time, built from plans originally researched by Thomas Wood Stevens for the Chicago "Century of Progress" in 1933, the Old Globe opened in San Diego on May 2, 1935. The opening coincided with that of the California Pacific International Exposition, which continued for two years. During this time, audiences in the at-first authentically roofless theatre for the fifty-minute-long "cut" versions of various Shakespeare plays which Stevens felt were dramatically unimpaired and more acceptable to modern audiences. Prior to each performance, "Queen Elizabeth and her court" viewed traditional morris dances performed in a recessed area in front of the theatre. After the play, the audience could retire to Falsaff Tavern, which at that time provided refreshments now available on "the green," and the spectacle of the "Queen" flinging nearly-gnawed bones over her shoulder in the best tradition of her royal father, Henry VIII.

At the close of the Exposition in 1936, however, the three buildings which comprised the theatre were sold to a wrecking company for $400. Incensed citizens leaped to the defense, and despite the Depression still in full swing, raised $10,000

49:1. Miriam Lennard, "The Old Globe, Living Theatre in a City in Motion," in Old Globe 1970 souvenir program (San Diego, 1970).

in only a few weeks for the purchase and renovation of the buildings to meet building codes and other requirements for a permanent theatre. The San Diego Community Theatre, a non-profit organization, was chartered by the State of California on February 3, 1937. Months of fund-raising and remodeling of the plant followed, and on December 2, 1937, the curtain went up on a four-performance "run" of John van Druten's "The Distaff Side." Total attendance was 701 persons, a far cry from the many thousands who now see each Globe main-stage production.

Four relatively uneventful seasons followed this initial success, but Globe production came to a halt with the beginning of World War II, when the buildings, together with everything else in Balboa Park except the Zoo, were taken over by the U.S. Navy, who continued to utilize the facilities for various purposes until 1947.

Finally, that year, the San Diego Community Theatre was able to resume, under director Craig Noel, whose first production was William Saroyan's "The Time of Your Life." 2431 theatre-hungry San Diegans attended the nine performances, and with each successive season, the Old Globe began to enlarge its scope to the present season of five-stage productions, with a minimum of 25 performances each, seen by a total of about 45,000 play-goers.

In addition to these major productions, the Old Globe brought new theatrical creativity to the community through its arena productions, first staged in La Jolla but in 1963 brought back to the Falstaff Tavern. Funds provided by the Globe Guilders, the women's auxiliary, made possible a large patio and lounges to complete the comfort and usability of the Arena. There, were presented experimental, *avant-garde*, or "theatre of the absurd" plays, together with lesser-known works of traditional playwrights, which attracted an audience with somewhat more esoteric fare than that presented on the main stage.

In 1949, shortly after the post-war reorganization of the theatre, the directors joined with San Diego State College to present a summer Shakespeare Festival. The first season presented *Twelfth Night,* under the direction of B. Iden Payne, an influential Shakespeare scholar and director who had participated in the Exposition productions. The following three years saw two plays presented each summer, but in 1953, the project was abandoned because of apparent lack of audience interest. Instead, the Old Globe presented "Mr. Roberts," which was then a new Broadway smash hit, to 25,000 spectators during 69 performances . . . a record for attendance and number of performances at the Globe.

As in 1936, however, lovers of the traditional theatre rallied to the Bard's cause, and the National Shakespeare Festival was reinstated in 1954, using some paid actors in order to obtain more skilled interpretations. The trend toward a professional repertory company has continued to develop over the last several years until currently, all major roles are taken by professionals, with smaller roles filled by scholarship personnel and apprentices, whose participation is made possible by contribution-supported grants which provide financial assistance to young actors still in training.

In its unceasing effort to bring the finest in theatre arts to the community it serves, the Old Globe in 1966 completed a $300,000 building program which included a new rehearsal hall, dressing rooms, costume construction and storage facilities, scenery and property construction and storage, and administrative offices, as well as new lounges. Nearly one-third of the funds were received from COMBO (Combined fund-raising project). The newest addition to the old Globe Theatre complex is the 245 seat Cassius Carter Centre Stage completed in January of last year at a cost of more than $120,000. It is dedicated to presenting the new and unusual in play-going fare.

The winter season program is discussed in the following article by George Waldo, written in 1968:

49:2   During each winter season, the Old Globe Theatre presents nine contemporary plays to enrich San Diego's year-round program of legitimate theatre. Now completing its twenty-seventh year, the community theatre presents non-professional local talent under the supervision of Craig Noel.

Unlike most community theatres which are dependent on civic or private financial endorsement, the Old Globe is completely self-sustaining, a rarity in the theatre world. In 1937, following the Pacific International Exposition in Balboa Park, $10,000 was raised to save the theatre buildings from destruction. On December 2, 1937, the newly formed San Diego Community Theatre presented four performances of "The Distaff Side," for an audience of 701 persons. The season totaled 41 performances playing to 6,650 patrons and ending with a surplus of $17.70 in the summer of 1938.

Plays were produced each season until the beginning of the Second World War, when the U.S. Navy took over all the park buildings for hospital facilities. Returned to the community theatre after the war, refurbished inside and out by volunteer workers, the theatre re-opened on October 29, 1947 with "The Time of Your Life," which was "guest" directed by Craig Noel. Fortunately, the guest has stayed, and since 1947, a total of 112 major productions have been mounted on the Old Globe Theatre stage.

Memorable productions over the intervening seventeen seasons include the first box office smash hit "Chicken Every Sun-

day" in 1949, the seven original musical revues "Caught in the Act"; the all time champ "Mr. Roberts," playing 13 weeks during the 1953 summer to 25,000 patrons; the eleven week hit of "The Boy Friend"; and eleven weeks of the surprise hit comedy "Under the Yum-Yum Tree." Selected outstanding artistic successes which failed to generate box office appeal included "Montserrat," "Death of a Salesman," "A View from the Bridge" and "The Fantasticks."

The 1963–64 winter-spring season at the Old Globe offered nine productions, four comedies and five dramas, for 195 performances entertaining 49,684 theatregoers.

Today, as in 1937, every facet of the theatre welcomes volunteer workers. The actors, backstage crews, refreshment crews, box office personnel, usherettes and doormen contribute their time and talents because of a love of theatre, a desire to be with others striving toward a common goal of entertaining the public. A dynamic woman's committee, the Globe Guilders, organize, decorate, promote and function at social activities and raise funds for necessary theatre improvements.

The twenty member Board of Directors (civic leaders, professional men and business executives) govern the Old Globe Theatre to determine policy and plan future growth, implemented by a professional staff.

Visitors to San Diego are frequently surprised as they wander through the fourteen hundred acre expanse that is Balboa Park to come upon a little "village green," surrounded on two sides by buildings in the style of the sixteenth century. But even more surprising is the value of this small group of buildings to the community as a center of dramatic entertainment.

And the Old Globe has met this challenge squarely. Season after season it presents the best in comedy and drama. Recently it has expanded the number of

49:2. George Waldo, "When Winter Comes . . .," in Old Globe 1964 souvenir program (San Diego, 1964).

46. Interior, Pasadena Playhouse, Pasadena, Calif., 1925. Published in *Theatre Magazine* (June 1926). Courtesy of The Hoblitzelle Theatre Arts Library, The Humanities Research Center, The University of Texas at Austin.

47. Cleveland Play House, Drury Theatre, Cleveland, 1927. Courtesy of the Cleveland Play House.

48. Barter Theatre, Abingdon, Va., 1965. Photograph by Patterson. Courtesy of the Barter Theatre.

49. Old Globe Theatre, San Diego, 1966. Courtesy of the San Diego Public Library, California Room.

49. Stage, Old Globe Theatre, San Diego, ca. 1938. Courtesy of the Historical Collection, Title Insurance and Trust Company, San Diego, California.

productions by presenting seldom performed plays in adjacent Falstaff Tavern. Six main stage, five arena productions and three Shakespeare plays give San Diego the most varied year-round theatrical season in the United States presented by a single producing organization.

The Old Globe Theatre is an ever-exciting and stimulating organization, committed to presenting the finest theatrical entertainment every year for San Diego audiences and visitors.

In 1968 an auxiliary stage was added to the Old Globe—the Cassius Carter Centre Stage, named for an attorney who was an outstanding authority on the works of Shakespeare. An account of the new stage appeared in the 1970 souvenir program:

49:3   Falstaff Tavern was originally constructed in 1935 for the Pacific International Exposition as an Old English restaurant for the Shakespearean plays performed in the Old Globe Theatre.

A great hearth dominated the room where costumed waitresses served hearty roast beef and yorkshire pudding, steak and kidney pie, mutton chops and assorted side dishes.

Destruction began in the fall of 1936 after the "Expo" closed. The hearth was dismantled before public spirited citizens realized the beauty and usefulness of Falstaff Tavern and the Old Globe Theatre. The buildings were saved through hastily contributed funds and the wrecking crews were sent away.

In the late thirties, Falstaff Tavern was utilized as living quarters for the Old Globe resident manager and as a storeroom for scenery and properties. When World War II became a reality in December, 1941, a prompt evacuation was necessary as the U.S. Navy took over all of Balboa Park for hospital facilities. Falstaff Tavern became a ship's service store.

49:3. "Cassius Carter Centre Stage," in Old Globe 1970 souvenir program (San Diego, 1970).

Returned to the Old Globe Theatre in 1947, the much used structure became the rehearsal hall for actors and an intermission refreshment area for patrons. An occasional experimental play was staged between productions in the main theatre.

To expand production activities at the Old Globe Theatre, a three play schedule was presented during the 1963 season in Falstaff Tavern. During the ensuing five years, twenty-five productions were staged for more than 250 performances. In this temporary arrangement two hundred chairs were placed on wooden platforms.

With continuing audience support of unusual, significant plays, the productions were expanded until the need for improved audience and stage facilities could not be delayed.

Completely reconstructed during the fall of 1968, the former Falstaff Tavern was brilliantly conceived as an intimate theater-in-the-round by architect Victor L. Wulff.

The Cassius Carter Centre Stage is nearly symmetrical with 245 seats in four sections surrounding the 12′6″ x 16′6″ stage. More than $120,000 was invested for the rebuilding of this unique and intimate theatre-in-the-round.

With this latest addition to the Old Globe Theatre building complex, more than $500,000 has been spent in permanent buildings during the past five years. Funds for these expansions were derived from contributions as well as profits from stage productions.

50. BUCKS COUNTY PLAYHOUSE
New Hope, Pennsylvania
Opened July 1, 1939

Named the State Theatre of Pennsylvania in 1959, the Bucks County Playhouse is of particular interest because of the many theatrical phases through which it passed. It was a repertory company, used the star system and package shows, and later under producer Lee

R. Yopp reverted to a permanent repertory policy on a year-round basis. A nonprofit organization, in 1967 it started a program of classical plays for high school students as well as a commercial program for adults.

The following account of the theatre appeared in the Sunday New York *Times* of July 19, 1964. (The Playhouse changed hands in 1969.)

50:1   FROM RED BARN TO
           PACKAGE AND TENT

In the historically fly-by-night business of summer stock, a few 'old-fashioned' theaters—like the Bucks County Playhouse —make money. But the trend is to 'star packages' and musicals.

by Emily Coleman

However improbable it may seem, there was a moment in summer-theater history when Edward Everett Horton played "Springtime for Henry" for the first time —and not for the 100th, or the 1,000th, or even the 2,000th. It happened in July, 1939, just 25 years ago. The place: the Bucks County Playhouse, which was also making its eager debut on the summer-stock scene. For the gala opening, a crowd of 1,000 jammed the narrow streets of New Hope, Pa., although only about 400 Broadway celebrities and literary lions could be crammed into the small new playhouse.

There were other problems that night. The company was barely able to get its own curtain up. A matter of some hours before the distinguished guests were to arrive, the building—a 265-year-old remodeled grist mill—and its grounds were chaos. Construction debris was all about, freshly painted sets were hanging from the limbs of trees, the seats and carpeting had not been installed, and the rest rooms were filthy. Local stockholders—who included the town plumber and druggist—worked with a will, went home and changed into evening clothes, and came back and labored again.

50:1. New York *Times*, July 19, 1964.

It goes without saying that, in the best tradition of the theater, the show finally did go on—an hour late. St. John Terrell, the theater's first manager, told the audience that, "after cooperative combat between cast, stagehands and assistants, we finished the building a few minutes ago." Venerable Richard Bennett, the company's director, said, "If a man with seat covers rushes in during the performance, get up nonchalantly and let him put them on— the seats, not the audience."

More seriously, Terrell announced that the undertaking which they had embarked upon was "no neighborhood drama league. This is to be a theater. It's just that the air is a little fresher and the grass a little greener."

It is doubtful that Terrell, then only 22 and some 11 years away from launching the first tent-show musical, had any real idea of how prophetic his words were to be. But the Bucks County Playhouse did indeed grow up to become a theater in the best sense of the term, surviving World War II, and a succession of revolutionary changes which have all but transformed ye olde artsy-craftsy red barns into supermarkets dispensing prewrapped cellophane packages of movie and TV stars on the hoof.

Several factors enable the playhouse to celebrate its 25th year of existence in a fearfully fly-by-night milieu. Its locale, for one thing, is very nearly ideal for a summer theater. Located in the heart of the so-called "genius belt," it has always been able to count on a climate favorable to the arts. In the beginning, various actors and playwrights like George S. Kaufman, Moss Hart and Jack Kirkland lived nearby. "We played as a truly resident company," actress Haila Stoddard remembers. "Most of us lived there."

Some of the names have changed today, but the atmosphere is equally beneficent. S. J. Perelman, James Michener and Pearl Buck are just three of the 186 local authors whose books are pridefully displayed in New Hope's bookstores. And for sightseeing and bargain-hunting matinee ladies, Main Street and Mechanic Street are sheer delights, for historic monuments abound (Washington crossed the Delaware just a few miles away) and there are Greenwich Villagey shops named Tow Path Antiques, Workshop of the Queen of Sheba, Simply Elegant Junk, Now and Then General Merchandise, the Gilded Lily Salon and Historic Logan Inn (built in 1727 or 1734, depending on which sign you read).

More practically, New Hope is ideally situated to draw audiences from population centers like Philadelphia and its suburbs, Allentown, Trenton and Princeton. Although the town itself has a population of only around 1,000, an estimated five million people live within 50 miles of the theater. And furthermore, Broadway, whence most casting in the summer circuit springs today, is only an hour and a half away.

The Bucks County Playhouse is the official State Theater of Pennsylvania, a designation which was conferred five years ago. The theater, read the official citation in part, "is recognized throughout the nation as a leader in its field, maintaining an artistic tradition that brings great credit to itself and to the State of Pennsylvania.["]

The man most responsible for bringing this accolade to the Bucks County Playhouse is Michael Ellis, a 46-year-old Pennsylvanian who has been its director since 1954. An erstwhile actor turned producer, Ellis came to the playhouse with the somewhat dubious distinction of having co-produced five Broadway flops in a row, including Jean Kerr's first play, "Jenny Kissed Me," and "Two's Company," with Bette Davis. The experience changed his theatrical philosophy drastically. "I felt it was foolish to try out a play on Broadway first," he now says. Most people disagreed. They felt is was better to have a flop on Broadway than

try out elsewhere. I feel it's better to try out here and not waste somebody's money."

Since coming to the Bucks County Playhouse, Ellis has tried out nearly 50 new plays, a policy which won him the 1962 Margo Jones Award for being the producer who had done the most to encourage new playwrights. "Ten years ago you could hardly get a good play to try out," he explains. "Now, it's no loss of prestige to an author to try out in the summer. It costs $7,000 to $9,000 to try out a play here; it costs $110,000 to $150,000 to try out in New York. Most other summer-theater producers claim they can't do new plays, that people won't come to see them. That just is not true."

Ellis's record for picking a good play is impressive, considering the staggering odds which are stacked against any new play's eventual Broadway success. In 1959 he tried out "Never Too Late," now on Broadway, and in 1960 he produced "Come Blow Your Horn," which also went to Broadway. "I made more money from 'Come Blow Your Horn' than in 10 years of operating the theater," comments Ellis. In 1961, he staged S. J. Perelman's "The Beauty Part" with Bert Lahr, which many admirers felt would have made it in New York in 1962 except for the newspaper strike and too many changes of theater. Ellis also tried out "The Advocate" in the summer of 1962; it made Broadway only briefly last season. From last summer came a play called "Nobody Loves Me," which is a current hit as "Barefoot in the Park," and a play called "The Absence of a Cello" which will open in New York in September.

This kind of experimentation, which also occurs in Westport, Conn., where the Theater Guild owns the Country Playhouse, is one of the few encouraging artistic signs of life to be seen around the summer circuit today. The stock company has all but disappeared in the larger houses, commercialism is rampant, and the sound of musicals is heard throughout the land.

Years ago, in the mid-thirties before the Bucks County Playhouse opened, the summer theater was looked upon as the proper setting for art for art's sake. There, the stock company, which had died in the cities during the twenties, found a new life. Veteran actors got jobs, and bright young things like Henry Fonda, James Stewart, Joshua Logan, Margaret Sullavan, Katharine Hepburn and Bette Davis learned their first lessons in stagecraft in summer theaters all over New England.

When the Bucks County Playhouse began in 1939, however, something called the star system had already begun to plague the summer circuit. Aging movie and theater queens who couldn't get regular work in the winter began to set house records in the summer by playing revival after revival of plays like Noel Coward's "Private Lives." Traveling alone, or with a leading man, they would move grandly into a new playhouse on a Sunday afternoon (after closing in another the night before). If the management was lucky and the hangovers not too severe, a rehearsal or two with the resident company might be managed before the Monday night opening.

Aside from sloppy performances, this method of operation also cost more and more money: By the mid-fifties stars like Helen Hayes, Gertrude Lawrence and Tallulah Bankhead were getting weekly salaries in the thousands plus a percentage of the gross.

Right from the start, the Bucks County Playhouse put a ceiling of $1,000 on its top salary for an actor or actress. The theater's small capacity—432 seats— makes anything higher out of the question. The figure did not inhibit such actresses as Ruth Chatterton, Lillian Gish, Jane Cowl, or even Miss Hayes, who played in "Alice Sit by the Fire" in 1944, a produc-

tion which was directed by Joshua Logan and featured the stage debut of Miss Hayes's daughter, Mary McArthur. But the $1,000 ceiling has deterred some, notably TV personalties Arlene Francis and Bert Parks.

In time, the touring star supported by a resident stock company was replaced by what is now known as the "package." A package is a star or stars with a complete supporting cast which is generally recruited in New York and which moves *en block* from theater to theater. The package appealed to most theater managers. It was more economical, far less trouble and the show was generally of higher quality, since it represented a rehearsed unit instead of a pick-up operation.

But packaging broke the back of the big resident stock companies. Five years ago, for example, the Lakewood Theater in Skowhegan, Me., founded in 1901 and the oldest summer theater in the East, dropped its resident company entirely. "It was an economic necessity," says Henry Richards, production director. "Casting a season of 11 different plays was impossible with transportation costs and high rehearsal pay. This way we get complete shows with stars and share with others in preproduction and transportation costs."

The package show, of course, was ideal for the television celebrity. Hopefully, if he had his own unit, his inexperience on the live stage might not be exposed too glaringly. For reasons that are still not quite clear, summer audiences are quite frequently more avid to see masters of ceremonies like Merv Griffin and Allen Ludden, or panelists like Peggy Cass or Betty White (Ludden's wife), than they are to watch a relatively authentic television dramatic actor or actress.

Richards of Lakewood has his own ideas of why his audiences in Maine invariably flock to see some TV panelist like Henry Morgan. "They are simply curious," he says. "They feel they know them as people, but they are curious to see if they can act and they are curious to see what they look like from the waist down."

The Bucks County Playhouse under Ellis takes a surprisingly tolerant view of nonacting celebrities, a category which embraces not only TV types but also disk jockeys like Gene Rayburn (of the old WNEW team of Rayburn and Finch) and night-club entertainers like Shelley Berman, who starred in a recent tryout of a new comedy, "A Perfect Frenzy." "I've made a kind of fetish of putting people in plays for the first time," Ellis says. "I try to get the best people I can to do the plays I want to do. Merv Griffin came here to try his wings; I put him in "The Moon Is Blue," and he broke the house record [9,800 for one week] last summer."

Ellis has learned that there is one kind of tryout he cannot attempt—a full-scale musical. "We tried one—Cole Porter's 'Out of This World,' " he recalls. "It was a disaster. We just can't handle the problems of a big-book musical."

But Ellis's disaster has become the musical tent's bonanza. Ever since 1949, when St. John Terrell put up his first striped circus tent in Lambertville, N.J., just across the Delaware River from the Bucks County Playhouse, musical tents have proliferated like rabbits. Ten years ago, there were nine such theaters which played to an audience of 800,000 and grossed $2 million. This summer there are 32 in operation, and the prediction is that an audience of seven million will bring $20 million to the box office.

Since this is clearly big business, it was inevitable that chain ownership and operation would enter the picture. There are several musical chains, but the biggest is the Philadelphia firm of Guber, Ford and Gross which runs, among others, the Westbury Music Fair on Long Island and the Valley Forge Music Fair in Pennsylvania.

Oddly enough, Ellis doesn't think that Terrell's extravaganza across the river has cut into his audience at all. "There have never been any competition problems," he says. "The audiences are different. We are the only proscenium theater in the area. In two weeks I get as many people as he does in four performances." Terrell agrees: "He has a much more cerebral group than I do. Musicals appeal to a more fundamental instinct in people than plays."

Needless to say, the musical tents usually use package shows with stars although Terrell produces his own on a no-star policy. The hottest musical of the summer is "My Fair Lady," which has been released to the summer circuit for the first time, and will play proscenium houses as well as arenas—the Bucks County Playhouse, of course, being a rare exception. An estimated 230 theaters will see a staggering assortment of Eliza Doolittles and Professor Higginses.

Actors Equity is one organization which is more than delighted at the growth of both packages and musical tents. Before the boom started, about 1,100 union members were employed in the summer. By last season, the figure had risen to 1,900. Marvin Poons, Equity's business representative in charge of stock and off-Broadway productions says: "I feel that summer theater definitely reflects Broadway in the increase of musicals and television and star names. To an extent, it is regrettable that there is not the opportunity there once was for experimentation and the development of actors, but from the union point of view I can't object to increased employment and improved salaries and working conditions."

The desire of the unions to cut into the

summer theater's cheap road to Broadway may well prove its downfall. Laurence Feldman, a former New York trial lawyer who has turned theater producer and manager at Westport, at the Mineola Playhouse on Long Island and at the Paper Mill Playhouse at Millburn, N.J., anticipates that union costs eventually will break summer theaters as they are today. Surprisingly enough, the change may mean going back to the old times, to the old resident company, either Equity or non-Equity, if the unions will go along.

Ellis, whose theater is too small and too rural to attract much union pressure, views the future in different terms. "One of the things I hope for," he says, "is that summer theater can extend their seasons. Some of the managers in the resort areas say this is not possible, that vacationers don't come early enough, but it should be possible in many areas. Another thing that has been economically healthy is the extension of the summer theaters on a professional level to parts of the country that never had them before. The Cherry County Theater in Traverse City, Mich., for example, is 10 years old this summer. It's had a hard time getting stars to come; transportation costs were large, and it wasn't worth a star's time. Now things are better, for other theaters have started in the Middle West. As they grow, they can provide more work in shorter jumps; they can operate so that one feeds the other. It's the pioneer out there all alone who has the tough time. All together, they can provide entertainment for a whole area.

Ellis also is hoping to stretch his own season by sending out touring shows in October and mid-March "to cover cities in Pennsylvania of under 75,000 population and reach people who obviously haven't had professional shows in many years. It would be a step forward in making clear that Pennsylvania should have a council on the arts. Some 16 states have, or have in formation, such councils. New

York State, of course, is way ahead. But if we can tour, the people in Harrisburg can see and be influenced."

As might be expected, the most practical prediction for the future comes from the musical tents. Prediction No. 1 in that world is that more and more of the billowing canvas will turn into permanent concrete year-around operations, providing solid, permanent structures which will serve conventions as well as "My Fair Lady." Says Lee Gruber, the tent mogul: "I think you'll find more and more theater in the suburban areas rather than the pastoral. The trend is to follow the path of the shopping centers. I think Broadway is kind of ridiculous. People don't live on 44th Street. It's true we're a paperback theater, but we're out there where the people are at the prices they can afford."

51. DALLAS THEATER CENTER
Dallas, Texas
Opened December 27, 1959

One of the most exciting regional theaters is the Dallas Theater Center, which combines regional professional theater with an academic program leading to a graduate degree in theater. Paul Baker, who was a professor at Baylor University, was the guiding force in the creation of the center and worked closely with Frank Lloyd Wright in designing the playhouse.

The following paragraphs explain something of Wright's architectural concepts in regard to the center:

51:1   In designing the Dallas Theater Center, Frank Lloyd Wright intended to excite the viewer with anticipation of the dramatic experience inside. His avoidance of right angles and employment of 60 and 120–degree angles was a conscious design to create a feeling of constant activity and, thus, provide a subtle, ever-present atmosphere of expectancy in the audience.

51:1. "New Directions in Theatre Design," in Dallas Theater Center pamphlet (Dallas, 1960).

To the modern viewer, accustomed to rectangular rooms, this use of sloping walls, off-set angles skirting away from the rigid line into the gentle or massive curves, gives a definite emotional and aesthetic experience. It demands that the viewer see the whole rather than the member parts. This unity, the essence of Mr. Wright's design, carries into every possible detail, even to the use of color. The architect selected an outside and inside finish of one shade, persuaded that color-emphasis in the theater should center on the stage and its auditorium.

The building itself is a concrete shell formation. Cantilever construction predominates the design, from the rock levels determining the building's placement to the 127-ton concrete stage loft, one-half of which hangs out above the stage. This circular over-hang, considered an architectural marvel, is almost out of the audience vision and projects upward some 40 feet into the grid system of the stage.

The outside propection of this drum is the highest point of the many-angled building. It is around the circular dome that the other areas of the theater have been designed. All attention seems to focus on the necessary center of the attention in any theater—the stage itself.

After the visitor gets past the ornamental fountain at the main entrance, he becomes aware of the movement of the lobby towards the auditorium. The spacious lobby curves into the stained wooden doors of the auditorium, an incredible combination of intimacy and spaciousness, of flexibility and concrete quality.

Continuing the cantilever design, 404 seats are arranged in eleven rows, each row rising five inches above the row in front of it. Overhead is a lighting plenum which, with its multitudinous rows of lights, provides space for a man to stand and walk. These rows, like giant circular ribs, parallel the stage and permit access by catwalk to the first row of lights above the stage.

All of these wonders are, of course, servants and glorifiers of the stage, with its central 40 foot circle and two side balconies, reaching forward into the audience with Elizabethan flavor. Inside the 40 foot stage is a 32 foot turntable. Three complete stage settings may be carried on this turntable at one time, thus facilitating changing of scenery with minimum wait and noise.

To the public the Frank Lloyd Wright building is a work of art; to the theater artist it is a living space offering each individual the environment for imagination and growth.

The idea for the center was conceived in 1954 by a group of Dallas citizens interested in theater. Robert D. Stecker, president of the Dallas Theater Center, and one of the original group, recalls something of the history of the theater.

51:2 The Dallas Theater Center and the Kalita Humphreys Theater—this rare combination of school and theater—stand as a tribute to an idea.

Its story is the creation—the conception—the unfoldment of this idea. This compelling purpose and the devotion of a dedicated group working together as an instrument for the realization of an idea. Bigger than any of them, bigger than the group, bigger than all the obstacles and stumbling blocks.

For over five years this idea has been going forward. So many people giving so much in so many ways—time, talent, energy, money—always working together; each trial, each obstacle, bringing added courage, determination and dedication. Each need bringing forth a person who could help meet the need. Each need for support bringing forth someone to furnish the support. Always the faithful few —year after year, after year—with the

51:2. Robert D. Stecker, "Recognition of a Need," in Dallas Theater Center dedicatory brochure (Dallas, 1959).

presence of the One Creator always in evidence.

Frank Lloyd Wright said that every good building should be "at home on its own site like a swan on a lake," and this building surely fulfills Mr. Wright's requirements. But, for almost five years, the swan paddled on dry land, or fought stormy waters. Each step was taken, always the idea moving forward. Labels of "dead duck," "dead horse" and the like never killed the duck or the horse or the swan.

The idea first appeared in 1954 at a backporch meeting. Dallas Little Theater old-timers blended their thoughts with newcomers, and new ideas. More meetings—ideas enlarging—the group enlarging, probing, digging—and finally emerging with the recognition of a need and developing the idea to fulfill the need.

Here was the need: No place seemed to exist for the drama major to carry forward his developed interest in the theater after graduation from college and prepare him for life in the professional theater. Acting schools aplenty, and good ones, exist, but still no place to take the individual and develop him completely so as to bridge this big gap between the college theater and the professional theater—readying him for useful citizenship in the theater world—in acting, directing, producing, and for becoming competent playwrights and technicians. This school would be in every sense a recognized graduate school giving university degrees. To fulfill this need became the prime purpose of the organizers of the Dallas Theater Center.

This school when organized would then develop and support a repertory company that would provide for Greater Dallas an exciting theater season delivering a fresh and experimental quality of performance of professional excellence and developing for America its first great resident repertory company.

To carry out this high purpose, the group formally met and formally organized in January, 1955. The hard core of this group, plus those who joined soon after comprise for the most part the officers and executive committee of the Dallas Theater Center. One name does not appear—that of the beloved Margo Jones, who, after hearing the purpose of the group at the organizing meeting, said, "Glory be to Betsy! I second the motion. Let's get started."

We did.

Affirmation, confirmation, and encouragement for the idea was found to be unanimous in checking at the top of the New York theater world. The checking also brought many suggested names for the all-important post of the director, and many were considered.

But the idea, the dream of the Dallas Theater Center and Paul Baker as director were made for each other—their marriage was inevitable. All the circumstances were right, the time, the place, and an understanding parent, Baylor University. Paul Baker was allowed to continue his work at Baylor, and still become immediately the integral pivot of the Dallas Theater Center, and Baylor University became the first University to arrange for granting graduate degrees at the Center.

The idea of the organizers was also Paul Baker's idea. The school and the theater were to be headed by Baker and his staff. About his staff, Baker said, "I wouldn't be much good without them." About talent in his school, he said, "I look for character before talent, and aim to build that."

Obviously the commitment was to the best—the highest—at every step. Through the generosity of Sylvan T. Baer, the ideal site in beauty and accessibility was donated to the theater in honor of Mr. Baer's parents. Important conditions to the gift were two conditions eminently fair, namely $100,000 in a building fund in two years, and starting the building by three years. These two conditions shaped the history and directed events during those three years to follow, and furnished the urgency —the compulsion—without which the goal might not have been achieved.

Frank Lloyd Wright, of course, was the natural, spontaneous and right choice as architect. This building, his last great one, strangely enough was his first theater. Mr. Wright had designed a theater which even had some of the same principles to be found in the Dallas Theater Center, for Hartford, Connecticut, in the 1930's. This theater failed to be built because of law suits, difficulties in obtaining building permits and fund-raising troubles. History repeated itself—almost—the same problems—law suits, building permits, fund-raising—tried hard to stop a Frank Lloyd Wright theater again, but this time, these obstacles strengthened the cause rather than weakened it. They helped build instead of destroy.

A great building must blend the necessities of the client with the creativeness of the architect. The client, in this case, was the director of the Theatre and his imaginative committee. Replying to a direct plea regarding the Dallas Theater Center Building, Mr. Wright said, "I will build a building that Paul Baker can work in and grow in, and that those who follow him can work in and grow in." He did.

Frank Lloyd Wright designed what Burgess Meredith has called the most beautiful theater in the world. He designed the building from within—the secret of the building is not in the walls, but in the spaces to be used for creating within the walls. He incorporated in the design the background and the challenge for the creative contemporary theater.

The story would be incomplete without special tribute to the building committee and the builder, Henry Beck, who believed in the project and understood the building, and to his men who, within a year after the ground breaking, had readied the building for its actors and students.

The concept of the school had grown to include a children's group and an adult education group. And now, over 300 students and theater artists were using this great space, even before is was finished. Principally, of course, was the graduate school forming the professional repertory company. International in scope, bringing actors and theater artists from many parts of America, from England, South America, the Philippines and Formosa—talented—intelligent—eager—alert and all articulate in expressing their gratitude for the school, the staff and for their opportunity.

The opportunity is individual development and the emphasis of the school on the individual. . . .

Before the Dallas Theater Center was ready to open, *Theatre Arts* magazine issued a progress report by John Rosenfield.

51:3 . . . Recently, on a temporary wooden platform, the actress Julie Haydon addressed students of the Dallas Theater Center in the Frank Lloyd Wright playhouse, more properly the Kalita Humphreys Theatre of the Dallas Theatre Center, designed by Frank Lloyd Wright. It was the first event in the structure, which has attracted nationwide attention even though the Center itself was still far from ready at this writing. No prefabricated stock materials can go into a Wright building. The shell is already up in a lovely wooded section overlooking a stream with the flavorsome name of Turtle Creek. Skeleton drama classes are in session under the direction of Paul Baker, head of the drama department of Baylor University in Waco, a hundred miles south of Dallas. Children and adults are meeting on a once-a-week schedule in nearby Lee Park, using a building that is a replica of General Robert Edward's Arlington, Virginia home. Nostalgia and the Confederate tradition do not seem to

51:3. John Rosenfield, "Theatre, Dallas," *Theatre Arts* 37:71, 74 (Dec. 1959); by special permission of Jovanna Ceccarelli, Publisher.

influence the most *avant-garde* theatre activity in Texas.

The Theatre Center is backed by a large civic group, organized as a nonprofit corporation with Robert Stecker, merchant, and Waldo Stewart, investment man, as ramrods. They "gave" the project to Paul Baker, whose novel and adventurous productions at Baylor, a Baptist university had attracted attention. The Theatre Center is primarily a graduate-school annex to Baylor, although it accepts any student on a fee basis, and awards Baylor credits for work achieved.

The expense of the Wright building has been a problem. A small group of contributors appears willing to see it through in yearly installments. There is no apprehension that the theatre will not be completed and that its supporters will not "go around" indefinitely until all dreams are realized. But the backers would like to hurry it along. It has been scrounging funds for more than four years. The theatre proper was named Kalita Humphreys after an actress from a wealthy old family who died in an airplane crash a decade ago. The family wished to memorialize her (she was a force in Dallas resident-theatre circles) and made an initial contribution of $100,000.

Baker's specialty has been dramatic production rather than drama itself, and he has liberated the stage imaginations of students and faculty in Waco. His *Othello,* with each role broken down into three characters who moved about the stage together; his *Hamlet,* with some double-casting and a constructivist scheme for five stages, and his use of some native folk drama for staging tours de forces have been admired.

When the Frank Lloyd Wright theatre is ready for use, Baker will present his own dramatization of Thomas Wolfe's *Of Time and the River,* given at Baylor last season. His professor of playwriting, Gene McKinney, will contribute an original, *The Cross-Eyed Bear.* Ramsey Yel-

vington, Baylor graduate who has written stimulating plays on local historical themes, will offer a new script about the Texas founding father, General Sam Houston. Oscar Wilde's *The Importance of Being Earnest* also is on the back-burner.

It is an error to assume that the late architect's only theatre in America is an adaptation of the plan once considered in Hartford, Connecticut. Though there are resemblances, the new project goes back to the specifications of a book published by Wright in 1928. The core is a scenic workshop, below the stage, and a stage fed by ramp or hydraulic lift. Although the acting platform permits use of a proscenium curtain, it is circular, with an opening forty feet in diameter. There is a revolving disk, thirty-two feet in diameter, which is quartered, and each section is on a lift. The stage thrusts closely to the audience, within three feet of the front row. Unusual acoustical resonance is made possible by an ingenious Wright shell-support provided for the acting platform. Side areas for acting also tie to the central stage, humoring Baker's predilection for stages that surround a public—an arrangement in his Studio One at Baylor, built many years ago with funds from a Rockefeller Foundation gift. Lighting is controlled centrally; lamps are located on the underside of the balcony and in an encircling light gallery.

For the audience there will be 366 lounge chairs with backs, side arms and no legs to stumble over. The seats will be cantilevered from concrete tiers that rise stadium-fashion. The outer material of the building is concrete and stucco, tinted buff. There are separate roof promenades for audience and actors. Liberal space has been provided for greenrooms, lobby, comfort rooms and the like. The building will be air-conditioned, of course, and suitable for year-round use. The site is a hillside, favorite topography for a Wright building. This structure hugs the configuration of the land; one stubby, jutting tower will remind some of Wright's Guggenheim Museum in New York.

It is one of the last Wright projects, and he took it reluctantly. Characteristically, he left Baker and the board of directors with a message: "No matter what you expect to put into this theatre, the theatre will take possession. Then the drama will be what it should be—like nothing else the world has seen." . . .

Some of the architectural aspects and technical innovations of the Dallas Theater Center are discussed in the *Architectural Record:*

51:4 Frank Lloyd Wright never gave up what he considered a good idea, and the Dallas Theater Center is an outgrowth of two earlier experimental schemes. Around 1917 he planned a theater for Aline Barnsdall to be built in Los Angeles near her famous Hollyhock House at Olive Hill which he designed. The project fell through and he didn't get another chance at a major theater for many years until he developed a scheme for West Hartford, Connecticut, based on an earlier theater project for Broadacre City. It was never realized. A number of auditoriums have been included in his schemes. Both Taliesins have them, and several years before he died Wright erected a dance pavilion for his wife Olgivanna at the desert camp. The Olive Hill and Hartford theaters, however, can be considered prototypes of the new building in Dallas, the former in the fact that its basic concept provided for experimental theater and the latter in its use of a ramp system within a hexagon, as well as a circular revolving stage.

Of more importance to the design of the Dallas theater than these early models was a particular attitude strongly held by Wright. He believed in the dignity of manual labor, not only in the service

of handcraft, but for its own sake. He was indifferent to mechanical contrivance, and did not want the form of his theater to be determined by the highly developed mechanics of modern theatrical production. In this design flats were to have been painted and stored in the basement workshop and lovingly toted by hand up one ramp, installed on the stage, and after the scene carried back down the opposite ramp to the basement. Unfortunately the turning radius in each ramp was determined by considerations of exterior mass and volume rather than function, and it became apparent that most pieces of scenery however gently carried by hand would be too long to round the bend. One of the ramps, therefore, is not used as such, and a mechanical lift has been installed across its width.

While a careful examination of the plan and section reveals other functional problems, it must be said that Wright has nonetheless made a significant contribution to theater design. He erected for Dallas the first building in America to function as an Elizabethan apron type theater. Apron type stages and theaters in the round have been erected in tents as well as in barns and other reconverted structures, but no contemporary theater building had yet been constructed to provide any arrangements other than those afforded by the proscenium type stage. Theaters constructed in the Western world since the end of the sixteenth century have been of the proscenium type and this means that for all this time the creation of theatrical illusion has been contained within a rectangular frame. While this arrangement is ideal for many types of performance, theater designers and directors are beginning to experiment with more flexible kinds of staging and welcome the added dimension given by the projecting stage. They feel that a more intimate relationship is established between actor and audience where the stage is partially surrounded by seats and closer to the audi-

51:4. "Frank Lloyd Wright: Dallas Theatre," *Architectural Record* 85:161–66 (Mar. 1960).

torium floor. Wright's theater offers new possibilities to the creative theater director, but cannot be used for conventional staging.

At Dallas the 40-ft circular stage has a 32-ft revolving turntable. Wright's original idea was to bisect the revolving drum with a permanent screen dividing it into a forestage and a backstage. Sets would be carried up the ramp and changed behind the screen, the stage would revolve and a new scene appear. The diameter of the drum was too small, however, to allow it to be divided in half. The forestage would have been too shallow, the backstage too tiny to function as such. The dividing screen was never installed and the full depth of the stage is being used when needed. The revolving stage functions *as* scenery, not to *change* scenery.

When it became apparent that Wright's backstage didn't work, there was no where to go but up. Every good working theater has a fly gallery, but Dallas required a special one for two reasons. With no backstage, most set changes have to be made from the flies. The system of raising and lowering flats had to be kept free from the circular wall or cyclorama at the rear of the stage because it is used as a screen for the projection of backgrounds and had to be kept clear of paraphernalia. Special winches were installed to raise and lower flats. These comprise a hanging system which is free of attachment to stage house walls as it does not require the traditional sandbag counterweights which must run in channels along these walls. The movement of flats is electronically controlled by a device developed by theater designer and engineer George C. Izenour who also developed the special winch. The mechanism can be pre-set to lower and raise scenery in any desired sequence or time span, and all preparation for staging may be set and ready while the performance goes on.

The narrow balcony or catwalk at the rear of the theater was originally intended to carry the stage lighting. A rule of thumb for the theater is that it should be possible to focus stage lights at a 45 degree angle. The rear balcony was too low to provide this angle so the indirect light coves which Wright had designed to light the auditorium were widened and made into front stage lighting positions. Additional lights have been installed on the inner surface of the fly gallery. The lighting control booth is at the center of the balcony at the rear. It houses another console with a pre-set memory designed by Izenour, which electronically guides the sequence of lighting combinations.

The theater was constructed at a cost of approximately $1,000,000.

The New York *Times* also gave an account of the new playhouse.

51:5   WRIGHT THEATRE OPENS TOMORROW

Architect's Only Playhouse, With Revolving Stage, Is Part of Dallas Center

Dallas, Dec. 25—The only theatre that Frank Lloyd Wright designed will open here Sunday to inaugurate the $1,000,000 Dallas Theatre Center.

The first production will be an adaptation of Thomas Wolfe's novel "Of Time and the River." It has been produced by Paul Baker, Texas dramaturgist and director of the new center.

Mr. Baker calls his theatre's unconventional revolving stage "the other actor" in the show. Actually the entire building —and the Kalita Humphreys Theatre— promises to be the star attraction.

Visitors compared the theatre, with its crowning dome, massive cantilevered balconies and avoidance of right angles, with another Wright legacy, the Solomon R. Guggenheim Museum in New York. The Guggenheim is on Fifth Avenue between Eighty-eighth and Eighty-ninth Streets.

51:5. New York *Times*, Dec. 26, 1959.

LONG WALK FROM CARS

From the parking lot at the theatre, it is necessary to walk almost entirely around the white structure to reach the entrance.

Mr. Baker said the theatre would not confront its directors and players with functional problems similar to those that the curators of the Guggenheim Museum were reported to have encountered.

"We ironed out all difficulties with Mr. Wright in the three and a half years before his death," Mr. Baker declared.

The architect visited Dallas and inspected the building for the last time three months before his death last April.

Burgess Meredith, the actor, who has promised to direct a play in Dallas early next year, says "the best ideas from the top theatrical minds in the world" have gone into the structure's design and equipment.

Charlton Heston, another performer who shows a lively interest in the Dallas center, predicts that "playing on this stage will spoil actors to any other stage in America."

The stage lacks a proscenium, the traditional frame-and-curtain dividing the spectators and the players. A thirty-two-foot central turntable stage is shielded in part by a disappearing screen, and finished by two side stages. The revolving stage and elaborate overhead and side lighting are said to permit unusual effects and quick scene changes.

Missing are the footlights that in the customary picture-frame theatre accentuate the separation between actors and audience. Wright said he was striving to create a "sympathic house."

The 440 spectators sit all around and above the forestage. The classical Greek and Roman theatres, the Elizabethan stage and the experiments of such modern dramaturgists as Max Reinhardt have been mentioned as possible sources of Wright's inspiration.

The stage has a total frontage of seventy feet. Its floor is only one foot above the level of the nearest seats, which are only three feet distant.

Wright, long interested in theatrical architecture had built a private stage in his home at Taliesin, Wis. Sponsors of theatrical projects in Hartford and California were unresponsive to his ideas.

So he responded eagerly when a group of Dallas business men and other prominent citizens approached him in 1954. The building rose on a wooded lot, not far from midtown Dallas. The theatre is named for Kalita Humphreys, a Texas actress who died in an air crash in 1954. Her mother gave $100,000 towards the project.

IRAQI PROJECT FOUNDERED

Shortly before his death, Wright was asked by the Government of Iraq to design an opera house and cultural center in Baghdad. Nothing came of the project, however, and the Dallas building is the architect's only playhouse.

The first season of the new theatre is ambitiously scheduled to last eight months. Eight productions by the permanent repertory company are foreseen. About fifty directors, actors and technicians, many of them Texans, will present a program ranging from "Hamlet" to a new play based on the life of Sam Houston, the Texas pioneer.

The new Dallas center includes a youth theatre for talented children and teen-agers and a graduate school of drama. It will offer evening lectures for adults and is also intended to serve as a laboratory for experimenting and developing new theatrical techniques. The graduate school began operations last September.

The theatre is wired for television and national hook-ups are planned. This would meet with Wright's wholehearted approval. His assistant in the Dallas project, Kelly Oliver, quotes Wright's notes as saying the legitimate theatre could hope for a new lease on life only if it were able to compete with motion pictures and television.

52. ARENA STAGE
Washington, D.C.
Opened October 30, 1961

Washington's Arena Stage has been one of the most vigorous, creative, and financially-sound of the regional professional playhouses. Henry Hewes, as drama critic of the *Saturday Review,* stated that the "Arena has raised its production standards to a quality unsurpassed by any American producing organization." This is high praise, and is almost incredible when one realizes that Arena Stage had only been organized as recently as 1950.

A brief history of the Arena Stage appeared in pamphlet form when the new Kreeger Theater was dedicated on November 29, 1970.

52:1   Winter, 1948—There is no professional theater in the nation's capital. Elsewhere in the country—in Dallas where Margo Jones is creating her theater-in-the-round, and in Cleveland and Houston—the first faint stirring of what will later become the "regional theater movement" are being felt. Zelda Fichandler, Phi Beta Kappa Cornell graduate (Russian language and literature) is soon to receive her master's in theater arts from George Washington University. She is among a small group of Washingtonians who want a professional company in town, and her 98¢ cardboard file box is the seed that will become Arena Stage.

THE HIPPODROME
The group included a policeman, a lawyer, a concert bureau executive, a tennis professional, a professor, a jeweler—40 people with no credentials or reputation as theater producers. But they did have the incredible drive to raise $15,000 in ten days, in time to exercise an option on an old movie house in downtown Washington.

She Stoops to Conquer was the first of 55 productions in the first Arena, be-

52:1. *Arena Stage 1950–1970: The First Twenty Years* (Washington: Arena, 1970).

tween August, 1950, and July, 1955. Through these first five years Arena Stage learned much about the rediscovered arena form, which proved economically and artistically well-suited to the twentieth century American theater. Directors, designers, actors and audiences fell in love with this "modern" theater shape, stunning in its simplicity and immediacy, its involvement with the audience around it, its major departure from the footlights and elevated distance of Broadway-style stages.

Young artists later to gain renown—George Grizzard, Gerald Hiken, Anne Meacham, Lester Rawlins, Pernell Roberts —and such memorable productions as *The Glass Menagerie, The Hasty Heart, All Summer Long, The Crucible* and *The World of Sholem Aleichem* stretched the possibilities of central staging and developed an ardent following for Arena.

The converted Hippodrome seated 247 on all four sides of the stage. It had its limitations: silly ones, like the fact that the actors had to run around the block to make entrances; and serious ones—though it played to full houses much of the time, the capacity was too small to support the costs of production. At the end of a successful American premiere run of Agatha Christie's *The Mousetrap,* Zelda Fichandler took the bold step of closing the theater for a year, to allow time for the search for a new home.

THE OLD VAT
November, 1956—The old Heurich Brewery in Foggy Bottom seems unlikely for a new theater, but the neighborhood at 9th and New York Avenue, N.W., wasn't so great either. And doesn't "in the forefront" mean that you create your own neighborhood? Sixteen months after the closing of the Hippodrome Arena Stage inaugurates the Old Vat with the American premiere of the full-length version of Arthur Miller's *A View from the Bridge.*

50. Bucks County Playhouse, New Hope, Pa., ca. 1960. Courtesy of the Bucks County Playhouse.

51. Kalita Humphreys Theater, Dallas Theater Center, Dallas, 1961. Courtesy of The Dallas Theater Center.

51. Interior, Kalita Humphreys Theater, Dallas Theater Center, Dallas, 1961. Color photograph by Karnegay. Courtesy of The Dallas Theater Center.

51. Interior, Kalita Humphreys Theater, Dallas Theater Center, Dallas, 1961. Courtesy of The Dallas Theater Center.

52. Arena Stage, Washington, D.C., after construction of the Kreeger Theatre in 1970. Photograph by Norman McGrath. Courtesy of Arena Stage.

52. Interior, Kreeger Theatre, Arena Stage, Washington, D.C., 1969. Courtesy of Arena Stage.

In the Old Vat, 500 seats surrounded what had been the brewery's ice storage area, and enthusiastic audiences warmed up the theater for 40 productions, including *Summer of the Seventeenth Doll, The Lady's Not for Burning, The Caine Mutiny Court Martial* and the American premiere of *The Egg*.

A subscription plan was conceived to free Arena artists from the hit-or-miss syndrome of New York, creating a basically stable theater audience who would participate in the development of each work, rather than shop for "hits." The production schedule stabilized at a fall-spring season, with the summer reserved for planning. National recognition came to Arena, and the Ford Foundation made grants first to Zelda Fichandler personally, then to underwrite the production of a new script, and then to encourage the growth of a permanent acting company.

Artistically, financially, administratively, the theater's period of learning was matched by its growing popularity in Washington, and its reputation in the world of theater. This was necessary acceleration for the big leap to a new home, because the Old Vat was slated for demolition: it lay in the path of a new freeway network that soon would link downtown Washington and the suburbs with the New Southwest area of town.

A PERMANENT HOME

October 18, 1960—"Our aim is no less than this—to bring life to life. And by this aim we are urgently indissolubly connected to the world we live in and to the people we live for. We are a theater for audiences. We are not an idle or esoteric experiment. We live to illuminate life and make it more meaningful and more joyful."—Zelda Fichandler on the occasion of the groundbreaking for Arena's new home.

Few Americans were qualified as theater architects in 1960, because no new theater had been built on a new site in this country for over 50 years. Few people in the world were qualified as designers of arena staging. But in one of America's most noted architects, Harry Weese, Zelda Fichandler found a sensitive intellect, willing to experiment, to work with her in designing the first theater ever built around the ideals of an existing professional theater company.

Eight hours of tape-recorded conversation with actors, directors, designers, technicians and administrative staff—and eleven years of experience in the Hippodrome and the Old Vat—were the basis for the award-winning design of the present Arena Stage. The design of all facilities, large and small, derived directly from the pooled knowledge of people who had pioneered in the development of the arena form.

The concretization of these ideas would cost almost a million dollars. With the expertise and energy of World Bank executive J. Burke Knapp and the full-time effort of economist Thomas C. Fichandler (Zelda Fichandler's husband and now executive director of Arena Stage), the money was raised through foundation grants of $300,000, other gifts of $75,000, the sale of $225,000 in bonds and a $250,000 mortgage. Among the contributing foundations, all of whom were impressed with the extent of general popular support for Arena, were the Arts of the Theatre Foundation, the Eugene and Agnes Meyer Foundation, the Old Dominion Foundation, the Rockefeller Foundation, the Philip M. Stern Family Fund, and the Twentieth Century Fund. James M. Rouse and Company arranged the mortgage from the American Security and Trust Company. The Redevelopment Land Agency made available a handsomely situated point of land along Washington's waterfront in the New Southwest section of town. A subsequent $863,000 grant from the Ford Foundation paid for the mortgage, repaid the bonds, purchased the site and allowed important improvements in the new building.

The present Arena Stage seats 811 in four tiers and eleven boxes surrounding the nearly square stage. Each tier is comfortably spaced into eight rows and backed up by the outer ring of box seats, all steeply banked to create involvement of "leaning into" the play. Entrances to the stage may be made through any of four tunnels from each corner, from under the stage, of through aisles in the house. Zelda Fichandler describes the stage as a neutral cube of space, rather than a flat playing area.

"The stage can be small or large. With light it can alternately expand and contract within one production. It can be sunken or raised. Platforms can be built up into one or all four of the tunnels, or into none of them. The space may be used as one place; or, because of the capacity of light to define numberless places within a totally neutral cube, it may be used as an infinite number of places."

Because there are artistic advantages to end-staging, where the audience surrounds on three sides, the Arena was designed for additional flexibility; one of the four tiers is movable—not concrete like the others but on wheels for easy removal —permitting a variety of endstage possibilities, in theory. But the total architectural design was too perfectly created for a neutral cube of space. When Joan Littlewood's *Oh, What a Lovely War* was presented with the tier removed the effect was novel and exciting—but clearly a compromise with the architecture. Though the movability of the tier continues to provide some flexibility for scenic designers, it has never since been removed in its entirety.

Among the many memorable productions in the present Arena were the world premiere of *The Great White Hope* and the American premiere of *Indians,* both of which went to Broadway with their Arena productions virtually intact; and productions of *The Caucasian Chalk Circle,* which inaugurated the theater in 1961, *The Devils, The Iceman Cometh, Dance of Death,* and *No Place to Be Somebody.*

Subscriber rolls grew steadily and so did the scope of Arena's special projects. Living Stage expanded from a theater-in-education idea, involving tours of professional improvisational theater at no cost to inner-city neighborhoods, a teacher training program that is in demand across the country and improvisational theater workshops for all ages at Arena. A driving interest in theater with particular meaning for black theater-goers has led to current discussions concerning a Black Repertory Theater based at Arena. Other activities have included plays for children; training programs for the professional resident company; internship training for high school and college students; programs in local prisons and detention centers; special performances for student groups; staff-member services as panelists and consultants; and the loan of Arena facilities to civic organizations.

These activities filled the theater to overflowing. Rehearsals took place on the lawn, in the theater lobby, in a nearby school building. Living Stage conducted classes in the basement of a neighborhood church. Set construction cluttered the parking lot. Actors used backstage corridors for dressing rooms. A one-bedroom apartment across the street contained the public relations department. Audiences filled the theater for overall season averages of 90–95%. It became obvious that there wasn't room for Arena at Arena.

THE KREEGER THEATER

Zelda Fichandler broke ground for the addition to Arena Stage on August 28, 1968. Stage II, as it was called before Washington philanthropist David Lloyd Kreeger pledged $250,000 toward its completion, was made possible by an $800,000 Ford Foundation grant; other major contributors were the Old Dominion Foundation, the Eugene and Agnes E. Meyer Foundation, and the Twentieth

Century Fund, supported by hundreds of smaller individual gifts. The Kreeger Theater was designed by Harry Weese. One of America's most noted architects (and the designer of Washington's Metro system), he worked with Mrs. Fichandler, executive director Thomas C. Fichandler, designer Robin Wagner and others to create the Arena complex in the new Southwest area of Washington.

The Kreeger Theater fulfills the need for more room at Arena.

THE STAGE

The flexible endstage and its 500-seat, fan-shaped house, is strikingly different from the Arena. The stage has a back wall and wings. The seats are a lively purple, the carpet a burnished gold, the long curved auditorium wall richly paneled in a brown velour—as contrasted to the Arena where a vivid ambiance would distract the audience on the other sides of the stage. The houselights, unlike the muted ones in the Arena, continue the marquee motif used in the Arena and Kreeger entrances.

There are also significant similarities. The steep rake of the Arena seating is approached in the Kreeger, particularly in the low encircling balcony. The stage is fully trapped and any part of it can be set at any level. A full grid and flyspace over the entire stage permit set pieces, props, even actors, to be flown into and out of the playing area. Three exposed lighting catwalks over the audience plus side and onstage lighting positions provide an Arena-like capacity for design by light.

While the Kreeger stage, like the Arena, is conceived as a neutral and flexible space, it is defined chiefly by the back wall which gives to the stage a single focus.

Panels on each side of the stage may be pulled in to shutter the playing space to 30 feet; or they can be rolled out of the way, widening the space to 42 feet. There is no permanent proscenium. When desired, one can be created as part of a particular scenic design. The same holds for a house curtain, a cyclorama, masking devices, and other traditional theater features. The first two rows of seats are removable and the stage can be thrust further into the audience.

The addition of the Kreeger Theater not only gives Arena artists and audiences another way of looking at things, but also permits the scheduling of a wider variety of theater events—plays for children, musical concerts, productions by a D.C. Black Repertory Theater, films, and events that are still unimagined—as well as a regular season of plays in two theaters.

THE REHEARSAL ROOM

The Rehearsal Room is a duplicate of the Arena Stage—the same size, fully trapped, with access aisles angled like the Arena's tunnels. A complete set can be put in here, used throughout rehearsal period, and then moved overnight into the Arena, following the closing of the previous show. This means that complicated sets can be used for many weeks before the show opens; in the past—as in most other theaters—rehearsals took place on drop cloths marked for platforms, steps, elevators, turntables and the like, until two or three days before performances began.

This room was also created for the production of experimental theater, works-in-progress, dramatic readings, panel discussions—a place where 125 theater people can participate, from fold-away theater seats, in the development of new works and new ideas.

THE OLD VAT ROOM

A 200-seat restaurant, with adjoining kitchen facilities, was provided in the design, to serve the Arena company, staff and patrons before and after the show. There are provisions for a cabaret stage, and when funds are available to finish this room it will be another outlet for the talent at the Arena.

THE SHOP, WORKROOMS, STORAGE AREAS, OFFICES AND DRESSING ROOMS

A floating floor, designed to minimize noise interference, a high ceiling, and imaginative devices for storage and set construction characterize the new shop. Oversize doors lead from the shop to the Kreeger and Arena stages, the Rehearsal Room and the freight elevator which connects the three levels of the new building.

There are workrooms and storage areas throughout the building. One of them is a large triangle of space under the southwest lawn along Maine Avenue. Another is an oddly shaped room under the auditorium which connects to the pit under the Kreeger Stage; another is the costume storage area, across the corridor from the administrative offices on the second floor.

The offices extend from a reception/switchboard room in two directions: along the north wall of the building are a business office, a design office and a library/conference room, and these are on a corridor leading to the Kreeger balcony; along the Potomac waterfront are a string of brightly lighted rooms for the directors and staff, and a kitchen for staff use. A large file room faces the central secretarial area. The intent of the office design was to eliminate physical separation of as many administrative and production functions as practical.

Dressing rooms, showers, and a "green" room form a curved corridor near access stairways to the stage, on the bottom level of the building.

Work remains to be done in most areas of the new building, and funding is still needed to complete many of the rooms. But the building has already created a new freedom of unhampered creativity for every Arena Stage function.

The reviews of Arena Stage productions were uniformly good, as indicated by the following, which appeared in *Newsweek* November 13, 1961.

52:2   In most American cities, live theater ranges predictably from the secondhand (touring versions of Broadway hits) to the second-rate (amateur excavations from the Samuel French play catalogue). In Washington, D.C., however, theatergoers for the past eleven years have frequently been privy to live productions that were neither, thanks to the tenacious repertory group called Arena Stage. Housed first in a 247-seat converted movie theater, so cramped that actors sometimes had to run around the block to make their entrances, and later in a brewery meeting hall with a comparatively generous 500 seats, Arena Stage since 1950 has put on 90 productions. Only a very few of these ("Three Men on a Horse," for one) were staged for their obvious popularity. A great many were chosen for their originality ("Epitaph for George Dillon," "Summer of the Seventeenth Doll") rather than their commercial appeal.

Last week, in a bulldozed former slum area on the Potomac waterfront, Arena Stage moved to a gleaming new $850,000 home. For the first play on its traditionally rectangular stage (surrounded now by 800 seats) the company offered a sumptuous, stylized production of "The Caucasian Chalk Circle," Bertolt Brecht's sprawling morality parable. (The moral of this rarely produced work, as encapsulated by director Alan Schneider: "A thing belongs to the person who deserves it.")

Circles and Classics: David Hurst and Melinda Dillon—both newcomers to Arena Stage's permanent company—were widely acclaimed in the leading roles, but Brecht's panoramic style still left some opening-night ticketholders going in circles themselves. Presumably they will feel more at home with some of the plays scheduled for production later in the sea-

52:2. "Repertory: D.C. Housewarming," *Newsweek*, Nov. 13, 1961, p. 94. Copyright Newsweek, Inc., 1961.

son—classic items like George Bernard Shaw's "Misalliance" and Anton Chekhov's "Uncle Vanya."

Although the Kennedys missed the new theater's black-tie opening, the New Frontier's next-highest echelon made the scene. Treasury Secretary C. Douglas Dillon and his wife sat in the Presidential box as guests of J. Burke Knapp, World Bank vice president and an Arena Stage sponsor; Jackie Kennedy's press secretary, Pamela Turnure, was accompanied by artist William Walton, a frequent White House visitor; and FDR's Attorney General Francis Biddle was there with his wife.

For trim, dark-haired Zelda Fichandler, Arena Stage's prime mover and producing director, the occasion culminated two years of questionnaires, tape-recorded conferences, and directives to architect Harry Weese, all designed to assure a theater exactly tailored to the special needs of the company. With the three-way financing job completed (contributions as large as the Rockefeller Foundation's $100,000, a $225,000 bond issue, and a $250,000 mortgage), Mrs. Fichandler could congratulate herself on a job well done. But she made plain that her appetite for work was still unsatisfied: "I'd like to start all over again, from scratch, in another area."

53. GUTHRIE THEATER
Minneapolis, Minnesota
Opened May 7, 1963

The opening of the Guthrie Theater in 1963 marks a significant date in American theater history, since this was the first massive attempt to bring outstanding repertory theater to the heart of America, the Midwest. The Twin Cities of Minneapolis and St. Paul launched a major effort to provide their area with the very best in theater, and through their endeavors were able to raise the money for a $2,250,000 theater plus ticket sales and sub-

scriptions to guarantee a financial success for the first season.

The playhouse represented a break with traditional theater architecture of the past in America, and by use of an asymmetrical thrust stage and an unusual design an exciting piece of architecture was achieved that won worldwide publicity. This excitement is reflected in articles on the theater in various national magazines. Several of the articles are reproduced here.

The artistic director of the theater originally was Sir Tyrone Guthrie, D. Litt., noted director and innovator. Sir Tyrone, committed to a classical repertory, was largely responsible for the final shape of the theater, which he claimed to be much better suited to the production of the classics than the usual proscenium stage.

53:1 In designing an auditorium, the prime consideration should be the relation of performer to audience. Since the middle of the seventeenth century when Italian opera took Europe by storm, theaters have been designed almost exclusively in the manner best suited to operatic performances. Such designs have a raised platform in front of which is a horseshoe-shaped auditorium, usually in several tiers of seating. Between stage and auditorium a great gulf is fixed, literally a pit, in which the orchestra plays. The stage of the opera house is further removed from the audience by a partition with a large hole through which the spectators view the performance. This proscenium opening is often decorated as a picture frame to enhance the illusion that the performance is a picture in which figures magically move, dance, or sing. When the performance demands that the picture be changed, a curtain falls and appropriate pulling and hauling prepares the stage for further surprises to delight the audience. When all

53:1. Tyrone Guthrie, "A Director Views the Stage," *Design Quarterly* no. 58 (Minneapolis: Walker Art Center, 1963), n.p.

is ready, the stagehands are replaced by painted mummers in fine raiment, and the curtain is raised. For many years I worked in such theatres, and it never crossed my mind that a theatre could or should be otherwise. When I was in my early thirties, I was hired to direct the Old Vic Shakespeare Company. Gradually it became clear to me that trying to put Shakespeare's plays into the conventional framework for opera was wrong. The plays were written by a master craftsman for a theater of altogether different design. It was certainly possible to adapt them to the requirements of conventionally planned theatres. It seemed more desirable, however, to adapt some commonplace building than to adjust a masterpiece. As is often the case, the obviously sensible building plan was too expensive to execute. Yet I realized that a more logical and easy way to stage these plays existed. It led to an examination of the whole premise of illusion which is the basis for the proscenium stage.

It has always seemed to me that people do not submit to illusion in the theatre much after the age of ten or eleven. They are perfectly aware that the middle-aged lady uncomfortably suspended on a wire is not Peter Pan but an actress pretending to be Peter Pan. For a performance to attempt to create an illusion is as gallant but as futile as Mrs. Partington's attempt to sweep the Atlantic Ocean out of her parlor.

In planning the Tyrone Guthrie Theatre, it was necessary to decide whether the stage should be the conventional platform separated from the auditorium by a proscenium arch or whether it should be an open stage such as the Elizabethan theatre and the ancient Greek and Roman theatres. A third alternative was available. We might have asked our architect to create a flexible design which could adjust to both types. We rejected this, however, on the ground that an all-purpose hall is a no-purpose hall—that insofar as a purpose is flexible, it is not whole-hearted; that it was better to be firmly and uncompromisingly of one kind than to attempt a compromise between opposites which we considered to be theatrically irreconcilable. We argued for the open stage for the following reasons: first, our intended program is of a classical nature, and we believe that the classics are better suited to an open stage than to a proscenium one. Second, the aim of our performances is not to create an illusion, but to present a ritual of sufficient interest to hold the attention of, even to delight, an adult audience. Third, an auditorium grouped around a stage rather than placed in front of a stage enables a larger number of people to be closer to the actors. Fourth, in an age when movies and TV are offering dramatic entertainment from breakfast to supper, from cradle to grave, it seemed important to stress the difference between their offering and ours. Theirs is two-dimensional and is viewed upon a rectangular screen. The proscenium is analogous to such a screen by forcing a two-dimensional choreography upon the director. But the open stage is essentially three-dimensional with no resemblance to the rectangular postcard shape which has become the symbol of canned drama.

No claim is made that the open stage is better than the proscenium stage for every type of play. But, in our opinion, the open stage is more desirable for the kind of plays we propose to perform and the kind of project we propose to execute.

53:2   The location of a permanent repertory theatre company of high artistic standards in the Midwest held challenging potential, not only for theatre, but for the region. It was a challenging opportunity for me to design the building for this new venture. We wished to design a theatre that would seat about 1,400 persons and that would accommodate open stage produc-

53:2. Ralph Rapson, "The Artist Design," *Design Quarterly* no. 58 (Minneapolis: Walker Art Center, 1963), n.p.

tions. During the inactive winter months of the repertory company, Walker Art Center would frequently use the theatre for its own cultural programs. The new structure had to be connected physically with the existing Walker building in a manner complementary to each other, but with separate entrances, circulation and control. Thus, visually conflicting structural forms were not considered. By expressing the form and shape of the theatre through the glass wall and abstract frame, we have attempted to provide an exterior which would anticipate the stimulation of the activities within the theatre itself.

The design and construction of a theatre is composed of a complexity of ideas, techniques, and functions. The architect must draw upon his own experience and that of others while searching for new ideas, directions, and solutions. Preliminary discussions with Dr. Guthrie established his preference for open stage production and the wish always to have one wall to play against, which eliminated the possibility of a theatre-in-the round or any great degree of convertible theatre. Dr. Guthrie also wanted to seat as many people as possible close to the stage to achieve an intimate actor-audience relationship. After consultation and analysis, it became the problem of the architect to translate this research into a specific design. I felt that the interior of the theatre should dramatically set the scene for the performance, anticipating and enhancing a stimulating event without overpowering the actual performance. The balanced but asymmetrical seating plan, the confetti-like color pattern of the seating, and the acoustical ceiling "clouds" express this idea. Since balcony patrons have too often been considered "second-class citizens," an attempt was made to eliminate this distinction by fusing the orchestra and balcony into one unbroken slope on one side. Elsewhere seating is designed in broken sections which lend variety and dynamic form to the interior.

The shape and size of the house, the seating layout which provides an arc of 200-degree seating about the open stage, the slope of the floor, the inclination and shape of walls and ceiling "clouds," the location of aisles and actors' entrances, and the flexible stage wall are all the result of many studies, sketches and models. The house design also grew out of exhaustive consideration of good sight lines, sensitive acoustics, flexible lighting, fire and safety codes, structural and air conditioning factors, and a variety of other requirements. Scale models of the interiors were built to visualize and test, by light readings, the exact nature and character of all parts of the space. Since existing theatre seating units were not suitable for the design of the theatre, a new chair was designed with the help of various manufacturers. It is being used for the first time in this building.

The unstable nature of the subsoil of the site and the proximity of the existing Walker Art Center building posed special structural problems. Because of the long spans and heavy loads and the soil conditions, much of the structure is built on deep concrete piling, with no loading permitted on or close to the Walker foundations. Light steel framing was chosen for lightness and economy.

Many people have given time and effort to the design and construction and many others have contributed towards the financing of the project. The achievement of a repertory theatre is a great ideal and one that will add to the cultural growth of the region.

53:3   The Tyrone Guthrie Theater opened on a note of éclat. The main streets of Minneapolis were festooned with white pennants with an heraldic crimson "G", and the monogram was repeated throughout the building, on the tickets and the program and on the blazers of the youth-

53:3. Richard Gilman, "The Stage: View from the East," *Commonweal*, May 31, 1963, pp. 282–83.

ful ushers, where it took the place of a Princeton shield or the emblem of a yachting or rowing club. And in fact there was an air of a regatta · or some other clean, wholesome public activity about the event, whose importance is that it brought to the Midwest its first permanent professional repertory company, together with a theatre built expressly for its purpose.

When Lincoln Center's theatre opens here, there will be far less innocent enthusiasm and naive pride; too many of us are already skeptical of its program and the people who are running it, as well as of the very possibility of being extricated by any single enterprise from our condition of theatrical arrangement. But out in those great new spaces all was optimism and exuberance.

The city, ecstatic with sudden glory, turned out in tuxedos and evening gowns, cheered the theater, the performers, the directors and the occasion, drank champagne at two successive open houses and felt itself to have entered the big time overnight. For the visitor, sophistication was a burden; if you couldn't jettison it all, if you kept making distinctions and applying criteria that in the general euphoria weren't being applied, there was nevertheless an infectious quality to the enthusiasm.

And there was reason for it. To begin with, there was the theatre itself. That it should have been built where it has been is the most impressive, although also the most precarious, fact of all. For what is being tested in Minneapolis is of course the idea of decentralization; if the Guthrie Theatre takes hold and works, if its standards are high and the response to its efforts substantial and continuous, then it may be the fountainhead of a new era in the American theater. But if it fails, we are all going to have to get right down to our skins and start all over again in a barn.

The building, which one feared might have been ugly and unuseful, is the answer to a great many prayers. Modeled in basic ways after the Shakespeare Festival Theatre in Canada, it is quite beautiful and admirably suited to a classic repertoire. Around its spacious Open Stage there is a steeply rising orchestra and a narrow balcony running five-sixths of the way; the seats (the capacity is 1,437) are covered in pastel-colored burlap, the acoustics are good and there is ample space for intermissions and easy access to every section. The whole thing gives rise to an atmosphere of bright, self-confident, non-competitive vigor and casual expertise—a theater open to whatever degree of technical ingenuity and dramatic imagination wishes to be exercised on its stage. . . .

53:4   The building, designed by Architect Ralph Rapson, looks as if Henry Moore had been doodling on it with a jigsaw. Through the holes of the outer facade peeks a structure drawn with a Modrian rule in a rectilinear austerity of charcoal grey, white and glass. Suspended over the stairs and lobbies are globes of light, a child's army of upside-down lollipops.

The stage itself juts forward like a mammoth home plate with a blunted tip, while a rear portico of four columns supports an upper platform. Around this arena stage sweeps C-arc of 200°, some tiers of the 1,437 seats rising as steeply as bleachers, others sloping more conventionally, none more than 52 ft. from the playing stage. The seats come in twelve shades of color. Above hover the scattered grey clouds of the acoustical panels, some of which house the spots that stab the stage with light.

Minneapolis' Tyrone Guthrie Theater, Midwestern home of a repertory company exclusively committed to the dramatic classics, is a token of light: the light of

53:4. "In the Land of Hiawatha," *Time*, May 17, 1963, pp. 87–88. Reprinted by permission from *Time*, The Weekly Newsmagazine; Copyright Time Inc., 1963.

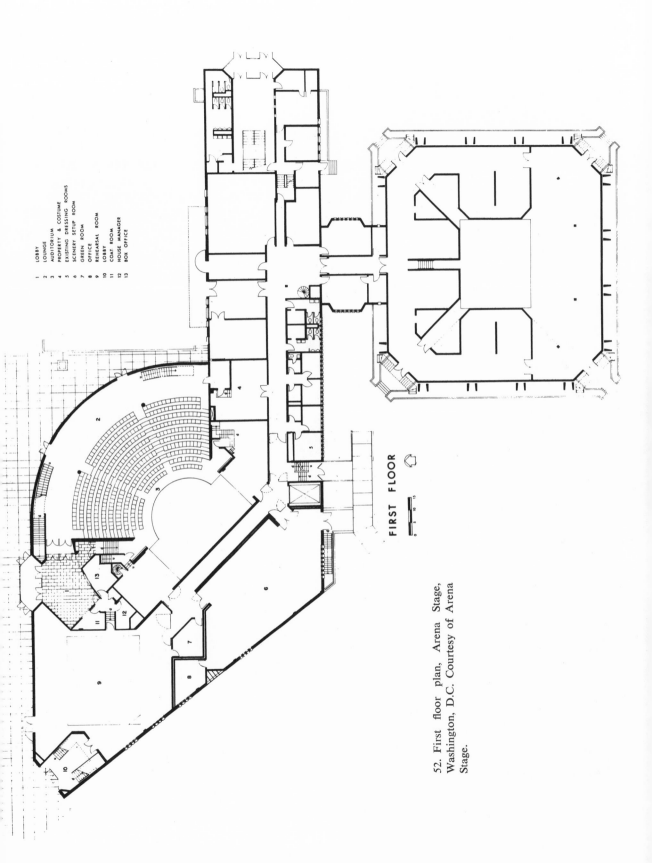

1 LOBBY
2 LOUNGE
3 AUDITORIUM
4 PROPERTY & COSTUME
5 EXISTING DRESSING ROOMS
6 SCENERY SETUP ROOM
7 GREEN ROOM
8 OFFICE
9 REHEARSAL ROOM
10 LOBBY
11 COAT ROOM
12 HOUSE MANAGER
13 BOX OFFICE

FIRST FLOOR

52. First floor plan, Arena Stage, Washington, D.C. Courtesy of Arena Stage.

53. Guthrie Theater, Minneapolis, 1963. Courtesy of The Guthrie Theater.

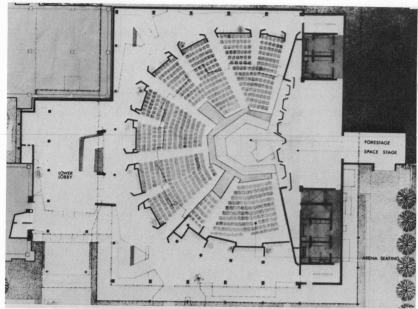

53. Plan of orchestra level, Guthrie Theater, Minneapolis. Courtesy of Design Quarterly.

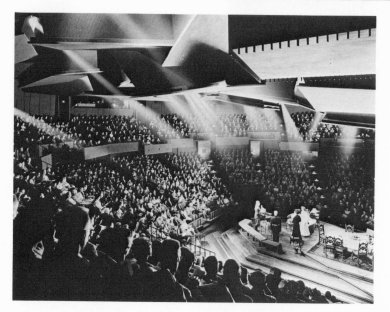

53. Interior, Guthrie Theater, Minneapolis, 1963. Scene shown is from Chekov's *The Three Sisters*. Courtesy of The Guthrie Theater.

ever quickening U.S. cultural interest, and the light of a theater seeking its better self far from Broadway's glaringly commercial White Way. Two questing Manhattan producers, Oliver Rea and Peter Zeisler, along with Tyrone Guthrie, were drawn to Minneapolis as a city immune to Broadway's manic-depressive boom-or-bust psychology. Guthrie, a restlessly inventive director, had already been the chief architect of Stratford, Ontario's successful festival. The trio found a fervent ally and a doggedly gifted fund raiser in Minneapolis Editor John Cowles, Jr. Prophesied Guthrie, who carries his 6-ft. 5-in. frame like a queen's grenadier guard in mufti: "Minn will come through."

Minn did. The T. B. Walker Foundation donated the land and a grant of $400,000. The Ford Foundation added $337,000. A Sunday school class in Mankato, Minn., sent 37¢. Out of a pyramid of effort, a $2,250,000 theater was born. To keep it alive for a four-play May through mid-September season costs $660,000. Already $331,150 has been raised in advance sales.

What is the value of a classical repertory theater? In Guthrie's view, it offers playgoers the chance to see "American expressions of the human spirit." As for actors: "How can actors develop other than personality cults if they don't measure themselves against the past?" . . .

53:5   Certainly the opening of the Tyrone Guthrie Theatre is an important landmark in theatre history. It is important as an example of what large urban community can do to enrich its life. And just as the Twin Cities recognized the feasibility of the project after seeing the even harder-won achievements in Stratford, Ontario, in Dallas, Texas, in Washington, D.C., and in New York's Central Park, so other cities will benefit from the results here.

53:5. Henry Hewes, "Northwestward Ho!" *Saturday Review*, May 25, 1963, p. 24. Copyright 1963 Saturday Review, Inc.

But it is also significant as a part of the nationwide spread of superior professional theatre. In Sir Tyrone Guthrie Minneapolis has a director who insists upon high standards, and who brings with him Tanya Moisewitsch, one of the world's great stage designers, and corps of technicians who guarantee that the production standard here will be as high as anywhere in the world. And, attracted by such excellence, many stars of our stage will be eager to spend a season performing here.

A third, more special importance of this theatre lies in the experimental extension of its open stage beyond the design of the stage at Stratford, Ontario. It would have been quite easy and safe for architect Ralph Rapson to copy that exciting and beautiful theatre with its symmetrical shape. Instead, this $2,500,000 theatre has tried to discover whether there may be some virtue in an asymmetrical seating arrangement and an irregular stage with a special geography of its own.

The theatre may take several seasons to evaluate fully. While the building itself, with its gay assortment of 1,437 brightly colored seats wrapped 180 degrees around the polyhedral tongue of its stage, is exciting on first entrance, one realizes after a few hours that considerable modification will be necessary before this theatre is as effective as its Canadian predecessor. For instance, because of the installation of bright aisle lights in the steeply pitched steps at one side of the auditorium, half the audience sees the plays against a distracting background of glare. Similarly, the polished, light-colored stage floor competes with the actors for our attention. And the architect's ceiling of permanent gray "clouds" creates an oppressive climate. Furthermore, asymmetry of the stage turns it into a too specific setting, instead of suggesting an area that the audience might imagine a number of poetic locations. And for some reason the scenes played against the back wall or on the little balcony seem terribly remote. . . .

54. THEATRE ATLANTA
Atlanta, Georgia
Opened November 2, 1966

Theatre Atlanta started as a community theater but later decided to become a professional company. There was, however, no permanent playhouse for the company, and seemingly no possibilities of one. At this point Frania T. Lee, who was on the board of directors of the group, donated a site and the money necessary to begin building. The new edifice opened its doors on November 2, 1966, to good critical acclaim for both the playhouse and the company. Unfortunately, financial difficulties caused the theater to close and it was put up for sale.

The New York *Times* announced its impending opening:

54:1 ATLANTA WILL GET A NEW PLAYHOUSE

Commercial Income to Help Support
Nonprofit Theater

---

by SAM ZOLOTOW

A nonsegrated, nonprofit legitimate theater is scheduled to open in Atlanta as a result of the efforts of a local drama buff.

Mrs. Frania Lee, widow of John W. Lee, a petroleum engineer, is contributing the site—a vacant lot between 17th and 18th Streets and West Peachtree Road—and the cost of the 700-seat house, which she estimates will be about $1 million, with loans and mortgages on reasonable terms. It will be called Theater Atlanta.

"We need a theater immediately to keep pace with a rapidly mounting population, now about 1.9 million, the construction boom and the cultural explosion," she said yesterday. "I became interested because the community has shown a wonderful spirit."

The ground-breaking ceremony is scheduled for Aug. 30, with occupancy about March 1. It will have a glass facade, a

54:1. New York *Times*, Aug. 16, 1965.

four-deck parking garage for 165 cars, three floors of office space, a gourmet restaurant, an after-theater cocktail lounge and a two-level promenade lobby.

COMMERCIAL USES HELP

According to Vincent Piacentini, consultant to Albert Ordway, architect, Theater Atlanta is probably the first example of a resident repertory theater that was made possible by the commercial development within the property.

As far as he could ascertain, he said, the project was the first direct application of a recommendation by the Rockefeller Panel Report on the Performing Arts that business and commercial activity should support a nonprofit theater.

However, a deficit for the 1965–66 season is anticipated. According to the prospectus, expenditures of $130,000 will be offset by $103,000 from direct income sources, such as season subscriptions, box-office sale and program advertising. The balance is to be covered by donations, a municipal appropriation and industrial and foundation support.

Jay Broad has been signed to a three-year contract as managing director.

"It is not our intention," he said, "to create a theater of 'instant culture,' whereby we would hire a company of ready-made actors, in ready-made plays and thereby achieve ready-made success.

TO REFLECT COMMUNITY

"We want to build a theater company, not an organization that simply presents 'shows'; a theater company that through nurturing and growth, will reflect the needs and desires of an Atlanta audience."

A core of 10 or 12 professional actors, preferably from Atlanta, will be hired on a full-time basis. Other players also are to be drawn from local talent.

Mr. Broad, a 35-year-old native of Newcastle, Pa., used to be an actor, but he gave up acting, he says, by "popular demand" to become a director. He was represented here last year by the Off

Broadway production of "Life Is a Dream."

Theater Atlanta will utilize a thrust stage that will bring the action closer to the audience. It will be 100 feet from wing to wing with a depth of 70 feet.

The auditorium is to be named in memory of Mrs. Lee's daughter, Mrs. Helen Cartledge, who was killed in 1962 with her husband, W. W. Cartledge when an Air France Boeing 707 jet crashed and burned while taking off for New York from Paris's Orly Airport.

There will be modern dressing rooms for 60 performers, a large workshop for prop and scenery construction and storage space.

Theater Atlanta was formed in 1957 as the result of a merger by the Atlanta Civic Theater, the Atlanta Theater Guild and the Playmakers.

54:2 THE OPENING of the new professional organization, Theatre Atlanta, is noteworthy for a number of reasons. The least dramatic but perhaps most valuable one is the way it has managed to finance itself in this rapidly growing community where so many new public projects are seeking the citizenry's philanthropic dollars.

Like the Studio Arena Theatre of Buffalo, Theatre Atlanta began as a community theater before deciding that it wanted to step up its quality with an Equity company and a new playhouse. Raising the required $1,000,000 quickly was impossible. However, one member of the board of directors, Mrs. Frania T. Lee, donated a site in memory of her deceased daughter, Mrs. Helen Cartledge, and was therefore able to borrow the construction money from the bank. This left the board with the much less formidable task of raising some $55,000 a year in order to pay Mrs. Lee a nonprofit rental

54:2. Henry Hewes, "The Conquest of Peachtree Street," *Saturday Review*, Nov. 19, 1966, p. 72. Copyright 1966 Saturday Review Inc.

sufficient to cover the carrying charges on her loan. Indeed, the amount may not be that much, for the theater, which is reconciled to an additional operating deficit of some $30,000 a year, will recoup considerable funds from a restaurant concession, three floors of rented offices above the theater itself, and parking fees from the 165-car garage, which is built below the main floor.

Theatre Atlanta also grew in a healthy way artistically. Its board found thirty-five-year-old director Jay Broad, who impressed them with his production of *Advise and Consent* with their non-Equity company, and he agreed to assume the leadership of the new company. Working with architect Albert Ordway and theater consultant Vincent Piacentini, Jr., he asked for an open-stage theater similar to the one at Stratford, Ontario, but, of course, much smaller. The result is handsome and works extremely well. None of the 775 spectators are more than 38 feet (fourteen rows) from the performing area, and, happily, this theater has include the all-important tunnels that permit actors to enter and exit from the two front corners of the stage.

HOWEVER, it hasn't all been easy. A carpenters' strike and a sheet-metal workers' strike delayed construction so that the theater, on its scheduled opening night, November 2, had facilities which were barely sufficient. Its restaurant was still a naked, cement room, portions of its lobby were still unplastered, and its heating system was not yet functioning.

To make things even more difficult, director Broad selected one of the most demanding plays of our time, Peter Shaffer's *The Royal Hunt of the Sun*, for the initial production. It is a tribute to both the theater's staff and its company that the presentation emerged as a consistently thrilling triumph.

To begin with, Mr. Piacentini devised three huge "ironing board" units, which he placed at the rear of the stage. When these are lowered halfway, they act as suspended platforms or "diving boards" on which the Inca god Atahuallpa and his priests can stand and view the approach of Pizarro and his tiny army. Later they can be let down all the way to form ramps, thereby creating the possibility of a dynamic flow of action through the stage area.

But *The Royal Hunt of the Sun* is total theater in which the scenery can become the actor, as it does with the lowering of the ramps, and the actors can become the scenery, as they do during the spectacle of Pizarro's men crawling along the stage floor, which gives us a sense of their scaling the forbidding and frozen Andes. Indeed, because Atlanta happened to be suffering a freak cold snap on opening night and because the heating system was not working, the totality of the experience was emphasized in a way certainly not anticipated by the playwright.

Of course, a company like this has its weaknesses, the principal one being a lack of depth in experienced and talented performers. Nevertheless, the two leading roles are so well played that it does not matter, and values emerge here that were not apparent in either the London or the New York pproduction. As Pizarro, a young, Laughtonesque actor named Clarence Felder is tormented and powerfully earthy. Despite an occasional overdoing of his passion, Mr. Felder gives us the sense of a historical figure struggling to find his true identity in an alien world. Since Mr. Shaffer is a realistic playwright, neither Pizarro nor his biographer, the disillusioned Martin, ever does find this identity. But in the struggle so fully portrayed here, he comes a great deal closer to it than do most men.

Even more rewarding is Frederick Congdon, who, as Atahuallpa, proved far superior to his Broadway predecessor. Mr. Congdon portrays the pagan ruler as a very shrewd and fiercely direct man, and his kinship with his reluctant murderer

and betrayer seems to surpass all other considerations. It is not a Christian kind of love, as Shaffer defines it, but in the highest sense of the word a sharing of understanding, a breakthrough that is possible, perhaps, only between two illiterates.

One can only say bravo to Mr. Broad and his audacious company, which includes distinguished actress Julie Haydon. That Miss Haydon is happy to play a tiny role in this first play suggests that this is a dedicated theater rather than just one more theater dedication.

The people of Atlanta were justly proud of their new dramatic facility. The Atlanta *Constitution* reported the opening:

54:3 $1,250,000 Theatre Atlanta Opens
With Gala Premiere
by Diane Thomas

Theatre Atlanta opened the doors of its new $1,250,000 home Wednesday night with a black tie premiere and Peter Shaffer's "Royal Hunt of the Sun."

The evening marked the turning point for the theater from an avocational civic group into the Southeast's first permanent professional repertory company.

The building at 1374 West Peachtree St. was financed by Atlanta's Mrs. Frania T. Lee in memory of her daughter Helen Lee Cartledge, who was killed with her husband in the 1962 Orly plane crash which took the lives of more than 100 Atlantans.

The auditorium will be named for Mrs. Cartledge.

In a gala pre-play ceremony Wednesday night, the doors of the theater were opened by Mrs. Bettey Sanders, wife of Georgia Gov. Carl Sanders, and the wife of Atlanta Mayor Ivan Allen. Vice Mayor Sam Massell Jr. presented the keys.

The opening attracted an impressive roster of celebrities. Among them were actor Bert Parks; composer-arranger

54:3. Atlanta *Constitution*, Nov. 3, 1965.

54. Theatre Atlanta, Atlanta, 1970. Courtesy of Mrs. Frania T. Lee.

54. Main stage, Theatre Atlanta, Atlanta, 1965. Color photograph by Chuck Sussmen. Courtesy of Mrs. Frania T. Lee.

55. Music Center Plaza, Los Angeles, 1964. In the foreground, "Peace on Earth," a sculpture by Jacques Lipschitz. Courtesy of Music Center Operating Co.

55. Music Center of Los Angeles County, Los Angeles, 1967. On the left, the Dorothy Chandler Pavilion; the Mark Taper Forum is the circular building (center right); on the right, in the Ahmanson Theater. Courtesy of Music Center Operating Co.

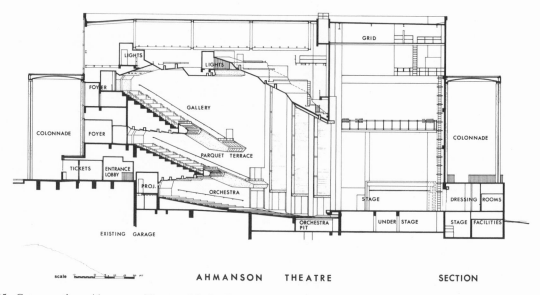

55. Cross section, Ahmanson Theatre, Music Center of Los Angeles County, Los Angeles, 1967. Architect's drawing. Courtesy of Welton Becket and Associates, Los Angeles.

Skitch Henderson, Butterfly McQueen of "Gone With the Wind" fame, New York playwright Harry Garnick, Stanley Young representing the President's Commission on the Arts, Gov. Sanders and Mayor Allen.

The building, still awaiting finishing touches, is the first built to house a legitimate theater in Atlanta in more than 65 years.

Standing five stories high, including three parking decks, the building contains, in addition to complete theater facilities, a 7,000 square foot area to be leased as a restaurant and cocktail lounge and some 10,000 square feet earmarked for commercial office space.

The plans are to extend the building an additional three to five stories for rental office space.

The auditorium itself, patterned after Tyrone Guthrie Theatre in Minneapolis and the Vivian Beaumont Theatre in Lincoln Center, New York, represents the combined efforts of New York-based theatrical architectural firm of Albert Ordway.

It features a 75-foot thrust stage with a 92-foot wing spread. The auditorium grid ceiling, 25 feet high, allows unlimited freedom in light placement.

The cost of the lighting equipment, including remotely controlled dimmers, is estimated at $27,000. The auditorium is done in charcoal brown with gold, rust and charcoal seats. It is surrounded by a promenade and exhibition area.

JAY BROAD HIRED

Last year Theatre Atlanta's board of directors engaged New York producer-director Jay Broad as their managing director. It was Broad who pushed for a permanent repertory company.

The core group of professionals now numbers 10, including four Atlanta actors. Avocationals fill out the roles.

Mrs. Lee describes the theater as "a dream come true." She and her daughter had always wanted to establish a drama

school for young girls. Now an acting school is included in the Theatre Atlanta program.

A LOT OF GUTS

"But what everyone has failed to realize," the petite, silver-blonde woman continues, "is the work, the struggle and the effort behind it all. It took a lot of guts."

It also took the cooperation of civic and business leaders, which was freely given.

At one point the group decided to give up the idea of a new theater and lease the building to office space, but the backers said, "no." The money was obtained for a theater and that's what they wanted it to be.

"The Royal Hunt of the Sun" kicks off a 34-week season of repertory, which will include Jack Kirkland's adaptation of "Tobacco Road" (opening Nov. 9), Jean Anouilh's "Waltz of the Toreadors," G. B. Shaw's "Caesar and Cleopatra," Arthur Miller's "After the Fall," and Bella and Sam Spevak's "Boy Meets Girl," Orson Welles' "Moby Dick, Rehearsed," and a final original production to be selected from manuscripts submitted in a Theatre Atlanta playwrights contest.

55. MUSIC CENTER OF LOS ANGELES COUNTY
Los Angeles, California
Opened April 12, 1967

The Music Center of Los Angeles County has been one of the most praised cultural centers in the United States. The architectural concept is efficient and beautiful and the three theaters not only artistically attractive but acoustically perfect. The first of the theaters to open was the Dorothy Chandler Pavilion, which was dedicated on April 9, 1964, primarily for operas, concerts, and ballets. It was not until three years later that the Mark Taper Forum and the Ahmanson Theatre were opened, but it was estimated that in the first three years, with only the Dorothy Chandler

Pavilion in use, the Music Center served 3,-967,981 persons, certainly an outstanding record.

A description of the center was published by the center, and the following excerpts are from that publication:

55:1 The Music Center is comprised of three theatres—the 3,250-seat Dorothy Chandler Pavilion, 750-seat Mark Taper Forum, and 2,100-seat Ahmanson Theatre. The Dorothy Chandler Pavilion, dedicated on December 6, 1964, contains unexcelled facilities for staging symphony orchestra concerts, opera, recitals, musical comedy, and dance programs. The Mark Taper Forum, dedicated on April 9, 1967, provides for intimate drama, recitals, lectures, and civic presentations; while the Ahmanson Theatre, dedicated April 12, 1967, is designed for drama, musicals, and ballet.

Planned, designed and engineered by Welton Becket and Associates, architects, engineers, and interior designers, and constructed by Peter Kiewit and Sons Company, general contractors, the three buildings are arranged on either side of the sweeping Mall Plaza with its reflecting pool, fountain, and evergreen trees. The Mark Taper Forum and Ahmanson Theatre are joined as a unit by a graceful colonade. Beneath the complex are four split levels of parking for 2,000 automobiles.

THE DOROTHY CHANDLER PAVILION presents a series of sculptured, fluted columns, faced in white quartz, extending the full length of the building and continuing around its entire periphery. Dimension of the six-level building are on a grand scale, 330 feet long, 252 feet wide, and it rises 92 feet from the Mall Plaza to the sculptured overhanging roof.

The Pavilion's auditorium is outstanding in its complete flexibility of acoustics, lighting and staging. It is capable of accommodating with equal ease opera, which utilizes a mammoth overhead stagehouse in addition to natural acoustics, musical comedy, which requires electrical amplification and a smaller, highly efficient stagehouse, and symphony concerts, which require natural acoustics as well as an acoustical shell enclosing the Orchestra and isolating it from the stagehouse.

A key to the auditorium's acoustical flexibility is a unique canopy which projects outward from the top of the proscenium and is adjustable to three different positions. In its lowest position, the canopy radiates sound to all seats in the house. This position is used for symphony concerts, opera and recitals. For musical comedy, which usually requires amplification, the canopy is raised to the second position, uncovering the speakers of the five-channel stereophonic system. The third position is similar to the second in that amplification can be used, but the canopy moves, exposing a light gallery for special stage lighting effects.

In sharp contradiction to the rule of thumb that a fine concert hall should be rectangular in shape, this auditorium is virtually square, providing an unusually intimate feeling for a house its size. Seating is on four levels—Orchestra, Founders Circle, Loge, and Balcony. Ninety per cent of the audience is within 105 feet of the stage. Seating on the Orchestra level is in the continental fashion, without front-to-rear aisles.

The stage of the Dorothy Chandler Pavilion is one of the largest in the nation —169 feet wide and 64 feet deep. It opens to a 40-foot by 172-foot rear stage and to a 40-foot by 60-foot side stage. 120 scenery battens are located beneath the 94-foot grid.

The orchestra pit is in two sections for flexibility and is hydraulically located so that the orchestra can be lifted into position from below stage level.

There are star dressing rooms on stage and mezzanine levels. On the Grand Ave-

55:1. Souvenir brochure published by Music Center of Los Angeles County, n.d.

nue level, there are dressing rooms for 200 dancers and chorus members, with complete wardrobe facilities, as well as press room, a first aid room, lounges, a music library and areas for instrument and scenery storage.

Offices for the Music Center Operating Company, Southern California Symphony –Hollywood Bowl Association, Los Angeles Civic Opera Association, Southern California Choral Music Association, the Music Center Opera Association, the Los Angeles County Music Center Coordinator, and the Los Angeles County Music and Performing Arts Commission are contained on the third and fourth floors.

The fourth floor also contains four large rehearsal halls, one of which is equal in size to the playing area of the stage.

The fifth floor of the Dorothy Chandler Pavilion is devoted to dining facilities. The Pavilion Restaurant has been designed for elegance and comfort. Its dining room offers buffet and Continental service with a sweeping view of the surrounding city. Two banquet rooms, the Blue Ribbon Room, seating 220, and the El Dorado Room, seating 170, are available for special parties. Another dining room, the Curtain Call Restaurant, decorated with mementos of early Los Angeles theatrical life, is located on the Grand Avenue level.

Major public areas include the magnificent Grand Hall, Oval Room and The Founders on the second floor and the Green Room on the Grand Avenue level. A mirrored Grand Stairway rises from the Grand Avenue entrance to all seating levels.

THE MARK TAPER FORUM anticipates the needs of the small theatre without imposing limits on flexibility of space and facilities. The circular structure rises from the center of a 175-foot-square reflecting pool, with the building's upper 27 feet cantilevering outward from its base to a diameter of 140 feet. Four broad walkways span the pool, with entry from the Mall Plaza across the south walk-

way beneath an aluminum canopy. Enclosing the upper portion of the building is a large, precast concrete mural suggestive of the forms and movement of the theatre. The mural was created by Beton Form Designers of San Francisco with design consultant Jacques Overhoff. Contrasting with the white panels of the mural are the dark precast panels which sheathe the Mark Taper Forum's circular base.

Entry to the theatre itself is into a main lobby dominated by a 60-foot curved wall faced with abalone shell cut into small squares and set as mosaic tile, executed by Tony Duquette. A bronze bust of Mark Taper by sculptor Robert Berks stands in the lobby.

A pentagonal thrust stage creates the focal point of the Mark Taper Forum's auditorium. This stage offers exceptionally good sight lines from the 14 rows of seats which rise steeply from the floor in a semi-oval around the stage. The stage, which extends 28 feet outward from the curved north wall and has a maximum depth of 30 feet, is a simple platform three steps up from the house floor. Completely without proscenium or stage curtains, the stage gives broad latitude to the production and permits the audience to become virtually a physical part of the presentation. Enhancing this stage is the combination of an arc-shaped cyclorama projection wall at the rear, movable open aluminum screens in front of the cyclorama wall, and a moving floor system between the screens and the wall.

A broad range of stage lighting is made possible through the inclusion of 300 lights in the ceiling above and between the acoustical panels. Additional lighting effects are made possible through the use of a lighting gallery at the rear of the house, a row of recessed lights above the cyclorama screen, and lights recessed into the face of the stage which are used to conceal onstage changes from the audience. A cyclorama projection room is located above the acoustical panels in the center of the house, on the same level as the light and sound control booth. Dressing rooms and scenery storage areas are behind the cyclorama wall. Additional storage areas and two quick-change rooms are on the main floor, and ten dressing rooms are located on the second level.

THE AHMANSON THEATRE'S 73-foot-high facade is enclosed by a full wall of dark gray glass, allowing patrons in the lobby and two upper promenades an excellent view of the Mark Taper Forum and its reflecting pool. In the evening the Ahmanson Theatre's exterior appearance is enlivened by the movement of patrons inside the building seen through the glass wall. The other three walls of the structure are precast concrete panels textured with off-white onyx aggregate.

The achievement of maximum intimacy of audience with performer guided the design of the theatre. The auditorium's depth is equal to its width. A bowed stage can bring the performance closer to the audience than in most theatres its size. The proscenium is as wide as the auditorium at the stage wall and runs the full height of the theatre, eliminating the formal proscenium arch. Thus, the physical barrier which separates audience from performer has been removed.

Added to these enhancing factors are the excellent sight lines from all seats. This is accomplished by using a square rather than the usual tunnel-like auditorium.

Grand stairways on both sides of the lobby lead downward to the 1,000-seat Orchestra level, which is below Mall level, and upward to the 500-seat Parquet Terrace and 600-seat Balcony. The first 13 rows of the Orchestra are arranged in continental fashion to create a dress circle. Entry to the Orchestra's continental seating is from both sides, while all other seating levels are entered from promenades at the rear of the auditorium.

The stage playing area is 40 feet wide and 45 feet deep, with the total inside stage width extending to 110 feet. A 75-foot-high grid provides 98 battens from which to fly scenery, curtain and props. The proscenium is 42 feet high and the house curtain raises to 30 feet to create an informal proscenium arch.

Acoustical flexibility is provided by a 20-by-60-foot canopy suspended from ceiling mounts above the proscenium. The canopy can be lowered to within 30 feet of the stage. When sound reinforcement is desired, a speaker border with a three-channel stereophonic speaker system can be dropped from behind the house curtain.

The orchestra pit is adjustable in two sections to accommodate up to 70 musicians who enter from the basement level, which houses locker rooms for orchestra members, a music library, and mechanical and electrical equipment. When not required for a presentation, the orchestra pit can be closed over with hinged decking on which removable seats can be placed.

A wardrobe room and dressing rooms are located on stage level. Two rehearsal rooms, one on the second floor and one on the third, allow a double rehearsal schedule in addition to onstage rehearsal. There is a suite of offices for the Center Theatre Group on the west side of the fourth floor. The fifth level is devoted to lighting galleries and electrical equipment. Additional stage lights are located on either side of the proscenium, behind walnut screens.

56. PLAYHOUSE IN THE PARK
Cincinnati, Ohio
Opened July 18, 1968

The Playhouse in the Park had been a favorite entertainment spot of Cincinnati playgoers since 1960. The original theater was a pavilion in Eden Park converted for use as a thrust stage. It was also quite small with a seating capacity of only 255, scarcely adequate

55. Interior, Mark Taper Forum, Music Center of Los Angeles County, Los Angeles, 1967. Courtesy of Music Center Operating Co.

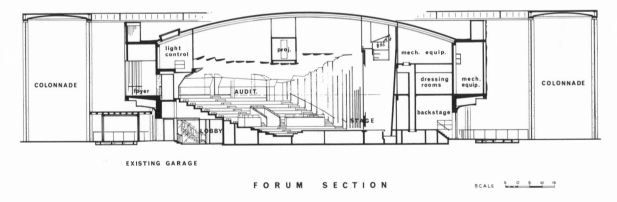

FORUM SECTION

SCALE

55. Cross section, Mark Taper Forum, Music Center of Los Angeles County, Los Angeles, 1967. Architect's drawing. Courtesy of Welton Becket and Associates, Los Angeles.

56. Playhouse in the Park, Cincinnati, 1968. In the center, the Robert S. Mark Theatre; in the foreground, the Shelter House Theatre. Courtesy of Playhouse in the Park.

for the needs of the public. A new theater was added to the old one and opened on July 18, 1968.

The Cincinnati *Enquirer* described the new playhouse:

56:1 Two days prior to the political bedlam of its National Governors' Conference, Cincinnati, Thursday, July 18, will become the theatrical focal point of the nation. On this date Playhouse in the Park christens its new $900,000 Robert S. Marx Theater in Eden Park. In more than forty years, the new theater is the first built for professional legitimate theater production and performance on a year-round basis. There have been new theaters constructed for campus, community, and summer musical operations.

The Marx Theater of the Playhouse will open with the first regional professional production of Tennessee Williams' 'Camino Real'.

The new theater is a giant step forward for both the American regional theater movement, and Cincinnati—creating the city's first two-theater complex. It has room for major productions in the Marx Theater and experimentals, original and children's theater in the nine-year-old converted shelter house which has served until this year.

A seating capacity of 672 in the new theater triples the number of people who can enjoy the work of this widely acclaimed resident professional company.

Audiences will enter the functional building, designed by Hugh Hardy of Hardy, Holzman and Pfeiffer, New York, across a plaza dotted with a random pattern of airport landing lights. Black and yellow doors give access to a lobby which is interesting not because of its decor, but because of the functional architecture which creates a decorative touch. A carpeted ceiling matches strips laid on the floors, and cuts a swath toward the main entrance to the auditorium itself. Theatri-

cal make-up lights, industrial shields and fluorescent strip lighting emit only white light in contrast to the deep blue of the landing lights on the plaza.

The lobby is walled with plain concrete blocks and figuratively shattered into five distinct levels where theater-goers may move during the pre-show or intermission. These levels are tied together visually with the impact of floor to ceiling mirrors.

A wall of glazed tiles bears the signatures of many patrons and businessmen who contributed $25 each to join the graffiti vanguard—among them Celeste Holm and Tallulah Bankhead. This signature wall stretches the height of the lobby area for 40 feet.

The auditorium is a gently sweeping arc broken by a cross aisle. The seats face three sides of an irregularly shaped acting platter upon which the shows are mounted. Again carpeting seems to be the only luxury. The ceiling is open, baring air conditioning ducts, electrical conduits, and a maze of catwalks from which the stage lighting is hung. The seats are comfortable, and spaced so each row can see over the head of those in front. The inner area creates an excitement of its own with a tilted seating bowl and angular stage to enhance the audience-actor relationship.

Most regional theaters, even the Playhouse in the Park, have had to live in buildings which are converted warehouses, lofts and other structures not designed, but adapted, for theater. Some of these, like the Shelter Theater, served admirably for the purpose, others are desperately inadequate and all regional theaters look forward to the time when they can move into a brand new plant of their own.

Playhouse in the Park not only joined the trend of new theaters and art complexes across the country, but has been prompted by a phenomenal growth. Unlike most performing centers, the demand for additional seating led the board of di-

56:1. Cincinnati *Enquirer*, July 7, 1968.

rectors and Brooks Jones, producer, in the direction of planning the new house.

Building the locally-financed showplace is more than an architectural feather for the Cincinnati area, or a dream-come-true for a group of culture-minded residents. It is concrete and convincing proof of the rapidly increasing importance of the regional theater to the arts in America. Walter Kerr of the N.Y. Times has accused the traditional Broadway theater of "suffering from this terrible sense of sameness." More and more actors and directors are realizing that the commercialism of the New York Theater is not atmosphere for experimentation and creativity.

The regional theaters are a convincing cure, for they can offer a well balanced diet of drama, mixing G. B. Shaw, Giraudoux, Beckett and Moliere with original offerings and musicals. That is why a regional company such as Cincinnati's Playhouse can attract actors like Al Freeman Jr., Ed Zang, Ellen Holly, Lynn Milgrim, David Hooks and Michael Lipton, directors such as Word Baker and Michael Kahn, and set designers like Ed Wittstein. The new Playhouse gives them evidence that an audience does await them, and these audiences are prepared to back them by overflowing houses and financial help to build the new theater.

Playhouse producer Brooks Jones has been with the theater here for six years. He calls it a "maverick operation," which in spite of its daring has shown artistic and financial success. "The new theater expands our capabilities immensely, and it is primarily the work of a few local people who want good theater, here in Cincinnati and now," he says.

Julius Novick of The Nation has said. "I left the Playhouse with a sense that something had happened to me—a rare feeling enough in the American theater."

An article in *Theatre Crafts* explained the design concepts for the new playhouse:

56:2 The coming together of the brave new breeds of producers and architects, each with their own concepts of what a theater structure should be, has produced some interesting new approaches to housings for the drama.

One of the underlying questions remains however—after the plans and model have been approved by the clients and all involved, and the theatre is up, and in operation—how successful has the new approach proved in producing a new theatrical experience. Has the new structure contributed to the dramatic experience or to the interpretation of drama, or has it complicated it to the degree that a traditional proscenium solution would, in the final analysis, have been more desirable?

CINCINNATI'S PLAYHOUSE IN THE PARK

The city of Cincinnati is one interesting place to look for some answers to these questions—to look at a new kind of theater that has been put up, and discover how one set designer works within that new performance space.

There are two theatres on top of Mount Adams in Cincinnati—all as part of a project begun by a small group of citizens to bring good, live theatre to that city. In the first phase of the project, the architects, Hardy, Holzman, Pfeiffer Associates, took an already existing Victorian structure and remodeled it into a 225 seat theatre—the Old Shelter House Theatre. Later the new Robert S. Marx Theatre was added to form the complex known as the Playhouse in the Park. The larger, 672 seat, new theatre (opened in 1968) is an exciting excursion into vital ways of conceiving a theatre project.

Perhaps the most interesting aspect of this new Robert S. Marx Theatre is how this essentially new approach to housing the drama relates to the people working

56:2. Patricia J. MacKay, "Settings for a New Stage Shape," *Theatre Crafts*, Jan./Feb. 1971, pp. 15–21, 34–35.

within the theatre. Both producer/theatre director Brooks Jones and architect Hugh Hardy thought that their plan "would make possible more imaginative and flexible productions." Architect Pfeiffer also notes that Brooks Jones did not feel a need for "many of the elements that theatre people have been trained to work with. The room was shaped and oriented in a way that would force people working there to reinterpret, rather than repeat, all the gimmicks and ways of setting up scenery of the part."

A number of designers have worked in the new Robert S. Marx Theatre since its opening. Among the most interesting designs are those of Ed Wittstein for *Volpone, Good Woman of Setzuan,* and *He Who Gets Slapped.* His use of materials, color, and stage space indicates a good understanding of the visual and architectural effects of this new theatre. . . .

OLD SHELTER HOUSE THEATRE

Ed Wittstein first went to Cincinnati several years ago to mount productions of Moliere's *The Miser* and Henry Living's *Honor and Offer* in the Old Shelter House Theatre. The old Victorian building had been converted into an intimate ¾ round theatre. The 225 seats were ranged on three sides of the stage space. However, the conversion had left an industrial chimney in the center of the stage around which Wittstein worked his set designs.

Their production of *The Miser* was updated to New Orleans as it stood before the Civil War. The set was constructed from raw wood and canvas—with yellow, white, black and grey as the main colors. The industrial chimney became the natural focus around which the basic set—a New Orleans fretwork balcony—was built.

In *Honor and Offer,* designer Wittstein reinforced the intimacy of the small theatre. The play, he felt, called for a "cottagey English Country Garden" feeling. His solution—a very realistic orchard with real trees and flowers was placed in front of the standing industrial chimney. The set was extended to the walls of the theatre where Wittstein had plants and flowers growing, and under the first few rows of seats where the audience found grass and flowers underfoot.

About working in Cincinnati, designer Wittstein comments, "I found the experience of getting out and working out of New York so refreshing that I have been going back ever since." A tribute not only to the city, the audience, the people he worked with, but, no doubt, to the two theatres in which he worked—the Old Shelter House as well as the new Robert S. Marx Theatre.

ROBERT S. MARX THEATRE

Since the completion of the new, large theatre, Wittstein has designed three productions there—*Volpone, Good Woman of Setzuan* and this past summer's production of *He Who Gets Slapped.* In talking out the most recent designs Wittstein highlights his approach to this theatre. "The whole theatre became the set and the set was a direct outgrowth of the theatre. All three productions that I have done there have been approached in that way. I have used modern materials which marry very well with the inside of the theatre. They accommodate the theatre, and don't work against it."

THE ARCHITECTURE

This new theatre has received a great deal of notice, by both the architectural and more general press. Producer/director Brooks Jones, under whose supervision the plans and requirements for the theatre were worked out has some very definite ideas about theatrical staging and the theatre stands very much as a testimony, in concrete, to those ideas.

First, this was to be a theatre in which the actors and the audience were in the same room, i.e., that there was to be no picture frame through which to view action. Secondly, that although the actors and audience are in the same room, there should be a distinct separation of their areas. Thirdly, as architect Hugh Hardy explains in *Architectural Record,* the stage was like a bookend. This means not looking at the stage wall straight on, but looking down at the floor and the back wall—seeing the floor and the wall together.

The result, architecturally, of this input was an asymmetrical thrust stage—at the time, it was only one of a few thrust stages built. The stage is separated from the audience seating by a moat or pit which Hugh Hardy points out "works well for Brooks Jones' style of production. Actors and audience do not intermix. He thinks this demeans the actor. He wants actors to be larger-than-life-sized people."

The asymmetry is evident in the stage shape as well as in the seating plan. About this asymmetrical stage architect Hardy has said that "once you put a performance into a room with an audience, the performance becomes a three-dimensional thing which depends on the movement as well as speech. There should be the opportunity to move in all sorts of ways which an asymmetrical stage provides."

Reinforcing the physical stage is the seating and shape of the house itself. The seats are ranged at different levels around the stage so that an actor moving to stage right finds himself looking down on the audience, whereas when he moves to stage left he is looking up at them.

In an auditorium such as this, where the arcs of seats terminate at the side wall, these walls become visually important. While in another time and place they might have been decorated and gingerbreaded, the architects devised a "porous" wall scheme which makes them functional. The several levels, perforations, and projections of these side walls work for the performance and provide, in conjunction with the vomitories and normal stage en-

trances, 24 ways of entering the stage areas.

The industrial "decoration" of the exterior and the lobby is carried through into the auditorium. There cat walks, structural metals, ladders and lights are all exposed. Concrete blocks are also exposed inside and out. . . .

ARCHITECTURAL QUESTIONS

The various designers working in this new theatre encountered some difficulties which bring up a few questions about the design of the building. The primary of these difficulties is the lack of direct connection from the scene shop to the stage and the lack of facilities for flying scenery.

The scene shop is below ground level and finished scenery must be hoisted up, brought around and then into the theatre. In discussing the problem architect Norman Pfeiffer points out that it was necessary to build that way because that one shop serves both the theatres in the Playhouse complex. That means that it is in use almost constantly. The only way to operate the shop without interfering with performances in the Robert S. Marx Theatre was to change the level, and seal it off with a two foot thick soundproof wall.

Although designer Ed Wittstein understands that theoretically rigging is seldom necessary in a thrust theatre, he comments "sometimes you do a production that requires a certain theatre magic." One example of that from his own work is the *Good Woman of Setzuan* for which Wittstein put in a rig so that the gods could fly to heaven at the end of the play.

Architect Pfieffer points out that at the time of designing the building they consulted with the people who were going to use the building. They could foresee no necessity for flying anything larger than a chandelier.

These are the kinds of questions that always arise between architect and potential user, and, no doubt will continue to

56. Interior, Playhouse in the Park, Cincinnati, 1969. Photograph by Ron Cochran. Courtesy of Cincinnati Enquirer.

57. Alley Theatre, Houston, 1968. Below, the large stage. Photographs by Ezra Stoller. Courtesy of the Alley Theatre.

come up—especially when budgets are limited and certain sacrifices have to be made.

It is an old problem, but a pertinent one: architects design for certain clients —to fit their particular and expressed needs for a given building. New people coming into a building brings with them other ways of working. Architect Pfeiffer comments that "problems will arise in any theatre when new people come in and apply their training to it. Theatres—proscenium or thrust—are designed with a particular point of view in mind and can seldom be forced to do something for which they were not designed."

The last word goes to Ed Wittstein who sums up his feelings about the playhouse by saying, "I am basically very happy with this theatre because there is an honesty, a relation between the outside and the inside and the function of the building, and it works very well as a theatre. Designing for the stage is becoming less concerned with putting up a lot of stuff. This simplicity is hard to find but it is the most satisfying and gives the most breadth to a production."

57. ALLEY THEATRE
Houston, Texas
Opened November 28, 1968

From the time the original Alley Theatre opened in 1947, the group headed by Nina Vance stood for excellence in theater. The building opened in 1968 was the third structure used by the group in its climb to national recognition. Nina Vance began with her group in a rented dance studio. Later she moved to a converted fan factory, where the group remained for over a decade, winning plaudits from critics throughout the country for their imaginative and well-chosen productions.

The subsequent magnificent playhouse, one of the best in the country, was financed by a $2,500,000 grant from the Ford Foundation and $1,000,000 raised by the people of Houston.

The following articles appeared in a commemorative brochure published in 1963. Brooks Atkinson wrote glowingly of the Alley, a theater in which he was vitally interested, and of its founder.

57:1   When I was visiting the Alley Theatre a decade ago, as drama critic of The New York *Times,* I asked Mrs. Vance how big she thought her potential audience was. "Fifteen thousand," she said. Since the population of greater Houston then was over a million, I was indignant. It seemed to me inexcusable that so few people in such a large city were interested in an intelligent theatre that put on significant plays so creditably.

Was Mrs. Vance too modest in 1958 or has Houston changed? For something —something admirable—has happened. The Alley Theatre subscribers now number over 20,000, which would be its active audience; and the potential audience must be at least twice as many. Now a radiant little institution that has lived so long in a refurbished fan factory is moving into a substantial modern building in the center of Houston, near Jesse H. Jones Hall, which is a dynamic building; and Mrs. Vance has not one theatre but two in which to squander the energy that has made the Alley Theatre one of the two best residential theatres in the United States.

I sometimes wonder why it is that women are so often the most effective in establishing residential theatres. The late Margo Jones was the pioneer among chatelaines. She founded her theatre in Dallas in 1947. Mrs. Vance organized the Alley Theatre of amateurs in a dance studio the same year. Arena Stage in Washington is the enterprise of Mrs. Zelda Fichandler who, incidentally, will also have two theatres to work in within a year or two. Why is that women have

57:1. Brooks Atkinson, "A Radiant Little Institution," in Alley Theatre commemorative brochure (Houston, 1963), p. 8.

155

been so conspicuously successful in this field?

I don't know; perhaps there is no reason. But Margo Janes was and Mrs. Vance and Mrs. Fichandler are women who have, not only talent for and a willingness to succeed slowly. They have durable nerves. It takes a long time to establish a residential theatre. It takes a long time and infinite work to create a reputation that has local acceptance.

If Mrs. Vance did not have patience as well as professional integrity she would never have survived the early crises when she was establishing a theatre that few people in the community realized that they needed. During the twenty-one years of the Alley, other theatres in Houston have come and gone and it was not because they lacked talent.

As an old friend of the Alley I should like to salute Mrs. Vance and all her associated friends and subscribers. The move into the new building—probably "complex" is the proper word, since there are two theatres—represents a victory for everyone, and the Alley Theatre is now going to be host to a larger part of the city population.

But everyone is permitted to feel a little nostalgia and gratitude to that cramped but hospitable rabbit-warren on Berry Avenue. Architecturally, it has no distinction. It is not even an efficient theatre plant. But the mood was cordial there. It was an extension of the personality of Mrs. Vance—friendly, modest, womanly, cautiously confident, humorous and dedicated. It is impossible to assess the value of what she has contributed to the civilization of Houston by staging so many plays in so many styles.

The Alley Theatre is genuinely cosmopolitan. It produces the best from everywhere. Nothing human is alien to the Alley Theatre where the subscribers can have a good time and also stretch their minds a little. When the new theatres open

they can stretch their minds wider than they could on Berry Avenue. Good Luck!

A local drama critic, Ann Holmes of the Houston *Chronicle,* had attended the first performance of the Alley in 1947 and wrote with perception about the theater's growth.

57:2   The Alley's tatters-to-towers history ought to prove something—that the Alley has been good in its 20 years, good enough to merit this Big Change.

But what is it that, out of its wildly varied list of 157 plays, has made this theatre which began as a flyer in a rented dance studio in 1947 worth the dollars and the interest of so many Huston people and important foundations in Houston and New York?

The answer has to lie with Nina Vance —but it ineluctably belongs to her public in Houston, too. Despite the fact that she is hard to track down by phone and seldom lingers long in the lobby area for the public to glimpse, she is not separable from the people who come to the Alley.

She doesn't know most of them in a city of millions. But almost 20,000 of them signed up for subscriptions before she'd even announced the titles of the plays.

An unspoken collaboration has existed between the people of the Alley and the uncharted audience out there since the first night in that dingy uncomfortable little studio room with the tree sprouting out of its ceiling. I was there to cover the play, "A Sound of Hunting," on November 18, 1947. The production must have been pretty tentative as I think back. But at the time, it signalled a new era. Odets and Lillian Hellman at the Alley were to put to rout an outmoded Noel Coward at the Little Theatre. For a generation of young people—and others with

57:2. Ann Holmes, "An Unspoken Collaboration," in Alley Theatre commemorative brochure (Houston, 1963), pp. 9–10.

vision—this spelled theatre of reform and change.

Looking over the list of plays offered since then, one notes it was a peaceful revolution, if indeed it was one—not much scandal, no bloodshed. Even that scurvy fellow, the fire marshall, who closed down the first theatre inadvertently provided a superb ending for act one and heightened the drama of The Cause.

When in the 'new' building, a regenerated fan factory, the theatre opened with Lillian Hellman's "The Children's Hour" a few eyebrows may have arched. But the theatre audience was ready for it and greeted the production with a storm of prolonged applause.

Once settled in its make-shift theatre, the Alley and its director could get down to the business of growing up—and they did. Some productions naturally were better than others. Only once, in "The Hostage," were audiences infuriated enough to huff and rattle themselves out of the theatre during the action. And in that tiny, close theatre, getting out took a lot of dudgeon.

A contact at the theatre phoned me and said, "It's terrible, the people are literally leaving the theatre in the middle of the act." I assured my friend that this was probably the greatest moment in the theatre's history, and urged him to go back and relish the bustle of it all.

This is what theatres are for—to stimulate and to make fantasy on that stage come so dynamically close it moves your mind, your heart, your bias, even your feet.

Consistently the Alley's seriousness grew evident and its productions deepened in techniques. This theatre, like a good play, has undergone a significant change, in this case the cumulation of growth. Suddenly—but rightly—it is moving out, into the clothing of maturity.

The tiny theatre's momentum and its magic, never quite consistent before with its physical facilities, hopefully can be sustained in the striking new turreted palace—which could be a set for "Henry V." And why not? Nina Vance is very much there. Underneath her easy laughter, her soft Texas accent, her luminous good looks and engaging manner, often self deriding, she conceals a disarming theatrical drive. It is like TNT in Emba mink.

She is so constantly alert to and responsive to new needs and new breezes that even veteran staff members don't try to second guess her.

Because she is a scholar and restless searcher for the right word she can be expected to cast out translation after translation and finally end up with a home brew of her own. If she goes after a particularly gifted guest director—she comes back with another one she liked better. But the greatest single quality of this woman and the one which has most profoundly shaped the theatre is her instinct for the human thing. This, blended with her sense of scholarship and her now sharpened theatre craft, makes her a fine director—and an apt administrator.

Critics don't watch play rehearsals. But on two rare occasions sans portfolio, and once on a research grant, I saw Miss Vance in action.

She sits quietly in the dark—watching, mostly watching. There is no shrill correction, no badminton of interrupting commentary. Occasionally, she'll stop rehearsal to make suggestions, redo some blocking, discuss a large meaning or a small one.

She has a developed sense of character, enjoys the ridiculous and invents funny scenes. Rehearsals tend to bubble and to keep their spontaneity. She never says do it this way and never walks an actor through a part. She has met with each player earlier, talked over the whole. And during the working hours she is teacher and a critical but engaged private audience which actors need. And afterwards in her office she became confidante, psychiatrist and final authority.

In a pre-rehearsal session of Chekhov's "The Three Sisters," she once asked each actor to write down on a slip of paper his private dream. No one would ever see it, she assured them. Reluctantly they wrote. When she asked someone to collect the notes, the actors went suddenly apprehensive. Was this some trick; would they be read? Instead the papers were burned ceremoniously unread, and the actors were urged to imagine their dreams going up in smoke.

This was a Nina Vance method of bringing home to them the intensity they must experience in the later parts of the play.

To maintain a theatre of novelty and small revolt would never have been enough for Nina Vance, though it was just right at the moment the Alley was born. In moving toward a major institution, dealing with works of quality and classic strength, she has characteristically taken the hard course.

If a glance at the list of works played during 20 years indicates a slight leaning toward the romantic, a closer look shows it has also been a list that favored high purpose and was frankly keen on literature. At few points was there sentimentality. The underlying grace of it has been a sense of the personal combined with a drive for excellence. That human concern made the Alley's comedies especially pointed, made its O'Neill glow and its Chekhov something special.

An official history of the Alley Theatre was commissioned by the officials of the playhouse and William Beeson hired to write it. Chapter 5, "Thresholds," described the new theater that opened in November 1968:

57:3   One is most careful about those to

57:3. William Beeson, "Thresholds," reprinted in Alley Theatre commemorative brochure (Houston, 1963), pp. 52–58.

whom one entrusts one's dreams. Particularly when those dreams are to manifest themselves in something as lasting as concrete. It is understandable that Nina Vance, Alley Theatre's founding director, took time before naming an architect for the building that would provide a home for the Alley Theatre.

In Ulrich Franzen she found a spirit that was, while not closely allied to her own, one that strongly complements some of its most deeply-rooted beliefs. From the beginning, it was plain to her that Franzen was no follower. He was out to change the face of American architecture. Implicit in his desire to do this was a feeling for the life of our nation's cities; a concern for the comfort and pleasure of those who spend the better part of their working lives surrounded by it. A collaboration between architect and future occupant requires that each probe the semantics of the other, often a most delicate business. More than this, it requires a searching instinct ready to plumb to the depths two distinct philosophies. The relationship established between an architect who has never before designed a theatre and a theatre director who has never before been in contact with an architect, demands much of them, both as craftsmen and people.

To facilitate Mr. Franzen's understanding of the Alley Theatre and its needs, taping sessions with the professional staff and company took place two weeks after the architect's appointment. During these sessions, members of the staff discussed their needs at some length. Often, at Mr. Franzen's insistence, the discussion went into the basic ideas behind their jobs: what their functions were, both as administrators/artists and as people. Frequently, what they idealized was torn apart in staff discussion and found to be both impractical and vague. Slowly, definitions were arrived at, often to the surprise of those involved. As people, we all have a tendency to take our jobs for granted. It is only when we are asked to explain what we do that we flounder and sputter. The sessions with Ulrich Franzen were valuable in two ways: they gave him an idea of what was required to make a theatre plant function smoothly; and they gave the staff time to reflect on their areas of responsibility and the expansion of those areas in the period ahead.

It was at first thought that a design consultant should be hired to assist in the development of the two theatres the new building would house. Several prominent designers were interviewed in extended conferences. Gradually, it become apparent to Nina Vance that she could not abandon this vital role to a stranger. It was at this important moment that Paul Owen, Alley Theatre design director, entered the history of the building. In the years that followed, time and time again, he was to prove invaluable to Mrs. Vance and Mr. Franzen, both as interpreter and consultant. It is Mr. Owen's enviable ability to see both sides of a question; to view a design with regards to the theatre's needs and its effectiveness as pure design.

There ensued a prolonged dialogue between director and architect. To Nina Vance it was essential that the theatre convey the male-female relationship, a relationship more vital than any, one that dominated the foundation of her theatre. Then, too, she had always regarded the theatre as a temple, a place of rites and worship, a place offering safety; protection from the too-swift currents of life.

Franzen reinforced the idea of safety; he felt it necessary to protect man's individuality through such a building. Not only must it offer protection, but it must strive to give the more introverted person small, enclosed areas in which to enjoy intermissions; at the same time, it must offer the more public person an aura of grandness, openness, potential space to be filled. Man's sense of identity could not be violated by a vast building that dwarfed his sense of self.

It was determined that the building should reflect its presence in the Southwest. This could be done by a rusty or tawny exterior, one that, in Franzen's words, suggested something "as ancient as stone . . . as modern as Houston." This feeling could be maintained throughout the structure by textures of fabrics, use of woods, by the very sense of limitless space encountered so often in this part of the world.

Too few buildings today elicit emotions in us as spectators. Paul Owen feels that the Alley Theatre, in its fluctuation of shapes, achieves an emotional aura throughout. "There are reductions of space, followed by explosions. The spectator becomes absorbed in getting to his destination. When he does, it comes as a surprise. The space provides this surprise. It also is a period. At all times the fluctuation is peripheral; subtle."

The Southwest emerges, too, in the feeling of earth, water and air, all employed to advantage in choice of materials, vistas from the porches, the almost aqueous undulation of the grand staircase.

As the design conferences continued and sketches and models began to emerge, the towers of the building developed the theme of marriage: of male and female, father and mother. The building's exterior, according to Paul Owen, "is a marriage of all geometric forms." This, he is quick to admit, could have become a disaster. It did not. Today one can readily see that the structure's soft, feminine curves are broken by stern, monolithic facing or the monumental towers. This juxtaposition was important throughout the building; it became a discipline strictly enforced, one that produced a building that sings viewed from any point.

Prior to all this, the large room was talked into shape. It was decided to retain the Alley arena and not out of sheer sentimentality. Franzen and the world had found it "an unusually effective stage.["] The new arena was to seat 300. It would retain the configurations of its original home on Berry Avenue. "However," stated Franzen, "the obsolute structure and equipment have, of course, been replaced with modern equipment, comfortable seating and spacious facilities, its architectural character will be that of a masonry-vaulted, intimate chamber, tucked away in the safe confines of a great building.

"The Alley's artistic commitment is to the open stage tradition. This calls for a single-form room where actor and audience enjoy a maximum of shared experience. The inhibitions of the theatre-in-the-round on one hand, and the lack of intimacy as well as the inefficient stages of some apron stage theatres on the other, were to be avoided.

"The division of labor, so common in proscenium designs where the architect designs everything in front of the curtain and the theatre designer everything in back of it, was neither wanted nor possible."

The large stage took a year to be born and the word "multi-space" crept into parlance as it became reality. No better term describes it. Basically, of course, it is a thrust stage, but its total effect is one that envelopes the audience. Its central playing area can be elevated, lowered or partially closed off with screens, depending on the production. Whole scenes can arise in minutes by the use of a giant hydraulic lift under the main section of the stage. Directly before it is a small lift, serving the purpose of the time-honored trap-door, reached by a separate staircase. Rising at either side of the central area are entrances which form balconies, promontories or towers, playing areas which can be divorced from the rest.

In promoting the sense of audience envelopment, Nina Vance recalled the runways she had seen in the Japanese Noh drama. These were integrated into the stage's final design as calipers, or side stages, which go to the very back of the theatre. Street-fights, crowd scenes or pageant-like parades might take place here. They also form an effective bridge to the main scene center stage . . . or a brief interim between important scene changes there.

A huge cyclorama looms imposingly at the rear of the stage. Before it is a trough for a projection screen onto which whole settings could be flashed or, a la Brecht, explanatory notes and legends. There is, of course, the possibility of combining cinema with live drama, utilizing an art form still in its infancy.

The audience would reach the magic place, prepared for grandeur by the ascent of the grand staircase, with vistas of pure, lofty space; just as, in the descent to the small theatre, it is gently prepared for a more intimate theatre experience: carpeted stairs, indirect lighting, space that is confined, but not confining, emerging into a space that creates niches rather than vast chambers.

The large room would seat 798 people in 17 gently sloping rows. More than two years of design study went into the development of seating for the new Alley Theatre. Called the Continental Chair, it was developed from fundamental criteria defined by George C. Izenour, Director of the Electro-Mechanical Laboratory at Yale School of Drama and designer-engineer consultant for the Alley. The chair has a contoured cushion for form-fitting support of both extremes of body shapes—from the tall, thin person whose support is concentrated on the lower pelvic bone and not too much of his own cushioning, to the short stout person whose weight will be considerably more and require more weight distribution. The new chair allows the luxury of backing up out of a row space to allow easy access for those passing in front, and yet not crowding the row behind.

The unparalleled intimacy of the old Alley Theatre was to be kept at all costs, for Mrs. Vance felt it to be one of her (and the actors') greatest assets. (Today, standing center stage in the large theatre, one instantly is aware of how successfully this objective was achieved!)

In housing two theatres in one building, Franzen was to avoid what might be considered the easy way out. He could have given each theatre separately functioning box offices, lobbies, dressing rooms and shops. It is to his credit that this did not happen. He has stated: "The proposed design arranges the public lobbies as well as the backstage areas in such a manner that they simultaneously serve both theatres with equal efficiency. This has been achieved by designing a slightly raised podium near street level containing the shops and dressing areas. The small theatre is located in this podium immediately adjoining these facilities. The main room and the major public facilities are carried piggy-back fashion on top of the service element and are readily accessible to it. It has therefore been possible to enter both theatres through the identical vestibule and to purchase one's tickets at a single box office. From this vestibule, one descends into the small theatre lobby and walks up to the main theatre foyer.

Backstage, there are seven dressing rooms, each with brightly painted doors. Ideally, each room accommodates two actors, but is capable of containing four. There is a large main dressing room for twelve; this number can be doubled for a massive, full-scale work. The Green Room, where actors meet the public, is dotted with toadstool-like seats of varied heights. The actors have a large room of their own for company conferences or relaxation between the acts or between Saturday and Sunday performances. The decor, according to Paul Owen, is High Camp, but utterly tensionless. Adjoining this is a roomy kitchen with stove, refrigerator and sink.

The shop facility is cavernous. One can imagine three entire productions being mounted there at once. The central construction area, where settings are built, is flanked by offices and rooms devoted to auxiliary stagecraft. There is room for sewing and cutting costumes, as well as fitting them. Nearby one discovers a wig room, millinery room, properties and upholstery rooms. The paint room, where new properties and scene pieces are built, has its own air conditioning vents to prevent paint and fumes from the fiberglass oven from circulating through the rest of the plant. The Alley in its long history has acquired thousands of costumes. These, together with the theatre's imposing collection of furniture, have been given more than adequate storage space in the plant, quickly accessible, yet set off from the main areas of activity.

Ann Holmes of the Houston Chronicle, taken on a tour of the building, remarked on its resemblance to a feudal city. Her observation contains more than a grain of truth. The desire was to create a facility where the Alley could produce everything that they would need. Again the idea of a castle and its self-contained life is interjected.

Technically, the lighting for both theatres is unrivaled in the nation today. It represents the culmination of twenty years' study by George Izenour in an attempt to devise a system controlled by an analogue digital computer. It is extremely economical compared to other such systems and unlike them, used stapled cards, rather than the hole-punch variety. The first installed effort in this system is now in use at Lincoln Center's Vivian Beaumont Theatre. Alley Theatre's is a more simplified version of it.

Above the audience in the small theatre is a light wire mesh, capable of offering support to one crew member or many at once. The particular mesh employed here was developed over a long period of time and was severely tested for dura-

161

bility and tension. It gives the lighting designer the ability to illuminate any section of the stage; a totality of flexibility denied most arena lighting designers. More importantly one can actually sculpt with light here; one is not forced to resort to flat, conventional lighting.

In the large theatre the lighting system is hidden by a series of sculptured, undulating, semi-circles, which, in Paul Owen's words, "form a chandelier by their configurations." As in the small theatre, areas can be plunged into instant darkness; others pinpointed, even followed by remote control spotlights. The key word, again, is flexibility, the ability to create magic in a second.

The administrative offices occupy the last two levels of the building. They have been carefully situated facing the plaza and Jones Hall, with the skyscrapers of Houston beyond. Most offices look out onto terraces planted with trees and bushes that serve to relieve the basic contours of the building and complement the gentle swirl of the porches. On the third level are offices accommodating the executive director, artistic administrator, director of board relations, publicity, mailroom supervisor and receptionist. There is a large open space for the stenographic pool. This level also contains the conference room, a most attractive place, with a superb view of the city.

On the fourth level one finds the artistic director's suite and that of her assistant. Mrs. Vance's suite is comprised of a small conference room or salon; an inner office; and dressing room and bath. Mrs. Iris Siff's suite contains a reception area; study and library; and an inner office. Moving toward Prairie Avenue on this level, one discovers a public area in which the Alley staff hopes to establish a club where they, members of the company and members of the theatre's Board of Directors may entertain friends and visitors. This club would enjoy several large terraces, in addition to a dramatic view of the grand staircase from a compelling height. It will be, if plans are implemented, one of the city's loveliest and most popular meeting places!

The public areas are dotted with coffee bars and spaces for bookstalls where Alley publications and other material of interest will be available. As has always been the policy, latecomers will watch the production on television in a separate viewing room.

Besides giving its facade a great strength, the nine towers of the new Alley Theatre accommodate stairways required by fire laws and contain air conditioning units, thus keeping the noise away from the integral areas of the building.

In inclement weather, theatre-goers can park underground in the Civic Center garage and take an elevator up to the public areas of the Alley. In doing this, they will pass through the famous Alley gates, so long a symbol of 709 Berry Avenue. Today, refurbished and re-hung, they connect the Alley's happy past with an even happier future. . . .

58. ATLANTA MEMORIAL ARTS CENTER
Atlanta, Georgia
Opened October 29, 1968

It was a tragic plane crash in Paris on June 3, 1962, that gave impetus for building the great Atlanta Memorial Arts Center. In that crash of a chartered Air France plane, 122 of Atlanta's most culturally minded citizens, members of the Atlanta Art Association, perished.

As a memorial to those members, the Arts Alliance (the combined Art Association and Atlanta Symphony Orchestra), supported liberally by citizens of Atlanta and particularly by the Emily and Robert Woodruff Foundation, built a magnificent cultural center, the first in the South. It cost well over $13,000,000.

A pamphlet published by the Alliance introduces the center.

58:1 Under one big roof on Peachtree Street you can paint a picture, or buy one; act in a play, or see one; sing in an opera, play in a concert, or hear one; dance in a ballet, or watch one; see a movie, a mobile, or a piece of sculpture.

The roof is that of the Memorial Arts Center, a $13 million complex built by the arts, devoted to the arts, consisting entirely of the arts. The Center houses a museum, the High Museum of Art, a school, the Atlanta School of Art, an orchestra, the Atlanta Symphony Orchestra, a theater company, the Atlanta Repertory Theater Company, a ballet company, the Atlanta Ballet and an opera company, the Atlanta Opera.

The Atlanta Arts Alliance is the supervising organization which built the building and sees to the overall operation of the various companies housed in it. The Alliance under the able chairmanship of Richard H. Rich was formed by the merger of the Atlanta Symphony Orchestra, the High Museum of Art and the Atlanta School of Art.

The Center, quite literally, rose from the ashes of the Orly plane crash of 1962 which took the lives of 122 Atlanta Art Association members who were touring art centers of Europe. The crash caused predictions that the city's cultural growth would be stunted for a hundred years. Six years after the crash, the Center, a Memorial to those who died, opened with an array of cultural achievements which is unparalleled in the South.

Symphony Hall, a 1900 seat concert hall is the permanent home of the Atlanta Symphony Orchestra, under the direction of Robert Shaw. Alliance Theater which seats 800 serves the combined companies of Atlanta's Municipal Theater: the Atlanta Opera Company, under the artistic direction of Blanche Thebom, which presents four fully mounted operas each year; the Atlanta Ballet Company, under

the artistic direction of Robert Barnett and David Blair, which offers four complete ballet productions each year; and the Atlanta Repertory Theater Company, under the artistic direction of Michael Howard, which mounts eight plays each season. The theater also operates a 200 seat studio theater on the lower level of the building.

In addition to these performing areas, a galleria 50 feet wide, 230 feet long, extending the full length of the building, connects the halls with the museum. This galleria serves as the main lobby for visitors and spectators.

A harmonious and stimulating background is provided for the students enrolled in the Atlanta School of Art. All equipment is the latest design, including shelving, work tables, and kilns in the sculpture area. The building also contains a film resource library and is equipped with the latest in motion picture projection equipment: the presentation of fine films is a regular activity of the Center.

Furnishings for the Center combine color and design with utility and serviceability. Every effort has been made to create a striking environment which adds to the enjoyment of the performing and visual arts by visitors, performers and students.

The Atlanta Memorial Arts Center, built from the tragedy of Orly, is a place where the immortality of art is exemplified in a hundred ways, where the visual and performing arts combine their programs and facilities to enrich one another and the community. It is, in short, the house that Art built.

The Atlanta *Journal* reprinted the comments of Paul Hume, writer for the Washington *Post* News Service.

58:2   THEATER OUT OF TRAGEDY
TRIPLE-THREAT ATLANTA TEAM DRAWS
SHOUTS OF ACCLAIM

58:1. *The Arts in Atlanta* (Atlanta: Arts Alliance, n.d.).

58:2. Atlanta *Journal*, Oct. 30, 1968.

Atlanta has created, out of tragedy, one of the nation's handsomest centers of the arts. Its $13.5 million Memorial Arts Center was built in memory of 122 citizens of this city who died in a plane crash in 1962 at Paris while in Europe to survey arts centers there.

Opened last week with a concert by the Atlanta Symphony under Robert Shaw, the center Tuesday night put on a triple-threat show that combined, in an American premiere, the Atlanta Ballet, The Atlanta Opera and the Atlanta Repertory Theater. The show was the ultra-spectacular operatic entertainment "King Arthur," by the greatest poet and composer in England at the end of the 17th century, John Dryden and Henry Purcell.

The piece comes from the time when English opera was a three-way affair in which actors acted and spoke, singers sang, and dancers danced. This was a perfect vehicle to show off the alliance theater which is the 800-seat auditorium that shares the new center with an 1,800-seat symphony hall.

THE AUDIENCE was a specially invited assemblage whose $100 tickets will help make possible lower-priced seats in the weeks to come.

Blanche Thebom is artistic director of the operatic wing, Robert Bennett, the ballet, and Michael Howard, the theater. The Dryden-Purcell piece gave them equal time in which to show the strengths they have brought to Atlanta. Jonathan Sternberg is the musical director. They make a formidable team.

"King Arthur" has everything in the way of gods and demons, and magic spirits, including, of course, Merlin. One of the famous scenes is that of King Frost and his cohorts turning into spring's warm, sunny flowers through the power of love. The final curtain is nothing less than Britannia rising triumphant from the waves to wildest acclaim, an acclaim joined in and shouted by Tuesday night's audience.

The production's national acclaim is seen in this thoughtful review by Walter Terry, dance editor, *Saturday Review*:

58:3 THE MERRY MONARCH lived to see only a preliminary rehearsal of a royal extravaganza which had been planned, by the poet Dryden, to honor and flatter him. If, nearly 300 years later, Charles II could return, not to the Palace at Whitehall in London, but to the new Atlanta Memorial Arts Center on Peachtree Street, it is certain that he would be both honored and flattered by a production which cost $250,000, called upon the talents of hundreds of theater artists, represented one of the most dazzling spectacles devised for today's theater, re-created the fascinating effect of being "excellently adorned with scenes and machines" (as it was originally described), and managed to be marvelously merry.

Dryden's original *Albion and Albanius* dropped its initial score by Louis Grabu, was rewritten to wholly new music by Henry Purcell, changed its title to *King Arthur* (or *The British Worthy*), and had its world premiere at the Queen's Theatre in 1691. On October 29, 1968, the masque was given its U.S. premiere by the newly formed Atlanta Municipal Theater, composed of the Atlanta Ballet, the Atlanta Opera, and the Atlanta Repertory Theater.

Both the handsome $13,000,000 Center (with its four auditoriums: Symphony Hall with 1,848 seats, the 868-seat Alliance Theater—where *King Arthur* is on view—the Studio Theater seating 200, and the 440-seat Walter Hill Auditorium in the thirteen-year-old High Museum which forms the core of the new center) and the performances to be held within it do honor to the memory of those 122 artists and patrons of the arts, all members of the Atlanta Arts Alliance, who

58:3. Walter Terry, "Excellently Adorned," *Saturday Review*, Nov. 23, 1968, pp. 72–73, 85. Copyright Saturday Review, Inc.

were killed when their plane crashed at Orly in Paris in 1962.

King Arthur will be given for a total of five weeks—although I think it would attract theatergoers and tourists from all over the country for more like five months —and after that, for forty weeks, the constituent company will have their own repertory seasons of ballet, drama, and opera. It is an especially gala year for the Atlanta Ballet, which has just dropped the "Civic" from its name as it moves into the ranks of America's professional dance companies. It is nearing its fortieth birthday and is America's oldest regional ballet troupe, founded by Dorothy Alexander, who now serves as its loved and indispensable consultant, and with Robert Barnett as its artistic director. (Blanche Thebom heads the opera enterprises and Michael Howard the repertory theater.)

But now to the resplendent masque itself. The task which confronted the new Atlanta Municipal Theater was enormous. The three companies had not worked together before on a coequal basis; the theater plant itself was untried; how to mount a masque for a modern audience was a challenge; and at times they were afraid that they were spending a fortune for something they couldn't pull off. There were reports of strains and tiffs and some lack of organization, and certainly several in authority were glassy-eyed at the $100-a-ticket gala opening. But they needn't have worried, for they came up with a sumptuous spectacle which was eye-filling, wholly entertaining, and a marvelous exhibition of what might be described —in words once used by Lady Peel herself (alias Beatrice Lillie)—as "pomp and peculiar circumstance."

Multiple credits go to Miss Thebom, who adapted *King Arthur;* Mr. Howard, the director; Jonathan Sternberg, musical direction; Joyce Trisler, choreographer (Josias Priest was the designer of the dances three centuries ago); Richard Gulliksen, settings; Kurt Wilhelm, cos-

tumes; Nananne Porcher, lighting; Robert Joyce, properties and masks. No one of these was more important than the other in providing actors, dancers, and singers with the magic tools for making unforgettable theater.

The old masques of England, along with the court ballets of France, relied heavily on effects created by stage machines, among them flights to and from heaven, transformation scenes, appearances and disappearances. Atlanta's production of *King Arthur* could well have left Ben Jonson, Inigo Jones (great makers of masques), and Charles II fairly boggle-eyed. I know that I was continuously captivated by a cascade of striking, and usually funny, stage effects. Let me recount some.

Not only did the fairy Philidel swing across the top of the stage on unseen (or barely seen) wires as she poured forth a remarkable array of soprano pyrotechnics, but she also made rendezvous with a giant dragon and a magician up there in the air. There were also such goodies as a waterfall (worked on the principle of a kitchen roller towel) which poured into a pool from which sirens emerged to lure Arthur from his quest (you'll be glad to know that he tore himself away while exclaiming, "But duty calls!"); a green forest which changed before your eyes to a kingdom of snow and ice presided over by an icy being who rose from the earth to the roof of the stage filling the void with a towering cone of glacial majesty, later to shrink, melt, disappear; trees whose branches were arms and whose trunks could talk; and, of course, a swelling sea of lovely blue, capped with white scallops from which emerged, in the finale, a towering Britannia in full charge of ruling the waves.

As for the dances, I should point out that Miss Trisler has quite properly rid herself of the steps of the late 1600s— they were technically limited by our standards, with no toe shoes at all—and settled for the spirit of the period with mock battles, in which warriors. knock each other out with near-slapstick konks over the head; episodes involving the jugglers, acrobats, and tumblers which king and court savored; a pastoral ballet no closer to the sheep pens than a fun Trianon; duels, buffetings, and swordplay; nymphs and satyrs engaged in an orgy which would not shock the guests at a church supper; and a multitude of other lively, tongue-in-cheek gambols and capers. Indeed, because this *King Arthur* is somewhat closer to ballet than to opera, it should be classified not so much as a masque as an anti-masque, as the major dance ingredients were once described.

By way of making this truly stunning spectacle intimate and amusing, the producers ignored today's theatrical artifices and, fortunately, re-created the scenic wonders which you can still see at the perfectly preserved Royal Court Theater in Sweden's Drottningholm (where twelve stagehands rotate blue-and-white-painted wooden rollers intended to depict a churning sea) and introduced their masque with a prologue which included a pitch for funds (expressed in Restoration-period verse) and the appearance of a foppish duke, who occasionally strolled into the realm of Arthur and out-declaimed the singers with his penetrating counter-tenor, along with his deliciously inebriated lady. Shrewdly, then, the wonder-workers in Atlanta succeeded in retaining the quaint beauties, the idiotic plot involvements, the lightheaded gallantries of another era, while brushing the whole fey affair with subtle contemporary accents.

The Alliance Theater—with superb acoustics, a steeply raked auditorium that makes for unimpeded viewing, a thrust stage with graceful ramps, and other pluses offstage, onstage, and backstage— is a perfect setting for *King Arthur,* but I am certain that it will frame with equal effect *The Cherry Orchard, Tristan und*

Isolde, Swan Lake, and other upcoming presentations.

And I think it should also be noted that in this great new arts center in the Southland's most aristocratic capital city, a racially integrated cast caused neither stir nor comment as whites and blacks pooled their high acting, singing, and movement talents. Curiously pertinent was a phrase spoken by Merlin as the British Arthur (played by a white actor) and the Saxon Oswald (played by a black actor) end the conflict which provides the masque with its theme: "Britons and Saxons shall be once one people; one common tongue, one common faith shall bind our warring hands in a perpetual peace." Just an ancient echo? Hopefully, this an omen.

Because of financial difficulties encountered within a few months following the opening, the enterprise was taken over by the Atlanta Arts Alliance, and the name changed to the Atlanta Memorial Center. The organization compiled the following fact sheet:

58:4   ATLANTA ART ALLIANCE

What is it?

> The alliance is exactly that:
> an organization designed to weld
> the performing and visual arts
> into one interdependent whole.

Its founding members:

> The Atlanta Symphony Orchestra
> The High Museum of Art
> The Atlanta School of Art

Its affiliates:

> The Municipal Theater Inc. consisting of:
>> The Municipal Theater
>> The Atlanta Ballet Company
>> The Atlanta School of Ballet
>> The Atlanta Opera Company

Its officers:

> Richard H. Rich, Chairman of the Board of Trustees

58:4. Fact sheet published by the Atlanta Arts Alliance, n.d.

Charles H. Jagels, President and Executive Officer

Its functions:

The creation and the continuing administration of the Atlanta Memorial Center; to provide through a single annual appeal, the maintenance funds for the Atlanta Symphony Orchestra, the Atlanta School of Art and the High Museum of Art.

When was it founded?

The Atlanta Arts Alliance was founded in 1964 when the 60 year old Atlanta Art Association joined forces with the Atlanta Symphony Orchestra.

The plane crash at Orly Field, Paris in June 1962, which took the lives of 122 members of the Atlanta Art Association provided the impetus. As a memorial to these cultural leaders, it was proposed that an Atlanta Memorial Center be built. The Atlanta Arts Alliance was formed to bring this about.

THE ATLANTA MEMORIAL CENTER

What is it?

It is a place—unique in the United States—in which the performing and visual arts come together under one roof.

It is an expression of, and a participant in, the concept of the interdependence of all the arts.

It is a center for education in and about the arts—a center not only for its immediate community, but for the entire Southeast region.

Location:

1280 Peachtree Street, N. E., Atlanta

Site:

Six acres
This site contains the High Museum of Art, built in 1955. The museum

has been retained as the core around which the Center is built:

Size:

296,750 square feet

Height:

Approximately 50 feet on four separate levels.

Cost:

$13 million
The Center has been financed entirely by private funds.

Architects:

Toombs, Amisano and Wells, in association with Stevens & Wilkinson

Interior design:

Larsen Design Studio in conjunction with Edward Ross, Linda Pinto

Administration:

The Atlanta Arts Alliance, Inc.

Formed for the purpose of creating the Center, the Alliance is also responsible for its continuing growth.

The facilities:

Four auditoriums:

1. Symphony Hall: 1,845 seats

   This will be the home of the Atlanta Symphony Orchestra, and will also be used for large opera and ballet productions.

2. Repertory Theater: 890 seats

   The Municipal Theater will be in residence here, with a 40-week season for plays, ballet and opera.

3. Studio theater: 200 seats

   This intimate theater is designed for experimental productions.

4. Walter Hill Auditorium: 440 seats

   This auditorium, part of the existing High Museum, is used for film showings, lectures, and other events.

The High Museum of Art
The original museum has been expanded to 23,000 square feet or more than twice its present size.

The Atlanta School of Art
The school, opened in 1928, offers a four-year program leading to the Bachelor of Fine Arts degree

Its new home in the Memorial Center accommodates 300 students, and offers some of the most complete facilities for training in the visual arts (including all graphics, sculpture, and photography) in the Southeast.

An arts resources library
Capacity 40,000 volumes, plus slides, films and other resources. In keeping with the educational function of the Center, the library is planned to be the major arts research facility for the Southeast.

The Galleria
This great hall, 52 feet wide and 232 feet long, bisects the Center, linking museum, theater and concert hall. It will be used as a Promenade, for special exhibitions of art and sculpture, for galas and other community functions.

59. MUMMERS THEATRE
Oklahoma City, Oklahoma
Opened December 2, 1970

The Mummers Theatre in Oklahoma City opened as probably the most exciting playhouse architecturally in the United States. The playgoer could not fail to experience this excitement as he viewed both the interior and the exterior of the theater. The architectural concepts involved were bound to be controversial among theater buffs and particularly detested by traditionalists in theater architecture. One thing is certain: this playhouse will be a milestone in the history of the American regional theater.

The architect for the building, John M. Johansen, A.I.A., was graduated from Harvard College and the Harvard Graduate School of Design and conducted courses in architecture at such institutions as Harvard, Yale, Massachusetts Institute of Technology, and Carnegie Institute of Technology. He went on to become Professor of Architecture at Columbia University. In an article in the *Architectural Forum* he discussed his concept for the Mummers Theatre.

59:1   The Beaux Arts is still very much with us. Nearly all major buildings currently designed, built, and each year honored by our profession, are conceived according to those standards and values which we thought we had discarded after the architectural revolution of the '20s and '30s. Whether classically geometric or romantically amorphous, most of the work by architects, including myself, over the past ten years has been faithful to that old tradition which would have us concern ourselves with the "tasteful arrangements of compositional elements."

The "form giving" period is waning. Although one can still make convincing distinctions between the forms of classicists like Johnson, Yamasaki, Stone, or SOM, on the one hand, and of the more picturesque designers like Kahn, Rudolph, Giurgola Venturi or myself, there is really little difference: we have really all come from the same bag, when our work is seen from the vantage point of a totally new formative position now being established.

This new position is one which is concerned not with gestural form and with master works of architecture, but rather with processes, with action, with be-

59:1. Reprinted from the article "The Mummers Theater: A Fragment, Not a Building" by John M. Johannsen from May 1968 issue of THE ARCHITECTURAL FORUM, pp. 64–68. Copyright 1968 by Whitney Publications, Inc.

57. Alley Theatre at night, Houston, 1968. Photograph by Ezra Stoller. Below, model of the arena stage by Ulrich Ranzen and Associates. Courtesy of the Alley Theatre.

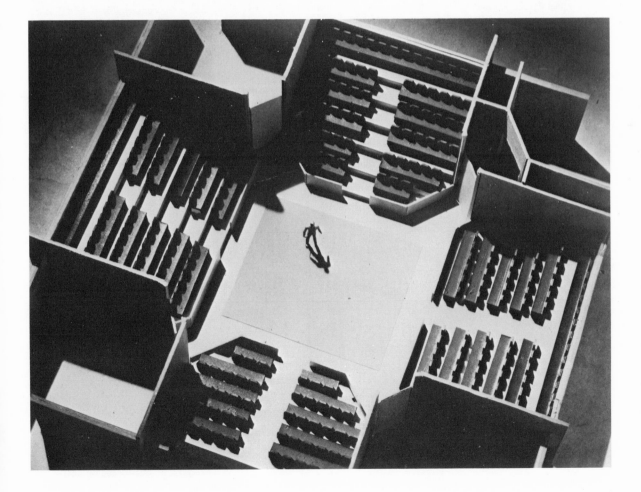

58. Atlanta Memorial Arts Center, Atlanta, 1968. Courtesy of the Atlanta Arts Alliance.

59. Mummers Theatre, Oklahoma City, 1971. Photograph copyright 1971, The Oklahoma Publishing Co. From the Oklahoma City Times, July 19.

havioral patterns, and how most simply all these may be accommodated. This new position is concerned with an "organizing idea," or "an ordering device." The idea of device will derive from motivating processes—processes of personal and of societal behavior, and of highly industrialized building techniques. Advocates of this position will strive to reconcile these now-more-carefully-examined living patterns with new technology. "Architecture," as we know it, is less and less a determinant in the organization of our buildings, of building complexes or of cities. Formalism, centrality, ordered sequence, and individuation of building design cannot deal with the demands that urban problems are now making upon the profession. "Architecture" as we knew it is no longer effective in its solutions, nor even compelling in its esthetic expression.

First of all, the scale of urban living is too large for one architect to conceive or to design as a totally determinate form. Secondly, permutational or open-ended programming will force a new concept, that of indeterminacy, in which structures may not look the same from year to year. There will be no time to compose and continually recompose for changing needs. In fact, there will be no need to compose once we shift to the idea of free, life-generated assemblages rigged on an ordering device—which may be structural, transportational, distributional, or any combination of these. The future city may look like one building; it will most certainly be continuous construction. The building, as a fragment, may look like many. Except for scale, the governing principles may be the same.

COMPONENTS, NOT COMPOSITION

The Mummers Theater complex, for Oklahoma City, is not a building as we have known it, but a fragment. The ordering device, or organizing idea, evolved (not surprisingly) from the processes of theater production and theater atten-

dance. The program, most simply stated, was a theater for 600, another for 300, and a school-rehearsal room, supported physically and organizationally by offices, common backstage facilities, and mechanical services.

Now one way of escaping the habits or design procedure in the "architecture as we knew it" (i.e., composition) is by feeding off cultural and technical situations in other fields. For me, the choice of another field of technology has been, as I have mentioned before, electronics. The danger in this process would lie in a mere imitation of forms. However, the borrowings of organizational systems or concepts, inspirational or appropriately adapted, may be valid. Further borrowings from the terminology of other fields are also helpful in forming for us new thought channels. To restate the Mummers program then, in terms of the organization of electronics devices, it is: three "components" with "subcomponents" attached, plugged into one "chassis" or "gate," and then connected by four "circuiting systems," superimposed at separate levels to avoid cross-circuiting.

With this organizing idea, the two theaters and school draw their services from backstage functions, having attached to them subcomponents varying in number and type—lounge, toilets, offices. And these components are connected by interlaced, circuiting systems—ramps, stairs, bridges, and ductwork. It matters little, once the organizing idea is determined, what the actual number, or forms, of these elements may be, or how they are connected, as far as esthetics go; from here on it is anybody's "styling job," for whatever that is worth. The design process, if the term can be used at all, is not one of composing but of rigging or assemblage. Each element, whether enclosed functional space, conveyor tube, or structural member, goes about its work directly and independently; sometimes with utter disregard for the other elements, or for occupants it is not required to accommodate at that place or moment. The way of dealing with functional elements, then might be to "position" them, i.e., to satisfy functional relationships; to "prop" them, i.e., to support with structure; and to "connect" them, i.e., to provide circulation and distribution.

ESTHETICS AND ORNITHOLOGY

Departing from the now common monolithic and ponderous concrete building, the Mummers Theater complex shows a marked division of its elements into "heavies" and "lights"—concrete for major structural elements, with light steel frame and cladding for cantilevered and spanning elements.

Although, as one witty artist has said, "esthetics is for the artist as ornithology is for the birds," the visual results of such an approach are still of some natural concern. The esthetic in this case must be a by-product of the direct solution described above. The specific programmed events and functions at work should suggest an appropriate organizing idea or device which generates, justifies, and becomes the esthetic. As McLuhan has said, ". . . all that is required as a basis for a work of art is the brush of one idea against another idea"—in the case of habitable structure, the brush of function against function. It is action: the infusion of human beings and the distribution of services, which is expressed clearly, usually directly from one point in space to another. It is the surprise, unexpected juxtaposition, superimposition, crowding, segregation, and confrontation, of elements which accommodates the human movement patterns which give whatever architectural quality this construction may have. The concern is that of reality, immediacy, honesty, economy. As the skeptical young say, "Cut the crap!"

The ordering device or idea, with its permutative possibilities, is determined early. However, the actual and final appearance is unpredictable. Elevations, if one can say they exist, cannot be drawn or studied; in fact, facets of wall, roof, and soffit are so numerous, with interface so prevalent, that their relationships may as well be left to chance. As in the new mathematics, we deal with "sets" of symbols and images; we recognize group effects, unplanned peripheral sensations, along with selected views—what is known at IBM as "pattern recognition." The impression is generally one of what Norbert Weimer called "organic incompleteness," and is altogether consistent with the current retraining of our perceptive habits under the influence of electronic devices.

Facets, not facades, result in bombardment of composite images; yet they are held together by the ordering device. Permutation, flux, change, whether by actual reassemblage in future years, or by suggestion of this possibility in concept, give the structure an aspect of "in-process." By making this vivid, the occupants may feel they participate, that they are involved, feel empathy, identify with, have, in fact, become part of the process.

Not only is the axially fixed station-point of the Renaissance out of date, but the moving station-point of Siegfried Giedion's space-time is out of date also, in favor of multiple simultaneous station points consistent with our present-experience world. In the Mummers building complex one will not only occupy, but assume many station points, and follow in the shaping of enclosing elements, the loci of other occupants in motion. The assemblage is volatile; elements may relate back to the same thing, yet not to each other. The relationship is organizational, not formal. Slang, not eloquence, is foremost. I choose slang because it has to do with what is brash, improvised but incisive, what involves firsthand experience, is an impulsive response to the immediate situation, and is said in a jargon that is out of accepted usage. This attitude is, I hope, free from cliché, free from overstudied or exquisite detail.

Ordering devices, or ideas, are found in all periods of architectural history. Today, however, the complications of mechanical services, transportation, fabrication, and construction techniques, as well as complicated living patterns, will require ordering devices which will be altogether determined by these processes— and not by a warmed-over Beaux Arts esthetic. The great proving ground of the organizing idea, or ordering device, will be the city. The Mummers Theater group is a relatively small individual structure —a fragment of city, a theatrical neighborhood. As such, it may illustrate a respect for human and technical processes as a generating force, for the stabilizing function of the ordering device, and a faith in the free, unpredictable development of resultant forces.

Whatever these forms might be, they will not look like the "architecture as we know it," from the same Beaux Arts bag in which most of us still find ourselves today.

The actual opening of the Mummers Theatre elicited many newspaper and magazine articles describing the new playhouse.

59:2   At the new Mummers Theatre in Oklahoma City, form does not follow function —it extends it and increases it. Not only does the building house and nurture theatrical performances, but it is, itself, a theatrical experience.

Opened in December, 1970, the theatre is the result of eight years of planning and work on the part of all those involved—including producer-director Mack Scism, stage designer David Hays and architect John Johansen. It is

59:2. Patricia MacKay, "Oklahoma City's New Mummers Theatre," *Theatre Crafts,* May/June 1971, pp. 6–12, 30–31.

a long way from the music tent in which the original Mummers group of eight amateurs opened in 1949. Throughout the transitions from music tent to warehouse theatre, producer-director Mack Scism has been the guiding force and personality of Mummers' activities. He put together a group which did the quality of work that gained national recognition. And in 1962, The Ford Foundation awarded the Mummers a $1,250,000 "challenge grant" to build and equip a new theatre, and $750,000 was raised within the community; Ford later granted a further $535,000 in building cost funds. The Mummers Theatre was to have a new home.

The resulting theatre, set in downtown Oklahoma City Park, is a complex of elements somewhat resembling a graduate level tinker toy-erector set, with colorful red and blue ramps leading to the drums and boxes of the structure. Two theatres —one small arena stage, one larger open-thrust stage, and a school-rehearsal hall are the main public elements of the structure. Attached to these are offices and lounges. All these elements are, in turn, connected by separate, circulation systems.

Mack Scism brought in David Hays as the stage designer, and with him formulated ideas about what the stage shapes should be, and how they should work them. Then, after these initial plans were worked out, architect John Johansen joined the team. Hays pointed out in a recent interview that his "authority started in the middle of the stage and faded as it reached the outside wall, and Johansen's was the reverse."

THE OPEN-THRUST STAGE

For the larger, 592-seat theatre, as designer Hays points out, producer-director Scism wanted an open-thrust, audience-stage arrangement, in which people encircled the stage 270 degrees. The form of the open-thrust stage is flexible, but not in the usual sense of the word—that is, the open-thrust stage cannot be transformed into a proscenium stage. Rather the inflexibility of this stage originates at the lowest level of the building—the basement. The entire stage is built up from that level.

The stage is supported on castored scaffolding from the basement level. It can be taken apart in sections and reshaped into new patterns to conform to a given play or style of staging.

Architect Johansen comments, "I like the idea that you strip down to the basement floor as a base level. If you have a stage, it is called 'staging' and not 'a stage.' It is not fixed. That becomes part of your stage design because you can design a stage everytime."

In addition, because the seating in the auditorium is not supported from below, but, rather, is in cantilevered concrete boxes, the stage can be rolled away completely.

David Hays pointed out, "I thought that a thrust theatre could be operated in such a way that it would have a similar flexibility to that of a proscenium stage. This staging can be radically altered during act-breaks or intermission just by pushing it out under the seats, and, in fact, the second production at the Mummers doesn't use the original stage shape at all."

The basement level also houses offices, dressing rooms, the greenroom, and workshops for scenery, costumes, and props. Scenery, seldom massive for an open-thrust theatre, can be brought up to the stage level by an elevator, stairs, or simply handed up through the "moat" in between the scaffolded stage and the seating.

Actors can enter the stage from a variety of locations. Designer Hays points out that it is "not the traditional, two or four, easily predicted tunnels." Hays goes on to comment that this flexibility in entrances was one of his original concepts

for the theatre. It was his hope that "the whole architectural concept be one that made the entrances part of the architecture —without necessarily telegraphing to the audience that this is *the place* the actor funnels in. The architectural solution permits six entrance spots."

Behind the staging area is a fixed backstage which serves as a point of origin for action, and for some movement of scenery. Architect Johansen feels that his background stage area is not suitable for proscenium work because of the width of seating in the house. The backstage area is generally closed off during production by a series of panels which move laterally on stage.

The ceiling over the main area in which the scaffolded stage can be arranged is made up of wooden panels of sections 1 foot by 3 feet. Installed partially because of acoustical considerations, each of these panels can be lifted out to permit scenery to be flown. "We cannot fly big pieces," designer Hays points out, "but, we can fly pieces almost three feet by ten feet."

These wooden panels also conceal a series of conduit pipes which are the basis of the stage lighting system. Stage design consultant John Gleason notes that "these pipes can hold a spotlight on either side and are equipped with an outlet every 18 inches."

Contiguous with the wood panels is a mesh of expanded metal grating extending to the outer wall of the auditorium, which functions as an open, continuous grid. Around the perimeter is a double row of permanent light ports. The continuous expanded metal grating enables a designer to focus lights for a show much more quickly than the ordinary cat walk system.

Talking about the lighting equipment for the theatre, consultant Gleason points out that his specifications for Kliegl Bros. Lighting included a 60 dimmer, 5-scene preset switchboard; 12 of the dimmers are 7,000-watts, and the remainder are 3,000-

watt. John Gleason also points out that all of the lamps are equipped with a pattern slot, and that 90% of the units all use the same 750-watt quartz lamps.

John Gleason designed for the theatre a basic lighting setup which was used for the first show, *A Man for All Seasons*. He goes on to comment, "the lighting was designed to work no matter how a stage designer moved the stage around, or what he threw at a lighting designer."

THE SEATING

Seating, ranged around the staging area in sections, does not form one continuous group; but, instead is divided into fixed "trays." These trays are essentially boxes, cantilevered at several different levels over the basement. The seating is in 8 to 10 rows in each tray. There are 592 seats in the house, and no seat is more than 10 rows from the stage. No tray interferes with the sightlines from another.

Designer Hays notes that when he started on the project one of his concepts was that, "the audience should be in seating units—three or four units—where they would be as tightly packed as possible." He also points out that this idea was inspired by the designs of a 16th century Venetian painter.

It was John Johansen's job to turn David Hays' idea into a architectural reality. Surrounding each tray is a small concrete parapet, which, while required by the fire codes, also gives, "a feeling of being boxed in and held there," as the architect points out. "But when you look over the edge of the tray, you realize that you are in space and it is 10 to 12 feet down to the basement floor."

In summing up his feelings about the open-thrust theatre David Hays comments, "it is an unusually flexible theatre, one that can be used in a lot of ways depending upon the imagination of the people who use it. It brings a lot of elements together. It is too bad that it took seven years to build because certain elements

of the design were more innovative when they were designed."

THE ARENA STAGE AND THEATRE

Complementary to the open-thrust theatre in design, size and function is the arena stage, which seats 240 people. The seats are generally arranged around four sides of the central stage. Entrances for the audience and actors can be made from the corners. However, that is only one way of arranging the arena. The seating, completely flexible, is designed so that parts, or all of it can be folded up and stored, or rearranged in other audience-stage relationships. David Hays comments that, "the smaller theatre can be set up in many ways; entrances for actors can pierce any seating block or corner."

The arena theatre echoes, in many ways, the old home of the Mummers Theatre. While it was not necessarily a conscientious intention, as designer Hays points out, "It was done to duplicate some of the atmosphere of the earlier theatre—to touch base with Mack Scism's old theatre and to bring in elements of other theatres, like the old Alley, that he admired." It was also to give Mack Scism the financial flexibility of having a theatre in which he could "fail" when he wanted to try more experimental works.

THE ARCHITECTURE

It is these two theatres—the 592-seat open-thrust and the 240-seat arena—in conjunction with the rehearsal hall–school that form the main components of the Mummers Theatre complex.

Architect Johansen's job consisted of translating the ideas that David Hays and Mack Scism had about the desired performance space; then, of massing these spaces in some sort of structure.

The traditional way of doing that would be to design these elements into one tightly packaged building. But architect Johansen reached beyond that. Borrowing from the imagery of electronics, as he comments in *Architectural Forum* (May

1968), "the Mummers Theater has three 'components' with 'subcomponents' attached, plugged into one 'chassis' or 'gate' and then connected by four 'circuiting systems' superimposed at separate levels to avoid cross circuiting."

It is this "circuitry" approach to the organization of the Mummers Theatre that makes it architecturally distinctive. Visually the structure resembles the proton and neutron structure of an atom, an assemblage sculpture, or one of the futuristic structures at Expo '70 in Osaka, Japan.

Having designed and dealt with the main components—thrust theatre over a supportive basement, the arena theatre, and the rehearsal hall–school; subcomponents (consisting of offices, lounges, and similar facilities) are then assembled and attached to the main components.

To move people from the outside world into these groups of main and subcomponents architect Johansen has designed different levels of the Mummers. At the lowest level is the basement area where the shops, dressing and green rooms have their own corridors and stairs. On the ground level, there is circuitry of automobile traffic which circles under ramps as cars park, or pick up and drop off people.

An arriving member of the audience would then proceed up one of the three main, blue sheetmetal ramps to a central courtyard. These ramps provide a public circuit which is a continuation of the city park paths, and permit people to walk through the building's open air central courtyard, but not necessarily to enter the building. The courtyard is glassed on the sides, and can be used for outdoor performances.

From there, a fourth circuit or red sheetmetal tubes leads members of the audience to a lobby where they can leave coats in yellow sheetmetal subcomponents. Theatre goers are then directed to the tube which will enter either the open-thrust theatre or the arena (each housed in a concrete drum), or the rehearsal hall. In the case of the open-thrust theatre, there is an ambulatory encircling the main concrete drum housing the theatre. At different points along the ambulatory are other tubes leading into the auditorium where the theatre goer then finds his seat on one of the trays.

The fifth major circuit system runs from the air conditioning systems in the three theatres to a water cooling tower, which is placed in top of the building complex like a contemporary assemblage sculpture.

Architect Johansen goes on to stress that he did not try to line up these systems in any particular way. "They all operate—doing their job, but disregarding each other, and you." Johansen continues, "The utter disregard of an element which is doing another job—not for you but for somebody else, or for you at another time —is an exciting idea. It is the opposite of a triumphal arch which is set up, static, and happens just once."

It is this excitement of interacting elements that contributes to the theatrical experience of theatre going at the Mummers. "The whole thing is performance for people, the moment they leave their cars. The building should be a dramatic performance, one of sequence, one of exciting events. The performance of theatre going cannot be detached from the performance on stage. I think it is the architect's responsibility to give a theatre building that experience," Johansen comments.

About the future directions of theatre architecture Johansen notes that he feels a lot of the old formality of theatre design is on the way out. There will be a greater flexibility in the arrangement of elements within the theatre itself.

It is too soon after the official opening to know how the Mummers Theatre building will work, architecturally, in practice. The response from the town has been enthusiastic. The set designs for plays going into the open-thrust theatre have extended and enhanced the unique, leveled atmosphere of the room.

There is, however, one very serious problem facing the Mummers. One that, at the time of writing, daily threatens to close the theatre—lack of money. Like far too many other outgrowths of the boom in cultural construction and cultural expansion there is the question—all too often faced only after the building is up—"do we really have enough of an audience to support this kind of facility?"

Grants and funding for construction are exciting things, but they do not necessarily guarantee an audience; that audience needs to be built too. Within about 6 weeks of opening, the Mummers Theatre began to realize that their deficit by the end of the season would be too large for them to cover. The Board of Directors had even posted the closing notices, when the theatre went into a last ditch effort to "Save the Mummers!"

Benefit performances, and benefit auctions, were staged. The townspeople responded with contributions of dimes and dollars to help the theatre. Twenty-three merchants of Oklahoma City have now donated 2% of their receipts for a 6 day period. The theatre has changed its programming so that they can cut production costs and appeal to a much wider segment of the townspeople. It now appears that the Mummers Theatre will be able to stay open until June. If they can build an audience to fill the new theatre, they will, of course, make it into next season. But now, even with their new building and their exciting entry a cultural experience, the Mummers Theatre needs the help of everyone interested in theatre.

The Mummers Theatre received excellent cooperation from the local press, as evidenced in the following article by Jon Denton, drama critic for the *Daily Oklahoman*. The brief history of the group, "It Started in a Borrowed Tent," appeared in the paper on Sunday before the theater opened.

59:3   As W. C. Fields might have put it, "Ah yessss, the Mummerrrrs!"

Yes, indeed. Can any other name evoke such mixed memories in Oklahoma City?

In two decades the acting company on Main street has incurred the stinging rebuke of local churches bent on erasing moral decay. It has stirred hearts to rapid beating with drama that also chilled the marrow. It has even become a most respectable thing, an institution of formidable impact on our City's cultural climate.

Can the Mummers survive success?

As the curious and the loyal advance to the new theatrical complex on W. Sheridan, will the Mummers deliver the same intimate appeal that winds, threadlike, through 20 years of theatrical history?

A look backward causes one to wonder.

It all started in a tent. Boredom played its part, because the summer of 1949 was unusually hot and dry, and without entertaining relief.

As Mack Scism recalls, producing a play seemed an excitable escape for eight young people. Scism was just out of the Navy. He was teaching speech at Capitol Hill High School. He was between semesters.

Scism had just acted in a play produced by the Scholar's Theatre, a one-year venture that folded with only moderate success. His venture on stage had been like sampling a potato chip: one bite was tantalizing, two might be tempting, but best of all might be the whole bag.

The group wanted to go to New York or the West Coast—anywhere except Oklahoma City. "We decided we would try to put on some plays and see if we couldn't get through the summer," he recalls.

Total resources were $8.40.

Scism knew a former carnival man who had a tent. A man he was buying gasoline from had a lot, vacant at the moment. Scrounging the dump yards produced enough scraps to put up a stage.

With the tent up at NE 22 and Eastern, business opened on a melodrama, "The Drunkard." Some of the excitement changed scenes to the city council room, however.

Melodramas like "The Drunkard," abetted by the likes of "Uncle Tom's Cabin," "The Streets of New York" and "Hawkshaw The Detective" spurred the interest of certain church groups.

"We no sooner got the first play on than a local church petitioned the city council to close the tent," Scism once told a reporter for Players Magazine.

The Mummers were charged with being lewd and licentious persons. The story hit the newspaper and new crowds flocked to the tent to see what was going on.

With the status of being labeled a public nuisance, Mummers prospered. The season's profit, $800, was quickly filed in the company's cash box—the glove box of Scism's car.

Mummers survived its first success, a pattern that was to follow in years ahead with astounding familiarity.

The theater had been nurtured by Mayde Mack Jones, later killed in an untimely auto accident. Originally christened the Mayde Mack Mummers, the singular title of Mummers Theatre was retained as an appropriate reminder.

Ancient mummers were wandering medieval actors and entertainers who traveled in troupes wherever their pockets and fortunes might be fattened.

With a fat, $800 bankroll, Mummers people tried three winter plays at Municipal Auditorium, then moved back to the tent for another summer of melodramas at Will Rogers Park. When no one pro-

tested, attendance slackened. Scism decided the moment of going-for-broke had arrived.

He quit his job as a teacher and scheduled six plays for the coming winter season. Melodramas were out. So was the tent. In 1950 new quarters were found at the Mirror Room of Municipal Auditorium, downtown.

The auditorium manager was an old friend, Scism recalls, who let the Mummers have a closet for an office. There were no windows, but Scism put in a phone.

Scism recalls "we fell in the round by accident, because there was no stage in the Mirror Room." Oklahoma City Symphony concerts were being held there. Collapsible risers had been constructed, in various shapes.

For four years, plays were held in the city building, with the Mummers arranging the risers, experimenting with various actor-audience relationships. An intimate rapport grew that continues as a Mummers hall mark.

Actors needed some administrative resources in the early Mummers maturity, so maybe Mayde Mack's father, C. Mack Jones, served as first president for six years. The first year staff was Mrs. Jim Bremkamp, vice president, Ruth Burgess, secretary, and Scism, treasurer.

Two other men became associated with the staff, a relationship that lasted through the years, with John Orr as business manager and Bill Dallas as technical director.

In 1951, after sharing directing honors with Lee Shirk, Scism became the only director, a position he has enlarged in responsibility to that of artistic director and producer-director.

By 1954, the Mummers faced another decision—again, a problem of success. The company had saved $6,000. Satisfaction with the Mirror Room had shrunken because the contract called for rental only between 6 p.m. and 6 a.m., six nights a week.

Everything had to be removed after each show, then replaced the next day. In Scism's words, "we wanted a place we could be in 24 hours a day."

A search led them to an oil field equipment warehouse at 1108 W. Main. It had room, although it was limited in acting facilities.

But the shape of the building was ideal. It suggested another arena stage area. So the abandoned warehouse became the Mummers' new home.

Theater was jelling in Oklahoma City and the Mummers prospered, drawing recognition and respect as weeks of hard board work changed to years of success.

A turning point arrived in 1958—or at least a sign of bigger things. In that year the Mummers Children's Theatre was established through joint sponsorship of Junior Hospitality Club and YWCA.

Scism was given a personal grant in 1958—$10,000 to make his own survey of the theater. He used the sum to travel through America, Europe and Canada.

The opportunity gave fruition to a desire born in the summer of 1949, when Scism decided professional theater was what Oklahoma City really wanted and deserved.

In his mind, he had it firm that the Mummers would someday be a professional theater, where the people doing the work would spend their days on a full-time job.

The sum of $244,000 was available to eight college drama departments and 16 theatrical groups.

That financial ripple in the pool of maturity eclipsed on Oct. 10, 1962, when Ford awarded the Mummers a $1,250,000 "challenge grant" to build and equip a new theater.

Jack Durland, president of the Mummers Board of Trustees until recently, met the immediate challenge by helping raise an additional $750,000 in three weeks. Then, to augment the initial grant, Ford boosted its backing with a 1965 presentation of $535,000 for building costs.

The grant was a notable exception to the way things go in the theater world. The Mummers is the only community theater in the Ford Foundation's $6 million program bolstering repertory theater in America.

Scism has made clear his attitude on the challenge—a stand that remains typical of his complete candor. He does not agree with people who say the theater was selected because the Mummers "were the best of something or other."

"It certainly was not the case with us," he has said.

He believes the Ford Foundation offered the grant "for the specific purpose of testing the feasibility and the possibility of a large, well-established successful amateur theater becoming a fully professional Equity theater."

No where does the contract say the Mummers cannot fail. Considering the challenge, the odds are heavy that the Mummers cannot succeed in as grand a manner as their new institution might demand.

And yet the odds have been stacked, skyscraper-high, against the Mummers since 1949. A tent, $8 and an opportunity were all the Mummers could originally claim toward success.

Only the challenge is left, plus some startling historical footnotes. The Mummers have never buckled under defeat.

The theater's future pivots on its ability to survive success. It has two decades for a running start.

60. JOHN F. KENNEDY CENTER FOR THE PERFORMING ARTS (NATIONAL CULTURAL CENTER OF THE UNITED STATES)
Washington, D.C.
Opened September 7, 1971

On September 7, 1971, perhaps the single most important event in American theater history occurred, the opening of the John F. Kennedy Center for the Performing Arts. For the first time Americans were to have a national cultural center in their capital city in which all the performing arts would be represented. The cost of this multi-theater venture was more than $66,000,000, making it the most costly complex yet built in the United States.

A brief history and description of the project was prepared by the staff of the center.

60:1   The founding fathers of the United States expressed the hope that the political capital of the new nation would be its cultural capital as well, and a national center for the performing arts in Washington, D.C. has long been the dream of many American citizens. Although the idea found considerable support over the years, it was only recently that positive action was taken.

HISTORY

Four American Presidents have played a direct role in the history of the national cultural center, recognizing that ours is the only major capital in the world without proper facilities for the performing arts. The Center was authorized on September 2, 1958 when the National Cultural Center Act was signed into law by President Eisenhower, who remained one of the Center's most steadfast supporters until his death in 1969.

"The Cultural Center belongs to the entire country," General Eisenhower said. "The challenge of its development offers each of us a noble opportunity to add to the aesthetic and spiritual fabric of America."

The theater of the Kennedy Center has been named for General and Mrs. Eisenhower in recognition of the General's extraordinary career and his role in initiating the Center.

President Kennedy gave ardent support

60:1. *The John F. Kennedy Center for the Performing Arts:* The National Cultural Center of the United States (Washington: The Center, 1969).

to the National Cultural Center and in 1963 signed amending legislation which extended the fund raising deadline three years.

"I look forward to an America which commands respect throughout the world not only for its strength but for its civilization as well," President Kennedy said a few weeks before his death. "I see little of more importance to the future of our country and our civilization than full recognition of the place of the artist."

President Johnson joined President Eisenhower and President Kennedy in wholehearted support of the Center and on January 23, 1964 signed into law a bi-partisan measure designating the National Cultural Center the sole official memorial in Washington to President Kennedy. The legislation renamed the Center the John F. Kennedy Center for the Performing Arts.

The original Act provided a government-owned site and specified that money for the Center's construction was to be raised by voluntary contribution. The John F. Kennedy Center Act authorized $15.5 million to match private contributions toward the Center's cost of construction, the first direct Federal grant in behalf of the performing arts. It also authorized a $15.4 million loan from the United States Treasury to finance underground parking facilities.

President Johnson broke ground at the Center's Potomac River site on December 2, 1964 and said, "This Center will brighten the life of Washington. But it is not, just as I have said, a Washington project. It is a national project and a national possession."

Construction began in 1966, after more than $15.5 million in private donations had been raised, qualifying the Center for the matching Federal grant. The Treasury loan became available at the same time.

Support for the Center has also come from President Nixon who has said, "This Center was conceived with full bi-partisan support as an effort to promote the per-

60. John F. Kennedy Center for the Performing Arts, Washington, D.C., 1971. Courtesy of the John F. Kennedy Center for the Performing Arts.

60. Model of the interior, Opera-Ballet House, John F. Kennedy Center for the Performing Arts, Washington, D.C., 1969. Courtesy of the John F. Kennedy Center for the Performing Arts.

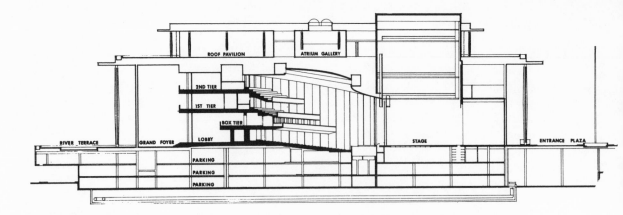

60. Plans for Opera-Ballet House, John F. Kennedy Center for the Performing Arts, Washington, D.C., 1969. Above, cross section; below, box tier level. Architect's drawings. Courtesy of the John F. Kennedy Center for the Performing Arts.

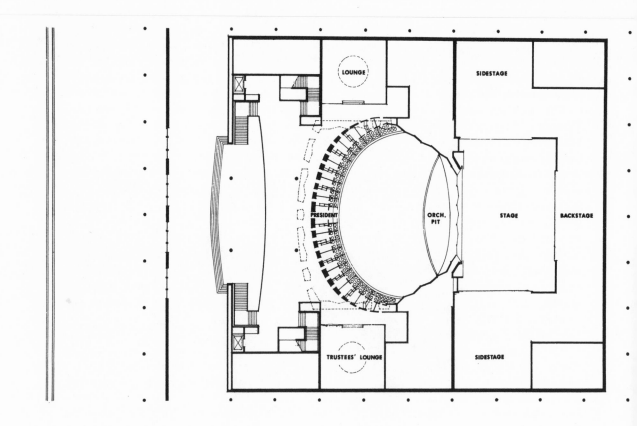

forming arts throughout the nation. I personally pledge full support to the successful realization of this project."

On October 17, 1969 President Nixon signed legislation which authorized $7.5 million in additional matching Federal funds and increased the Treasury loan by $5 million. These additional funds will help meet the meteoric rise in building costs since 1964.

The opening of the Kennedy Center, scheduled for September 1971, will at last place Washington among the major capitals of the world which provide a national focal point for the arts as well as government.

A LIVING MEMORIAL

The Kennedy Center is directed by an independent Board of Trustees whose members are appointed to ten-year terms by the President of the United States. In addition, there are ex-offico members of the Board drawn from pertinent public agencies and from the United States Senate and House of Representatives.

The Trustees have been charged by Congress (1) to provide a national stage for the finest in classical and contemporary music, opera, drama, dance, film and poetry from this nation and from nations abroad; (2) to provide facilities for lectures and other civic activities; (3) through imaginative programming, to develop new and ever broadening audiences not only for its own theaters by for theaters and concert halls throughout the nation; and (4) to provide opportunities for the growth and experience of young performers and young audiences, and to provide for other age groups as well.

The opening season of the Kennedy Center will feature the best of America's and the world's symphony orchestras, opera, theater and dance ensembles, concert artists, and the greatest personalities in the field of popular music. A festival of classic and contemporary films is planned for the film theater. A new major work by Leonard Bernstein will be premiered at the opera house and will officially open the Kennedy Center.

The American Ballet Theater, the Center's resident dance company, will figure prominently in the schedule of the opera house and will present three two-week seasons annually. The New York City Opera, which has become one of the world's leading ensembles, will perform regularly each season at the Center. The National Symphony Orchestra, under the leadership of its new and distinguished musical director, Antal Dorati, is the Center's resident orchestra and will present its full schedule of performances in the concert hall. In addition, the Trustees are setting aside time in the Center's theater for the other well-established performing arts companies of Washington.

A comprehensive education program is a high priority item in the Kennedy Center's public service plans. Many of the country's children will see their first live professional performance at the Kennedy Center. The center expects to continue to sponsor such programs as the American College Theatre Festival, which brought 10 of the nation's best university theater groups to perform in Washington in 1969 and 1970, and the National College Jazz Festival, first presented in 1970.

The Kennedy Center will encourage and foster the growth of the arts of our time while preserving our great heritage. Through its programs, and through telecasts and broadcasts, the Kennedy Center will seek to influence and invigorate the performing arts across the nation.

THE CENTER AND ITS FACILITIES

The John F. Kennedy Center for the Performing Arts promises to be one of the most distinguished architectural achievements of our time. Designed by Edward Durell Stone, whose work has graced the leading cities of the world, the Center's majesty and facile beauty will effectively symbolize our nation's regard for the per-

179

forming arts. As a national monument the Center also will be a fitting companion to the Washington, Lincoln and Jefferson Memorials, all within view of the Center's rooftop.

The Center is being constructed in a park-like setting on 17 acres of land along the east bank of the Potomac River opposite Theodore Roosevelt Island, a bird sanctuary which by law will be preserved forever in its natural state. To Mr. Stone, it is "one of the most exciting and glorious settings for a public building in the world."

Within the Center's single building will be an opera house, a concert hall, a theater (the Eisenhower Theater) and a film theater. Also included will be a small exhibit gallery, a multi-purpose pavilion, a restaurant and a coffee house. The substructure of the Center will contain a three-level, 1600-car parking garage.

While the Center itself is designated as the nation's official memorial to President John F. Kennedy, an area in or near the Center will be set aside for a specific memorial in his honor. The site and nature of the memorial are pending determination.

The Building

The size of the building alone—about 100 feet high, 630 feet long and 300 feet wide—will be awe-inspiring. It will be surrounded by sixty-six steel pillars encased in gold-finished aluminum. Its windows overlooking the Potomac will soar six stories from floor to ceiling, and the entire exterior wall surface will be faced with white marble, the gift of the government of Italy.

The Entrance Plaza, running the length of the east side of the Center, will provide the Center's main access. Germany has donated sculptured bronze panels to embellish the entrance area. Down the middle of the Plaza will be a long reflecting pool, sparkling fountains and planting areas for trees.

The two main entrances to the building will lead from the Entrance Plaza through two grand corridors, the Hall of Nations and the Hall of States, into the Grand Foyer. Flags of the countries recognized by the United States will be suspended from the ceiling of the Hall of Nations. Flags of the 50 states of the United States will be similarly displayed in the Hall of States. Floodlights in these halls will create a blaze of color to accent the white marble walls and bronze columns.

The Grand Foyer will run the entire length of the Center on the west side, opening onto the river terrace and overlooking the Potomac River. The foyer, one of the largest rooms in the world, will offer a spacious promenade beneath 18 magnificent chandeliers, a gift of the people of Sweden, and provide access to the concert hall and theater. It will also serve as the Center's main reception area.

Opera House

The opera house will be used primarily to present opera, musical comedy and dance. It will have walls of royal red with accents of gold to match the magnificent stage curtain, the gift of Japan. Its seating capacity of 2,322 is comparable to that of such famous opera houses as La Scala, the Paris Opera and the Vienna State Opera. Its crystal chandelier, measuring 50 feet in diameter, comes from Austria. The orchestra floor will seat 1,374, the box tiers will seat 423 and 419, respectively.

The stage of the opera house measures 100 feet wide and 65 feet deep. The stage and backstage areas, comparable in size to the Metropolitan Opera House at Lincoln Center in New York City, can accommodate four productions at one time. The orchestra pit, with room for 110 musicians, is designed so that it can be covered to provide either a forestage or space for additional seating.

The opera house will have one large rehearsal hall measuring 50 by 70 feet, as well as coaching rooms and two smaller rehearsal rooms.

Concert Hall

The concert hall, primarily for orchestra and choral concerts and recitals, will retain the conservative character and grand manner of such distinguished, time-tested halls as Symphony Hall in Boston, the Musikvereinsaal in Vienna and the Concertgebouw in Amsterdam. Eleven crystal chandeliers have been donated by Norway for the concert hall.

The concert hall's seating capacity of 2,761 is roughly comparable to that of Carnegie Hall in New York City. The orchestra floor will seat 1,638 persons, the box tier with 63 boxes will seat 246 and the two tiers above will accomodate 391 and 486, respectively.

The Eisenhower Theater

The theater, which has been named in honor of the 34th President of the United States and Mrs. Eisenhower, is intended primarily for drama. Comparable in size to major Broadway houses, the Eisenhower Theater will seat 772 on the orchestra floor, 64 on the box tier with 15 boxes and 306 in the upper tier for a total of 1142.

The stage of the theater measures 75 feet wide and 55 feet deep. The backstage area is more than half that of the opera house. The orchestra pit is convertible either to a forestage or space for additional seating and will accommodate 40 musicians.

The opera house, concert hall and theater each will have its own lobby, promenade and lounges. The lobbies opening off the Grand Foyer will be majestic in size. The lobby of the opera will be 145 feet wide and 35 feet deep. The concert hall and theater lobbies each will be 120 feet wide and 35 feet deep.

The tiers of the opera, concert hall and theater will have open balconies overlooking the lobbies. Reception and refreshment lounges will be located in convenient

places and will be open for service prior to showtime and during intermissions. Lounges on the box tier level normally will be reserved for special occasions and honored guests. The north lounge of the opera house will be decorated and furnished as a gift of the people of Denmark.

A Presidential box accommodating up to 12 will highlight the box tier of each of the major halls. They will have fully appointed anterooms and be reserved for the use of the President of the United States and his guests. The Presidential lounge of the opera will feature a Waterford crystal chandelier and four wall brackets donated by Ireland.

Each of the major halls is designed to permit film showings, and television and radio broadcasting, and can be used for lectures and meetings. Each will also have its own greenroom and stage door reception room, as well as a conductor's suite, offices for managers and technicians, warm-up areas and a canteen for performers and stagehands.

The Film Theater

The film theater, located on the roof terrace level directly above the theater, will seat 500. It will have the most modern facilities for the projection of 35 mm. and 70 mm. films. In addition, a moveable proscenium arch will make it possible to provide a completely open stage as well as a conventional one and thus permit the use of the hall for experimental theater, children's theater, poetry and drama reading, chamber music and experimental dance.

The film theater will include a greenroom and stage door reception room, offices, dressing rooms and storage areas. Elevators will provide access to the roof terrace level.

Other Facilities

In the middle of the roof terrace level, overlooking the Potomac, will be the Pavilion, a multipurpose room 130 feet long and 75 feet wide designed for exhibits, large receptions, band concerts, meetings and conventions.

The Atrium Gallery, a spacious corridor 130 feet in length and 40 feet wide, will run through the center of the roof terrace level. At the south end of the roof terrace level, with magnificent views of Washington and Virginia, will be the Center's restaurant, cafeteria and cocktail lounge.

FINANCING

Land

Approximately 17 acres of land for the John F. Kennedy Center for the Performing Arts was provided through the Act of Congress creating the Center in 1958 and subsequent legislation. The John F. Kennedy Center Act of 1964 granted $2.5 million for the acquisition of land not owned by the government to complete the designated site. This land includes eight acres for the building, surrounding property to provide a park-like setting, and approaches to the Center and its underground parking facilities.

Construction

Construction of the Center, exclusive of land, will cost an estimated $66.4 million. Congress appropriated $15.5 million to match private contributions under the John F. Kennedy Center Act of 1964. The law also authorized the Center's Trustees to issue revenue bonds to the United States Treasury to a value not greater than $15.4 million. These funds were designated for construction of the 1,600-car underground garage and are payable from the revenues accruing to the Board.

Public Law 91-90, signed by President Nixon on October 17, 1969, authorized an additional $7.5 million in matching Federal funds and an increase of $5 million in borrowing authority from the U.S. Treasury.

Private Subscriptions

The Kennedy Center qualified for the original matching Federal grant in 1965 when pledges and contributions were in excess of $15.5 million. The Trustees are currently seeking an additional $2.5 million from private sources in order to match the recent Federal grant.

Of the amount that has been raised entirely from private sources, the Ford Foundation contributed $5 million, the Rockefeller Foundation $1 million, Old Dominion Foundation $500,000 and the Joseph P. Kennedy, Jr., Foundation $500,000. About $5 million has been contributed by almost 400 industrial and business firms. There have also been a large number of gifts from individuals and from other foundations.

Foreign Gifts

Ten foreign nations have made substantial contributions to the Kennedy Center. Italy has donated all of the marble for the interior and exterior of the building, valued at more than $1 million, the largest gift to the Center from a foreign nation.

Austria will be represented by a magnificent crystal chandelier and associated lighting fixtures in the opera house. Belgium has given mirrors for the grand foyer, the opera, the concert hall and the restaurant. Canada's gift is a red and black woolen stage curtain for the Eisenhower Theater designed by Madam Mariette Rousseau-Vermette. The Danish government will decorate and furnish the north lounge of the opera house to represent Danish arts of the twentieth century. The German government is donating bronze panels sculptured by Jürgen Weber for the Center's entrance area.

Ireland is giving a specially designed Waterford crystal chandelier with matching sconces for the Presidential lounge of the opera house. A magnificent hand woven red and gold silk curtain for the opera house is the gift of the government of Japan and the America-Japan Society of Tokyo. Eleven crystal chandeliers fabricated by Hadelands Glassworks for

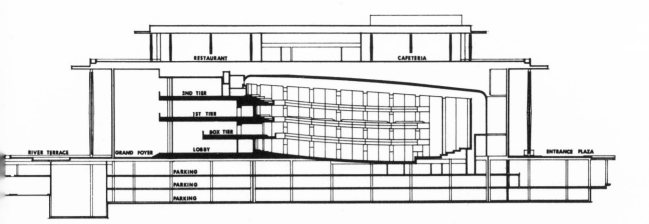

60. Plans for Concert Hall, John F. Kennedy Center for the Performing Arts, Washington, D.C., 1969. Above, cross section; below, the box tier level. Architect's drawings. Courtesy of the John F. Kennedy Center for the Performing Arts.

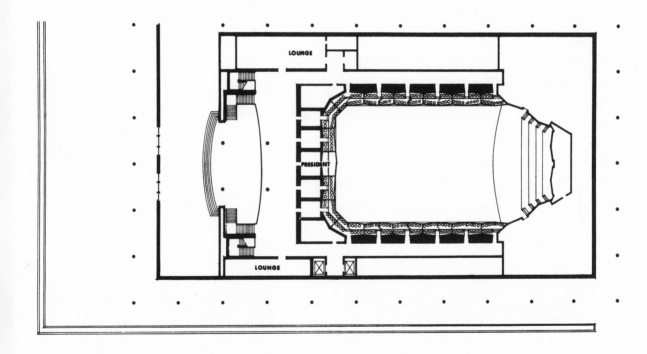

60. Model of the interior, Concert Hall, John F. Kennedy Center for the Performing Arts, Washington, D.C., 1969. Courtesy of the John F. Kennedy Center for the Performing Arts.

60. Model of the interior, Eisenhower Theater, John F. Kennedy Center for the Performing Arts, Washington, D.C., 1969. Courtesy of the John F. Kennedy Center for the Performing Arts.

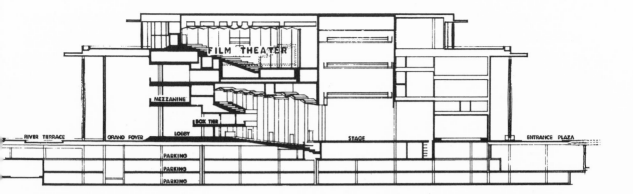

60. Plans for Eisenhower Theater, John F. Kennedy Center for the Performing Arts, Washington, D.C., 1969. Above, cross section; below, box tier level. Architect's drawings. Courtesy of the John F. Kennedy Center for the Performing Arts.

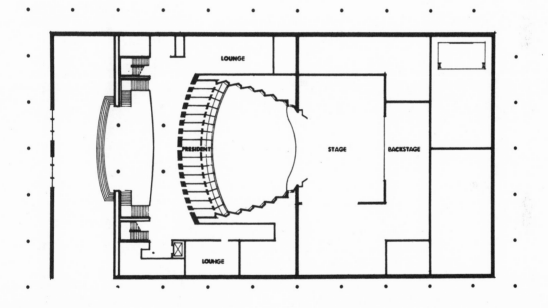

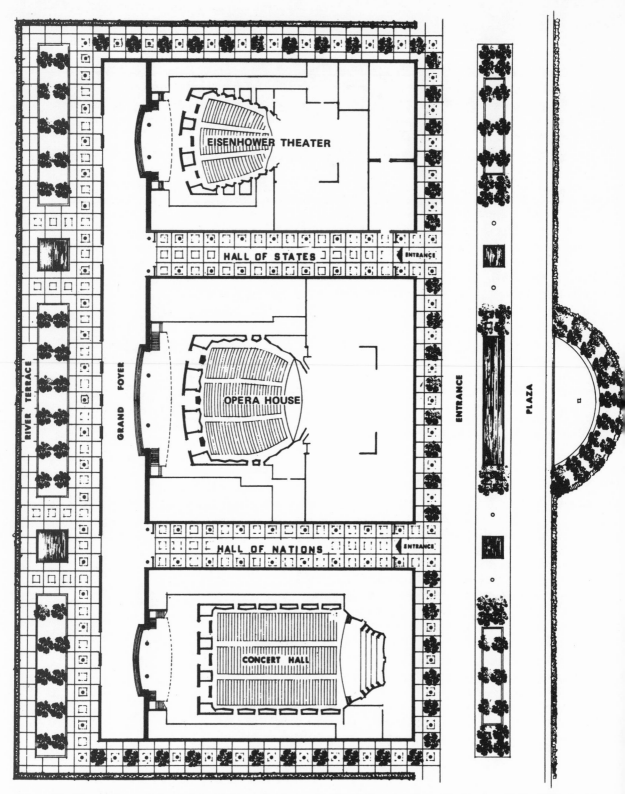

60. Plan of the main level, John F. Kennedy Center for the Performing Arts, Washington, D.C., 1969. Architect's drawing. Courtesy of the John F. Kennedy Center for the Performing Arts.

the concert hall are the gift of the people of Norway. Sweden has commissioned Orrefors Glassworks to produce eighteen crystal chandeliers for the grand foyer as her gift to the Center.

A number of other countries have indicated their wish to contribute to this national memorial and discussions with them are continuing.

The opening of the Kennedy Center elicited much adverse comment from the critics as well as from various theater historians and people involved in theatrical production. There was some protest that a theater center that cost so much money should have such old-fashioned physical facilities. Few of the many advances in theater architecture were evident in the theaters of the complex.

The center was opened with the performance of Leonard Bernstein's Mass. The following excerpt from *Newsweek* is rather typical of criticism of the center's architecture:

60:2 . . . Most of the barbs tossed at Bernstein's "Mass," however, seemed gentle alongside the bricks hurled at the center's architecture. For the building, practical as it may be, is beset with several severe esthetic problems.

First, there is the site itself. The Kennedy Center is located on the banks of the Potomac about a quarter of a mile upstream from the Lincoln Memorial. This sounds, on the face of it, marvelous and it does indeed make for handsome views from the building's terraces. But the place has been surrounded by such an assortment of visual and physical barriers as to make it nearly as forbidding as a medieval castle from the outside. From the Virginia shore, the prospect is obscured by Theodore Roosevelt Island, a thickly wooded bird sanctuary. On the Washington side, the center is hemmed in by the gargantuan Watergate complex and encircled by

60:2. *Newsweek*, Sept. 20, 1971, pp. 22–29. Copyright Newsweek, Inc. 1971, reprinted by permission.

the twisting strands of a freeway system. Viewing the building from a distance does not lure the visitor closer, but rather makes him wonder how to find his way to the entrance. As one newspaper critic noted, the building manages to be "isolated from city life."

Second, the exterior. Simplicity was to be the keynote of the structure—architect Edward Durell Stone was chosen largely for the elegant simplicity of his designs for the U.S. Embassy in New Delhi and the American pavilion at the 1958 Brussels World's Fair. But the Kennedy Center carries simplicity to the point of blandness. Its flat marble walls, relieved only by spindly steel column fitted with fins and painted gold, makes it resemble nothing so much as a rectangular white layer cake garnished with golden toothpicks.

And finally, the interior. The outside, at least, give some illusion of lightness to a massive edifice 630 feet long, 300 feet wide and 100 feet high. But any such illusion is rudely dispelled the instant one steps inside. Two vast marble-clad halls, each one 60 feet high, run the width of the building dividing it into its three components, the Concert Hall, the Opera House, and the Eisenhower Theater. Near the ceiling of both these corridors hang rows of silk flags, in one case those of the 50 states and the territories, in the other, those of the 120 countries recognized by the U.S. No other bits of décor (except the ubiquitous golden poles) break the relentless formality of these halls, which seem designed either for a treaty-signing or an Olympic foot race.

Both of them debouch into an even more gargantuan room, the Grand Foyer, running the entire length of the building along the riverfront. It is almost three times as long as Versailles' famous Hall of Mirrors, and fortunately it is blessed with a few pleasing details: eighteen Orrefors crystal chandeliers, hanging to within 12 feet of the floor; high Belgian mirrors for the inside wall; and a lively

7-foot bronze head of John Kennedy, sculpted by Robert Berks, standing opposite the opera staircase midway down the room. Nevertheless, the aura of spare giganticism persists.

This, it seems, is what architect Stone was driving at. He walked through the building last week with Sen. William Fulbright, a fellow Arkansan and one of the key sponsors (with New Jersey Rep. Frank Thompson) of the legislation that made the cultural center possible. "Its monumentality," he thought was the best feature of the place. "Just think, Bill," joshed Stone. "Here we are, just two snot-faced kids from the Ozarks, and we've built the world's greatest cultural center."

That sort of hankering after grandiosity seemed oddly out of place with the taste of the times. One of the center's problems may be that it was designed about ten years ago, when architectural tastes ran more to Stone's expansive and antiseptic "international" style than they do today. Another difficulty may be that, despite all the criticism of its opulence, it was built, essentially, on the cheap.

Stone's original scheme was far more elaborate, a giant $250 million complex of three halls radiating from one central rotunda. This was quickly scotched in favor of the simpler plan, whose cost was estimated at $30 million. Expenses have since soared to $70 million ($43 million of it from public grants and loans), and the center isn't finished yet—a 500-seat film theater is planned for the top floor. The overruns have not, in general, come from frills, but from expensive necessities such as soundproofing to seal out the noise of low-flying jets bound for nearby National Airport and sound-lock systems to keep the sound in one theater from setting up vibrations in the others.

The deluxe furnishings that recently moved columnist Jack Anderson to denounce the center as a "public works palace for the rich" are, for the most part,

gifts from foreign governments. The Italians, for example, donated all that Carrara marble, valued at more than $1 million. Sweden gave the Orrefors chandeliers, Belgium the giant mirrors, Japan an exquisite red and gold silk curtain in the Opera House, Austria the Opera's sunburst chandelier, and France two Matisse tapestries and two Laurens bronzes. Twenty-five other nations have also sent major presents or promised to.

Where money has been spent amply— and with such brilliant results as to redeem the center's other lapses of taste— is in the three theaters that are, after all, its heart.

The Opera House, the building's centerpiece, is a rich burgundy jewel box. The balconies and walls, entirely covered in deep red fabric, are bowed in a series of gentle arcs outlined by gilt studs to give the impression of luxuriant padding. There is no frame around the stage, which helps draw even patrons in the farthest seats into surprising intimacy with the performance. Despite its three balconies, it is a small hall as opera houses go— 2,334 seats as opposed to the Metropolitan's 3,800—and the sightlines and acoustics were pronounced superb by last week's audiences.

The same is true of the Concert Hall, a classically austere rectangular affair modeled on the highly successful acoustical lines of Boston's Symphony Hall and Amsterdam's Concertgebouw. The wooden walls are painted cream; the stage is backstopped by a huge Skinner Aeolian organ, its deep copper pipes stretching upward like wing feathers. The night after "Mass's" premiere, the hall was inaugurated with a concert by Washington's National Symphony, which has made immense strides under its new conductor Antal Dorati. President Nixon came to this one—he has a special fondness for the National Symphony, and pronounced himself well pleased. Violin virtuoso Isaac Stern, soloist in Mozart's G Major violin concerto, was ecstatic. "I had a ball," he said later. "I used the hall like an instrument, just letting the sound out and letting it float. It's fantastic."

The Eisenhower Theater (so named to honor the President who signed the center's original legislation—and also to coax Republican money into the project) is not yet finished; it will open next month with a performance of Ibsen's "A Doll's House," starring Claire Bloom. Here too every effort has been made to create near-perfect conditions for viewing and performing. "Everybody always said the Morosco Theater is the best in New York," says Roger Stevens, himself an experienced New York theater pro. "We asked the architect to make it like the Morosco."

And so, if the center can be regarded as a convenient protective shell for three first-class theaters, it is a triumph. Critics may—and have—denounced the very concept of such arts centers as cultural supermarketry. They may regret that the theaters were not built separately nearer the city's heart instead of perched out at its elbow. But the practical fact is that unless they had been invested with John F. Kennedy's name as a national memorial, and unless Roger Stevens had performed wonders of extractive engineering in raising both public and private money for the place during repeated moments of crisis, no one of these three theaters would ever have been constructed and the Capital would have remained a cultural wilderness. . . .

Chapter 3

College and University Playhouses

A peculiar phenomenon of the twentieth century has been the rapid development of the college and university playhouse with an accompanying dramatics program for which an academic degree can be earned. As early as the eighteenth century in America there was interest in drama in the universities, but this for the most part limited itself to the study of drama as literature or, perhaps, a reading of a play in public. It was not until the twentieth century that the universities began to take steps toward building playhouses and, concurrently, creating a theater arts program of academic value. Such pioneers as George Pierce Baker of Harvard and Yale universities, Frederick Koch of the Universities of North Dakota and North Carolina, Thomas Wood Stevens of Carnegie Institute of Technology, and Edward Mabie of the University of Iowa were able to fire the imaginations of students, alumni, and university administrations to allow them to teach courses in the theater arts and to erect proper playhouses for university productions.

Carnegie Institute of Technology was the first academic institution in the United States to offer a degree in the theater arts; other colleges and universities followed suit. The early playhouses, however, were not innovative in architecture and design of stage; any innovations were technical, as in lighting techniques and devices.

One of the first major departures in theater design was the Penthouse Theatre of the University of Washington, which offered a playhouse designed solely for presentation in the round. This theater was opened in 1940. The outbreak of World War II halted any further advances for a few years, but with the cessation of hostilities and the tremendous increase in college and university enrollment, new buildings were designed, edifices that were increasingly daring in breaking with the past. It became the general philosophy that the universities should lead the way in innovation, pointing new directions in theater.

These innovations were in design, certainly, but they were also mechanical. Under the inspired leadership of such a technician as George Izenour of Yale, the "theatre automatique" was developed at Harvard, offering the greatest flexibility yet seen in the American theater: by the touch of a button a theater auditorium could be changed from proscenium to arena to thrust stage. In other words, for the first time the theater could be shaped to meet the needs of a particular production, and the director was no longer hampered by having a particular type of theater.

Other exciting playhouses were erected on university campuses, and many small colleges, willing to experiment, invested in innovative theaters. One of the most interesting of these was the theater of Birmingham-Southern College with its turntable stage arrangement, which is described in this chapter.

The universities later entered the theater-complex era with the development and opening of the magnificent Krannert Center for the Performing Arts at the University of Illinois.

With the great number of students being trained in theater arts, the universities can be expected to contribute greatly to the shape of the playhouse of the future.

61. CARNEGIE INSTITUTE OF TECHNOLOGY
Pittsburgh, Pennsylvania
Opened April 23, 1914

The beginning of the college theater movement is usually traced to Carnegie Institute of Technology, the first institution in the country to offer a degree in the field of theater arts. The history of this important playhouse and department of drama was to be written by Elizabeth Kimberly, associate professor emeritus of the Department of Drama, Carnegie-Mellon University. Mrs. Kimberly, from her vast knowledge of this subject, wrote the following account of Carnegie Institute and that first department of drama.

61:1 Thomas Wood Stevens founded and developed the first degree giving Drama Department in this country, where theater training combined with a college curriculum. There was no precedent for this, or examples to follow when Carnegie Institute of Technology established its famous theater course.

Stevens, playwright, poet, artist, and dreamer, as well as teacher and practical

61:1. Elizabeth Kimberly, manuscript account, 1971.

man of the theater, came to Pittsburgh from the University of Wisconsin where he had been lecturer of Fine Arts. In Madison he had also been working in the pioneering venture of the Wisconsin Players. He was already well established as an author and producer of various plays and pageants, an avocation he continued while at C.I.T.

Stevens' background and formal education were varied. A native of Daysville, Illinois where he was born on January 26, 1880, he attended the Armour Scientific Academy in Chicago and graduated in 1897. He then entered the Armour Institute of Technology and took a three year course in mechanical engineering. His interests turned to the arts and he studied painting and etching with Bragwyn and Sorolla in Europe, founded the Blue Sky Press in Chicago, and became literary critic for the Inland Printer, the famous Chicago monthly. In 1903 he became head of the Departments of Illustration and Mural Painting at the Art Institute of Chicago, a post he held until 1912. While there he was associated with Donald Robertson in the production of plays and began collaboration on plays with Kenneth Sawyer Goodman.

In 1913, Arthur Hamerschlag, President of Carnegie Institute of Technology, and Russell Hewlett, Dean of the School of Applied Design, invited Thomas Wood Stevens to come to Pittsburgh to work out a plan for a school of stagecraft. Thomas Wood Stevens says, in Theater Arts Monthly, 1939:

"I took a long walk over the hills at Madison, thought it all over, and went to Pittsburgh with another scheme: not a school of scenery and lighting, not for applied design in the narrower aspect, but for a school of the theater—something more comprehensive and more difficult.

"To combine a college course with the technical training of a repertory theater.

187

To give the dramatic artist a general education with the interpretive activities of the stage."

To teach by doing—all students, no matter what their special talents or interests might be, would learn to know all phases of a play's production and all aspects of the operation of a theater.

The idea was revolutionary. This became the pioneer department in this country to give a degree in drama, and made quite a stir in professional circles. Many famous theatrical people came to observe, and educators to see how the curriculum worked.

The Department of Drama, then called the Department of Dramatic Arts, opened on February 9, 1914. Thomas Wood Stevens wrote, "We found ourselves in a palatial new building devoted to the arts. Along the front were five niches, with Architecture, Painting, Sculpture, Music, and Drama carved in stone over them. Eighteen students were enrolled, nine men and nine women. The students worked regularly in diction, elementary technic, history of art, history of costume, drawing, dancing, sight singing, English and rehearsal."

The student newspaper, *The Tartan* of April 29, 1914 reported: "The beautiful Design School Theater was formally dedicated on April 23, 1914." The play chosen for this occasion was "Two Gentlemen of Verona" by William Shakespeare. The dedication and first production had been planned to take place on the bard's birthday. Thus was inaugurated the tradition in the department of celebrating Shakespeare's birthday annually by the production of one of his plays. Directors for this first production were Thomas Wood Stevens and Donald Robertson, who had been brought in from Chicago as a visiting director.

It was a gala opening night. The audience was composed of trustees and officers of Carnegie Institute and other distinguished guests. The guests entered the building through the center niche of the five niches on the front facade. It led into a large and impressive foyer built of limestone with a high arched ceiling. The ground plan of Saint Peter's Cathedral in Rome was inlaid in the center of the marble floor outside the entrance to the theater. The ceiling represented an interesting and colorful historical study of architecture designed by James Monroe Hewlett, Arthur Hewlett, and Charles Basing of New York. All this combined to provide a most impressive foyer to the theater.

As the dedication guests entered the theater, to the right of this large, high ceilinged foyer, they found a beautiful room purveying an atmosphere of intimacy and warmth. The theater was elliptical in shape with a seating capacity of 450, built entirely of natural oak, hand carved in Greek design. On the oak doors of the three entrances, various theater symbols, including the masks of tragedy and comedy, had been carved. The ceiling was of specially designed plaster ornament and had a large stained glass skylight surrounded by a circle of lights. The seats were leather and wood, handcarved, divided into three sections on one level. There were two aisles and two small balconies, one on either side of the theater.

The principal decorative features of the theater were seven large panels, also designed by the Hewlett brothers and Charles Basing. The subject of the large central panel or curtain was Rome. At the left the guests viewed three smaller panels illustrative of Egypt, Assyria, and Greece and on the right they found three panels illustrative of Byzantium, the Middle Ages, and the Renaissance. The selection of Rome for the central panel was due, not merely to its chronological position, but especially to its significance as forming the connecting link between ancient and modern art. The curtain was steel, weighing about five tons and at the

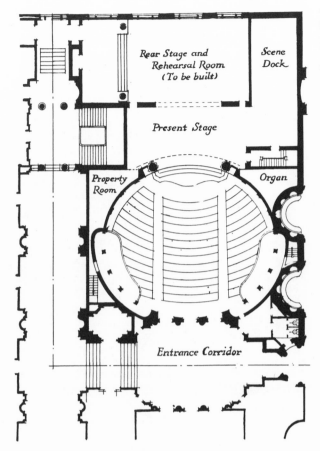

61. Plan of the Theatre of the School of Applied Design, Carnegie Institute of Technology, Pittsburgh, 1914. Architect's drawing. Courtesy of Carnegie-Mellon University.

PLAN OF THE THEATRE

61. Interior, Theatre of the School of Applied Design, Carnegie Institute of Technology, Pittsburgh, 1914. Courtesy of Carnegie-Mellon University.

62. Playmakers Playhouse, University of North Carolina, Chapel Hill, 1925. Courtesy of U.N.C. Photo Lab.

62. Interior, Playmakers Playhouse, University of North Carolina, Chapel Hill, 1925. Courtesy of U.N.C. Photo Lab.

time of its installation was one of the few of its kind in the country. There was an oak organ to the right of the stage.

The inscription over the proscenium read "Ici L'inspiration Deplois ses Ailes" —"Here Inspiration Unfurls Its Wings." On that first exciting evening, it truly did.

The first production which was most enthusiastically received was a thoroughly cooperative venture. The costumes were made by the drama students and the students of the Margaret Morrison Carnegie School under the supervision of Miss B. R. Stannard, Instructor of Pattern Modeling and Theory of Dressmaking in M.M. C.S. The programs were the product of the C.I.T. press. Thomas Wood Stevens wrote:

"The painting department came down in squads to make the sets. Among them came Woodman Thompson who was just graduating as an illustrator. He stayed on on the drama faculty (1914–1921) to be trained into a resourceful scene designer and executant."

Between the acts the Symphony Orchestra of the Department of Music, led by J. Vick O'Brein, gave a concert in the Exhibition Room, across the hall from the theater.

While the performance was in progress, the first Arts Ball was being given by the Design School. The theme was Roman Festival and it was held in the Architecture Department on the second floor. The decorations and the costumes were lavish and colorful.

As the curtain fell on "Two Gentlemen of Verona" a grand march proceeded to the foyer from the drafting rooms. Several dances were held in the foyer and then students and guests returned to the second floor where festivities continued.

The play was repeated the following night for the students of the four schools and again for the faculty. In April–May, 1915, it was revived for two performances, alternating with "Much Ado About Nothing" to celebrate the Tercentenary of Shakespeare's birth.

62. UNIVERSITY OF NORTH CAROLINA
Chapel Hill, North Carolina
Opened November 23, 1925

The *Christian Science Monitor* of July 28, 1925, devoted four columns to an article about the Carolina Playmakers, reviewing something of their history and describing the newly refurbished building that was to serve as their playhouse.

62:1   THE CAROLINA PLAYMAKERS, 1924–5

. . . The new playhouse which will be opened in the early fall is one of great significance to the group. The building was formerly the home of the law school, and is considered by authorities to be one of the finest buildings on the campus. Its classic design, resembling a Greek temple, is rendered different by unique and interesting changes. Instead of the usual acanthus motif on the capitals of the columns, native decorations are used in the conventionalized design. The hand-carved wooden capitals show long, graceful, leaves, curling up to reveal ears of corn.

The whole building is covered with vines and shaded by maple trees. Inside the finishing has been done in soft cream tones, with seats of comfortable design. Over the stage is a large Playmaker mask, and on either side of the proscenium arch are graaceful pottery vases. These were presented to the Carolina Playmakers by the Dramatic Club of Lincolnton High School. They were made in the pottery work at Jugtown, near Lincolnton.

Down in the basement are dressing rooms, the actors' green room, store rooms and wardrobes, completing the equipment. Over the front entrance are offices for the business staff.

It is planned to open the theater with a special celebration in the fall. Francis Gray has written a play to be used on this occasion. The old building was used as a ballroom in the days before the war, and the play is laid on the night when the students were called to arms just as they were celebrating their graduation in '61. . . .

The story of the development of the theater program at the University of North Carolina is a fascinating one. It was recorded by Harry Davis in a booklet, *Adventures in Playwriting: A Record of the Writing and Staging of a Thousand Plays by Student Authors*, published on the occasion of the 200th bill of new plays presented at the Playmakers Playhouse on March 30 and 31, 1963. An excerpt from the booklet follows:

62:2 In conservative circles the theatre and the people who work in it have usually been held suspect. So it is not surprising that the formal study of the theatre arts, for academic credit, is a relatively new subject in the curricula of institutions of learning. We are proud of the fact that the University of North Carolina, the oldest state university in operation in our country, and one which has frequently led the way in widening the scope of higher education, was among the first to give academic recognition to the study of theatre and drama.

As a matter of historical interest, the first dramatic performance ever to take place in a state university occurred in Chapel Hill, when two plays were presented in Old East in July of 1796 by the Dialectic and Philanthropic Societies as part of the Commencement exercises.

62:2. Harry E. Davis, "How It All Began." *Adventures in Playwriting: A Record of the Writing and Staging of a Thousand Plays by Student Authors* (Chapel Hill: Univ. of North Carolina, Dept. of Dramatic Art, 1963), pp. 3–7.

This production had come about through the efforts of William Augustus Richards, an erstwhile strolling player who had become a teacher in the preparatory school of the university.

Unfortunately Richards' efforts in behalf of the theatre were short-lived, for his work brought down the wrath of a prominent trustee of the university, General William Richardson Davie, after whom the Davie Poplar is named. In a letter to James Hogg, dated August 3, 1797, General Davie wrote:

"As to the acting of plays at the university, I think they are by no means as well calculated for the improvement of elocution as single speeches. . . . Single scenes from some of the best plays might still be used to advantage, but the acting of a whole play is absurb and unprofitable from every point of view. If the faculty insists on this kind of exhibition, the trustees must interfere. Our object is to make the students men, not players."

General Davie's influence must have been reflected in the passage of an act by the General Assembly of North Carolina in 1835, which read:

"No person without permission in writing therefor, from the president of the university or some member of the faculty, seven days beforehand, shall exhibit at Chapel Hill, or within five miles thereof, any theatrical, sleight-of-hand, or equestrian performance, or any dramatic or artificial curiosities, or any concert, serenade, or performance of music, singing or dancing."

Fortunately this act is long since out of date. But with the extinction of Richards' "brief candle," not much in the way of dramatic activity happened on our campus for over a hundred years. It is due to the vision of one of the university's great teachers, Dr. Edwin Greenlaw, who headed our English Department from 1913 to 1925, that dramatic art was finally given a fair chance to prove itself academically respectable. One of Dr.

Greenlaw's interests was creative writing; he was disturbed by the lack of any significant activity in the arts in North Carolina, and in the South as a whole.

Dr. Greenlaw had heard of some amazingly successful work that was being done in original playwriting at the University of North Dakota by a young instructor, Frederick Henry Koch. Mr. Koch had formed a group called The Dakota Playmakers, and had inspired his students to create their own plays from native materials close at hand. Dr. Greenlaw reasoned that if Mr. Koch could produce such patently good results in the limited cultural environment of the Dakotas, he might do far more in North Carolina, where a much richer body of history, legend and folklore was at hand. With the help of President Edward Kidder Graham, Dr. Greenlaw persuaded Mr. Koch to join the English faculty at Chapel Hill.

World War I was nearing its end when the new instructor began his teaching in Capel Hill in the fall of 1918. With Dr. Greenlaw's blessing, he introduced three new courses into the English curriculum: Shakespeare, Modern Drama, and Dramatic Composition. In the catalog the latter course is described as follows:

"English 31-32-33, Dramatic Composition. Credit 1½ courses. Fall, Winter and Spring Quarters. A practical course in the writing of original plays. Emphasis is placed on the materials of tradition and folklore, and of presentday life. The essentials of stagecraft are illustrated in the production, by The Carolina Playmakers, of selected plays written in the course. The course is limited in number."

If we remember that the bitter battles of the Argonne and of Ypres were being fought when these courses were initiated, it is not surprising to learn that only one male student enrolled in Mr. Koch's first class, along with twelve girls. The male student was Thomas Wolfe, a lanky mountain boy from Asheville, who had been rejected for service because of his unusual height. With the end of the war, the enrollment returned to its normal preponderance of male students. Among these, in the first years of Mr. Koch's teaching, were Jonathan Daniels, George Denny, Hubert Heffner and Paul Green.

The student who enrolled in the Dramatic Composition courses found a teaching approach radically different from the norm. He was handed a list of plays and told to read them; he was also told that he would soon be writing a play himself. Students and instructor sat together around a long table; there were no formal lectures, and no particular discussion of dramatic theories or techniques. Plays were read and discussed, and the student was urged to think about dramatic happenings in his own life, and to put them down on paper. As Mr. Koch himself later put it:

"I believe that when the Good Book says 'God created man in His own image,' it means that He imparted to man somewhat of His own creativeness; in a sense He made man a co-worker with Him—potentially an artist! In our way of playwriting we try to cherish the creative spark of the student. We encourage him to examine, with understanding and imagination, the eventful happenings in his own life, the characters in his own neighborhood. Then we guide him in shaping the materials in an appropriate and interesting pattern for the stage."

There were two fundamental features of Mr. Koch's teaching philosophy. First, he believed that the young writer is most successful when he uses material close at hand, material that he knows intimately from his own experience. Indeed, he believed that the most dramatic events in life are those associated with everyday experience. "Write what you know" was his constant admonition. As he later stated it:

"We have cherished the locality, believing that if the locality is interpreted faithfully, it might show us the way to the universal. For if we can see the lives of those about us with understanding—with imagination—why may we not interpret that life in significant images for all. It was so with the Greeks before us, and with our English forebears. It has been so in all lasting art."

It was natural that the early plays written by Mr. Koch's students were strongly regional in flavor, since most of the writers were boys and girls from rural backgrounds in North Carolina, or in the South. To identify such plays, drawn from the life of the common people, Mr. Koch employed the term "folk plays."

A second and equally firm principle on which Mr. Koch insisted was that a play is not a play until it has been presented by actors before an audience. Simultaneously with the establishment of his university courses he founded The Carolina Playmakers, a community-wide producing group through which the playscripts of the student writers, as well as standard dramatic works, could be presented to the public.

In 1918 the university had no suitable place where plays could be staged, so Mr. Koch obtained permission to use the high school auditorium in the new public school building. With the volunteer help of faculty, students and townspeople he extended the lecture platform there, erected a proscenium arch and curtain, and installed homemade footlights and spotlights. The new facilities were dubbed "The Play-House," and there, on March 14, 1919, the first bill of one-act student plays was presented by the Playmakers. They were: *When Witches Ride*, by Elizabeth Lay (now Mrs. Paul Green), *The Return of Buck Gavin*, by Thomas Wolfe (with Wolfe in the leading role), and *What Will Barbara Say?*, by Minnie Shepperd Sparrow.

On the inside page of the playbill of this memorable first production of new plays Mr. Koch printed an inspiring "An-

nouncement." Among some of its statements were these:

"The Carolina country from the mountains to the sea affords a rich stone of tradition and romance for the making of new literary and dramatic forms fresh from the soil. Among these are the legends of the 'Lost Colony' and the Croatans; the tales of the intrepid pirate, Blackbeard; of such indomitable pioneers as Daniel Boone, Flora McDonald, and the Town Builders of Old Salem; the lore and balladry of the mountain folk—a wonder field for the maker of plays and songs of our people. . . .

"Already a number of interesting plays have been written in the University course in Dramatic Composition, three of which have been selected for presentation in this program. These are native plays in the full sense of the word. . . .

"Being adjustable and portable, the stage equipment of THE PLAY-HOUSE may be readily adapted to any town hall or school auditorium. We are hoping that it may serve the people everywhere as a radial center, a creative center—that it may carry the idea of folk playmaking throughout the state and beyond. . . ."

There is clearly a note of prophecy in these and the other statements of the "Announcement." In a rapid flow of developments, the dramatic life of the state began to grow and spread. In May of 1921 The Carolina Playmakers made their first tour. Travelling by train, the Playmakers presented three plays in six towns in North Carolina. The plays were: *The Miser*, by Paul Green, *When Witches Ride*, by Elizabeth Lay and *In Dixon's Kitchen*, by Wilbur Stout.

In 1922 Henry Holt and Company published *Carolina Folk Plays*, *First Series*, a collection edited by Mr. Koch. This was to be followed by a Second Series in 1924, and a Third Series in 1928. In 1922, also, the Bureau of Community Drama and the state-wide Carolina Dramatic Association were started as a joint undertaking of The Carolina Playmakers and the Extension Division of the university.

In 1925 Smith Hall, one of the oldest and most beautiful buildings on the campus, was remodelled into a small theatre and turned over to Mr. Koch as a permanent home for The Carolina Playmakers. A grant from the Carnegie Corporation, secured with the help of Augustus Thomas, provided the new theatre with up-to-date lighting and staging equipment.

In 1927 the Pulitzer Prize in Letters was awarded to Paul Green, a recent student of Mr. Koch's, for his play, *In Abraham's Bosom*. In a later tribute to Mr. Koch and his catalytic effect on the dramatic life of the state and the nation, Mr. Green wrote:

"Then in 1918 Proff Koch came riding in from the Dakota prairies, his arms full of plays and his head full of dreams. In no time a stage was set up, and everybody near and far, little and big, black and white, realized for the first time that he, said body, was an artist of some sort —mainly a dramatic artist. I chose the last. And after a few productions I was caught fast in my choice and had struck acquaintance with all the bat-like terrors that inhabit the shadows of the stage."

Ten years after the founding of The Carolina Playmakers, in April of 1928, Mr. Koch organized a Southern Regional Conference on the Drama, a two-day meeting which brought to the campus some of the leading figures in drama in America, including Barrett Clark, Howard Mumford Jones, A. M. Drummond and George Pierce Baker. Prominent in this conference were local residents Paul Green and Archibald Henderson.

1928 saw also the first issue of a new quarterly magazine, *The Carolina Playbook*, published jointly by The Carolina Playmakers and the Carolina Dramatic Association. It usually featured the publication of a new play, and carried articles on theatre and drama by such writers as Archibald Henderson, Maxwell Anderson, Paul Green, Lynn Riggs, Barrett Clark, Montrose Moses, Brooks Atkinson, Percy Mackaye and Walter Pritchard Eaton.

The Federal Theatre Project, established in 1935, with the creation of a national people's theatre as one of its aims, recognized the vitality and originality of the native theatre movement which had developed out of Chapel Hill, and named Mr. Koch as Regional Adviser for the Southeast. During the three years of its existence in North Carolina, the project, under the state and local administration of Playmakers alumni, sought ". . . to carry out the ideas planted in this state over the past several years by Frederick H. Koch, director of The Carolina Playmakers, an exponent of native drama. . . ." To the campus, on a Writers Project, came Betty Smith, Robert Finch, Herbert Meadows and Grace Murphy.

By 1936 the burgeoning dramatic arts program at Chapel Hill had added two assistants to Mr. Koch to the role of the English Department, and the original three courses had expanded to include courses in acting, directing and stage production. With the blessing of the mother department, an independent Department of Dramatic Art was established, headed by Mr. Koch.

The busy and productive years rolled on, and the fame of the Carolina Playmakers and their plays continued to spread. Students came to Chapel Hill from Canada, Mexico, England, Norway, Germany, Egypt and even from China, to write about their native soils. In 1937 Paul Green, by then one of the leading dramatists in America, completed the script for *The Lost Colony*, an historical drama which opened in the outdoor Waterside Theatre on Roanoke Island in

July of that year. In dramatizing the story of Sir Walter Raleigh's ill-fated colonists, Mr. Green developed a fresh and vigorous approach to the pageant-drama, and set the pattern for a new form of theatre which is now flowering in America.

In 1940 the "coming of age" of The Carolina Playmakers was celebrated with a week-long Southern Regional Drama Festival, held in the Playmakers Theatre. To Chapel Hill came three hundred visitors, including Clifford Odets, DuBose Heyward, Howard Mumford Jones, Arthur Hobson Quinn and Norris Houghton. As in the previous conference, Chapel Hill's own Paul Green and Archibald Henderson were prominent. In Mr. Koch's welcoming address the first twenty-one years of The Carolina Playmakers were reviewed, and the record was an amazing confirmation of his belief that the key to the universal lies in faithfulness to the particular.

Through the inscrutable irony of fate Mr. Koch's career in Chapel Hill began at the end of one World War, and came to its close near the end of another. On August 19, 1944, while on a visit to his eldest son, he suffered a fatal heart attack while swimming at Miami Beach. Frederick Henry Koch was physically a small man, but with his passing a giant spirit was stilled.

One of Mr. Koch's many gifts was his ability to enlist on his staff the talents of exceptionally skillful and able people. One of these was Samuel Selden, who joined the Playmakers staff in 1927. Quiet and unassuming, he had been largely responsible for the high professional standards maintained in Playmakers productions, and for the firming up of the academic courses in dramatic art.

Succeeding Mr. Koch as director of the Playmakers, and chairman of the Department of Dramatic Art, Mr. Selden faced some dilemmas. The pioneering days were over; original playwriting and

the theatre arts were now an accepted and respected part of the university curriculum, not only here, but in hundreds of other institutions over the country. The post-war student was likely to be more sophisticated, more cosmopolitan, than his forerunners. To many students the war had brought a cynicism, a sense of frustration and futility, a craving for new gods, or for no gods at all. It was more difficult to focus the interest on the local and the particular, on the simple everyday life. The aeroplane, the radio, and television had broken down the barriers of communication, and the student felt himself a citizen of a diversified and often confused world, rather than the citizen of a particular locality.

Despite the disruptive effect of the war and the necessity to readjust to the changes brought about by it, the staff of the Playmakers and the department has continued to put its faith in creative playmaking, and in the artistic strength and integrity of the individual and the particular. However distractive the political, social and scientific developments of our present day may be, the solution to its problems still lies with the individual, and the future belongs to the young.

In celebrating that point in time when The Carolina Playmakers present their 200th Bill of New Plays, we look in two directions. With fondness and with pride we look back over the forty-four years of the past, in which seven hundred and thirty-two new one-act plays by students have come to life on our small stage, in which forty-six new full-length plays have been produced there, and in which our colleagues in the Carolina Dramatic Association have presented there two hundred and twenty-five new plays by their members. And with confidence and expectation we also look forward to the future, in which the insight and imagination of the new playwright, with the help of his fellow artists in the theatre, will continue to enrich, to enlighten, and to exalt our daily lives. As Mr. Koch would have said, "It has always been so."

63. YALE UNIVERSITY
New Haven, Connecticut
Opened December 10, 1926

The defection of famed Professor George Pierce Baker from the Harvard faculty to that of Yale University signified the beginning of the strong drama program at Yale. Baker had been famous for his "Theatre 47" workshop at Harvard, teaching playwriting under that title in the Department of English. Despite his own deep interest in the theater, however, he could not gain the interest of the Harvard Corporation in building a playhouse for him, so when Yale offered him that inducement he joined the faculty there.

The Yale University Theatre opened on December 10, 1926, and the New Haven *Evening Register* reviewed the play and the playhouse the following day.

63:1   "THE PATRIARCH" WELL RECEIVED
AT YALE THEATER

―――――――

Broadway and University Folk
Thoroughly Enjoy Opening Performance
By Baker Pupils

―――――――

Drama took its place with the fine arts last night when 700 dignitaries of Yale University and of Broadway gathered in the Yale University Theater for the formal opening of the gift of Edward S. Harkness. Sitting in the third row, directly in front of President James Rowland Angell, the benefactor saw the curtain rise on "The Patriarch," two short years after he had announced his gift of a million dollars to Yale for the establishment of a department of drama and for the construction of a Yale theater.

Behind the scenes, Professor George

63:1. New Haven *Evening Register*, Dec. 11, 1926.

Pierce Baker, head of the department, saw his dream of nearly two score years fulfilled. The little "47 Workshop" at Harvard, which he had made a center of academic theatrical interests all over the country, and which had been closeted in a tiny room in Massachusetts Hall at Cambridge, had grown into this, a complete modern theater, through the generosity of Edward Harkness.

In the audience were delegates from Broadway, there to welcome the academic theater to the professional theater, for, with the opening of the complete theatrical unit as a part of a university the profession had recognized a new influence in its ranks. That influence, that bond was sealed with the announcement last night that John Golden had bought the play from Boyd M. Smith, the author, for production within a year.

It was a story of tragedy in the loneliness of the Allegheny Mountains, tragedy judged by a Patriarch according to the laws of God and the word of the Bible, though it meant the death of his last son. Where Mr. Smith treated his main theme, the struggle in a torn soul between justice to God and the love for his son, the treatment was deft yet restrained. The difficult first act, in which he laid the foundation which was to justify the Patriarch's decision to follow God's words and kill his own son, was successful in its purpose.

The third act, in which the devotion to God gave him the courage to make the sacrifice, was immense in its tragedy. Only in the second act, when the motivation of the sub-plot leading the son to kill his brother on suspicion proved insufficient, did the play fall down. Then only was there a note of unreality, but when Mr. Smith switched again to his main theme, the struggle within the patriarch, real tragedy followed.

Herbert J. Biberman, playing the part of Abner Gaunt, the patriarch, had a dignity, the determination, the restraint, which was necessary for the success of the part. Herschel V. Williams, Jr., contributed to the part of Joe Gaunt, the son who killed his brother and faced his punishment with a smile, a fiery passion for justice which he used to help the play over the weak point, the insufficient motivation for the killing.

The bravery of a mountain woman, the love of a mother who had to give all for the cause of justice to God, was brought out with telling restraint by Katherine T. Clugston.

The part of Leah Tanner, a tigress of the mountains, whose four-year stay in the city had only accentuated her fierce, cruel temper, left nothing to be desired in its portrayal by Gretchen H. Steiner. Her father, played by Andrew N. Lytle, was the simple mountaineer, who was willing to submit to justice, but the ease with which he played his role was a little incongruous with the temper of his malicious daughter.

Not only the acting but the scenic design, lighting, production, costuming, in short, everything in connection with the performance, was done entirely by members of the department.

Donald Mitchell Oenslager, a recent graduate of Professor Baker's Workshop at Harvard and now an assistant of his, who has already carved a name for himself on Broadway by designing scenes for two successful productions there, designed the scenery for the play.

In his treatment of the scene for the first and the second act, Mr. Oenslager, in co-operation with Stanley R. McCandless, who handled the lighting, brought something new to the theater in his combined indoor and outdoor effect for the purpose of impressing the solitude of the mountains. Like everything new, a note of incongruity was hard to forget, in the picture, but his purpose was attained. The scene for the third act the top of a mountain that space, was in perfect keeping with the spirit of the play. A jagged bush, silhouetted against the blue of space, harmonized with the struggle in Joe Gaunt's soul before he killed his brother.

The play opened with a prologue by Lee Wilson Dodd, New Haven's dramatist-novelist, who gave credit where credit was due dedicating the theater to Mr. Harkness. It closed with an address by Professor Baker who spoke of the new opportunities which the gift had made possible and again thanked Yale's benefactor.

The costumes were designed by Rose Bogdanoff, while the technical details were taken care of by Philip W. Barber. The rest of the staff was as follows: Stage manager, Lemist Esler; assistant stage manager, Daniel Coxe; stage carpenter Dean Holden; assistants in lighting, Ruth Chamberlin Barber and Maurice Onesin; properties, Harry L. Burnett. The play was produced by Professor Baker. The play will be given four, possibly five more times, with a performance this afternoon and tonight.

The building itself, known as the first university theater of gothic design in the country, is unique in its construction, for it combines the practical structure of a professional theater with the necessary work shops of a university school of the theater. The entrance or hall way leading into the main auditorium are simply finished in a quaint gothic fashion. The auditorium itself is also simple, excellently arranged so that practically every seat in the house gives a satisfactory view of the stage.

There is little decoration either on walls or beams; but the entire house is given a touch of great beauty and richness by two large tapestries hung on either side. These tapestries are indeed treasures; they were given to the theater by the same Mr. Harkness whose generosity provided the theater itself and the tapestries are the more significant in that they come from the original family of Elihu Yale.

Hangings throughout and the great stage curtain are of heavy velvet, in a beautiful maroon shade. The seats, which are very comfortable, are also finished in a shade of corded velvet to harmonize with the curtains. The lighting fixtures, both at the entrance and in the auditorium are of quaint lantern design, to carry out the Gothic style of the whole.

Directly underneath the auditorium is the lobby, finished also with maroon velvet hangings. This room, large enough to seat 200 persons, is also used during the year as an experimental theater, where the practise productions of the department are given to the theater's regular audience. It is equipped with a smaller stage which has a cupola horizon, to be used experimentally since the height of the small stage does not allow the workers to fly their drops and settings.

In the back of the lower floor is a large rehearsal room, a coffee shop for the students and a large lecture room for classes. There [are] also storage rooms, and a rehearsal and storage room for the Yale Dramatic Association, which occupies the southwest corner of the building, with its offices and green room on the main floor.

The stage entrance at the side of the building leads directly to the section most used by the students. There is an information booth, a green room, interestingly furnished in green and maroon and yellow, with the walls covered with photographs of famous theatrical personages and scenes from former plays given by the 47 Workshop. The green room is the club or lounge room of the department. A door leads directly onto the large stage from the entrance way, and in back of the stage, visitors were shown the carpenter and paint shops, the property and electrical rooms and the design room where there are on exhibition model theaters of the Greek and Medieval periods, made this year by the students. The green

room is the club or lounge room of the department. A door leads directly onto the large stage from the entrance way, and in back of the stage, visitors were shown the carpenter and paint shops, the property and electrical rooms and the design room where there are on exhibition model theaters of the Greek and Medieval periods, made this year by students in the class in scenic design.

There is throughout the entire building a decidedly professional atmosphere. The equipment everywhere is the best of its kind, and is complete. The tower above the stage, 75 feet in height, gives opportunity for the flying of whatever amount of scenery may be desired. A great cyclorama is used in the present production.

The production of "The Patriarch" has been done entirely by the students of the department of drama, under the personal direction of Mr. Baker and his staff. The settings were built and painted in the shops by the students; properties have been assembled including some genuine and very valuable antique furniture which has been loaned for the production by several New Haven dealers. The lighting has been worked out by students in the lighting classes. The entire organization of the stage force was worked out by students.

The playhouse and its design received excellent coverage in the press. The following article is from *The American Architect*:

63:2   THEATRE FOR YALE UNIVERSITY,
NEW HAVEN, CONN.
Blackall, Clapp & Whittemore,
Architects

The Department of the Drama is a function of the School of Fine Arts of Yale University. The University Theatre is a part of the School of Drama and an adjunct to the teaching and administering of all of the arts connected with the drama

63:2. "Theatre for Yale University," *American Architect* 122:347–51 (Mar. 1927).

and the theatre, including everything from the writing of plays to the actual production thereof. It is not a public theatre in any sense, but is more like a laboratory, for a selected audience, and everything that takes place in the theatre being a part of the work of the Department. But being a laboratory theatre, it is arranged and equipped to give actual working conditions under which plays would be mounted and presented. It is in no sense a place for amateur performances, though such may be given, but it is a serious establishment of absolute standards in stagecraft.

The exterior of the building is designed in a Gothic style intended to be in harmony with the Harkness Memorial, the more recent Harkness dormitories and the proposed Yale library, being carried out in combinations of cast stone of a warm buff color. Weymouth seam-faced granite with weathered faces and Holland brick of dull red and brownish yellow tones. The relative amounts of stone and brick vary from nearly all brick in rear to nearly all stone on the front. The photographs published show the building in its condition at this time, March, 1927. The drawings, however, show the front as it will be when completed during the coming Summer, the additional work consisting of a porch on the left of the facade connecting to a lateral cloister leading to the administration rooms, also including an archway on the right of the front connecting the theatre facade to the enclosure of the adjoining Chapter House which is in the same style, and also including niches to relieve the simplicity of the front and some incised ornament around the central portal. All of this additional work was contemplated when the building was contracted for, but the actual execution was deferred until the final cost could be definitely determined. The mass of the tower which marks the portion over the stage is entirely of brick with the exception of a few slight bands and capping stones. The small turret at the corner of the stage tower encloses a 10,000 gallon sprinkler tank and is a practical necessity which is utilized to cover up the severeness of the stage tower. The low portions of the building on the left of the front are occupied by the administrative offices, the dressing rooms, etc. The entrance to the theatre is through the central portal on the front and through the porch on the left, the entrance to the offices being through the porch and cloister. The stage entrance is toward the rear on the side passage. The Yale Dramatic Association, an undergraduate organization entirely distinct from the School of the Drama, but with a notable history of its own, has quarters in the rear on the left with separate entrance.

The main entrance from the street gives into a small vestibule with ticket offices on each side. Beyond the vestibule is the main lobby extending across the front with stairs to the balcony at each side. The lobby is finished with a very simple plaster wall treatment, an arched, beamed ceiling and stairs of concrete with iron railing. The floor is of linotile in tile patterns, the whole being very quiet and simple. Beyond the lobby is the auditorium consisting of a parquet and a single balcony with total accommodation for 700 seats. The seats are from 20″ to 24″ wide and the rows from front to back are spaced 34″, giving very liberal accommodation. No provision is made for orchestra, the seats being carried right up to the stage front. The interior of the auditorium was intentionally kept very simple and there is almost a complete absence of anything like an architectural treatment. The walls are plain plaster; almost the only woodwork consists of the balcony front, which is of light oak, and the only decoration is afforded by some large Persian-Chinese tapestries, donated by Mr. Harkness and hung on each side of the proscenium. But there is no proscenium properly so called; there are no mouldings at all around the stage opening, and the ceiling beams which traverse from side to side are kept as simple as possible, only a slight amount of cornice being carried around the side walls. It was intended that nothing in the auditorium should compete with or detract from the presentation on the stage, all the interest being concentrated in the play, even the sight lines being arranged so that the two sections of the house above and below cannot see each other. If only a small audience is present, as on some occasions, they could fill the entire floor without being conscious of the emptiness of the balcony seats, and the audience would count simply as spectators and in nowise detract the attention from the stage.

The stage curtain is of silk velvet unrelieved by any ornamentation, hung in simple, heavy folds and is of a dark, rich plum color, almost black in ordinary light, this particular shade having been chosen after repeated experiments with different colors of light. It is the only strong note in the auditorium. The curtain will lift up as a whole, loop back partially for curtain calls or loop back on the sides wholly if desired. The tormentors and the teasers are of the same material so that they go with the curtain as a unit instead of competing with it. The colors in the auditorium are light, warm plaster tones, with stippled surface on the walls, light warm-colored oak on the front of the balcony and a dull glazed gold very deep in tone over the whole of the ceiling and the ceiling beams, this same tone being carried down over the slight cornice work on the side walls. The carpet in the aisles is a gray heather tone; the woodwork of the seats is a gray walnut and the upholstering of the seats is a neutral brown so that the whole effect is very quiet and unobtrusive, with no accent except the main curtain and the two tapestries.

The lighting of the auditorium is by fixtures of dull bronze hung close to the ceiling, arranged with lights to throw up for indirect lighting and some exposed lights for direct work. There are no brackets and no lights to shine in the eyes of the spectators.

Each of the beams across the ceiling is hollow, contains a runway accessible from the upper portion of the stage and is equipped with numerous pockets for spot lights to throw illumination on the stage at different angles. At the rear of the balcony there is a compartment which will be used as a moving picture booth when desired, and also serves as an observation stand for Professor Baker from which he can see the stage and be in telephone communication with the stage manager. Also spot lights can be thrown on the stage from this booth. In addition to this the front of the balcony contains a continuous trough with outlets at frequent intervals in which connections can be plugged for spot lights to be placed on the front of the balcony and to illuminate the stage.

The stage is 40 feet deep from the curtain line to the back wall and the full width of the house. The curtain opening is 34 feet wide and 24 feet high. There is a clear height from the stage floor to the gridiron of 75 feet with ample space above that to arrange the rigging, etc., and the usual ventilating skylight in the roof. There are no fly galleries. The rigging is carried down to the stage level with a counterweight system controlling border lights, the drops, etc., all operated directly from the floor, the curtain likewise operating from the stage level. On the left of the curtain opening is the stage switchboard. The stage floor throughout the central portion is built in sections, any one of which can be moved as desired for stage settings. On each side of the proscenium beyond the curtain is a small door connecting directly to the stage and with the auditorium, intended to be used in the giving of Elizabethan plays when the actors pass in review in front of the curtain. At the rear of the stage is the scene dock and carpenter shop connected to the stage through a wide opening so that additional depth can be given to the stage when desired, to a total depth of about 70 feet. The scene dock and carpenter shop is equipped with a very complete set of woodworking machinery and has on one side wall a large paint frame which slides down into the basement in a wide slot and carries up to the roof of the second story, permitting the mounting and painting thereon of any desired size of scene. Opening from one side of the scene dock is the electrician's room and property room, and in the rear on one side is a large room used for instruction and for the making of stage models. The stage manager also has an office at the rear of the scene dock.

In the basement under the main auditorium reached from the main lobby is what is known as the experimental theatre, used for rehearsals, tryouts, etc. It is equipped with a stage with the same curtain opening as the main stage but very much lower. This stage has as complete an electrical equipment as the space will allow and has a background arched overhead and rounded in plan to serve as a cupola horizon. The audience room would seat about 250 people. When performances are given in the main auditorium, this experimental theatre is available as a coat room or foyer, and in close proximity thereto are the public lavatories for men and women.

The space under the stage of the main auditorium is utilized as a rehearsal room. It has no special fittings, simply an undivided space available for this purpose.

The stage entrance is on the side street giving into a hall, with a custodian's office and stairs leading up and down, this hall leading directly to the rear of the stage. The Department of the Yale Dramatic Association also opens from this corridor. Adjoining this toward the front of the building is a Green Room, a place

of reunion for the students and the artists, equipped with comfortable chairs and tables. This Green Room connects directly with the stage and also toward the front connects with the business office of the Department, this business office also being reached from the cloister on the front. Professor Baker's private office adjoins the business office.

In the basement under the Green Room is a large recitation room used by the Department. In the rear under the Model Room is a complete cafeteria kitchen equipment which furnishes meals to the students, the tables being set in the rehearsal room under the stage. The balance of the basement under the carpenter shop is used for storage. The ventilating apparatus is located in a portion of the space under the main stage.

In the second story along the side are several private offices for the teaching force of the Department. Toward the rear is a library for the use of the students and beyond that are arranged the wardrobe rooms, costume rooms and a complete dye establishment, a large chorus room for women and one for men, and a number of individual dressing rooms with the necessary toilets, etc. Each dressing room is for two persons and has a bowl with hot and cold water, a steel make-up table, two mirrors and the necessary illumination. The walls of the dressing rooms are of terra cotta painted; the floors throughout are of concrete stained and varnished.

The construction of the building is fireproof throughout in strict conformity with the requirements of the Building Department and with the best usage in such constructions. The framework is of steel, the floors of reinforced concrete.

There is a complete system of heating and ventilation supplying fresh, warmed air to all public portions of the house and removing the air from the auditorium and the experimental theatre, the balance of the building being heated by direct radiation. Steam is taken from the University plant located at some distance from the theatre, brought to the building under pressure into a room under the porch. A tunnel is carried entirely around two sides of the building for distribution of pipe, etc., and also to give access for supplies to future buildings which are contemplated in the rear. Electricity is taken partly from the City supply with an alternating current, and partly from the direct plant of the University. There is a stage switchboard for the experimental theatre and an unusually complete board for the main stage. The lighting of the stage, in addition to the projection lights previously described in connection with the auditorium, includes footlights of the X-ray type and tormentor bridge with almost unlimited capacity for attachment of spot lights, with tormentor lights on each side, also the usual provision for border lights overhead. There are also floor pockets on each side and in the rear. The total capacity for electricity in this theatre is more than the total capacity of all the rest of the buildings of the University put together, it being found desirable to provide for any desired amount of illumination in connection with the stage settings, though at no time would all of the lights be put on.

The building was erected by Sperry & Treat Co., builders, of New Haven, Conn., from the plans of Blackall, Clapp & Whittemore, architects, under the immediate superintendence of D. W. Clark, Jr., of the said firm.

64. UNIVERSITY OF IOWA
Iowa City, Iowa
Opened November 7, 1936

The movement for an academic theater began early at the University of Iowa and can probably be traced to a meeting held in 1920. After a period of sixteen years, which included much work, some heartbreak, and certainly a scaling down of plans, the new theater building was opened. The importance of the playhouse was stressed by Edith Isaacs in *Theatre Arts Monthly*:

64:1   The importance of the new Iowa University Theatre is measurable not only by what it means to Iowa now but by what it may bring, in the future, to the American theatre. In essence the project consists of three theatres, all of them designed for specific university uses but at the same time scaled to the artistic needs and financial resources of varying communities. For example, the main theatre, which will house the auditorium, is to be built within a cost limit of $65,000 to $75,000, so that a region able to furnish that amount to build a theatre may take this university unit as a model. The second is planned to a cost of $32,000 to $38,000, and the third to a cost of $14,000 to $18,000. These two smaller units will be given over to the manifold technical and educational requirements of a university theatre. Studios, workshops in lighting, design and so on will be housed in the north wing. The south wing will include a small auditorium for experimental productions of new plays. On the west side of the building space will be provided for offices, classrooms and playwrights' studios. Located in a tract of thirty acres overlooking the Iowa River, the main structure will be supplemented by two reconstructions, one of an Elizabethan theatre (probably The Fortune) and the other of a Greek theatre. Grant Wood, as interior decorator, will design a series of frescoes based on the dramatic materials of the region for lobby, lounge and auditorium.

The day following the dedication ceremonies, a review appeared in the Iowa City *Register*:

64:1. Edith J. R. Isaacs, " A New University Theatre," *Theatre Arts Monthly* 18:702 (Sept. 1934).

64. University of Iowa

NEW THEATER IS DEDICATED

---

400 Persons See Play As S. U. I. Guests

"Two Hundred Were Chosen," a play by Mr. Ellsworth P. Conkle of the university dramatic arts staff, was given in premiere performance Saturday night as part of the formal dedication ceremonies of the new university theater before 400 persons who witnessed the play as guests of the university, including many notables in the field of dramatic art who were attending the three-day national fine arts conference which ended that evening.

The play, which is also in rehearsal for production on Broadway within two weeks, pictures the government's recent colonization of a valley in Alaska. In showing the reactions of the characters, an assortment of persons who have been "picked up out of the debris of the depression and transported, hopeful or dour, into the promised land," the author really portrays the emotional and intellectual growth of the farmer from stubborn individualism to social consciousness.

RECEIVED WARMLY

Mr. Sydney Spayde's acting in the role of Per Slocum was received warmly by the audience. Leading parts were played by Mr. John Chandler Bartlett and Miss Jane Fifer, and the cast also comprised Misses Marie Park, Jean Cowman, Dorothy Brown, Florabel Houston, Nona Seberg, Derelle Atkinson, and Sara Ann Carr, Mrs. Paul Siman, two children, Donald Jackson, Richard Davis, and Messrs. Bramer Carlson, Virgil Baker, Rodney Stewart, Max Ellis, Dwight Thomas, Jack Chase, LaVern Adix, James Butcher, Ronald Van Arsdale, Walter Fleischmann, Carl Weber, Don Tornquist, Le Mar Hoaglin, Robert Whitehand, Richard Smith, Robert Bigham, William Leeney and Robert Moore.

Displayed to advantage in the production was the highly flexible system of

64:2. Iowa City *Register*, Nov. 8, 1936.

lighting control in the new theater. The building as a whole is said to be one of the finest and most practical of its kind in the country, including in its equipment a revolving stage.

RAISES CURTAIN

Prof. Edward C. Mabie, head of the school of dramatic art, director of the play, raised the curtain Saturday evening with a speech of gratitude. In his dedicatory address the director expressed thanks to a long list of his colleagues who had made possible "this realization of the dream of his 16 years' experience with the theater here." He also accepted floral tributes from the state universities of Wisconsin and Missouri.

Persons in the audience at the play were also guests at a formal dinner in the memorial union at which President-Emeritus Walter A. Jessup of New York City, president of the Carnegie Foundation for the Advancement of Teaching, received a golden mask from Purple Mask, national university dramatics organization, in recognition of his work in the development of the theater.

The theater and its relation to the community was discussed by Gilmore Brown, director of the Pasadena, Calif., playhouse, on the after-dinner program. George T. Baker of Davenport, president of the state board of education, made the presentation of the building, and President Eugene A. Gilmore spoke briefly in acceptance.

A program prepared for the dedication ceremonies in 1936 contains articles about the theater, three of which are included here.

UNIQUE EQUIPMENT

The ideal modern theatre is judged by the excellence of its architectural design and by the usefulness of its equipment. Architects George Horner and R. C. Sandberg have contributed a design which

64:3. Dedicatory brochure published by the University of Iowa Theatre, 1936.

63. Yale University Theatre, New Haven, Conn., 1927. Courtesy of the Yale University School of Drama.

64. University of Iowa Theatre, Iowa City, 1936. Courtesy of the State University of Iowa.

64. Interior, University of Iowa Theatre, Iowa City, 1936. Below, cross section. Drawings published in dedicatory brochure. Courtesy of the State University of Iowa.

is honest and beautiful. It is honest with theatre functions and its stage machinery is unique.

The first unit of the theatre contains the auditorium seating approximately five hundred, the lobby, the foyer, check room, offices and costume shops. The stage itself is 42 feet deep by 56 feet wide and adjoining it is the wagon stage area which is 42 feet deep by 75 feet wide. This area is being used as a temporary scene shop until the North unit which will contain the shop, paint room and class rooms is added.

The stage equipment proper includes a gridiron 56 feet above the stage floor, a counterweight system of 18 sets of lines, rigging for the asbestos curtain, main curtain, light bridge and cyclorama. The stage has a built-in, 36 foot revolving stage which is crossed by a double set of imbedded steel tracks for the sliding stages that run the full length of the stage and wagon areas.

The counterweight system is an arrangement of rigging that permits scenery to be suspended in the flies above the acting area and counterbalanced by weights hung offstage. Provision has been made for supplementing the present number of counterweighted units as the need arises. Several complete settings may be shifted by this method.

The turntable revolves upon sixteen flanged wheels running on a circular track. This is supported by a heavy concrete ring which rests upon a foundation independent of the foundation of the building. It will be capable of an entire revolution in one minute. Several small settings may be mounted on it at the same time, and by rotating the stage a new scene or setting can be brought into view of the audience in a matter of 20 or 30 seconds. One use of this machine may be tested in Ibsen's *John Gabriel Borkman* where the playwright calls for the audience to see the characters walk from one setting to another. This of course can be done by slowly revolving the stage in full view of the audience.

The sliding stages are large, low platforms or wagons mounted on flanged wheels that can be rolled on either of the two sets of tracks running the full length of the stage house. On these wagons may be built large settings or particularly heavy exterior scenes. The major part of the ramp in *Two Hundred Were Chosen* is so mounted. By using the revolving stage as a turntable one of these sliding platforms can be moved from its position in back of the proscenium arch to a corresponding position directly upstage where it can be rolled off on the second set of tracks. At the same time another wagon with its setting may be rolled into position in back of the curtain from the first set of tracks where it has been stored.

These stage machines which may be used separately or in combination comprise a plant adapted to a variety of uses. They provide flexibility and speed and facility for handling heavy scenery found in new modern theatres.

—A. S. Gillette

The unusual system of lighting in the new University Theatre is called flexible remote control. In the rear of the auditorium is a glass-paneled control room affording a perfect view of the stage for the lighting control operators. Here is the small control-board consisting of 48 individual dimmer circuits and eight master dimmers with finger-tip sized handles all within easy stretch of one person's arms. The height of the board is such that a person of average height can comfortably see over the top for an excellent view of the stage. In this position with controls of such small size and capable of subtle movement, accurate timing of lighting cues and smooth blending should be a common-place in stage lighting of superior quality.

Controlled remotely at the rear of the auditorium, the actual dimming will be done by reactance dimmers and Thyratron electronic tubes in a remote control rack under the stage. This is connected also to an interconnecting panel offstage left where the one hundred outlets, distributed about the stage, can be connected in any combination to the 48 dimmer circuits on the control-board.

The outlets to which any lighting instruments, such as spotlights, can be connected, are located in the stage floor, on the lighting bridge, in the ceiling beam of the auditorium and so forth. A spotlight and other lighting instruments will be mounted in this ceiling beam on the lighting bridge hanging from the gridiron just back of the act curtain (controlled vertically from the counterweight), on other pipe battens hanging from the gridiron by the sets of lines mentioned above, and also mounted on a tower 18 feet high that can be moved about the stage on casters. The tower is especially useful for sunlight and moonlight effects. A battery of floodlights overhead will change the large cyclorama (55 x 102 feet) from day to night or vice versa, and striplights on the stage floor will produce dawns and sunsets on its surface. Linnebach projectors and lens effect machines will decorate the cyclorama with distant mountains, clouds, rain, or other effects required by the drama.

As the store of lighting instruments is gradually increased this highly flexible system of lighting control should be capable of producing the most effective lighting imaginable.

—H. D. Sellman

THE MAIN AUDITORIUM

Seating capacity is approximately 500. Chairs are arranged in solid formation not broken by longitudinal aisles through the center. Aisles are placed along the side walls. Six entrances lead from the foyer through vomitories which are outside the structural supporting walls of the building. Rows will be spaced 40 inches

apart to provide transverse aisles. Seats will be a minimum of 21 inches wide and selected for comfort. Each row is elevated more than 10 inches over the one in front, so that sight lines from each seat will be as nearly perfect as careful arrangement can make them. Acoustical characteristics of the room are being given careful study by experts working with several different interests and purposes.

THE STAGE

The stage is 126 feet long and is 52 feet from front to rear wall. It is equipped with three scene shifting devices. The first is the conventional counterweighted gridiron which serves the main stage area, a space 56 feet by 52. In this area also is a revolving stage designed to increase the speed of scene changes. The turntable of this revolving stage is 36 feet in diameter. It is constructed of trusses and operates upon sixteen 16-inch wheels on a track bed of reinforced concrete. Special care is being given to the elimination of all noise and vibration from its operation. The third scene shifting device which makes possible the handling of heavy equipment is a system of wagon stages. The principal units are two wagons, 16 feet by 33 feet, operating upon steel tracks. Adjoining the wagon stage area on the north is a workshop 40 feet by 60 feet. The stage, and the auditorium as well, will be lighted by a system of recent design. The operator's control board will be at the rear of the auditorium. The sky illusion and effects will be secured through the installation of a cyclorama, in design similar to that which Adolph Linnebach has installed in many recently constructed theatres in Europe.

64:4 . . . by March 1, 1938, the costs for

64:4. Paul W. Davee, "Definition of the Philosophy Underlying the Recognition and Teaching of Theatre as a Fine Art in the Liberal Arts and Graduate Curricula at the State University of Iowa" (Ph.D. diss., Univ. of Iowa, 1950), pp. 353–55.

building and equipping the theatre had come to $176,483. Of this last amount $50,000 had been provided by the Rockefeller Foundation, $56,900 by other gifts and grants, $27,600 by the Federal Works Administration, and $41,982 from state funds.

For this money, a building was provided with a 477 seat auditorium, a stage 42 feet deep by 55 feet wide adjoining a workshop area 42' x 75'. The stage and workshop adjoined so as to provide an unbroken floor area of 42' x 130'. The building contained a foyer, lobby, lounge, two checkrooms, two dressing rooms, box-office, two public washrooms, a design classroom and workshop, a dye room and a costume shop. Space under the stage, one small room and some additional space under the auditorium floor could be used for storage. A lighting control board room, projection room, and small organ loft and two small storage rooms were provided at the rear of the auditorium. The seventeen rows of seats were arranged in single tier unbroken by aisles and with plenty of leg-room between. Access to the auditorium for the audience was by 3 archways on either side, each fed by a separate ramp or stairway from the lobby. An electronic control board with 48 individual reactance-type dimmers, individual, group master and grand master control was provided. This control board was wired to an inter-connecting panel, which made possible the connection of any of the 100 stage lighting outlets to any of the 48 dimmers. This provided extremely flexible use for the board. A movable, steel light bridge was located just to the upstage side of the proscenium arch. A gridiron and counterweight system fitted with 18 sets of lines was provided. There was a revolving stage floor 36 feet in diameter, and a cloth horseshoe shaped sky cyclorama encircled the entire stage. These were some of the principal features of the new theatre as of March of 1938.

In June of 1941, plans were made to add the present north shop wing to the building, which now houses the costume and scene shops. Funds used for this construction were $12,000 of accumulated surplus in the University Theatre Operating Account and $13,000 of accumulated interest from the Mark Ranney Memorial Fund. This added $25,000 to the cost of the theatre plant making the total come to approximately $201,500. Mr. Mabie has recently stated that the investment in the building, its services and equipment to date have amounted to a total of nearly $240,000.

65. UNIVERSITY OF WASHINGTON
Seattle, Washington
Opened May 16, 1940

As theater started to come of age in the universities, it began a very fruitful period of experimentation in architecture and stage design. The University of Washington was one of the leaders in the movement, completely breaking with the proscenium stage tradition in its new Penthouse Theatre.

Glenn Hughes, who was chairman of the drama department and one of the prime movers for this theater, describes the novel playhouse.

65:1: The Penthouse Theatre, situated on an elevation overlooking Lake Union, surrounded by beautiful landscaping, is a white, one-story building with an elliptical, dome-roofed central unit, and with rectangular wings. Its dimensions are 112 by 84 feet. It is of frame construction, and the exterior is weather-proof plywood. The interior is plastered throughout. Its design, which might well be termed modern classic, is purely functional.

Having no precedent for a building to house drawing-room comedies performed in circus style, we allowed our needs to

65:1. Glenn Hughes, *The Penthouse Theatre* (Seattle: Univ. of Washington Pr., 1950), pp. 24–29.

determine the plan. We took as our starting point the center of the theatre—the acting area. We did not want this area square or rectangular because the corners would interfere with our desire to swing the audience around the stage. We dismissed the idea of a perfect circle as being uninteresting and also ill-adapted to the representation of a drawing-room. Searching for a clue to the proper dimensions, I said one day to the architect, "A typical drawing-room is one in which you can put a 12 by 18 rug. Therefore lay out a rectangle of those dimensions and swing a row of seats around it symmetrically, leaving three feet clearance at each corner." This he did. "Then," I added, "swing two more rows of seats around the first one, and you have the dimensions of the auditorium."

"Only three rows?" he asked. "Yes, only three rows. It has been our observation that at Penthouse plays people in the first three rows are really *in* the play. With the fourth row they begin to feel themselves outside it. And we must not succumb to the temptation to enlarge our audience. How many will this plan seat?" He made a quick estimate of 175. "Plenty," I said. "Practically ideal. I wouldn't agree to less than 150 and certainly not to more than 200. Please come as near as possible to 175." (The actual seating proved to be 172.)

The auditorium that resulted from these limitations turned out to be a somewhat elliptical room measuring 42 by 48 feet. I say somewhat elliptical because an ellipse is a two-centered circle, and our circle has three centers, or six, according to how you figure. At any rate it looked right, and we proceeded to cut it into four equal segments by inserting four doors symmetrically at the ends and sides of the circumference.

Our next problem was the foyer. It seemed to me that it would be pleasant and artistically appropriate to have the foyer encircle the auditorium. Most foyers are dead-end streets. And I remembered the circular foyer of a theatre in Paris, which gave one the surprised pleasure of a return to the starting point without obstruction. Another advantage of the circular foyer would be that it would allow the audience access to a rear porch or balcony, with a view of the lake. All right, we will draw a foyer right around our auditorium. How wide shall we make it? Not too wide. The audience will not be large, and most people like being rather crowded. Besides, there will be a free flow around this corridor-like foyer, and congestion will be extremely unlikely. How about eight feet? Let's make it nine for good measure. Nine it is.

Now we have nothing to do but locate the utility rooms. Box-office, directors' office, dressing-rooms, property room, furniture room, check-room, rest-rooms, furnace-room and kitchen. Some of these, the smaller ones, can be set into the curved façade, which should follow the curve of the foyer. Box-office, check-room, and perhaps one rest-room are the logical ones for this location. Furniture and property rooms should have access to an outside entrance other than the main entrance. Therefore we will extend a wing to take care of them. A wing with square corners, to balance the curves of the central unit. Then, inevitably, a similar wing at the other end, and this provides two large dressing-rooms, one for men and one for women. The kitchen and the other rest-room can be fitted into corners on either side at the back. A small basement under the furniture room will take care of heating and ventilation equipment.

At this point we began to worry about waiting-rooms for the actors. Having cut them off from the auditorium by our circular foyer, we were now faced with the prospect of their using the public foyer. And this we did not like. Besides, there should be a service-room for hand-props adjacent to the auditorium, and likewise a light-control booth.

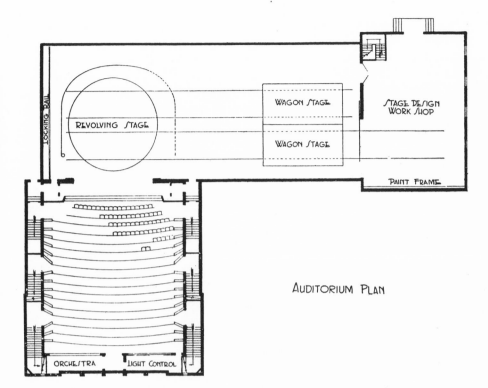

AUDITORIUM PLAN

64. Floor plans, University of Iowa Theatre, Iowa City, 1936. Above, auditorium plan; below, basement plan. Architect's drawings. Courtesy of the State University of Iowa.

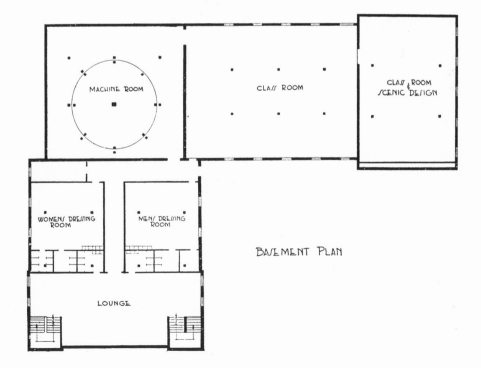

BASEMENT PLAN

65. Penthouse Theatre, University of Washington, Seattle, 1940. Published in *The Penthouse Theatre* (Seattle, 1950). Courtesy of the University of Washington Press.

65. Interior, Penthouse Theatre, University of Washington, Seattle, 1940. Published in *The Penthouse Theatre* (Seattle, 1950). Courtesy of the University of Washington Press.

65. Floor plan, Penthouse Theatre, University of Washington, Seattle, 1940. Published in *The Penthouse Theatre* (Seattle, 1950). Courtesy of the University of Washington Press.

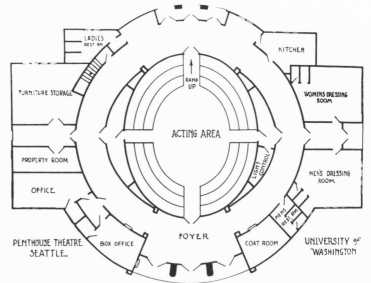

There was only one solution to these problems: a pair of enclosed rooms between the auditorium and the foyer. By making these crescent-shaped, and fitting them to the curves of the auditorium walls, they were rendered almost unnoticeable. And they are extremely practical. It is true, of course, that at the beginning of an act the actors must cross the foyer, but this movement is of only a moment's duration, and takes place after the audience is seated, so there is no conflict. During the act most of the entrances and exits are made to and from these waiting-rooms, although occasionally they must be made from the front and back entrances (opening directly into the foyer).

So much for the floor plan. Details of construction and equipment were then settled one by one. I will enumerate a few of the more interesting items.

The three rows of seats in the auditorium are each raised six inches, so that the acting area is eighteen inches below the level of the foyer. Ramps lead down from each of the four entrances.

In order to avoid expensive steel trusses, we asked the University engineers to devise a method of supporting the domed ceiling of the auditorium with wooden construction without the use of pillars. Our request was granted, and the problem was solved by the construction of eight laminated trusses set against the walls of the auditorium and meeting in the center of the dome to form, in effect, four arches. These trusses follow the side-walls straight up for thirteen and a half feet, then curve with the dome to the center, which is twenty feet above the stage floor. Architecturally, they are simple and effective.

The lighting problem we considered very important. Particularly anxious were we to avoid the use of lighting fixtures within the auditorium. We wanted the room clean and free of both utilitarian and ornamental detail. Our technical director met the challenge beautifully. His first request was for a space at least four feet high between the ceiling and the outer roof. His second was for a set of forty holes in the ceiling, arranged in a pattern of his own devising, each role approximately four inches in diameter. Above each hole he placed a spotlight equipped with either a Fresnel lens or an ellipsoidal reflector, adjusted to achieve a focal joint at the ceiling hole. The lamps in these units average 400 watts in strength. Thirty-two of the spots cover the acting area, eight cover the audience. They are hooked up in circuits of four units each. In addition to these ceiling lights, there are outlets around the base of the first row of seats, into which floor lamps and radios used on stage may be plugged.

The lighting is really beautiful. There is no glare in the eyes of the audience, and the system is so flexible that any reasonable intensity of light may be obtained in any portion of the auditorium.

The light-control booth is equipped with one-way vision windows, permitting the electrician to watch the action of the play, but preventing the audience from seeing into his booth. And these include not only offstage effects and radio music onstage, but also the broadcasting of the play to the utility rooms of the theatre. Loudspeakers are installed in box-office, directors' office, kitchen, and dressing-rooms, and everyone connected with the production is therefore in touch with the play at all times. The system is used, too, for calling the actors on-stage at the beginning of an act.

Inasmuch as we make a feature of coffee-service during the main intermission, we arranged for a commodious and completely equipped kitchen, with a service door leading to a bar in the foyer. Not only at this bar, which is near the back porch, but also in the front foyer, at a portable bar, we serve black coffee and attractive candies free to the audience.

Believing in the advertising value of a well-lighted exterior we installed outdoor flood-lights around the entire building, the lighting units themselves concealed by a hedge of Portuguese laurels. The all-white building stands out in the night brilliantly, and is visible from a number of boulevards. And as a contrast to the white mass we constructed two hollow columns of glass brick at both front and rear entrances, and these are lighted by violet and green neon tubes concealed within the columns.

The interior decoration and furnishings I shall summarize briefly. The auditorium walls and ceiling are uniformly off-white. The chairs are upholstered in cherry-red, with ivory leather seats. They are of the best modern design and construction, and are of the self-rising type. The entire acting area and the ramps are covered with a well-padded carpet of champagne color, with an unobtrusive self pattern. Drapes at the doorways match the seat upholstery.

The floor of the foyer is of rubber tile, in two contrasting colors—turquoise and marbleized white. These colors alternate in large, symmetrical masses. The inner wall of the foyer is light turquoise—a solid mass of color, without trim. The outer wall is off-white, relieved only by the turquoise masses of the sets of doors in the front and rear of the foyer. Venetian blinds cover the windows of the rear foyer. And at either side of the front entrance to the auditorium are shelves with supporting panels extending straight down to the floor, on which attractive arrangements of flowers are always present. Panes of glass set in the shelves cover light units which illuminate the flowers.

Dressing-rooms are equipped with indirect lighting at the make-up tables, and each has its lavatory and shower. The chairs are chrome. The kitchen is done in yellow, cream, and copper. The demi-tasse cups of the coffee service are of solid colors—black, yellow, blue and green, and the candies served are cream wafers in pastel shades. The powder room is in chartreuse. The offices are in white, with furniture of chrome, red, and natural wood. Everywhere the atmosphere is modern, clean, airy. It is also gay. And the audience reflects this gaiety even before the play begins. Thus the mood is set for comedy.

66. HARVARD UNIVERSITY
Cambridge, Massachusetts
Opened October 15, 1960

Harvard University, which in 1925 had lost George Pierce Baker because it would not provide him with a playhouse, in 1960 presented the nation with the most revolutionary university playhouse that had yet been seen. It was the only completely flexible playhouse, and for the first time a theater could be arranged to suit the nature of a play.

On October 9, 1960, Harvard proudly announced the opening of its Loeb Drama Center.

66:1   The doors of the new Loeb Drama Center will open on Saturday, Oct. 15, to a performance of Shakespeare's "Troilus and Cressida" by students of Harvard and Radcliffe.

In the nation's newest theatre, they will act out the tale of love and war in ancient Greece on an Elizabethan stage, reminiscent of the theatre of Shakespeare's time.

For other plays, as the new Loeb Drama Center moves through its first season, the 588-seat auditorium may be converted easily, in minutes, to theatre-in-the-round or to be conventional proscenium stage.

The main theatre of Loeb, set in a red-brick and glass building on Brattle Street decorated by aluminum screening, will be

66:1. Loeb Drama Center publicity release (Cambridge, Mass., 1960).

the show-place of the energetic, lively and talented extracurricular drama which has kept Harvard and Radcliffe theatre-conscious for 15 years. This activity has contributed some actors, writers, directors and producers to the professional stage, but primarily it has provided experience of the drama for future scholars, scientists, lawyers, doctors and businessmen.

Three or four major student productions will be offered the public in the Loeb Drama Center each term. For this fall term, the schedule will include: "Troilus and Cressida" (Oct. 15), "The Pirates of Penzance" (Nov. 17), and "The Caucasian Chalk Circle" by Bertold Brecht (Dec. 8). These will be produced by the Harvard Dramatic Club and by the Harvard Gilbert and Sullivan Players. Each production will run two weeks.

The drama center, one of the goals of the recent $82.5 million Program for Harvard College, is named in honor of John L. Loeb of New York, a member of the Class of 1924, and of his family. Mr. Loeb's generous gift, along with contributions by other friends of the college drama, made the center possible. A pre-opening performance of "Troilus and Cressida" will be given, by invitation, to benefactors and friends of the Center on Friday, October 14.

Behind and around the main theatre, the Loeb Drama Center will be filled with student activity related to the theatre. In a small experimental theatre whose flexible stage can be set up anew to suit each offering, students will present two one-act plays each week, on Thursday afternoons and on Friday and Saturday nights. The experimental theatre will hold about 100 spectators. Panels of scenery are lowered from the ceiling, to change the space relations on the stage. The entire room is black, to suggest, when only the playing area is lighted, what one of the directors calls "an island of action suspended in infinity." Three rehearsal rooms also are included in the Center.

Assoc. Prof. Robert Chapman, co-author with Louis Coxe of "Billy Budd" and other dramas and Director of the Loeb Drama Center, will guide student playwrights and actors in workshop programs. A workshop for student directors will be conducted by Stephen Aaron, who is Assistant Director of the Center. Mr. Aaron directed a number of undergraduate plays before he received his A.B. from Harvard in 1957, and after a year at Oxford he directed plays for the Boston Repertory Theater before returning to Harvard.

Sound-proof booths at the top of the main theater provide a conference room where a class may discuss a play while watching its action; a recording room for taping the sounds of a play for study; a television studio for the broadcast of Loeb Drama Center productions over educational station WGBH of Boston; and a lighting console from which the more than 100 lights of the stage and theater can be controlled by pre-set signals as many as 10 cues ahead of the action. Technical workshops are directed by Technical Director Donald Soule, an engineer and designer who worked at Yale with George C. Izenour, designer of the stage, lighting and technical equipment for Loeb.

Behind the theater, a sound-proof building houses other workshops, for scenery design and for costume design. The costume supervisor is Mrs. Olga Liepmann, formerly with the Brattle Theater of Cambridge. She is assisted by Lewis Smith, who has worked with the Cambridge Drama Festival.

Performances may be given simultaneously in the main theater and in the experimental theater, and the two lobbies are independent. All seats in the main theater will have a single price: $1.50. Admission to experimental theater productions will be without charge. Curtain time for both theaters will be 8 p.m.

Laying down broad policy for the Loeb Drama Center, the Faculty Committee said this:

"Since it is important that the Drama Center be used to encourage the highest possible level of undergraduate activity, and since initiative and responsibility are essential in good undergraduate dramatic effort, the Director will consult freely with students and will seek to leave them as much responsibility and opportunity for initiative as possible, subject to his basic responsibility as an officer of the University."

The Faculty committee, under the chairmanship of Dean McGeorge Bundy, includes: Prof. Alfred B. Harbage, Shakespearean scholar; Prof. Harry Levin, literary critic; Prof. Archibald MacLeish, poet and playwright; Prof. Elliott Forbes, Director of the Harvard Glee Club; Professor Chapman, and Dean Robert B. Watson. Mr. Aaron is executive secretary.

The Center, designed by Hugh A. Stubbins Associates, is located at the corner of Hilliard Street and Brattle Street in Cambridge.

The mechanical flexibility of the new playhouse received critical acclaim throughout the country. A description of the operation of the theater and its potential is found in *The Architectural Forum*:

66:2 Harvard's new theater wraps three plans and the gamut of advanced stage, lighting, and rigging systems into a single package.

There is little in the unobtrusive and polite exterior of the new Loeb Drama Center on tree-lined Brattle Street in Cambridge to indicate that it encloses the most revolutionary new stage and equipment in the U.S. today. Indeed, the auditorium itself does not suggest, when seen

66:2. Reprinted from the article "Theatre Automatique" from the October 1960 issue of THE ARCHITECTURAL FORUM, pp. 90–96. Copyright 1960 by Whitney Publications, Inc.

in one of its incarnations, that it can be changed automatically into two other basic forms—a proscenium and an arena —during a single performance.

These features, arranged with apparent ease in the confines of the 515-seat theater by Architects Hugh Stubbins & Associates, are made possible by the first complete installation of the systems of noted Stage Technician George C. Izenour.

Radical as the means may be, the end was envisioned in the 1957 statement of a Harvard-Radcliffe faculty committee headed by Dean McGeorge Bundy and Professor Archibald MacLeish: "We see this building as an opportunity, not a fixed definition, as a working instrument, and not as a separate institute. We see a theater flexible and spacious, so constructed that it can adapt itself to future techniques while at the same time maintaining its role as a place of meeting and community for the two colleges."

This goal of having a theater *without* a drama school has been a Harvard-Radcliffe hope ever since the late famed George Pierce Baker took himself to rival Yale to form such a school. Over the years community theater in extracurricular form has thrived in Cambridge in old movie houses and converted gyms. Occasionally, and with luck, the auditorium of a technical high school was available, but if necessary the play went on in lecture halls and student commons. This long exile from a real theater, perhaps, caused the committee to realize that "the play's the thing." The committee went on: "The building should not be so architecturally exciting and excited, as building, that the plays produced will be overshadowed by their frame."

The newly finished product fits the directive explicitly. Instead of closing itself in a campuslike setting, the building opens right off the sidewalk of Brattle Street by way of deep setbacks off the first floor, forming a porch somewhat like an arcade. The sides of the building are opened, again, to a garden court on the one side, and to a spacious terrace on the other. Because the high stagehouse is backed by lower workshops and by a 100-seat experimental theater and tryout room, the rear of the building, facing directly on a residential cul-de-sac, is almost domestic in scale.

The foyer and lobbies inside continue the simple, yet luxurious, application of concrete, brick, and travertine. The main auditorium is entered from the sides. The area behind the bisecting ambulatory is banked stadium-fashion with 12 rows of fixed seats with a total capacity of 359 persons. The forward seven rows are split into two banks of 78 seats each. These seat banks can be brought up to backstage level by elevators and then can be pivoted 90 degrees to face each other, or even 180 degrees to face the back bank of fixed seats. In this position, the seats occupy a place on the main stage. In this case, then, a new platform stage is formed in the area originally occupied by the seats. The platform elevators which raised the seats are used to raise the floor in segments to form several patterns.

On the second floor of the building are three rehearsal rooms, offices for the director and coaches, and a library, used in conjunction with the Harvard library system. The building contains 53,482 square feet of floor space and is constructed on a 173 by 220 foot site. The construction cost per square foot was $33.08. Total construction cost: $1,770,000.

The main feature of the Loeb Drama Center is that it is the first complete integration in a theatrical structure of the revolutionary electro-mechanical systems of Yale's noted theater design-engineer, George C. Izenour. With this building, the U.S. moves well ahead of Europe in establishing the prototype of the flexible, fully mechanized theater of the future, likely to affect theatrical design for years to come. The new mechanics comprise three separate yet interacting systems.

Lighting. From an electronic push-button console and preset panel, a single operator controls over 400 stage lights, manipulating their color and intensity in any predetermined pattern. By means of the preset panel or "memory" unit, the console operator can follow a lighting score for the drama, molding its moods and settings.

Rigging. From another console, a single operator controls 30 compact, synchronous, electric winches, ranged around the backstage perimeter, to rig and fly all stage sets. This system eliminates stagehands and the old parallel-set, space-consuming maze of ropes and counterweights, unchanged for three centuries, to allow flexible overhead rigging from a grid network, placing sets in any desired position or juxtaposition.

Staging. From two control points, two operators using special analogue controls actuate an underlying hydraulic lift and pivot system, to change the theater in a matter of minutes into any one of three forms: a conventional proscenium theater, an Elizabethan theater with apron stage thrust into the audience, and a modified theater-in-the-round. The hydraulic mechanism lifts or lowers two front sections of seats, which also pivot on aircraft wheels, to accommodate the various stage conformations, these also being hydraulically operated.

The result is a theater which, leaving all mechanical functions to automation, with lighting as the integrating element, becomes completely flexible to the purposes of the play. Two or three operators can run the whole show. Though the cost is about $70,000 over conventional installations, there are other outweighing economies. For one, the rigging system allows a much lighter beamed roof, and saves about a third of the stage's once wasted cubage, which can now be put to such useful purposes as rehearsal rooms. And, of course, the total is three theaters in one.

THE LONG PULL

Izenour has been over 20 years in single-minded pursuit of this flexible theater. A husky, blond six-footer, he emerged from college in the depression thirties, an English major with an intense interest in the theater, and went to work for the old, ill-fated WPA Federal Theater Project. It struck him at once that antique stage techniques were rigidly limiting the growth of the theater, that the stage, in fact, was "a technical desert," relatively untouched by all the modern developments in lighting, electronics, and automatic machinery. His first chance to put forth his idea of a flexible theater was in a multi-purpose, quick-changing theater for San Francisco's 1938 Golden Gate International Exposition. This ran only six months, the whole federal arts project being chopped off by Congress, but it was long enough for him to get the attention of the Rockefeller Foundation, which offered him a grant at any university of his choice to continue his work.

Since 1939, Izenour has been at Yale, assisted from time to time by various foundation grants, heading an Electro-Mechanical Research Laboratory in the Yale School of Drama. He patiently taught himself step by step the electronics and engineering necessary to work out his inventions. The main problem, as he saw it, was to free the theater from its rigid framework and from slave labor, elevating the human operator as the important element to close the control loop. The ideal was to break down the barriers to the audience, push stagecraft out to the very theater walls, make space and light and mood wholly plastic. No isolated gadgets could do this, but only integrated systems, foolproof in their automaticity, teachable to almost anyone, and embracing the theater as a whole.

Izenour's first systems design was electronic lighting, installed in Yale's drama school theater in 1946, and since become standard in about 100 theaters and television studios. Next came the synchronous electric winch system, first installed in Hofstra College Playhouse, and making a major appearance in Frank Lloyd Wright's Dallas Art Theater (FORUM, March '60), whose unconventional drum shape had to be matched by equally unconventional rigging. Finally, he worked out the hydraulic lift system, adapted from elevator design. All systems designs came together in the Harvard theater, and all are now licensed and available from cooperating manufacturers.

The new systems have little chance in the present commercial theater, which has become simply a New York real estate holding operation in a cluster of obsolete, unreconstructable Broadway houses. No new Broadway theater has been built in close to 40 years. Broadway's inflated investments, backward building codes, and featherbedding labor practices preclude anything so radically new and creative. Indeed, the Loeb theater was built over the opposition of Broadway advisors. For, as more flexible theaters are built, it will become only too plain how shoddy, overpriced, and uncomfortable Broadway really is. And Izenour sees in the sharp rise of experimental university theaters, along with the new off-Broadway, community, and summer festival theaters, and centers for the performing arts, a building renaissance that will return excitement, poetry, and substance to the theater, and may eventually topple Broadway.

Izenour's own work is a good index. In addition to the new theaters in which his systems already have been built, he is working on 11 more projects, most of them university or art and community center jobs, including the Julliard Theater and Metropolitan Opera House in New York's Lincoln Center. Three of the

66. Loeb Drama Center, Harvard University, Cambridge, Mass., 1960. Courtesy of Harvard University News Office.

66. Interior, Loeb Drama Center, Harvard University, Cambridge, Mass., 1960. Courtesy of the Harvard University News Office.

67. Fred M. Roberts Theater, Grinnell College, Grinnell, Iowa, 1961. On the right, Fine Arts Building. Photograph by Baltazar Korab. Courtesy of Grinnell College.

67. Interior, Fred M. Roberts Theater, Grinnell College, Grinnell, Iowa, 1961. Courtesy of Grinnell College.

new projects are posthumous Wright designs, in one of which, the Monona civic art center for Madison, Wis., scenery will fly in on a trajectory, due to height limitations, by a modification of the synchronous rigging system. In another project with Architect Paul Schweikher he is working on a design in which the whole floor of the theater will consist of 178 hydraulically operated platforms for the ultimate in flexibility.

The next big problem Izenour will attack with or without architectural aid is structure, in order to get, along with his mechanical systems, the most economical theater possible. He is ready to experiment with precast systems, Buckminster Fuller's octet truss, and any other ideas that promise a saving in structure. Theaters as presently built cost too much, and any reduction in costs would make it possible to get more of them built. "We've got to get the right kind of buildings," says Izenour. "If we don't, we will just ape the commercial theater, and the commercial theater is a losing proposition."

67. GRINNELL COLLEGE
Grinnell, Iowa
Opened October 1, 1961

By the late 1950s colleges and universities throughout the country were opening new fine arts centers, experimenting with flexibility in theater architecture and the shape and size of the stage. Grinnell, a small liberal arts college in Iowa, opened a fine arts complex with a theater containing one of the first open stages to be designed for a college theater.

67:1   GRINNELL'S LIBRARY
AND FINE ARTS CENTER
BURLING LIBRARY, ROBERTS THEATER, AND FINE ARTS CENTER • GRINNELL COLLEGE, GRINNELL, IOWA • SKIDMORE, OWINGS & MERRILL, ARCHITECTS • KEYES D. MET-

67:1. "Grinnell's Library and Fine Arts Center," *Progressive Architecture*, Sept. 1962, 147–53.

CALF, LIBRARY CONSULTANT • JAMES HULL MILLER, THEATER CONSULTANT

The Burling Library is the first building to be constructed at Grinnell under the directives of a development plan drawn up by SOM to increase the enrollment capacity of the college to 1100. The library site was unoccupied; two buildings that SOM determined obsolete were demolished to provide the site for the Fine Arts Center, which includes the theater. Together, the buildings form a new core for the academic area.

The library has an unpretentious exterior that fits in with the scale of the old buildings on the campus. Although three stories high, it appears to be lower: the grade on the entrance side rises to the level of the middle floor; a bridge at the entry spans a shallow moat that exposes the lower-floor windows.

Precast T-columns and tie beams support a roof system of precast double T's. The solid side walls are of brick; on the front and rear, the walls are of gray glass in specially-designed aluminum extrusions. The glass walls are set at the column line so that the T's provide deep overhangs above two balconies projecting from the main level. Students can read outdoors on the sheltered balconies in good weather. By this simple architectural device, the library becomes a symbol of an alma mater.

The basic idea of the building is that it can be experienced on the interior as a single large room: a mezzanine running through the main space is arranged so that the unity of the space is everywhere apparent. Except for the foyer, offices, cataloguing room, and the Twentieth Century Room (a reading lounge devoted to modern literature), the campus level and the mezzanine are arranged in an open plan. There is an interpenetration of books and readers—stacks, aisles, carrells, tables, reading lounges and alcoves—so that the entire space becomes a study area without hindering the privacy of the individual. Carrells ring the periphery of both levels; this placement orients some of the carrells toward views of the campus and others toward brick walls. Students can choose study areas according to the amount of concentration they require for their work.

Grinnell's Fine Arts Center, the second unit of SOM's development plan, comprises two buildings: the Arts Building and the Roberts Theater. The Arts Building, a two-story rectangular block that has a concrete structure with prestressed bents, contains classrooms, workshops, studios, and rehearsal rooms. Exterior walls are of dark gray brick and gray glass set in special aluminum extrusions.

The Roberts Theatre is a separate structure, joined to the Arts Building by a glass-walled connecting link that serves as a foyer for both. Except for the basement level, the 424-seat theater structure is separated from its auxiliary functions —lobby, toilet facilities, even some of the backstage storage areas such as wardrobe are in the adjacent Arts Building. The theater, in fact, is devoted almost exclusively to what the spectator shares with the performers, and this is openly shared; even front-of-house lighting is exposed. This purity of purpose is clear, and the separation from the classroom spaces neatly expresses the distinction between apprenticeship and performance.

The structure is composed of precast concrete columns and girders with a roof system of precast, prestressed T's. The T's are exposed on the interior and on the front and rear of the exterior. The building is horn-shaped, making it suggestive of its acoustic function, and is enclosed by dark gray brick.

The theater is designed with a single-form open stage that combines both the apron and caliper forms; that is, the stage has a fixed shape comprising an acting area that projects into the audience, and extensive side stages that surround the

audience. The stage is frameless; performers and spectators are in a single, unseparated chamber.

The stage is planned for free-standing set-pieces and for projected scenery so as to minimize the work of stage crews and to permit students to concentrate on the play itself.

This theater is an example of one of two significant new types to be developed in this century, the other being the mechanized multi-form theater. As such, it has been the subject of heated discussion in theater circles for some time. Because this controversy typifies the current status of theater design, we present an evaluation of the theater by theater designer Arthur C. Risser, and an answer to this critique by James Hull Miller, the consultant on the design of the Roberts Theater.

ARTHUR C. RISSER: The architecture of a theater should be dictated by the activities within the building. The Grinnell theater will produce plays of all periods; therefore, flexibility of equipment and techniques is essential. One particular theater form will not be universally satisfactory. Other stage arrangements would have been possible within the Grinnell program.

Several undesirable features may be noted in the theater. The designers have not been successful in their attempt to avoid a proscenium: in conjunction with the catwalk over the audience (immediately in front of the curtain track), the curtains, even when fully opened, create a proscenium effect. The long-span prestressed roof members serve a purely utilitarian purpose and are not treated as the finished ceiling of the auditorium and stage.

Inadequate sight-lines are immediately apparent upon examination of the drawings. In order to mask off-stage personnel, lighting instruments, and rigging hardware, the scene designer must use an inordinate number of masking units. Some theater designers maintain that masking is unnecessary; however, glare from a light, and both movements and objects irrelevant to the play, are disturbing to an audience and can shatter the impact of a scene.

Although the theater designer planned for projected scenery, he provided a screen that does not extend to the ceiling and that only partially encloses the acting area. To many persons in the audience, actors playing in any of the forestage areas will be unrelated to the scene projected on the screen.

The stage is shallow, with cramped circulation behind it. The narrow space provided behind the cyclorama is inadequate for scene construction purposes, and the storage spaces above will be partially visible to the audience.

No public restrooms are provided. The omission of public restrooms in a theater is inadvisable.

In the following examples of other possible arrangements, the same building envelope as that actually built is used, with the exception that the high portion of the ceiling is located over the stage area rather than over the rear of the auditorium. The two proposals incorporate all the required production facilities, and accommodate multi-form stages within that volume.

An orchestra lift provides a flexible forestage that may be used for an orchestra in a pit, for audience seating, or for playing area. A full cyclorama encloses the acting area. Seating for approximately 300 persons is provided, with only two outside aisles, in the Continental manner. The addition of a lobby separated from the auditorium eliminates noise. Larger areas for scene construction and storage are also incorporated.

The theater has a flexible arrangement that provides the advantages of the Grinnell stage, possesses the proscenium-and-forestage features of the first proposal,

and also offers an opportunity for the arena arrangement.

As a theater becomes more flexible, greater mechanization of the stage is required in order to reduce labor requirements; the result is that initial costs and maintenance costs are greater.

The foregoing discussion is not a recommendation of one particular theater plan but attempts to encourage the study of each theater in the light of the functions it is to serve. When the form of a theater is the result of the architect's desire to use a particular kind of building material or method of construction, the usefulness of the building for the production of plays is likely to be limited.

JAMES HULL MILLER: The Roberts Theater was designed to serve orchestra, chorus, drama, operetta, opera, children's theater, dance, forum, lecture, and classwork. As anticipated, the theater is in use continuously—morning, afternoon, and evening. What a college needs is a new kind of theater that will realistically meet the requirements of this complex new program. The Roberts Theater is interesting because its design represents this sort of new concept.

Four features, I believe, are important in making the theater fulfill its requirements: the single chamber containing both stage and seating, the caliper stage that surrounds the audience as well as forming the central performing area, the ceiling-roof combination, and the suspended lighting system. The architectural features create an envelope that favors a simplified stagecraft.

There are two schools of thought on what a theater should be to an audience. One feels that the spectator should be presented with an illusionistic slice of life. The other school believes that dramatic imagery is more intense when the spectator is completely aware of all the forces of playmaking. The techniques of the latter, the open-stage school, are based on a visual shorthand, in which associations stir up a complete imagery; these techniques are based on the principles of gestalt psychology. The history of theater is replete with rich examples of both experiences, thus giving the lie to the criticism that one is more limited than another.

Generically, there are two types of scenic design: one where the setting surrounds the acting scene, as in the proscenium theater; in the other type, the acting area surrounds the settings. Proscenium staging tends toward the display of successive scenes, stored to the sides and above the stage; often staging displays multiple settings, often simultaneously, within a larger space; off-stage storage spaces may be provided by arranging temporary screens. Open staging is, of course, the more traditional in the history of Western culture.

The stage lighting system at Grinnell is introduced within the total space, not above it, beyond a false ceiling. This solution also is determined by the philosophy of what a theater should seem to the audience. The pendant lighting plane in the Roberts Theater was initially designed as metal bar tracery, as a part of a sculptural pattern. I regret the "masked functionalism" which was executed, and also take exception to the abundant use of curtains. But I believe that the Roberts Theater is a milestone in the development of theaters for college and community activities. It is a theater that is economically feasible and practical to operate.

68. UNIVERSITY OF CALIFORNIA
Los Angeles, California
Opened March 14, 1963

The University of California at Los Angeles, long a leader in the teaching and practice of theater arts, opened its new theater complex in 1963. This much-anticipated event was announced in the Los Angeles *Times* of March 14.

68:1
UCLA to Open Theater Arts Building Tonight
Student Performance 'Girl of the Golden West', Scheduled at $2.6 Million Edifice
by Jack Smith

UCLA's theater arts department, which began 43 years ago with a public speaking class on the old Vermont Ave. campus, opens its new $2.6 million home to the public tonight at Westwood.

The new Theater Arts Building on the north campus will enter the cultural life of the community with a student performance of the period piece "The Girl of the Golden West."

This virile melodrama by the San Francisco-born David Belasco was chosen as the premiere production to symbolize the West's youth, vitality and emergence as a creative force in the nation's life.

PREVIOUSLY SCATTERED

The red curtain in the building's 500-seat Playhouse will rise at 8:30 p.m., to signal the start of a new era that offers greater scope for the development of theater skills and talents at UCLA.

Until now the 750-student theater arts department has been housed in scattered barracks-like bungalows and limited in staging its productions to Royce Hall and other auditoriums designed for other purposes.

The new Theater Arts Building is among the most advanced laboratories in the world for the student of the theater, the motion picture and the television and radio arts.

The great stage of the Playhouse, for example, is large enough to hold any two ordinary theater stages as mere sets, and it is equipped with lighting, sound and staging systems which are not only the latest thing, but something more than that.

68:1. First published in Los Angeles *Times* Mar. 14, 1963. Copyright, 1963, Los Angeles Times. Reprinted by permission.

LABORATORY AND TOOLS

Between the Playhouse and the smaller, more conventional Little Theater, the new building offers a laboratory and tools not only for tomorrow's new wave, but also for tomorrow's actor, designer or teacher in the small school, theater or workshop.

UCLA expects that this new laboratory will provide elbow room for a creative freedom and experimentation whose influence may go far beyond the campus.

"That's why it's right to have this on a campus, as we have advanced equipment in our science laboratories," said Ralph Freud, theater arts professor and director of "The Girl of the Golden West."

"The things learned here undoubtedly will find their way back into general use. We have created here an environment for research."

Prof. Freud said the faculty and students of the entire department will produce and present to the public six plays a year in the Playhouse, plus three during the summer session.

In the Little Theater, meanwhile, smaller groups will be at work. Here student playwrights, directors, set designers may work with their own ideas in production.

Major productions ranging from the Elizabethans to current Broadway playwrights will be staged for the public in the Playhouse.

The Little Theater, meanwhile, will be used for one-act plays, thesis productions and sometimes puppet shows.

LEARN OLDTIME METHODS

Dr. Samuel Selden, chairman of the department, emphasized that students will learn the old-time methods of sound, lighting and scenery handling so they may be "at home" in any theater, including the high school auditorium and the stock company barn.

Besides the theaters, the new building houses offices, classrooms, rehearsal halls,

dressing rooms for featured players and chorus, and a huge workshop (79x100') in which sets will be created and built.

"The Girl of the Golden West" will continue through March 23. Abby Kenigsberg, a graduate student, stars as the girl.

A review of the opening performance appeared in the Los Angeles *Citizen*:

68:2   UCLA Playhouse
Is L.A.'s Finest
by Gerald Faris

In the second act of "The Girl of the Golden West," Minnie wins the right to aid her wounded bandit-lover in a poker game with Sheriff Jack Rance, pulling three aces and a pair from her garter belt while his back is turned.

With the same kind of bravado, the UCLA Theater Arts Department Tuesday night managed to apply a similar sleight of hand to the whole play. The audience, like Jack, was "taken in"—but to its utter and complete delight.

David Belasco's 1905 saga served as the vehicle to open the university's new Playhouse, the gem of the theater arts department's $2,600,000 home. Without fear of exaggeration, one can call this theater a masterpiece of proscenium design.

It is certainly the finest legitimate theater in Los Angeles. The search for comparable showplaces of dramatic art would probably extend around the world.

Designed by UCLA's Edward Hearn, the theater is conceived in terms of the latest verticle handling and lighting control equipment. Maximum freedom in writing, direction and production is permitted. An outer foyer is dominated by a 15-foot-high "Tower of Masks," sculpted by Anna Mahler.

The auditorium, in which red fabrics

68:2. Los Angeles *Citizen*, Mar. 15, 1963.

are balanced against dark hardwood walls, seats between 500 and 589 people (extra rows of seats can be added). There are two hydraulically controlled orchestra pits, stage traps, a massive stage house, with a completely automated winch system for flying scenery, and behind the stage itself, readily accessible scenery and costume shops.

In a brief preperformance address Tuesday night, UCLA Chancellor Franklin D. Murphy noted the state of "maturity" attained by the fine arts in university life, demonstrated by the theater, and introduced a guest from the audience, James Kirkwood, who played Trinidad Joe in the first New York production of "Girl." The role last night was done by Ken Burtness.

And when the curtain did go up, it was not on a museum piece, but on a substantial, absorbing piece of dramatic Californiana which only occasionally seems dated. The melodramatic overtones never become so dominant in the company's "straight" rendition as to undermine the rather touching plot, and principal characters—Minnie, Jack and Dick Johnson—are more real than make-believe.

All of the play's weaknesses, it seems, are stored up until the third act, and then there's really no stopping them.

In the first place, it's anticlimax. (Minnie has already won Dick away from Jack and the miners, and it's rather apparent he'll escape the hangman even though he is a "thievin' road agent.")

Secondly, it's a deep dip into sentimentality, bested only by the Wilmington to Catalina swim, with or without a rowboat for a quick rescue. There's no rescue possible after Minnie pulls that third ace.

Abby Kenigsberg is charming and pert as Minnie, Mike Hoctor a rather poker-faced Jack (but he has a heart), and Jon Drury a suave, polished Dick Johnson, although his performance tends to become hollow and monotonous after.

68:3   THE PLAYHOUSE

This theater has been designed to allow maximum flexibility with the latest in vertical scenery handling and lighting control equipment presently available. The concept behind its design is to permit the theater artist the maximum range of creative freedom conceptually in the playwriting, direction, and design of a play. It is intended to serve as an advanced laboratory for research and production. The auditorium has been conceived to achieve the maximum in comfort, safety, visibility, and audibility for the audience by the use of continental seating. In the following article you will find detailed information about the building and its equipment.

The auditorium walls are of dark hardwood. The rear wall is ribbed hardwood. The side walls are designed as reflective surfaces for sound support in the corners of the auditorium and the rear wall is sound absorbent. The glass windows of the control and observation booths are angled to provide additional sound reflection for the rear rows.

The front curtain, seat upholstery, and a decorative panel at each side of the rear of the auditorium are red. The aisles are carpeted and the seating levels are of grey rubber tile on concrete.

The auditorium ceiling, of hard plaster, is in four panels on different planes, broken by three light wells running from wall to wall. The angle of each panel is calculated to produce the best reflective sound support and still permit proper lighting angles. There are six speaker ports located for binaural stereophonic sound distribution. Above, there are connecting catwalks in all lighting ports, control booths and the stage area.

There are 500 permanent spring riser seats arranged in twelve rows of conti-

68:3. Commemorative brochure published by Univ. of California, Los Angeles, Theater Arts Dept., 1963.

nental seating. Two portable rows of seats may be put in on each of two orchestra lifts for a maximum seating capacity of 16 rows and 589 seats. The depth of the auditorium from the proscenium to the back row is 67'–0"; the width of the audience seating fans to 80'–0" at the rear. The elevation of the stage is 38" above the auditorium floor; the difference in elevation from the first portable row to the last permanent row of seats is 5'–9".

There are three double exit doors on each side of the auditorium and entry to all seats is by ramped aisles running from the lobby to the stage.

The interior lobby is 62'–0" x 18'–0". The exterior wall is brick-faced with black marble columns. The interior wall is of ribbed hardwood matching the auditorium. Entry to the auditorium is by light-locked doors at either end.

The mezzanine lobby is 50'–0" x 12'–0" average width. It contains access to the light and sound observation booths, men's and women's lavatories, and a telephone booth.

The light control, sound control, and two observation booths are located on the mezzanine level above and behind the last row of seats in the auditorium.

The stage frame is of Korina hardwood plywood, adjustable from a minimum of 26'–0" to a maximum of 58'–0" in width. It is 22'–0" high, adjustable to 14'–6". A 5" thickness is maintained around the frame for any of the available proportions used.

There are side lighting ports running the full height of the side walls.

There is a forestage the full width of the auditorium.

Access from auditorium to stage is by portable steps.

There are two hydraulic lifts which serve as seating levels, forestage, orchestra pit, or stage elevators. They can be used independently or as one unit with a six position preset panel located in the wings. For safety, each exposed edge of

each lift contains an automatic microswitch stop which shuts off the entire system when the run is obstructed.

The stage house

Width overall is 105' from wall to wall, 48'–0" right of the center line, 56'–0" left of the center line.

Depth overall is 58'–0" from front to back wall, with 52'–0" from the effective proscenium frame line. (The first panel of the auditorium ceiling projects into the stage house 6'–0" to create a projection platform which is 40'–0" along the straight line of the proscenium.)

Height to the gridiron is 65'–0" over the entire stage. Above the grid there is 6'–0" of clear working space. In the up right and down left corners of the stage spiral staircases run from the basement to the grid with landings at the stage, the intermediate catwalk, and at loading platform levels.

Placed evenly at the center line of the proscenium is one series of traps 4'–0" wide running 60'–0" across the stage. Four additional rows of traps run 36'–0", divided at the center line, to make a total depth of 20'–0" of trapped area.

14'–0" upstage of the first five rows of traps is a single row 40'–0" centered on the proscenium line. Traps, lifts, and stage floor are constructed of 2" x 4" vertical grained Douglas Fir.

A 20'–0" high x 30'–0" wide soundproofed door is located in the upstage wall of the stage on the auditorium center line to connect the stage with the shop area of the building.

The side and rear stage walls and the stage ceiling are treated with one inch fiberglass acoustical formboard for sound absorption.

There is a 14'–0" difference in elevation from the basement to the stage floor. The basement extends under the entire stage, the lift area, and a 5'–0" walkaround area surrounding the lifts. The hydraulic pumps for the lifts are located in the basement stage right. At the basement level the lifts may be entered through wire-mesh enclosures on three sides. A slide gate with electric interlock is located at each end of the upstage lift, and a hinged gate with electric interlock is located near the center of the downstage lift. To allow full access to the upstage lift a metal guard railing, running the entire length of the upstage edge, pushes into the pit as the lift descends.

There are six permanent counterweighted lines, four of which are allocated to flying the valance of the adjustable proscenium, the act curtain, the downstage and upstage sides of the lighting bridge. In addition there are two free lines.

There are 50 grid winch units, two alternators, a two-scene preset for each alternator, in a Clancy-Izenour grid winch vertical scenery handling system, which is completely automated. 25 winches are mounted on the front wall, and 25 on the rear stage wall. The console is designed to expand to a total of 60 units. It is castered and portable with a 50'–0" cable attached to the center of the stage right wall.

Lighting control

There are three banks of silicon controlled rectifier type dimmers, containing at present 120 3KW and 6 5KW dimmers in the system; one bank in the basement, one on the side platform catwalk stage right, and one in the grid. Each dimmer has receptacles for patching two circuits directly into the dimmer. All dimmers are movable from dimmer bank to dimmer bank.

There are 256 20-amp twist-lock lighting circuits and 18 50-amp twist-lock lighting circuits distributed throughout the theater.

The control operation is a Century C-Card lighting control system. This system permits one operator to control all lighting from a position where the entire stage is visible in the same manner in which the audience sees it. There are two preset readers, Left (AB) and Right (CD). The console patch panel allows the connection of any dimmer (168 potential dimmer positions) by low-voltage patch cord up to a total of three dimmers, to any of the 120 control potentiometers which form a complete preset. There are four presets visible on the two preset readers at any time. Four cards form one preset. The card is a plastic unit that contains 30 printed circuit potentiometers and 30 adjustable contacts set by depressing a button, sliding it to its desired position, and releasing it. These cards, serving as memory units, may be removed for storage of a show being performed in a repertory condition. A motor drives each reader drum through 15 positions as selected by push buttons. When in the coupled position there are 60 presets of 120 dimming control circuits each. In the uncoupled condition there are 120 presets of 60 dimming control circuits.

Sound control

The primary purpose of the sound system is the reproduction and control of music, sounds and sound effects for stage production. The system will accomplish the reproduction and amplification of ten channels of monoaural or five channels of stereophonic sounds simultaneously or individually. It provides a flexible hook-up by patching and switching of any sound to six ceiling loud-speakers and/or ten portable loud-speakers. It contains two Ampex stereo tape recorders, two turntables with three stereo tone arms, a center arm for use on both tables, and four microphone inputs. It is designed to provide the mixing of sounds, stereo frequency controls and stereo units that reverberate the sounds.

THE LAB THEATER

Conceived as a basic laboratory, it is therefore of a more conventional design. It was built as the beginning theater laboratory but still provides the most advanced conventional equipment presently available. Auditorium seating, while of the more conventional radial type is still designed to achieve the greatest possible comfort, visibility and audibility.

The walls are of plaster, the rear wall of ribbed hardwood, containing a standing-room rail in the center section with acoustic panelboard behind. The side walls are designed for reflective sound support, the glass windows of the control and observation rooms are angled to provide additional sound support in the rear of the auditorium.

The front curtain, seat upholstery, and carpeting are gold.

The auditorium ceiling is in three different planes broken by two light wells running from wall to wall, calculated, as in the Playhouse, to produce the best reflective sound support and lighting angles. Catwalks above, connect lighting ports, control booths and stage.

178 permanent seats with spring risers are located in nine rows of radial aisle seating. There is a potential for two portable rows of seats on the orchestra pit floor when at auditorium level for a total seating capacity of 200. The depth from the proscenium line to the back row is 49'–0". The widest portion of the auditorium seating is 49'–0". The elevation of the stage is 40" above the auditorium floor, the difference in elevation from the first portable row to the last permanent row is 3'–4".

Exit doors are located on each side of the auditorium at the front, and at either side of the interior lobby, which also contains access to the rest rooms on the audience right.

Light and sound control and observation booths are located above and behind the last row of seats in the auditorium. Access to the booths is either from a corridor in the office wing of the building or from a staircase opening on to the exterior lobby.

The proscenium is made up of two-fold side wings of Korina hardwood plywood. These can be folded to regulate the side entrances and sight lines. The proscenium is 30'–0" wide x 16'–0" high. There are lighting positions the full height in the entrance portals on each side of the forestage and above the front audience exits left and right.

Access from auditorium to stage is by portable steps.

The orchestra pit floor is handset, constructed of a framework using 4'–0" wide platforms that can be arranged as a forestage extension, or as audience seating. In addition, scaffolding may be erected at the basement floor level to construct any orchestra pit depth required.

The stage house

Width, 70'–0" from wall to wall, 32'–0" right of the center line, 38'–0" left of the center line.

Depth, 30'–0" from the proscenium line to the back wall.

Height, 40'–0" from the stage floor to the gridiron. There is 6'–0" of clear working space above the gridiron. In the U.R. corner of the stage is a spiral staircase which runs from the basement to the gridiron with landings at the stage, an intermediate catwalk which provides access to the permanent adjustable light bridge, the beams, and to the grid. In the D.L. corner, downstage of the proscenium wall, is a spiral staircase which runs from the basement to the loading platform with landings at the stage, an intermediate catwalk which provides access to the bridge and the beams, and to the loading platform.

Placed evenly at the center line of the proscenium are a series of traps running 32'–0" across the stage, in four rows totaling 16'–0" of depth.

4'–2" upstage of the first four rows is a single row 12'–0" long by 5'–0" deep trap centered on the proscenium line. Traps, orchestra pit floor, and stage floor are constructed of 2″ x 4″ vertical grained Douglas Fir.

Centered on the backstage wall is a loading door 16′ high by 20′ wide, which gives access to a paved concrete driveway that runs to all storage areas, rehearsal rooms and the shop.

As in The Playhouse some stage walls are sound absorbent.

There is 14′–0″ of elevation difference from basement to stage floor under the entire stage and orchestra.

30 permanent counterweighted T-track lines are installed on this stage. There are four lines downstage of the bridge, two lines which handle the permanent bridge, and twenty-two lines upstage of the bridge, two of which handle the permanent cyclorama, and two to handle the tripping of the cyclorama.

Lighting control

A single dimmer bank is located S.R. in the basement which has places for 24 dimmers, 3KW capacity, 16 6KW capacity of the silicon controlled rectifier type. Any dimmer in the 3KW group may be interchanged. Any 6KW dimmer may be interchanged with any other 6KW dimmer.

There are 156 20-amp twist-lock lighting control circuits and 4 50-amp twist-lock circuits, distributed throughout the theater.

The lighting control console is a Century C–I two-scene preset board. The console is designed to be operated by two people with a fader between two manual presets.

Sound control

The sound system has six stereophonic amplifier outputs, with three stereo Rek-O-Kut pick-up tone arms, two Starlight turntables, two stereo Berlant Concertone tape recorders. The system is capable of mixing six stereo inputs and four microphone inputs in addition to four auxiliary stereo inputs.

Common spaces for both theaters

There is an outdoor lobby common to both theaters. It is 62′–0″ x 64′–0″, with a 30′–0″ by 30′–0″ opening to the sky. There is lobby seating of built-in concrete benches and a 30′–0″ planter at the rear of the lobby in front of the green room. Metal screen grating encloses the front of the lobby with openings on either side containing 13′–0″ high gates, 6′–0″ in width. The box office, 10′–0″ by 7′–0″ is common to both theaters and located at the front center of the lobby. Seating charts for each theater are etched on the windows facing the corresponding theater.

In the center of the lobby is a monumental sculpture 15′–0″ high, carved from limestone by Anna Mahler and entitled "Tower of Masks." It is lighted from the roof of the building and serves as a symbol of the department.

A green room is adjacent to the Playhouse theater and contains a kitchen unit.

There are two chorus dressing rooms each seating 20, one near each stage, and 10 dressing rooms seating from five to eight. All dressing rooms are located off a hall that connects the two theaters so any room can be assigned to either theater. Men's and women's shower rooms are located in the center of the dressing room area. A typical dressing room has one wash basin, full-length mirror, costume hanging space, make-up shelf and individually lighted mirrors.

Costume construction–storage area is located above the dressing rooms with a hoist which will transport a costume rack to the dressing room area.

The departmental construction shop which serves the technical needs of motion pictures and television as well as theater, is 79′–0″ wide by 110′–0″ long with 25′–0″ of clear height. It contains one 70′–0″ scene dock with plug storage above. A 20′–0″ high paint frame is built in two 30′–0″ sections that can be combined into one frame. There is a painting spray booth near the paint frame. A

68. Macgowan Hall, University of California, Los Angeles, 1963. Photograph by John Cauble. Courtesy of the University of California, Los Angeles.

68. Interior, Ralph Freud Playhouse, Macgowan Hall, University of California, Los Angeles, 1963. Stage set for *Crime and Punishment* designed by Robert Corrigan. Photograph by John Cauble. Courtesy of the University of California, Los Angeles.

69. Loretto-Hilton The-
atre, Webster College,
Webster Groves, Mo.,
1965. Photograph by Bill
Engdahl, Hedrich-Bless-
ing, Chicago. Courtesy of
Loretto-Hilton Theatre of
Webster College.

69. Interior, Loretto-Hilton Theatre, Webster College, Webster Groves, Mo., 1966. Photograph by Bill Engdahl. Hedrich-Blessing, Chicago. Courtesy of Loretto-Hilton Theatre of Webster College.

30'–0" wide roll-up steel door opens to the outside where a 30'–0" paved passage-way leads to the small theater, future motion picture and television sound stages and rehearsal and storage spaces. The bulk of the shop floor is constructed of wood with electrical outlets for both 120-volt and 208-volt circuits.

A stock-room–tool-room adjoins the shop proper. A drop and pipe rack is located along a 60'–0" corridor off which are additional flat storage docks, a prop room, welding room, light storage and repair. In addition on the ground floor reached from outside is a drapery storage room and a heavy unit storage space, plaster room and puppet laboratory. On the mezzanine level of the shop are located three offices, a student drafting room, a lighting laboratory, dark room and dressing room–shower rooms which contain individual student lockers.

The basements of the two theaters are connected by a 10' wide passageway.

In the office wing are located two rehearsal rooms approximately 40'–0" square. One doubles as a creative dramatics classroom with a one-way mirror glass observation booth. The other can be converted for central staging use. There is a technical lecture–demonstration room which contains 96 tablet arm seats, a projection booth, roll-down screen and facilities for scenery and lighting demonstration. It may also be used for rehearsal purposes.

There are three seminar rooms, one on each floor. There are 40 individual offices for the faculty and staff as well as space on the second floor for administrative offices. A reception area is located on the ground floor.

69. WEBSTER COLLEGE
Webster Groves, Missouri
Opened July 1, 1965

Webster College, originally operated by the Sisters of Loretto but from 1967 a secular

institution, opened a new playhouse in 1965. This theater is of interest for several reasons. Webster is a small college, for most of its history a college for women. Its budget was limited, and any plans for a playhouse had to include adequate classroom facilities. In addition to these problems, Webster also chose to integrate a professional repertory company into its theater plans.

Their efforts received acclaim from both academic and professional sources. The playhouse was described in the *Architectural Record*:

69:1 In this ingeniously developed concept, moveable sound proof walls, elevators and traps transform the acoustical and visual qualities of the space in a number of surprising ways. Webster College's $1,600,017 performing arts center now under construction and scheduled for completion in September, 1965, belongs to the Sisters of Loretto, and will serve the St. Louis community as well as the students of this 48-year-old Catholic school for women.* The center is named after Conrad W. Hilton, a long-time benefactor of the Sisters of Loretto, who raised $1,500,000 for the new theater.

The college could not justify the expenditure of the sum necessary to provide a fine theater without building into it some multi-use features to serve the other arts and the college as a whole. In addition, the college administrators required that no supplementary spaces sit idle much of the time, but that all spaces be independently and simultaneously usable. This need found expression in three sloping lecture rooms—two seating 125 and one seating 250—immediately adjacent to the main room. By means of delicately balanced, vertically bi-parting, moveable

69:1. "One Multi-purpose Theatre-Auditorium Adapts to Every Use," *Architectural Record* 131: 124–26 (Dec. 1964).

*This article is not entirely accurate. The total cost of the center was $1,900,000. Also, in 1967 Webster College became a legally secular, coeducational, liberal arts college.

wall sections formed as heavy steel girders, these normally independent teaching spaces can be opened into the main room, thereby expanding it to a capacity of 750 to 1,000 persons. By means of a simple treatment of the rear walls of each lecture area and the drama room sides of the girders, the acoustics of the entire space can be changed from absorptive for the spoken word to reverberant for musical performances. Between the flanges of the lecture room sides of the girders, concealed by sliding chalkboard panels, will be storage for seats, lecterns, screens and other equipment needed for classroom use.

Since the program required a variety of uses of the stage, and not all were compatible with the thrust stage, great flexibility was needed in this element. The entire thrust stage and forward gutter area can, by means of two lifts and boxing, be adusted vertically from 4 feet below the gutter level to 2 feet above this level, permitting many forms of both stage and orchestra pit in a wide range of locations. Four of these arrangements are shown.

The building contains 55,000 square feet of usable floor space, and is presently under construction at a cost, completely equipped, of approximately $29.00 per square foot.

Said George C. Izenour: "This is the first instance, that I know of, where an attempt has or is being made to divide a theater auditorium into smaller units by means of elements that are of sufficient mass as to render the spaces so divided completely isolated from each other acoustically as well as visibly. These elements as have been determined by previous measurement, must possess a unit mass of approximately 25 pounds per square foot and must provide in addition an air tight, or precision, fit to the opening they are designed to seal off. The solution here utilizes the density of steel fabricated in the form of plate girders of sufficient length and height to provide the required mass plus a neoprene gasketing system with sealed-in air to provide the precision fit between the moveable and static elements."

Research and consultation was made possible by Educational Facilities Laboratory, Inc.

Architects: Murphy and Mackey, Joseph D. Murphy, F.A.I.A. (partner in charge of design), Theodore J. Wofford, A.I.A. (Project coordinator and stage design); mechanical engineer: Paul Londe & Associates; structural engineer: Albert Alper; principle theater consultant for moveable walls, lighting and special equipment design: George C. Izenour; theater consultants: Sir Tyrone Guthrie, Jo Mielziner; acoustical consultant: Robert Newman of Bolt, Beranek & Newman, Inc.; general contractor: Gamble Construction Company.

The new center was cited by Henry Hewes in the *Saturday Review* as an outstanding playhouse.

69:2 The St. Louis area has several notable examples of modern architecture. There is the late Eero Saarinen's 600-foot-high steel arch. Yamonski's beautifully vaulted Lambert Airport, and the Climatron, a huge tropical greenhouse inspired by the geodesic dome of R. Buckminster Fuller. And last summer it acquired the Loretto–Hilton Center of the Performing Arts, designed by Murphy and Mackey after consultation with Sir Tyrone Guthrie, George Izenour, and Jo Mielziner.

This new building, which cost a little less than $2,000,000—compared to the $40,000,000 spent on the arch—is of special interest because it attempts to resolve the difficult problem of being an effective auditorium for both music and drama, with a range of capacities: 500,

69:2. Henry Hewes, "The Uncloistered Theater," *Saturday Review*, Feb. 18, 1967, p. 45. Copyright 1967 Saturday Review, Inc.

750, or 1,200 people. Furthermore, since it is a part of a small liberal arts college, the building has to provide classroom space for more than the theater arts department.

The problem of being effective for both plays and concerts was solved simply by the hanging of sound-absorbent curtains in front of sound-reflective walls. Then, thanks to a grant from the Ford Foundation Educational Facilities Laboratory, a plan was devised whereby one 250-seat classroom and two 125-seat classrooms could either become part of the auditorium or be sealed off by mechanically operating heavy steel walls that can be shut airtight by means of compressible copper stripping which resembles sponge rubber.

The basic auditorium seats 500 people in an open stage arrangement with the audience on three sides of the acting area. However, it can be turned into a proscenium stage by lowering the two hydraulic lifts that constitute the thrust portion of the stage, and manually filling this area with an extra 200 seats.

It is possible that the need for the most economic solution of its variable-size problem may have led to a shallower sloping of the seats than is found at Stratford, Ontario, or at Lincoln Center's Vivian Beaumont. Somehow this gives the auditorium less dynamic tension, less sense of expectancy, less feeling of commitment. Nevertheless, the theater as it stands seems to work reasonably well in the full thrust position.

Since July, the Repertory Theater of Loretto–Hilton Center for the Performing Arts has presented seven plays in alternating true repertory style. These include the premiere American production of Mario Fratti's *The Cage*. Now the company is embarking on a tour of nine Missouri cities with two of its most popular shows, Philip Minor's production of *Twelfth Night* and J. Robert Dietz's staging of *A Midsummer Night's Dream*. The

first sixty performances of the tour are guaranteed against loss by $25,000 from the Missouri State Arts Council, plus a matching $25,000 from the National Council on the Arts. Should the attendance be good, the company will be able to extend its tour an additional seventy performances before returning to Webster Groves in July.

The Repertory Company's artistic director, thirty-year-old Robert Flanagan, is properly pleased with the results of the first season's operation to date and with the way the sixteen professional actors have collaborated with the students and faculty of the Webster College Theater Arts Department. Both the college and Actors Equity have allowed maximum flexibility to the project. Thus, students have been able to play substantial roles in professional productions whenever the directors have found them capable of doing so. And a number of these students will receive a full semester of credits for their four months of work on the tour supplemented by papers they must write.

Mr. Flanagan is quick to credit whatever success the company has had to the wise and sympathetic leadership provided by Webster's president, Jacqueline Grennan. As Sister Jacqueline Grennan of the Order of the Sisters of Loretto, she obtained a donation of $1,500,000 from Conrad Hilton, who was educated by the Sisters as a child. Then, in January this year, Sister Jacqueline left the Order in a move designed to change Webster College into a secular institution. Just as she has voiced her own conviction that education can flourish best independent of church law and church authority, Miss Grennan also understands that theater education needs to be liberated from a tradition which too often has restricted the student to an educational rather than a professional approach. In creating the Center and permitting the college to subsidize 40 per cent of the professional company's budget until the community's citizens assume that responsibility, Miss Grennan has not only enriched the St. Louis area, but has stimulated the whole educational theater transition.

70. MACALESTER COLLEGE
St. Paul, Minnesota
Opened October 28, 1965

Another mechanized playhouse was designed for Macalester College in St. Paul by George C. Izenour, designer of the Loeb Drama Center at Harvard. This playhouse resembles the Harvard theater, but on a smaller and simpler scale.

At the time this theater was being planned, the Guthrie Theater had just opened, and so the people of the area were quite excited to hear that the Twin Cities would soon have yet another innovative playhouse. The following article appeared in the Minneapolis *Tribune*:

70:1   MACALESTER EXCITED BY THEATER
by Beverley Kees

One of the state's most exciting new theaters is scheduled to be completed a year from Christmas, according to Mary Gwen Owen, Macalester College director of the department of speech and drama.

Macalester's theater, still in the hole-in-the-ground stage, was designed by George Izenour, "one of the greatest theater designers in the world," Miss Owen said.

It will be part of a fine arts building complex which will include art, music and humanities areas—all connected by lounges and indoor gardens, she continued.

Miss Owen took off the school year 1960–61 to head a fine arts commission for the college. Under a grant from the educational facilities laboratory of Ford Foundation, she and other commission members traveled around the country, gathering ideas for the ideal theater.

70:1. First published in the Minneapolis *Tribune*, Oct. 24, 1963. Reprinted with permission of the Minneapolis Tribune.

IZENOUR worked with the commission's suggestions and designed a theater which can use the proscenium arch, theater-in-the-round or a three-quarter stage, Miss Owen said. Banks of seats will be moved by simply pressing a button.

There will also be an elevator in the pit which can lift the orchestra up or help move heavy material to the stage, she said.

Izenour designed the mechanical end of the theater for the greatest flexibility and ease of handling, she said.

THE THEATER section of the fine arts complex will also include an experimental theater, a dance studio, a large classroom and several small classrooms.

A new addition to Macalester will be the use of recording apparatus in the classroom so the teacher will be able to tape his comments on a student's performance and the student will be able to hear both when he is done.

Miss Owen is excited about the variety of uses the new building will have. She has tentative plans to open the theater with "Oedipus Rex" and "Lysistrata."

In Macalester drama, "we do all sorts of things," she said. The college players are currently rehearsing "The Alchemist" which will open Nov. 2.

Miss Owen came to Macalester in 1928 when plays were produced in the top floor of Old Main. The theater was later moved to an "Army surplus building," she said.

"The building had no splendor about it," she said, but it was all on the main floor and it was comfortable.

The Army building was recently torn down to make way for new construction and plays are now being produced in the old Macalester Presbyterian Church.

The *E.F.L. Newsletter* of October 1965 discussed the new arts center at Macalester. The E.F.L. (Educational Facilities Laboratories, Inc.) is a nonprofit organization established by the Ford Foundation to help schools with their physical problems.

70:2 JANET WALLACE FINE ARTS CENTER. Just completed, this group of buildings typifies one way to house the arts: separate but together. After three years in-depth planning that included establishment of a Fine Arts Commission to study the matter, visit other colleges, and consult with experts, Macalester's decision was to separate the facilities but cluster them in a single complex.

The complex consists of five structures: one each for theater-speech, music, the visual arts, the humanities. The humanities, as a closely related discipline, were included. By making the building part of the complex, humanities students are placed in direct contact with the other arts, routed by traffic patterns through the same exhibition areas, lounge areas, and the like. The fifth building is a 10,000 square foot common-use facility located in the center of the group. With its enclosed winter garden flanked by lounges for students and faculty, plus exhibition galleries, it serves as the architectural core of the complex and as a physical link between all the buildings.

In accordance with its donor's admonition to "get the best," each activity in the Center has a place of its own. The theater, permitted to be just that, need not be all things to all departments. It need not do double duty as a concert hall, a lecture hall, or anything else. The music building has a concert hall of its own, and lectures are given elsewhere. Neither must theater or concert hall divide or multiply to satisfy competing bids for use by numerous groups within their own departments. In both music and drama, rehearsals for one show can take place while performance of another is on, and student drama groups can freely experiment in still other spaces expressly designed for experimentation. So too are the

70:2. "Macalester College Fine-Arts Humanities Center," *E.F.L. Newsletter*, Oct. 1965, pp. 9–12.

demanding needs for storage space met separately in each of the buildings.

THE THEATER AND SPEECH BUILDING, a two-story and basement structure, has as its dominant feature the main theater itself, designed in consultation with George Izenour. Planned as a teaching theater, it enables students to be exposed to the broadest range of theatrical style, from the Greek drama on. Like Harvard's Loeb theater, Macalester's theater is mechanized for quick change—though it is smaller and simpler (placing it closer to the reach of a small college building fund). Basically a straight proscenium auditorium, stage and seating can be converted by means of a hydraulic lift system and pivoting seat banks to accommodate a three-quarter arena stage or theater-in-the-round. The entire theater can be changed over from one form to another in minutes by two operators.

For readers interested in how it works: One lift raises the orchestra pit, large enough to hold 20 musicians, to the level of the stage (or lowers it to a basement storage room beneath the stage to bring up props). Another lift raises to stage level a platform upon which the first five rows of seats stand. The banks of seats, divided into two sections, pivot on airplane wheels and fan out, one section to the left side of the hall and one to the right side, creating a horseshoe-shaped seating arrangement. The platform vacated by the seats is joined to the platform of the raised orchestra pit to form a stage apron thrust forward into the house for a three-quarter arena stage or theater-in-the-round. For the latter, portable chairs are placed on the back of the stage behind the proscenium.

The lighting system, also mechanized, makes use of the most modern theatrical lighting technology. In contrast to many theaters which require a number of men to manipulate banks of controls, here an automated preset system of light control makes it possible for one operator to manipulate a complex sequence of lighting changes. In addition, an integrated acoustic and lighting system provides extreme flexibility for hanging lighting equipment from the ceiling. The acoustic clouds, which are reflective or absorptive panels suspended from the ceiling, serve as mounting positions so light fixtures can be installed at any point over the acting area.

Acoustics in the house are tuned for articulate speech.

Neither the technological capability nor the interior of the auditorium itself is flamboyant. They are supportive features quietly designed so as not to upstage events onstage. The theater is first and foremost an actor's theater, calculated to focus attention on the players and the play, not the hall.

The house holds 250 in fixed seats arranged continental style; that is, with rows of seating that run from site to side of the hall uninterrupted by longitudinal aisles. Capacity can be expanded by an additional hundred for theater-in-the-round with the portable chairs.

Supporting spaces and equipment that contribute to the top quality are a two-story scenery production shop behind the stage equipped with a rolling platform for wheeling scenery onstage; basement rooms for storage of props and costumes (the planners figured on no less than 20 per cent of the building's space as adequate for storage); dressing rooms with showers and lighted mirrors; glass-walled rooms from which small classes can look down on the stage and discuss the action without disturbing the audiences; a greenroom where actors may relax before going on, wait between scenes, and meet friends during intermission and after the performance.

Other than the theater which is its shining star, the single feature most likely to endear the building to its users in the long run is its individual spaces for different functions, provided by three discrete areas in the basement. One of these is a 40 by 32 foot practice theater for student-directed experimental plays or rehearsals. Bare except for lighting equipment and chairs (some of which are in a balcony that runs around three sides), it is intended to stimulate creativity by forcing student directors to use their imaginations. Seating is for 100. Another space, for individual recitals, is essentially an oversized classroom with a platform and two spotlights. Still a third space is a 30 by 40 foot dance studio, mirrored on three sides and with practice bars—a special boon to the dancers who in most schools are relegated to the gym for practice. When not in use for dance, an operable wall permits the space to be divided into two costume and makeup rooms, one for men, one for women.

The top floor of the building contains six classrooms for speech, including a small suite for forensics. Like the dancers who need mirrors to view their work, speech students or debators can see themselves in action at the podium through closed circuit television. And an integrated sound system in each classroom simultaneously records an instructor's criticism while a student performance is being recorded, making it possible for students to hear both in playback on the same tape.

Total space in the building: 38,700 square feet.

71. TRINITY UNIVERSITY
San Antonio, Texas
Opened October 24, 1966

Paul Baker, director of the Dallas Theater Center, also became chairman of the Department of Speech and Drama at Trinity University in San Antonio. Here he helped design and plan the new Ruth Taylor Theater in the fine arts complex that opened in 1966.

70. Janet Wallace Fine Arts Center, Macalester College, St. Paul, 1965. Courtesy of
Macalester College.

70. Interior, Janet Wallace Fine Arts Center, Macalester College, St. Paul, 1965. Courtesy of Macalester College.

71. Ruth Taylor Theater, Trinity University, San Antonio, 1966. Courtesy of the Public Relations Office, Trinity University.

71. Interior, Ruth Taylor Theater, Trinity University, San Antonio, 1966. Courtesy of the Public Relations Office, Trinity University.

Like the Dallas Theater Center, the Ruth Taylor Theater is multi-form, with great flexibility.

Gynter Quill, amusements editor of the Waco, Texas, *News-Tribune*, had studied under Paul Baker at Baylor University. His analysis of the Ruth Taylor Theater reflects his close association with Baker and his work over a twenty-year period.

71:1   Bare space, without form, is a void, and of little use. But the creative mind can give form to space, can shape it to exciting uses.

Drama educator-director Paul Baker prefers to begin with sheer bare space in a theater—a formless arena which the writer, the director, and the designer must organize.

Accordingly, Trinity University in San Antonio has given to Baker and his staff three thousand square feet of stage space, distributed over a U-shaped area, bare, unencumbered by pillars or intervening walls, to work in, to create in.

The Ruth Taylor Theater, which Baker terms "the first truly American theater," provides surroundings that are tastefully beautiful without being distractingly lavish. It is a building which will play a dual role: a center of social life for both campus and community and a place of education.

A TEACHING THEATER

It is essentially a teaching theater and a place where Baker can continue his search for new forms and for new relationships between artist and audience . . . a place in which training for the budding artist may be flexible and where a great open space stimulates the imagination.

The $1,400,000 Ruth Taylor Theater, whose 55,000-square-foot bulk snuggles into the sloping terrain, is built on six levels of the same red brick that went into the 37 other buildings on the campus. It

71:1. Gynter Quill, *A Critic Looks at the Ruth Taylor Theater* (San Antonio: Trinity Univ., 1966).

is a dream made possible by Mr. and Mrs. Vernon Taylor of San Antonio, whose interest in the arts, all of them, was manifested several years ago by their gift of the conjoined Music Center and Art Building, both of which bear Mrs. Taylor's name. (Mr. Taylor is one of Trinity's 36 devoted, hard working trustees.) These two handsome structures form one side of Trinity's fine arts complex. The theater connects to them to form another, and a 2,900-seat auditorium for music and other University presentations, already on the drawing board, will soon be coupled with the theater at its service wing. Another corner of the auditorium will meet a wing of the Music Center to complete the enclosure of a large quadrangular space.

To use a term Baker is fond of, the building "makes a statement." It proclaims, inside and out, what it is and the philosophy of its designer. Here is a forthright invitation to the creative imagination: simplicity combined with flexibility in the arrangement of stages and seating; solidity and firmness in structure, standing apart from and yet in complete harmony with, its surroundings.

COOPERATIVE VENTURE

The basic design, particularly of the horseshoe stages and the auditorium and their relationship and proportions, is by Paul Baker. But all of it, from concept to completion, evolved through collaboration by the director with O'Neil Ford and his assistant Art Rogers. Mr. Ford is the University's design architect. "Trinity architects," Baker says, "are really interested in what happens in a theater." Their rapport was .of the closest, the director says, and Ford terms it "the best cooperative venture I've ever seen, so that I could not say where this idea or that one began or ended."

Working closely with them, not so much in a supervisory way but more as a mentor, was the University's president,

Dr. James W. Laurie, the one most aware of and concerned for the overall picture —the University's total function and the relation and importance of the theater and the drama department to it.

MORE THAN SERVICEABLE

Mr. and Mrs. Taylor's interest in the Ruth Taylor Theater extended to insuring that it is more than merely serviceable. Its appointments, the decorative as well as the utilitarian, they wanted to be the finest available, stopping short only of wasteful extravagance.

The swivel seats in the auditorium, desired by Baker for reasons beyond comfort, are one example. None meeting his standards was found in any catalogue, and few of the American manufacturers queried were interested in building them at a price thought reasonable. But one in Denmark was, and he replied with designs and then a sample. This was a chair of wood, upholstered with black leather, self-straightening, and pivoting on an air bearing of secret design. Despite the considerable cost, increased by shipping charges and customs duties, that was the chair selected by Mrs. Taylor because it was the best suited, the director asserted, to the uses of this remarkable theater.

The quadrangle formed by the fine arts complex—located a story below the street level because of the dropping terrain, and entered by way of a handsome stairway with curving brick walls—may be put to both functional and esthetic use, as patio and sculpture garden.

The patio is more than a vantage point from which best to view the imposing, arcaded facade of the theater building. It is actually an organic part of it, flowing directly through glass doors into the tiny Cafe Theater, which may be used for cabaret performances or, together with the open area, for social functions.

SIX LEVELS

The second level (the first houses mechanical equipment and storage rooms) is the principal one, containing the hexagonal main theater (Theater One) with its multiple stages and a 412 seat audience area (or up to 1,000 seats for arena productions, by shifting things about).

Entry to Theater One is from the third, or street, level, at its junction with the Ruth Taylor Art Building. One goes through the lobby, bypassing the office corridor, and enters the foyer. This 100-foot-long avenue is heavily carpeted; its curved interior is walled with three-quarter-inch, dark tan slats, rip-sawn and evenly spaced over gold burlap. The exterior wall of the theater lobby is a long expanse of glass, with doors opening onto a railed balcony overlooking the patio. A pair of opposing openings gives dual access to the auditorium of Theater One at the uppermost of its six tiers of fixed seats. Leading downward to the pivot seats (on the stage level) is a pair of sweeping, curved stairways . . . at the bottom of which, reflecting through the slatted walls, are large mirrors . . . so that the theatergoer may be startled at meeting himself coming downstairs.

On the fourth level, surrounding the auditorium, is a hexagonal balcony, half of it for seating, half for acting. In the north wing are the shop, storage areas, and the little Attic Two Theater. Classrooms and four of the building's ten faculty offices occupy the south wing; separating the two wings are the upper foyer and rehearsal classrooms. On the fifth level are more dressing rooms and the catwalks which lead to the lighting plenum and to the light-and-sound booth suspended from the ceiling above Theater One. On the sixth level, additional dressing rooms flank the loft. Here are the topmost of the three grids from which the theater crews service hexagonal Theater One's 52-foot working height.

MULTI-FORM THEATER

The building's focal, operating point, the horseshoe stage, is not copied from the theaters of New York or London, but evolves from Baylor Theater's rectangular Studio One, which Baker designed a quarter-century ago.

Though Baker and Ford agree that nothing now looks as old-hat as an arena theater, their new playhouse can be converted to that style by removing the pivot seats bolted to the floor.

Trinity's is a multi-form theater, allowing for past, present, and future—a defined space permitting several variations in the relationship of actor to spectator, in space boundary, and in audience seating.

A playwright-novelist, who was admittedly piqued by the difficulty of getting a new play into production on Broadway, predicted during a recent panel discussion sponsored by the National Theater and Academy, that "the universities will dominate theater in the next twenty years."

He may be correct, and there are signs pointing in that direction, or at least away from New York. But if he is right, it will not be because of superior buildings, no matter how greatly superior, but because of what goes on in those buildings and the direction that inspires the activity. If the universities dominate, it will not be by imitating what they are to replace, but by the force of new ideas.

THEATER OF THE UNEXPECTED

One must expect the unexpected in the Ruth Taylor Theater of Trinity University: stages enveloping most of the auditorium; an audience, whirling in swivel chairs, following the action from stage to stage; an Othello or a Hamlet divided among three players; actors scrambling up ladders to speak to other ascending or descending actors; a speaking chorus to comment, rhythmically, on a character or a situation; clusters of players, separated by scrim curtains, to be revealed by lighting when needed. These were not the conceits of a teacher-director content to play it safe.

Baker may agree with John Donne that no man is an island, living alone unto himself, but affects others and is affected by others; accomplishes more by the cooperative than by the hermetic life. But that reinforces rather than weakens the major premise of his philosophy—that man is first of all an individual with his own inner life to live; that he must live life in his own way, imaginatively and creatively, in his life-long search for truth about himself and about the universe in which he is a mere speck.

For all of Baker's experimenting, he has not set out to make over American theater on his own terms, and he most assuredly does not dislike the traditional because it isn't new. To risk the use of a dirty word, he has not feared to return the "theatrical" to the theater. He does not shun showiness or emphasis or direct appeal to the audience; and even when he uses the proscenium stage, his players are not loath to acknowledge the fact that there are people on the other side of that imaginary "fourth wall" and that they are not mere eavesdroppers through a transparent curtain.

There is danger in taking Baker at his word without knowing the man and the attitude behind the word. He speaks scornfully of doing "warmed-over Broadway plays," and the fact that he does Broadway plays makes him appear inconsistent. That some of what is done in New York is not worth doing is not disputed, but neither is the fact that much of what is first seen there is worth presenting elsewhere. The operative words are "warmed-over." The scorn is for those who copy the Broadway production, who move it, as it were, bodily into another theater or even into a different spatial arrangement without redesigning it, forcing it to fit; who slavishly imitate Broadway direction, accepting another man's viewpoint rather than restudying the play for values not perceived or for possibly an altered emphasis which would give it

231

more meaning, or for the altered statement it must make in a different environment.

Whether his presentation of "The Boy Friend" in Studio One at Baylor or of "Romanoff and Juliet" at the Dallas Theater Center was better or not is a matter of taste. But it was different, was evidence of the creative mind at work, and represented even if in a small way a reaction to the "store-bought culture and copied educational attitudes" that he says are symptomatic of the nation's dedication to brawn and materialism.

A PLAYWRIGHT'S THEATER

Baker has followed through with his maxim that "a theater without writers is only part of a theater" by retaining two on his Trinity staff. And he encourages others to write and produce. Significantly, he has designed a playwright's theater that is flexible enough and adaptable enough so that the writer is not bound to a fixed, arbitrary form of presentation but is inspired to define his own actor-spectator relationship.

The Ruth Taylor Theater lends itself to experimentation, but it is not itself an experiment. It is in large measure the result of experiments already made by the director in Waco and in Dallas. It is designed both to reflect and to implement an artistic philosophy and point of view already matured, and to house a theater group whose chief requirement is flexible space, subject to arrangement to communicate its point of view in whatever style best suits the chosen vehicle.

For the theater's design, Baker has not been unduly influenced by one stylistic tradition, but has made provision for all of them, not excepting even an approximation of the classical Greek, recognizing that there are important differences between the performance styles of different periods and making it possible to present historical as well as modern works without inconvenience to either.

UNLIMITED STAGE DESIGN

Major productions, such as the inaugural "A Different Drummer" by Eugene McKinney, designed by Virgil Beavers, can be served up to the audience on a broad, sweeping 110-foot angular front, whose abruptness is softened by four steps (which in addition to their unifying aspect may serve as playing area), and whose 30-inch height is still a foot or so below the audience's eye level.

The center stage has a 30-foot front at the steps, but the steps do not define its limit. It can be extended to 70 feet, to the structural supports which anchor the back walls of the side stages. The stage's open width is flexible and can be fixed by a second, traveling curtain, hung forward of the house curtain, which can be drawn or flown.

A 20-foot thrust stage can be added at the center, extending to the second row of seats, with some of the displaced seats moved to the side.

The back walls of the stages may be draped with black or blue cycloramas. But the most provocative innovation is the provision, in threaded inserts spaced at four-foot intervals in the rough, unfinished concrete, for mounting three-dimensional props to simulate any desired background.

The limits of the stage, without the proscenium, and with its 30-inch height from the floor belied by the four steps, seem to disappear into the auditorium, so that audience and actor are together, occupying the same space.

The auditorium is handsome, with its walls of ripped, deep-colored slats and ceiling painted warm brown, and with seats of black leather. It is not so ornate as to create the festival atmosphere of some of the world's major show places that compete with the performance. Rather, it appeals to an audience that comes to see a play. It invites the audience to participate, thereby supplying a fundamental ingredient of the living theater.

The nature of his operation, as part of a university, freed Baker and the architects from the insoluble consideration of intimacy and contact in terms of a large, revenue-producing audience.

AUDIENCE BECOMES PARTICIPANT

Essential to optimum workability of the three stages is the mobility of the relatively small audience enveloped by them. The audience is given the ability to shift in 140 pivot seats, along with the changing scenes, from stage to stage. Consequently, there is a heightened sense of participation as a natural accompaniment to the play. The theater-goer enjoys a frequent change of a perspective that comes with being near the action for one scene and seeing the next from a removed vantage point.

A large part of the seating is located just behind the swivel seats. The 186 fixed chairs are identical with the others, except that they do not pivot and do not rest on the floor, but are hung from the risers behind them—stadium style. The arrangement on steep banks gives another dimension to the view of the actors' placement on the stage. Eleven temporary seats can be placed at the rear, and the balcony will seat another 86 in double rows.

The seats were built, and their spacing dictated, with the comfort of the spectator in mind. (Cramped muscles can compete successfully with drama for attention.)

In an auditorium 76 feet at its widest point, no seat is more than 65 feet from the edge of the center stage and the nearest is six feet. The sight lines from every seat to every stage are perfect.

COMPLETE TECHNICAL EQUIPMENT

The broad sweep of the auditorium and stages creates a feeling of size and strength, of which light and sound are essential parts.

Lighting has personality in a Baker production, and there is ample provision for it from several hundred positions above the stage, in the balcony, and in the overhead plenum, controlled from the 60 pre-set dimmers in the booth suspended over the auditorium. Sound effects are also controlled there. In addition, the building is equipped with public address systems, an intercom system from booth to stage manager, and a monitoring system so actors in the seven dressing rooms and the green rooms can follow the progress of the play.

Baker's ability to make exciting use of a simple platform, facilities for seeing and hearing well, and protection from the weather, has not led to disdain for modern technology. In addition to sophisticated lighting and sound equipment, there are three booths from which to project scenery and special effects to all stages through openings concealed by the slatted walls of the auditorium.

Strategically located close to the main stage and on the same level so that heavy sets can flow directly to it—but shut off from the stage by a sound lock—is a large two-story shop (34 by 80 feet on the main level, 14 by 55 feet in the loft for prop storage). The shop has the only elevator in the building for bringing materials from the ground level and raising sets to the small theater on the fourth level.

ATTIC II

The diminutive Attic II Theater, which will seat 88 persons on its main floor and another 20 in its balcony, is primarily an experimental theater in which to test ideas for the larger Theater One. A multitude of possibilities is offered by its irregularly shaped small stage (36 by 18 feet, with additional playing room on the broad stairway to the balcony), backed by a series of movable panels hanging from runners from the wall four feet behind the stage. The theater's name carries over from the makeshift stage on the third floor of the Marrs McLean Science Center, which served the drama department for three years.

EDUCATION OF THE TOTAL PERSON

Since, by its Statement of Purpose, Trinity is dedicated to "the education of the total person," aiming through its liberal arts program at a balance among the humanities, the social sciences, and the natural sciences to instill in its students the ideals of a rigorous pursuit of truth, freedom of thought and investigation, and creativity in the arts, it is not unnatural that it should open its doors to one of its more illustrious alumni to join its faculty and then give him one of the finest teaching theaters to be found anywhere.

For the Trinity Purpose is identical with that of Paul Baker, who has earned an international reputation in its pursuit, and its expressed promise is a reward to him, even as his own ingenuity and philosophy and a theater designed by him and a department directed by him, are valued assets to the university. His theater program, for both public presentation and classroom exercise, is geared to the rigorous pursuit of truth; his curriculum, particularly the Baker-designed course, "Integration of Abilities," which encourages the student to discover and exploit his talents and whose keynote is freedom of the individual to think and grow creatively, is the Purpose in action.

CAPABLE, UNIFIED FACULTY

Though Baker properly dominates his department through force of genius and personality rather than because his name is printed on an office door, it is not a one-man operation. He has surrounded himself with a staff that is thoroughly imbued with his philosophy, whose thoughts are so closely attuned that, as Architect O'Neil Ford said of his and the director's collaboration on the building plans, in preparing a production it is difficult to say with whom this or that idea originated.

Nearly all of the drama faculty members are former Baker students, and of these all but the youngest have been his associates for years. The arrangement was not calculated to insure harmony or serenity in conference, for this is no collection of sycophants, but it does assure unity of purpose and continuity of doctrine.

San Antonio is now coming into its own. The cultural hub of a vast area, one larger than that served by any other southwestern city, the Alamo City has lacked a completeness in the performing arts that other communities had or approached. The HemisFair City began to take on a new distinction and promise in this vital dimension with the addition of Paul Baker and his drama associates three years ago to the brilliant renaissance on Trinity Hill.

With the completion by Trinity University of one of the finest theater facilities in the country, a city already rich in attractions and attractiveness has added one more gem. And those who have observed the achievements of the past can hardly wait for the coming of tomorrow, and tomorrow, and tomorrow. . . .

72. BIRMINGHAM–SOUTHERN COLLEGE
Birmingham, Alabama
Opened November 16, 1968

Perhaps the most revolutionary and innovative college theater to be developed is that of Birmingham–Southern College in Birmingham. The central concept of the stage design is a mechanical lift for a split turntable that makes changing of scenes a matter of a few seconds. The idea was proposed by the chairman of the Department of Speech and Theater, Arnold F. Powell. The theater and his concepts were explained in the following arti-

234

72. Theater, Birmingham-Southern College, Birmingham, Ala., 1968. Courtesy of Birmingham-Southern College.

72. Interior, Theater, Birmingham-Southern College, Birmingham, Ala., 1968. Architect's drawings. Courtesy of Birmingham-Southern College.

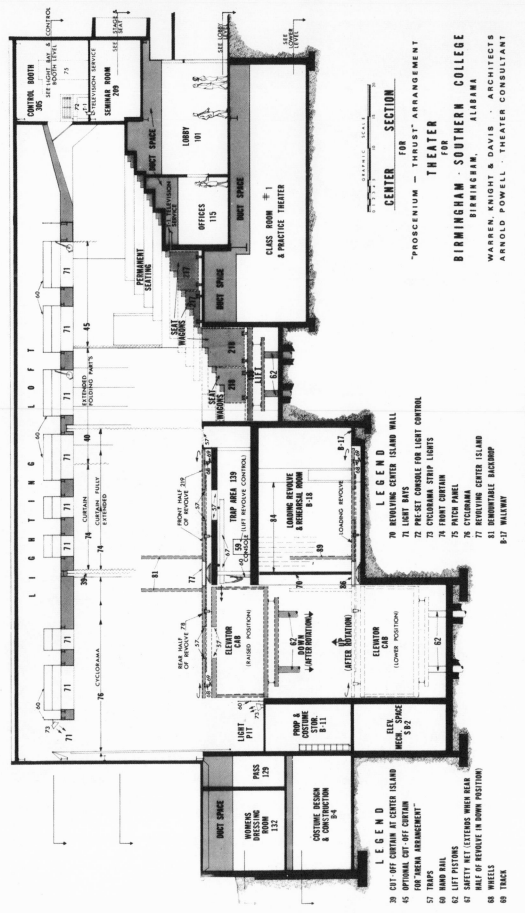

72. Cross-section, Theater, Birmingham-Southern College, Birmingham, Ala., 1968. Architect's drawing.

cle in *Birmingham*, the monthly publication of the Birmingham Chamber of Commerce.

72:1   "This is one of the most exciting stories ever told in Birmingham, if not the most exciting. There is no place like it that we know anything about. This is something that ought to be built in Houston or Atlanta, where you've got so many people who want the best, regardless of the cost. It can mean more to Birmingham than The Club. Powell is brilliant, and this is his design. I'm just making it work, and that's a job." John M. Davis Jr., architect.

"I've designed some complicated things in my life, but nothing as complicated as this." A visiting architect, unidentified.

"This is one of the most exciting buildings that ever will be constructed on this campus." President Howard M. Phillips.

The source is [of] these declarations of opinion and fact is a theatre which seats a maximum of 400, which is in the final weeks of completion on the campus of a private Methodist college, Birmingham–Southern, and which symbolizes the achievement and dedication of one man, if anybody, Dr. Arnold Francis Powell.

Professor of English, Director of the College Theater, Chairman of the Department of Drama and Speech, Arnold Powell, perfectionist, is seeing come to life his concept of the finest theatre in the world.

It retains the best features of the traditional proscenium, or picture-frame staging, yet embodies unlimited flexibility for staging. Part of the stage rests on an elevator, and a portion is a huge turntable. Actors may enter anywhere; up through the floor, out from the wings or in from the audience.

The fly-loft of the early theatre is eliminated and replaced by the concept

of stage-setting from below. This concept grew out of Powell's conviction "that a college theatre should be able to reflect in its productions the changing and developing theatrical styles of the past and present, as well as keep up with—or experimentally forge ahead of—the changes and developments of the future." All design efforts were bent to this end.

Basically, the theatre building is a utility structure built around a split-revolve-lift stage; a one-of-a-kind machine that will give the theatre maximum flexibility. This utility, however, creates a distinct beauty of its own which sets the theatre apart from other buildings on the Hilltop campus. With new art and music facilities already in operation, the theatre is the last building scheduled for the Hilltop's fine arts complex.

Underway nearly two years now, upon completion in March, the theatre will round out new facilities for presenting the performing arts, an integral part of 'Southern's liberal arts program.

Fan-shaped, accented with exposed aggregate siding and vast areas of glass, the building is literally imbedded in the east side of 'Southern's fine arts complex. More than half of the seven story structure is underground.

It is first an educational structure . . . a teaching building if you will. But the very subject matter offered there shapes the rooms, underground galleries and mechanical spaces by function, imparting to each its own character and design.

A case in point is the ceiling nearly thirty feet above the stage floor. At first glance, it is a skillfully-designed pattern of lights and darks not dissimilar from a suspended spider web. But look more closely. The dark spaces are openings through which spotlights illuminate the stage below. The white areas are catwalks for technicians.

There is little distinction in the building between the traditional stage and seating space for the audience. Stated

72:1. James M. Gillespy, "Newest Theatre in the World . . . and Best," *Birmingham*, Feb. 1968, pp. 8–12, 46.

235

simply, the stage is located anywhere the audience isn't. Yet there will be instances when the audience will be placed on the stage.

Virtually the full area of the main floor level is available for stage space. The floor, with all elevators at stage level, provides 6,840 square feet of usable space. It was designed to serve as a television studio and already installed in the walls, awaiting the day they will be needed, are metal conduits for television cables.

This area, this stage, fits an endless variety of dramatic configurations. Theatre in the round, square, rectangle or any other geometric shape is possible. The lower tiers of seats are on "wagons," so-called because they may be moved in groups or individually and spotted around the floor to vary seating.

Architect John Davis said one design problem was the possibility this theatre might be used for several years without repeating the same seating arrangement.

Davis is obviously proud of his achievement. He jokes that the building has thirty-five levels and no right angles. No one has taken the time and effort to tabulate the truth of the statement, but the building is complex.

The unique feature of the theatre is hard to spot unless you know where to look and are a student of theatre design. Powell sought to eliminate the well-known backstage arrangement with its vast, empty flyspace. He aimed, instead, to install the most flexible arrangement possible for shifting scenery and varying levels for acting areas.

Powell feels "the proscenium arch with the traditional fly-loft has long furnished marvelous and varied physical production facilities, but such an arrangement tends to shut the audience out, to discourage a feeling of immediate participation in the play.

"On the other hand, the arena or open stage reaches out and includes the audi-ence, but frequently becomes scenically rather bleak for lack of production facilities."

This theatre seeks to overcome both shortcomings. "As theatre," Powell says, "the new building attempts to offer the possibility of various combinations of the best features of yesterday's proscenium stage and today's or day-before-yesterday's open or arena stage, hopefully pointing the way toward a fuller, less limited use of tomorrow's stage."

Circular, the main pattern of the stage rests on a turntable which rotates 360 degrees. In addition, the stage is split, so that each half—or semi-circle—operates independently of the other. The rear half of the stage and turntable rests on the elevator.

Though the concept may be hard to grasp, there are three halves of the stage. Should the mathematics of this equation seem impossible, one must realize at least one of the halves is always underground, about thirty feet below the main level of the stage and waiting to be brought to the surface by the elevator.

Only a small part of the uniqueness is above ground. To see the whole, to visualize all of its mechanical wonders as a unit, it is best to start at the bottom. It is here the actors and technicians work. There is no better guide than Powell.

He conceived the idea for a split-revolve-lift stage after years of experience in college theatre, television and summer stock. President Howard M. Phillips has called Powell a genius and gives to the drama director full credit for conceiving the structure.

A graduate of 'Southern, class of 1936, Powell's enthusiasm for the theatre is enormous. He received his Master's degree from Vanderbilt in 1938 and his Doctorate from the same school in 1947, with some Navy war service in between. He studied television production at Yale, directed a summer television series for 'Southern for two years and has produced and directed more than thirty plays. He is a prize-winning playwright.

Powell's dramatic efforts far predate his academic pursuits. While a youngster and student at South Highland Elementary School, he produced a play to benefit the then-important milk fund for schoolchildren. His mother, apparently doubting his ability to draw a large audience, offered to match receipts dollar-for-dollar. The play was standing room only. In fact, said Powell, "they were standing on the porch looking in windows." He doesn't remember the amount exactly, but the play cost his mother about $50.

His enthusiasm for the theatre has never wained. He is, himself, an accomplished actor. And many of his students will admit to spending hours of vicarious enjoyment watching Powell directing them in a part.

His students and members of the College Theatre call him the Great White God, only half in jest.

The 1964 edition of the *Southern Accent*, Birmingham–Southern's student annual, was dedicated to him and editor Hubert Grissom said Powell "can give a ninety-eight pound girl courage to climb a sixty-foot ladder and hang curtains on non-existent rods." The *Accent* also classed Powell as a "fifty-year-old-boy wonder."

The title fits. He is jeered by many who believe his productions of the theatre of the absurd are too "far out." He is cheered by those who laud his efforts to try the untried.

The new theatre is the sort of place one would expect to find a boy wonder or a genius. It is awe-inspiring to a legion of College Theatre alumni, most of whom regard Powell with the veneration sometimes ascribed to the Oracle at Delphi. These former students see in the new theatre the Alpha and Omega of their dramatic dreams.

One ex-College Theatre actress, home from New York over Christmas, said the thing she missed most while here was touring the theatre building. It was closed during the holidays.

Powell's theatre alumni date back to the barely-adequate stage of the campus' old Student Activities Building. When the building was renovated and remodeled, the organization was without a home and moved to the College auditorium in Munger Hall where it operated successfully for several years until a clean-up and painting program again evicted the players.

Creating an Underground Theatre (as it was aptly named) in the basement of Stockham Women's Building, Powell and his troupe remained there for a year, finally suspending performances last Spring. Next curtain that rises will be on the grandest opening night the college has ever known, on April 4. The production, "Caucasian Chalk Garden," will be to the theatre group what a bottle of champagne is to a newly-finished ship. Those who raise eyebrows of criticism at the theater do so mainly because they think it is costing, proportionately, as much as a new ship. The price is rather high, measured strictly in terms of seating capacity: more than $1 million. Realistically, however, the scope of view should be broader than that.

Follow Powell's angular form through a side door and down a few steps into the Green Room. Here the players will await their cues. It is theatre tradition dating back more years than most can remember that this room is always painted green.

Further into the building, steps connect the Green Room with make-up and dressing rooms. An interior set of steps leads deeper into labyrinth-like storage areas for costumes and props. They are just inside the building shell, out of the path of stage hands and technicians who are constantly on the move.

Out of the Green Room and up a half-dozen steps is the main entrance to the stage. There are many ways to make an entrance in this theatre. The number of combinations is nearly unlimited as is indicated by the number of doors, traps and catwalks, all leading upwards.

Hurry on, keeping sight of Powell's thatch of white hair and craggy features. He hastens up the stairs near the theatre roof to unlock the wonders of sound and lighting booths which overlook the audience and stage. These necessary functions previously were performed by students crammed into tiny enclosures under the stage, behind the stage or nowhere near the stage.

Further upwards, balanced on a catwalk above the abyss, cross above the ceiling, dodge openings from which lights will hang, and come to the very center of the theatre.

Below is the stage, its dark pit at the rear where the elevator moves to change scenery. From here, see how the design of the stage, the turntable and the elevator blend into a complete unit unseen in any other theatre in the world.

Back across the ceiling follow Powell, this time to the east and plunge after him down a vertical circular stairway which spirals nearly seventy feet from the ceiling to the basement.

At the bottom is a cavern. That is the only way to describe it. Its function is purely technical. Here scenery is built and painted. Designed to handle fifteen-foot flats, the canvas and wood scenery pieces which hold a play together, the basement opens onto the third of the three halves of the stage. The other two are far above at stage level. It takes but the touch of a button to bring another half of the stage down here and take the third half up to the stage floor.

There is nothing below now but machinery to work the elevator, which was manufactured by Dover Elevator Company of Memphis. But around the side, by-passing big storage lockers and along a couple of curved halls, come back to the front of the building. This time it is

one level down, beneath the lobby, offices and spectator seats.

The smaller teaching theatre is here. Used often for student-written and produced plays, it consists of two large classrooms, for after all, this entire building is a classroom. Drama, speech and other performing arts are taught here and it also will be used for lectures and concerts.

Technical Director for the Theatre and the man who will watch over the machinery and wiring that make the building work, is John Kitchens, alumnus of 'Southern, 1961. Kitchens, a former actor in the College Theatre, received a Master of Fine Arts degree from the University of Georgia in 1966 and in preparation to joining the Birmingham–Southern faculty, worked for the Peter Albrecht Company, of Milwaukee, which installed the turntable mechanism.

Powell says this building, in its own way, follows the trend which has brought theatre into a new focus from primitive beginnings. "Though it is somewhat of an oversimplification," he says, "theatrical production styles have come full circle from the open, ritualistic, participatory performances of the primitive and ancient time; through the removed, framed, observed performances of proscenium or picture-frame realism; back again to open, more-or-less ritualistic participatory performances."

Those who really believe he is a Great White God might also tell you they are sure he was either acting in, or directing, the very first open, ritualistic, participatory play, whenever it was. And though he didn't have at his disposal the masterpiece of a theater he has today, his disciples might also tell you that he damn sure was planning it.

72:2   WHAT MAKES
THE BIRMINGHAM–SOUTHERN COLLEGE
THEATRE UNIQUE?

72:2. Fact sheet published by Birmingham-Southern College, 1966.

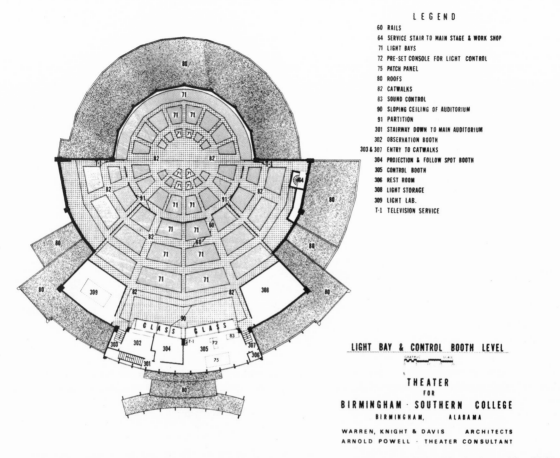

LIGHT BAY & CONTROL BOOTH LEVEL

GRAPHIC SCALE

THEATER
FOR
BIRMINGHAM · SOUTHERN COLLEGE
BIRMINGHAM,   ALABAMA

WARREN, KNIGHT & DAVIS   ARCHITECTS
ARNOLD POWELL · THEATER CONSULTANT

72. Plan of the light bay and control booth level, Theater, Birmingham-Southern College, Birmingham, Ala., 1968. Architect's drawing. Courtesy of Birmingham-Southern College.

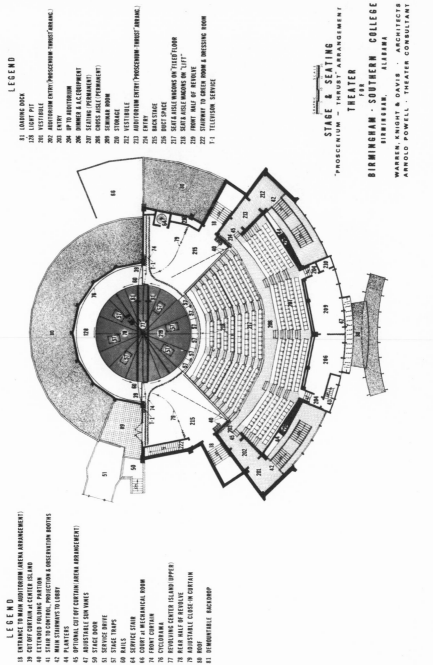

72. Plan of stage and seating, Theater, Birmingham-Southern College, Birmingham, Ala., 1968. Architect's drawing. Courtesy of Birmingham-Southern College.

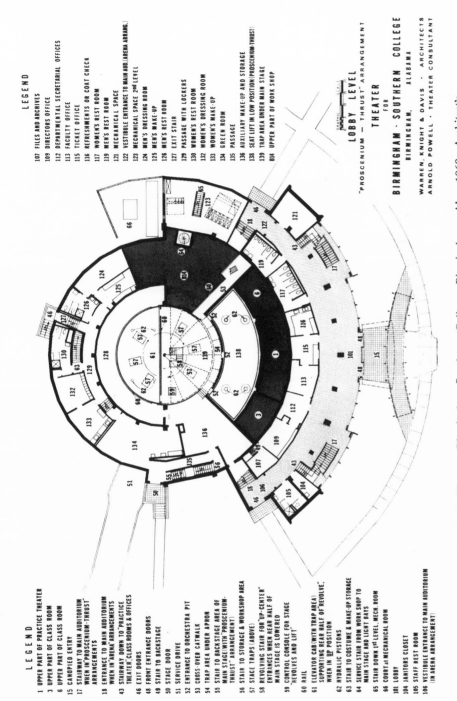

72. Floor plan of lobby level, Theater, Birmingham-Southern College, Birmingham, Ala., 1968. Architect's drawing. Courtesy of Birmingham-Southern College.

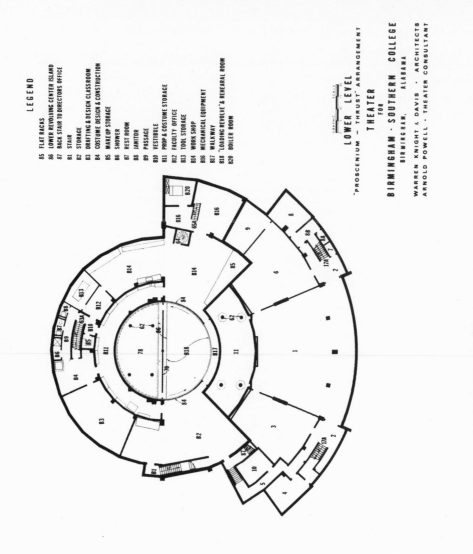

LEGEND

85 FLAT RACKS
86 LOWER REVOLVING CENTER ISLAND
87 BACK STAIR TO DIRECTORS OFFICE
B1 STAIR
B2 STORAGE
B3 DRAFTING & DESIGN CLASSROOM
B4 COSTUME DESIGN & CONSTRUCTION
B5 MAKEUP STORAGE
B6 SHOWER
B7 REST ROOM
B8 JANITOR
B9 PASSAGE
B10 VESTIBULE
B11 PROP & COSTUME STORAGE
B12 FACULTY OFFICE
B13 TOOL STORAGE
B14 WORK SHOP
B16 MECHANICAL EQUIPMENT
B17 WALKWAY
B18 "LOADING REVOLVE" & REHEARAL ROOM
B20 BOILER ROOM

GRAPHIC SCALE

LOWER LEVEL
"PROSCENIUM — THRUST" ARRANGEMENT
THEATER
FOR
BIRMINGHAM · SOUTHERN COLLEGE
BIRMINGHAM,   ALABAMA

WARREN KNIGHT & DAVIS · ARCHITECTS
ARNOLD POWELL · THEATER CONSULTANT

LEGEND

1 PRACTICE THEATER
2 VESTIBULE
3 CLASS ROOM
4 FACULTY OFFICE
5 PASSAGEWAY & STEPS TO BACKSTAGE AREA
6 CLASS ROOM
7 STORAGE
8 DEBATE ROOM
8A STORAGE
8B ALCOVE
9 MECHANICAL ROOM
10 FACULTY OFFICE
11 UNEXCAVATED
17A STAIRWAY TO LOBBY
62 HYDRAULIC PISTONS
63A STAIRWAY TO MAKEUP & DRESSING ROOMS
64 SERVICE STAIR
65A STAIR TO 2nd LEVEL OF EQUIPMENT ROOM
70 REVOLVING CENTER ISLAND WALL
78 REAR HALF OF "REVOLVE" (DOWN POSITION)
84 ACCORDION DOORS

72. Floor plan of lower level, Theater, Birmingham-Southern College, Birmingham, Ala., 1968. Architect's drawing. Courtesy of Birmingham-Southern College.

1. The split-revolve-lift stage makes possible rapid changing of scenes (15 seconds). Three scenes may be fully pre-set at any one time.
2. The split-revolve-lift stage also makes possible the elimination of the fly-loft and its inherent separation of the stage area from the audience. One continuous, unbroken ceiling extends over the stage and audience.
3. This continuous ceiling—consisting solely of open lighting bays and catwalks—makes possible a highly versatile lighting system. Any spot can be lighted from almost any angle. All lighting is controlled from a five-scene, preset control system.
4. A seat lift for the first four rows, and the mounting of the first eight rows on movable sections, allows maximum flexibility of stage and seating arrangements. Practically any audience-stage confrontation in the history of the theatre—or even untried forms—can be arranged, including 360-degree arena staging.
5. Even in the open proscenium arrangement, the 90-degree spread and high risers for the seating (15 inches per row for the first eight rows, 18 inches for the last four) create a striking sense of intimacy between audience and stage, plus optimum acoustics and sight lines. The last row of seats is only 46 feet from the stage. (Maximum proscenium seating is 370; arena arrangements can accommodate approximately 500.)
6. With the removal of all portable seat sections, the theatre can become a very large television studio—with abundant lighting facilities, generous floor space and spacious control booths—for a live audience of 200.

73. UNIVERSITY OF ILLINOIS
Urbana, Illinois
Opened April 24, 1969

Undoubtedly the most ambitious of all university theater buildings was that of the complex at the University of Illinois—the Krannert Center for the Performing Arts, which was dedicated in 1969. The center contains a large auditorium, three theaters, and an outdoor Greek amphitheater.

Proposed plans for the $21,000,000 theater complex were discussed in the *Illinois Alumni News*:

73:1 Four separate units—an auditorium and three theaters—plus an outdoor theater created by the arrangement of the buildings compose the planned Krannert Center for the Performing Arts.

The central unit will be a music auditorium to seat 2,200, designed for use for many programs produced by students and faculty as well as for concerts by outside talent.

The other three are a music theater for 1,000, a drama theater to seat 700 and an experimental theater for 250. The outdoor facility will accommodate about 1,000 persons.

Major outlines of the complex, scheduled for completion during the 1967–68 academic year, were explained at the July 24 press conference by Max Abramovitz '29, the architect, who dismantled the model layer by layer as he detailed structural plans from the top down.

'A Teaching Arm'

"Functionally, the Center is planned as a practical teaching arm oriented to University and community audiences," Mr. Abramovitz said, "and it is my hope that an appropriate and pleasing architectural quality will develop out of the relationships of the individual forms which express the activities within and compose the complex as it rises from its series of elevated platforms which will be landscaped to relate to the campus surroundings."

The entire Center will be built on a man-made rise of ground to give it dominance over the surrounding area. Underneath will be two floors which will in-

73:1. *Illinois Alumni News*, Oct. 1964.

clude practice rooms, rehearsal areas, offices, dressing rooms, workshops and space for parking approximately 800 cars.

The rooms on the lower levels will be in constant use in the teaching programs in music, drama, the dance, opera and other fields, and the garage area is so designed that, by later remodeling, part of it could be converted into classrooms.

Natural lighting will be provided for the parking area from a specially designed clerestory, and it will also have natural ventilation. Cars can approach the parking [area] from several sides of the complex.

Steps Provide Seating

The main entrance to the auditorium will be at ground level, from the east, Mr. Abramovitz explained, with another entrance from the terrace level and still another at an upper level. From the west, or interior side, it will be approached by the dramatic flight of steps some of which provide seating for the outdoor theater.

The theaters, each visible from all sides, will have connecting corridors or walkways wide enough for benches and lounge spaces, and the walls of the connecting galleries will be designed for the display of materials related to the performing arts.

So that a maximum number of persons can enjoy them, provisions will be made for piping programs from the various theaters to other units of the Center.

Mr. Abramovitz related the Krannert Center to the recently completed Assembly Hall for which he also was the architect.

'Comparable to the Best'

"The Hall," he said, "was built for large functions and performances at which sound amplification facilities are generally required, while this Center for the Performing Arts will provide for smaller audiences tailored to the special qualities and capabilities of each of the performing activities where the various programs can be heard naturally without the need of any amplification devices.

"Together these buildings should have an exciting impact upon the University and the surrounding communities in the field of the performing arts and will augment the existing educational and scientific facilities which have contributed so much to the achievements of the University and its graduates."

"The Krannert Center," the architect said, "will provide the University of Illinois with modern facilities for teaching and experimentation and for performances in music, theater and dance comparable to the best among the universities in the nation."

73:2 The Krannert Center for the Performing Arts occupies a rectangle of ground 690 feet by 590 feet. The area was formerly occupied by residences and several business properties and was especially valuable because of its proximity to the campus. Operating through the University of Illinois Foundation, the University acquired a total of 44 parcels of land from private owners and the right-of-way to a block of California Street from the City of Urbana. Total cost of land acquisition in the area was $2,141,895.

The terrace gardens occupy 30,600 square feet of ground and the two-level underground garage covers approximately 227,000 square feet.

The main terrace level leads to a large public foyer which provides access to the four theatres. This large foyer envelops the four theatre entrances and offers interesting intermission and after-theatre areas for promenades. The main terrace also leads to an open air amphitheatre seating 1,000—an ideal spot for the revival of Classical Greek plays, or for admiring the California Street Mall—a gift of the Class of 1917.

73:2. Commemorative brochure published by the Krannert Center for the Performing Arts, 1969, pp. 45–60.

240

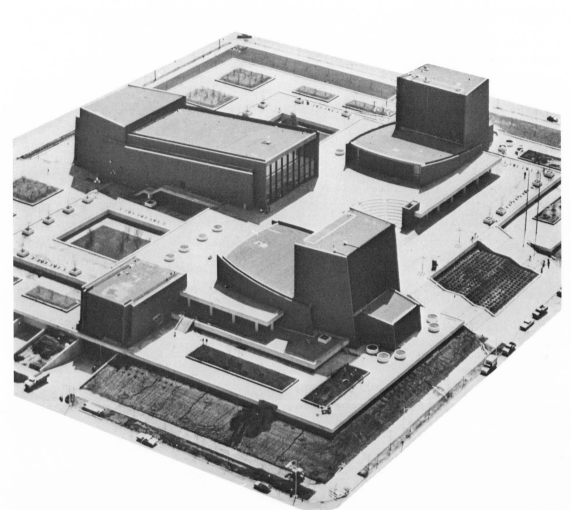

73. Krannert Center for the Performing Arts, University of Illinois, Urbana, 1969. Courtesy of the University of Illinois.

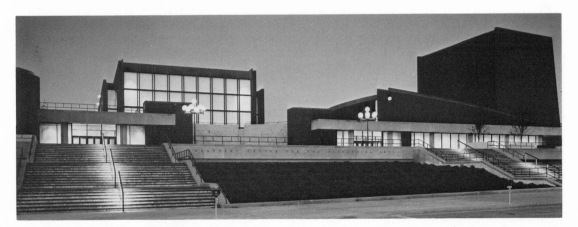

73. Krannert Center for the Performing Arts, University of Illinois, Urbana, 1969. Photograph by Harr, Hedrich-Blessing, Chicago. Courtesy of the University of Illinois.

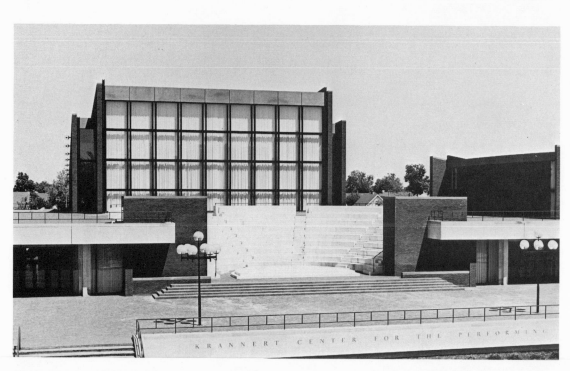

73. Outdoor amphitheater, Krannert Center for the Performing Arts, University of Illinois, Urbana, 1969. Courtesy of the University of Illinois.

73. Interior, Festival Theatre, Krannert Center for the Performing Arts, University of Illinois, Urbana, 1969. Photograph by Harr, Hedrich-Blessing, Chicago. Courtesy of the University of Illinois.

73. Interior, Playhouse. Krannert Center for the Performing Arts, University of Illinois, Urbana, 1971. Photograph by Bill Engdahl, Hedrich-Blessing, Chicago. Courtesy of the University of Illinois.

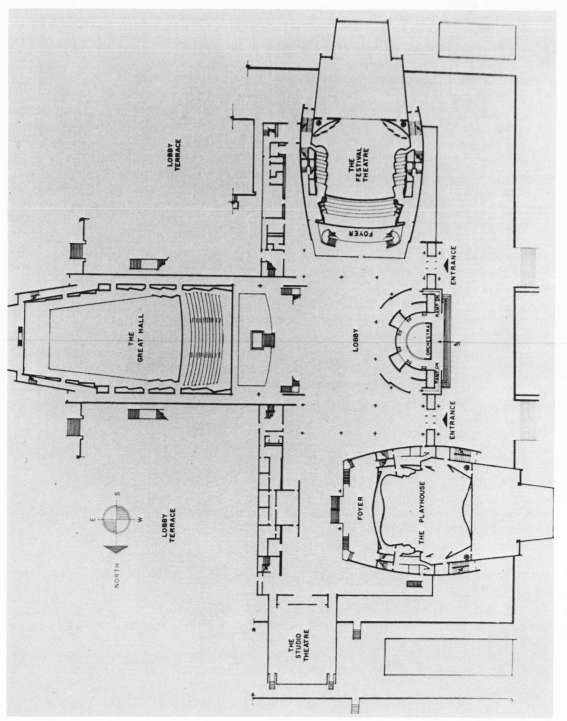

73. Plan of lobby terrace level, Krannert Center for the Performing Arts, University of Illinois, Urbana, 1969. Architect's drawing. Courtesy of the University of Illinois.

On the lower level of the Center are five major rehearsal rooms—each designed for a special need: For orchestra, chorus, drama, opera, and the dance. It contains some thirty offices for department heads and their staffs. The large shop for the construction of scenery would be the pride of any commercial enterprise. There are huge vaults containing electrical equipment. A machine room houses the heating and ventilating equipment, although the cooling tower was located on another building, nearby, so that mechanical sound would not affect the acoustics of any of the theatres. The workshops, offices, and service rooms occupy some 20 percent of the entire area of the Center.

Wide corridors connect the shop area with all the theatres, and scenery can be moved easily from workroom to stage along what virtually amounts to an enclosed highway.

Construction of the Krannert Center for the Performing Arts required 37,650 cubic yards of concrete, or enough to build a 4-foot sidewalk of normal 4-inch depth from the campus to the home of Mr. and Mrs. Krannert in Indianapolis. The Center contains 2,600 tons of reenforcing steel, which would fulfill the reenforced concrete needs of a modern industrial plant. It contains 1,720 tons of structural steel or enough to build a sizable railroad bridge.

Bricks in the Center number 904,580. Of these, 15,368 were brick made especially for this project. The structure contains 468,100 masonry blocks and 160,000 paving bricks. There are enough bricks here to build 90 residences and pave the streets around them. Walls and ceilings contain 45,000 square yards of plaster. The project used 131,000 square yards of aggregate, 3,200 square feet of granite for the stairs, 1,112 tons of Indiana limestone for various areas, 45 tons of Longmeadow (Massachusetts) brownstone and 70,460 pieces of Ludowici

tiles. The amount of aggregate would pave 3½ acres, or more than enough to cover the quadrangle on the Urbana campus.

The Center contains 220 miles of wire, some 50 miles of conduit, 38 miles of low voltage wire.

The floors of all four theatres are of teakwood, 18,186 square feet of it in the Great Hall, 6,406 square feet in the Playhouse, 7,170 square feet in the Festival Theatre, and 3,394 square feet in the Studio Theatre. Wood for the rehearsal room covers 15,252 square feet. The teak, which came from India, Ceylon, and Burma, consists of very small pieces of wood glued together by hand. Nine such small pieces form a piece of flooring 6 inches square and these, in turn, are pieced together to form the floor.

The butternut wood was acquired from Chester B. Stern at New Albany, Indiana, a hilly, wooded area in the southern part of the State. Six thousand butternut logs were examined critically to select forty-six logs of matching wood. The boards for the Great Hall walls had to match exactly, and the most careful selection was required for a perfect job.

More than three hundred men were employed in the construction of the Center. These included electricians, plumbers, iron workers, stone setters, carpenters, laborers, pipefitters, sheet metal workers, excavators, roofers, masons, terrazzo workers, insulators, painters, tile setters, marble setters, and pavers. Strikes slowed down construction several times. One strike, of steel workers, off campus, meant hauling steel from Alabama, where there was no work stoppage.

Selected as the general contractor for the project was Turner Construction Company, of Boston, Chicago, Cincinnati, Los Angeles, New York, and Philadelphia, and the job was contracted through the University of Illinois Foundation on a cost-plus basis for maximum efficiency and economy. Each year Turner company completes more than thirty-five projects with a total valuation of $150,000,000.

The Festival Theatre (originally called the Music Hall) seats 985, and is intended for small-scale musical and musical-dramatic productions, particularly opera and dance. While it often will be used for public performances appropriate to a theatre of this size, it is more closely related to the educational program.

Walls of the Theatre are of a light parchment color with a cream colored ceiling. The seat fabric and carpeting are a special Krannert vivid red. The floor and seat standards are a dark monastral blue. The stage curtain is a special weave of red, gold, bronze, and beige threads presenting an irridescent effect. The balcony wood caps, the stage apron, and stage lifts are of American cherry veneer, as are the panels in the metal railing around the orchestra pit. The metal railing of the balcony parapet is of dark bronze.

The Playhouse (originally called the Drama Theatre) is the center of legitimate theatre at the University. Its seating capacity is 678, with optimum space and equipment backstage and on stage for all production activities and demands.

In the Playhouse, walls, floor, and ceiling are of the dark, monastral blue. The lower rear wall is carpeted for sound absorption, and is of matching special Krannert blue. The stage apron, the lift aprons, the pit railing, and railings at the boxes for paraplegics are in English burled oak. The stage curtain and proscenium curtains are an irridescent oyster color. The seats are scarlet cushioned. In this theatre, too, there is dimmer control for down lighting, the light beaming in the cones from the ceiling.

The Studio Theatre is a small experimental theatre, with a seating capacity of 250. (Of this number 132 are permanent seats.) It has maximum flexibility in its design and technical equipment. It is available to graduate students and faculty as a research laboratory for the theatre.

Walls, ceiling, and grid in the Studio Theatre are dark blue. The seats are movable, for various types of productions.

The carpeting in the foyer and lobby area of the Great Hall and in the lounge areas is beige. In the foyers of the Great Hall, the Festival Theatre, and the Playhouse the walls are of acoustical absorbent fiberglas behind a warm beige acoustical cloth, accented with vertical birch strips. The ceilings are white. The carpets of the Festival Theatre and Playhouse extend into the foyers and lounge areas to introduce the tone of these houses as the visitor approaches them.

The east wall of the main lobby is of Italian marble in whites, creams, and tans. The floor is of Thailand teak parquet. The five staircases opening off the lobby and leading down to the mezzanine level are of Italian Dotticino terrazzo. The conference room next to the director's suite and the screen walls around the coat room are panelled in black vinyl. Counter faces also are in this material. Counter tops in the box office and in the coat room are of Lo Glare Micarta in a grayish tan tone. Ticket control railings and stair railings are dark bronze. Black vinyl also is used in the elevator cabs, with the cab hand rails of teak, and metal parts and the doors are dark bronze.

One sees exterior face brick as he enters the lobby areas. All window frames are of dark bronze, contrasting with the off-white draperies in the director's suite and in the lobby and reception room. The same color is used in the draperies on the large west window of the Great Hall and in the smaller windows of the Festival Theatre, the Playhouse, and the Studio Theatre. The floor of the Center's reception room is of teak parquet. A specially woven rug has been placed in this room. Walls are of beige grass cloth panels, with teak on the doors. Benches and sofas in the lobby, the foyers, and lounge areas are of black vinyl, with table tops of Italian marble matching the marble of the lobby wall.

There is unity throughout the interior of the Krannert Center and yet each theatre has a character of its own. The entire complex has a warmth and quietness which have been achieved through the most careful planning and excellent taste on the part of those who, over a period of many months, gave careful thought to the project.

Chapter 4

Summer Playhouses

One of the most popular forms of theater is the summer theater, which is an old mode of entertainment for Americans. At the very beginning of the nineteenth century several popular summer playhouses opened in New York City and were attended by large audiences. As the population of New York grew and the city limits were pushed the length of Manhattan Island, the summer theaters gradually disappeared. By the end of the century, however, we find their reappearance.

Elitch's Gardens opened in Denver May 1, 1890, and as of 1972 was the oldest summer theater still in operation. The Lakewood Theatre in Skowhegan, Maine, opened in 1901, and other groups were quick to follow. The summer theater offered an opportunity for actors and actresses to work in the country and for summer vacationers to have enjoyable entertainment. Significant actors, directors, and designers came from this form of theater, particularly from such a group as the Provincetown Players and their Wharf Theatre in Provincetown, Massachusetts.

More recently there was great interest in the presentation of Shakespeare's plays, and several important summer festivals sprang up devoted to presenting them—notably the American Shakespeare Festival Theatre in Stratford, Connecticut, and the Oregon Shakespeare Festival Theatre in Ashland, Oregon. The Old Globe Theatre in San Diego, once a summer playhouse, commenced a year-round operation.

74. ELITCH'S GARDENS THEATRE
Denver, Colorado
Opened May 1, 1890

For several generations of playgoers, Elitch's Gardens Theatre has represented outstanding summer entertainment. The oldest operating summer theater in the United States, it opened May 1, 1890. Throughout its long history many of the most talented stage stars in the country appeared at this interesting playhouse, and Elitch's Gardens maintained its position as one of the outstanding summer theaters in America.

For the fiftieth anniversary celebration in 1941, a history of the playhouse was published. It is reproduced here.

74:1   When Mary and John Elitch arrived in Denver in 1882, looking for a site for

74:1. Souvenir program published by Elitch's Gardens, 1941. Reproduced by permission of John Gurtler.

244

their "dream" house, little did they believe that the place they were seeking would eventually become the most famous amusement area in America and its theater one to attain a world wide reputation.

The sixteen acre plot which they purchased after a quest of five years formed the nucleus of the vast amusement enterprise and floral gardens which today occupy thirty-two acres, with 160,000 square feet under glass where the famed Colorado Carnations are grown and shipped to all parts of the United States. Surely a far cry from the little farm where Mary and John Elitch began their married life among the majestic cottonwoods and apple trees. Some still are thriving to remind Denverites of another generation that here love and tender care nourished a vision that John and Mary Elitch cherished.

In her book, Colorado Pioneers In Picture and Story, Alice Polk Hill says— "The far famed Elitch's Gardens became a beauty spot in pioneer days. Mrs. Martha Hagar, with her husband and sons came to Colorado in the early times and settled at Empire, where they were constantly in dread of Indians. The town was then a distributing point of rations for the Utes. They passed through a period of merciless Indian savageries and butcheries and finally, after the death of her husband, Mrs. Hagar moved to Denver.

"Here she married William Chilcott and for many years the couple made their home on the property now known as Elitch's Gardens.

"Mrs. Chilcott, with her own hands, planted many of the shade trees that adorn the Gardens today. Through her continued labor and care the dreary desert place was changed into a pleasant ranch, which soon became famed for its beauty.

"The many fine reports of it caught the attention of John Elitch who bought the property and made it one of the beauty spots of Denver."

They occupied a comfortable farm, located in the grove of beautiful apple trees and here they planned and worked together. Nothing was done without careful consideration. And their labor of love progressed and in May 1890 the gates were opened to the public. The press of the state acclaimed the event. The people of Denver, proud of the new enterprise, flocked in droves to The Gardens and the grand children and great grand children of those early pioneers are the people today who make possible the yearly improvement and the enormous sum necessary to maintain the theater.

Nat Goodwin, famous comedian of another day en route to an engagement on the Pacific Coast, stopped off in Denver to wish his old friend, John Elitch, good luck. John Elitch was an actor, prior to his marriage, and knew every one of note connected with the theater. Stuart Robson, playing in Denver at the time, was among the throng that witnessed the first vaudeville performance on the second day. That doughty showman P. T. Barnum, himself was present. A friend of John Elitch, he was his advisor and comrade and his suggestions and sound advice proved invaluable. Mr. and Mrs. Tom Thumb, house guests of John and Mary Elitch, were also present. May Irwin of beloved memory and that ever gay person Eugene Field, then a member of the staff of the Denver Republican were present also.

Peter Satriano's band provided the music for the picnic that preceded the vaudeville performance. It should be mentioned in passing that during the construction period of the theater, James O'Neill, father of our distinguished dramatist today, Eugene O'Neill, visited the Gardens and promised John Elitch, that he would return some day and put on a play.

Even a sketchy picture of the history of Elitch's would not be complete without printing the program of the inaugural performance in the famous playhouse. The theater that in years to come was to find its place in the history of the drama in America and to give to the acting profession many gallant and noted artists, who still boast that they played "Elitch's." The program follows:

Opening Performance
Elitch Amusement Gardens.
May 1, 1890
Comedy Sketch—Banjoists
Mont——The Montgomerys——Mamie
The Little Athletic Wonder
Miss Minnie Zola
The Great Knock-about Comedians,
Singers and Dancers
Bailey and Reynolds
Charles W. Goodyear
Comedian
Van Auken and La Van
Champion Triple Horizontal Bar
Performers of the World.
Bijou Mignon
America's Youngest Singing and Dancing
Soubrette
Charles E. Schilling
The Quaint Comical Musical Genius
Miss Rosa Lee
The Gifted and Refined Balladist
The San Francisco Twins
Ed——Nealy and Sully——John
Australian Marvels
The Family Zola Troupe
Most Expert and Daring Artists
That Have ever visited This Country.

John Elitch did not live to see the first dramatic performance in the theater that still maintains his name. The Gardens theater had become so successful with its vaudeville performances that first summer that he determined to give all of his future to the theatrical business. He organized The Goodyear, Elitch and Schilling Minstrels and toured the Pacific Coast. While playing at the Alcazar Theater in San Francisco he contracted pneumonia and died on March 10, 1891.

Determined to carry on alone Mrs. Elitch continued to present the best vaudeville and followed with light opera for several seasons. She then decided to organize her own stock company and the first performance on May 30, 1897 was a brilliant event. The first plays were "Helene" by Martha Morton, author of "Fool of Fortune" which the late W. H. Crane had played successfully, and "A Bachelor's Romance" made famous by Sol Smith Russell of beloved memory.

George Edeson directed the first play. James O'Neill, keeping the promise he had made to John Elitch, returned to play the leading role. Jane Kenmark was his leading woman. Others who appeared during that season were Walter Edwards, Margaret May, Ernest Hastings, William Burress, Rolinda Bainbridge, Lenora Bradley and Lillian Dailey.

George Edeson, the first director of the stock company was the father of Robert Edison, later to become one of New York's most renowned stars.

A set and never violated rule laid down by Mr. Edeson was that the members of his company must be artists of experience and that the women members of his cast must always dress well. That rule is still in vogue today. Arnold B. Gurtler, present titular head of the vast enterprise has never engaged an actor or actress for his summer season who was not a competent member of the profession. As no one has ever refused a bid to come to Elitch's for the summer, Mr. Gurtler has always had hundreds of applicants from which to assemble his casts. With salaries on a par to those paid in New York for the regular season, members of the profession have found it not alone profitable to spend a summer in Denver but an ideal vacation resort.

In reading this brief history of the highlights of Elitch's one must remember that it would be utterly impossible to stress every season with an accurate account of the problems involved as the enterprise flourished and blossomed into the famous institution it is today. A half century's history of an organization as famous as "Elitch's" cannot be retold in a story, which the writer is trying to tell in the limited space permitted. He has tried to tell briefly of the glories of the Gardens and the fame of its theater. Much of the story retold here he has gleaned from the history of Elitch's as told by Caroline Lawrence Dier, in her delightful book "The Lady of the Gardens," which was published in 1932. He is grateful to his good friend and co-worker, George Somnes, who was kind enough to suggest that he read the story, so that he might be familiar with the history of the theater and its people.

A veritable gold mine of anecdotes of folks now distinguished in the theater, a few may be retold as a person is permitted to become reminiscent during a Golden Anniversary. The story of Antoinette Perry, producer of many New York hits, is typical of the history of Elitch's. At the tender age of eleven Miss Perry read her first lines on the Elitch stage. Her training here gained for her the enviable position of leading woman for David Warfield. Following her brilliant career as an actress Miss Perry startled New York with a series of plays which she staged expertly. "Strictly Dishonorable" and "Kiss The Boys Goodbye" were produced by her. Her daughter, Margaret Perry, may be remembered as she too has followed in the footsteps of her mother and has been featured in the cinema in Hollywood and on Broadway.

Theater folks know that the late Douglas Fairbanks' first experience was acquired on the Elitch stage. Hearing that a Shakespearean production was to be given and not having sufficient money to purchase a ticket, the lad, he was twelve then, asked permission of the janitor, to do some work that would gain for him enough money to purchase a seat. When told no work was needed he asked if he

might scrub the stage. The stage was scrubbed and the boy received his ticket. Later he became a pupil of Margaret Fealy and a few years later the lad who scrubbed the stage was an accredited member of the company. His first role was that of "Reginald Lumley" in "Cousin Kate." In later life he often retold the story of the boy who loved the theater so dearly that any menial job was a pleasure if the reward was a seat to see a play.

In the early days of The Gardens its zoo was world famous. And the stories of the animals and their antics is intertwined with some of the noted players of the period. Frederick Perry, matinee idol of grandmother's day, was an Elitch favorite. Time meant nothing to Perry and he was usually late arriving for a performance. Hurrying to the theater for a matinee one afternoon, he sensed a bulky form beside him. He barely reached the stage door as "Sam", a large black bear, had managed to get out of his corral and had other plans for Mr. Perry. "Sam" was good natured and harmless but Perry was terrified and the play was almost over before he regained his composure.

A number of fine lions were born in the zoo and many later found their way to famous collections. Rex, the king of all the beasts in the Gardens zoo, was known all over the world and was the model for the great marble guardians of the entrance to the Chicago Art Institute.

One of the first ostriches to be broken to harness was trained here; and hitched to a light wagon, would be driven around the Gardens by Mrs. Elitch, much to the delight of the visitors.

Walter Edwards was the leading man for one of the Garden's most prosperous seasons—1898. The opening play was Frances Hodgson Burnett's "Esmeralda." Margaret Dibdin, noted beauty of the time, was the leading woman, coming to the Gardens fresh from her New York triumph as leading woman for E. H.

Sothern in "The Prisoner of Zenda." Others in that never to be forgotten company included Meta Maynard, Lenora Bradley, Daisy Lovering, Harry Leighton, Thomas W. Ross, W. M. Wadsworth, DeWitt Jennings, J. Rush Bronson, Robert Bell, Ray Southard and Laura Alberta. Truly a breath taking array of famous show folks.

The Spanish-American war was at its height and the floral beds depicting the American and Cuban flags was a sight long to be remembered.

Here too, during this season were shown the Warograph, animated pictures from the Menlo Park studios of Thomas Edison; the grand daddy of all the movies of today. The first to be shown in the West, they created a sensation.

Flushed with the success of the 1898 season, Mrs. Elitch, the following season produced one of the most celebrated productions in the early history of the theater. "Cyrano de Bergerac" had never been given in Denver and the ambitious little lady and her associates determined that Elitch patrons must see the play. It required a cast of one hundred. Undaunted the production was planned and the surrounding country searched for additional talent. The leading roles were enacted by a cast containing such famous artists as Howard Hansel, Henrietta Crosman, J. Henry Kolker, Frederick Conger, Scott Cooper, Brigham Royce, Herman Sheldon, Eleanor Robson, Lillian Dailey, Katherine Field and Madge Cook. Such an aggregation would demand recognition in any city in the world. In the cast of one hundred, the names of some folks may be found who afterward won their spurs in New York. They were playing tiny roles in that famous play. Some were amateurs, fresh from dramatic schools of the time. So they too, learned their first real lessons in dramatic art on the Elitch stage, now so rich in tradition.

The same season saw four of the original members of the New York cast of "Trilby" brought to Denver to play in the Elitch production of the play that had created a furore in the East. Miss Crosman in the title role was acclaimed. Howard Hansel portrayed "Svengali" and important roles were played by Frederick Conger and Frank McVickars.

Highlights of the season at the turn of the century was a series of concerts by the Adelman's Symphony Orchestra. For the first four months of the theater season the superb Herbert Kelcey and the lovely Effie Shannon were engaged to head the acting company. Others included J. T. Sullivan, William F. Owen, George S. Spencer, Brandon Tyna, Blanche Kelleher, Jessie Izett and Louise McIntosh. The beloved Neil Burgess and his New England company were brought to the Gardens later during the season for a weeks engagement of "The Country Fair". Then as a fitting climax Blanche Bates was brought from New York. She arrived with ten trunks, something sensational in those days. She played "The Dancing Girl" and even standing room was at a premium. Her second play was Augustin Daly's greatest comedy hit, "The Last Word". Miss Bates' supporting cast included Robert Drouet, Frederick Perry and John T. Sullivan.

The following season the consolidation of the Manhattan Beach Company and the Elitch Gardens Company was consummated. A splendid production of "As You Like It" was staged with Blanche Bates as "Rosalind." The rear wall of the theater was removed in order that the stage might be extended beneath the stars. "The ultimate achievement of forest and pastoral scenes" the Denver papers said the next day. And thus, without knowing it at the time, the Gardens had, for the first time in America, staged an out-of-door scene with the sky for a ceiling. The practice is quite common today.

The following five years were lush for the Elitch Gardens Theater company. Its fame having spread far and wide, it was not necessary to beg the theatrical folks of the period to come to Denver. They were honored to get the invitation. The 1901 season opened with "Sowing The Wind" with Hobart Bosworth and Eleanor Moretti playing the leading roles. E. J. Morgan played a two week engagement in "The Only Way" and capacity audiences cheered this grand artist.

In July of the same year Blanche Walsh began a four week term opening with the play that made her fame world wide, "Under Two Flags." A resident of Denver, Edward Elsner, had made the dramatization and the opening was one of the biggest of big nights. Miss Walsh also appeared in "Fedora" and "Romeo and Juliet." Miss Walsh played one of her noted roles, "Romeo," Maude Fealy, the "Juliet." She closed her season in "La Tosca." It was said at the time that Miss Walsh was receiving a weekly salary of $750, a sum unheard of in those days. But as standing room was the rule all during the engagement, it was apparent that Miss Walsh earned the sum paid her.

With the departure East of Miss Walsh, Mrs. Elitch tried to induce Blanche Bates to return to Denver and made her a fabulous offer. But Miss Bates was rehearsing a new play for Charles Frohman at the time and was compelled to refuse.

Closing the season in a blaze of glory, Rose Coghlan gave one of her entrancing performances as "Peg Woffington." She also presented "A Woman of No Importance," Oscar Wilde's comedy that is still revived today. She closed her season with "The Rivals." It was a summer season that will be recalled as long as Elitch's endures.

During the next five years the Gardens upheld the fine reputation its companies had achieved. Walter Clarke Bellows, who had staged a host of big hits in New York was brought to Denver. With him came such favorites of the day as John Mason, Lillian Lawrence, John T. Sullivan, Frederick Sullivan, Edmund Lyons,

William H. Tooker, Joseph W. Wheeler, Jr., Louise Rial, and Antoinette Walker.

The first play of the 1902 season was Frank Mayo's dramatization of Mark Twain's "Pudd'nhead Wilson." The press the following day hailed the company and play. The papers also spoke of the many improvements made in the theater. The stage had been widened, boxes rearranged and attractively redecorated. A beautiful presentation of "A Midsummer Night's Dream" followed the Mark Twain play, with John Mason as "Lysander" and Jessie Bartlett Davis. Miss Davis, whose superb voice was known all over America, created a sensation in Denver. At the time she was the star of that gallant organization known as The Bostonians, hailed by critics of the day as the most competent group of singers of the generation.

Hero worshipers followed Miss Davis on her shopping tours around the city and did everything to show their adoration.

Stanley Weyman's "Under The Red Robe," with Frederick Perry in the leading role, followed the Shakespearean production and later during the summer Herbert Kelcey and Effie Shannon played "Her Lord and Master" and "My Lady Dainty." These stage idols of the day are still remembered by the drama lovers of another generation.

Mrs. Elitch created another sensation that season when the largest balloon ever seen in the west was brought to the Gardens. Its designers preferred to call it an "Aerostat." Sixty-five feet in diameter and more than two hundred in circumference, one hundred and five feet high, with a lifting power of forty five tons, it was indeed a spectacular sight. The first ascension was cheered by every resident of Denver.

The season was also noted for the return of Maude Fealy, then known as the youngest American star. She had made her debut at the age of three on the Elitch stage and was returning after fifteen years to receive one of the largest salaries ever paid an artist in Denver. At that time she was the leading woman for that stalwart artist, E. S. Willard. Known all over America, a favorite in London, she was lionized by Denver society.

The gracious and brilliant Henrietta Crosman opened the 1903 season auspiciously; "As You Like It," "The Sword Of The King" and "Mistress Nell" were Miss Crosman's vehicles and in each she achieved the ultimate. Miss Crosman also startled the residents of Denver by driving her new "horseless" carriage. A reception tendered Miss Crosman in the Rustic Lane was attended by every socially prominent person in the city.

Aubrey Boucicault joined the company later in the summer and played "A Gentleman From France." Son of the famous Dion Boucicault, for half a century a London idol, the young leading man soon endeared himself and became a great favorite. His father was the first person to give a matinee in America. It was in New Orleans and the doors were opened at eleven "so that family parties might be nicely established and ready for the twelve o'clock curtain."

Denver also welcomed favorites of other seasons who returned. In the group were Marie Wainwright, Esther Lyon, Ada Dwyer, Channez Olney, Mabel Pennock, Ethylyn Clemens, Mabel Adams, William Humphrey, Theodore Roberts, J. Henry Kolker, Charles Mackey, Herman Sheldon, Hardee Kirkland and Joseph Kaufman.

In August, 1904, The Chicago Sunday Tribune said: "While the rest of the country has been in the theatrical dumps, the city of Denver has been the bright spot on the map. Much of the best of the fare given during the winter and spring to the east and middle west has been served to Denver theater goers since June 1, and served, too, under conditions nearly ideal from the popular viewpoint.

"What would Chicago think of a stock company containing such players as Theodore Roberts, J. H. Gilmour, Frederick Perry, Helen Tracy, Edward Mackay, and Julia Stewart." Praise well deserved.

Stars still came to Denver to augment the regular acting company. Magnificent support was given to Amelia Bingham, Maude Fealy, Edwin Arden, May Buckley, Edward Mackay, Frederick Perry, Blanche Walsh and others. Miss Fealy, by now "Denver's Own," was welcomed in two plays, "The Cavalier" and "When Knighthood Was In Flower." Later in the summer she played the dual role in "The Prince and The Pauper." At the conclusion of her engagement, Miss Fealy was presented with a handsome loving cup, the presentation speech being made by Governor Peabody of Colorado.

The season of 1905 proved a momentous one for the now famous theatrical institution. Minnie Maddern Fiske came direct from a thirty-one week season in New York to play "Leah Kleschna." Her supporting company included such brilliant artists as George Arliss, John Mason, Charles Cartwright and William B. Mack.

Sarah Bernhardt coming to Elitch's! That was the news that greeted Denverites in 1906. Startling news. Accustomed to the best, the news that the "Divine Sarah" was coming, proved more than sensational. And this great and beloved actress helped make Elitch history. The regular Elitch company were proud to serve as supers in Miss Bernhardt's French cast. "Camille" was given during a matinee and "La Sorciere" in the evening. Never in the history of the theater had such a group of "supers" walked on any stage prior to the appearance of Mme. Bernhardt. They included May Buckley, Olive Oliver, Olive Wyndham, Katherine Field, Julia Blanc, Edward Mackay, Frederick Paulding, J. H. Gilmour, Geoffrey Stein, George Boniface and Harry Stubbs. Years afterwards they would boast proudly, "I played with Sarah Bernhardt." Denver thrilled and ever remembered the two wonderful performances.

On thru the years. Great Stars. Superb Plays. The best always. 1908; David Belasco, always a friend of Elitch's sends his bright star, David Warfield, to play "The Music Master," the drama that had created a sensation in New York. Without doubt that famous line, "If you don't want her I want her," has been used more frequently than any line from any play in American drama history. Mr. Warfield also played another of his great roles, the old soldier in "A Grand Army Man." A former Denver girl returns to her home city as Mr. Warfield's leading woman, Antoinette Perry. It might be mentioned in passing, that Mr. Warfield is still with us. He lives in retirement in New York, spending his days and evenings in the Lambs Club, New York, playing bridge with his old friend, Benjamin F. Roeder, for half a century David Belasco's business manager and friend. David Belasco passed away May 14, 1931. Former members of his staff make annual visits to his final resting place at Linden Hills, Long Island, on the anniversary of his passing.

It's quite possible that a few folks still recall the terrific storm that held up the curtain for "The Music Master" for almost one hour. Street cars were halted, but drama lovers refused to permit the elements to keep them from a performance of David Warfield.

The surrounding towns proclaimed August 30 "Warfield Day" and excursions were arranged from Colorado Springs, Pueblo, Greeley, Fort Collins and even from Cheyenne, Wyoming. Surely a magnificent gesture that no one could possibly forget.

1911 brings William Collier, affectionately known to millions as "Willie," to Elitch's in plays that had established him as one of the great comedians of all times. "The Patriot," "The Country Boy," "Caught In The Rain" and "The Man from Mexico" were projected to capacity audiences. Mr. Collier had his now famous stepson, Willie Jr., as a member of his company. A wee lad then, young Collier is now a name in Hollywood. A writer in a New York paper said at the time, in speaking of the theatrical season, "It seems the cream of New York's players are to be seen in the 1911 Elitch Gardens Stock Company."

Milton Sills was the new leading man for the 1912 season and Louise Woods, the leading woman. "The Chaperon" was the first play and others of the season included "The Witching Hour" by Augustus Thomas, said to be the first play written in America, with mental telepathy as its theme. "The Deep Purple," "Seven Sisters," "Her Husband's Wife," "Salvation Nell," "Mother" and "The Awakening of Helena Richie" were among the plays presented. Others in that popular cast were Louise Woods, Jennie Eustace, Janet Dunbar, Walter Edwards, Forrest Winant, Clarence Handysides, Grace Carlyle, DeWitt Jennings, Robert Harrison and Geoffrey Stein. Helen Ware appeared during August playing "The Third Degree," one of this noted artist's best known plays.

On thru the years the standard of plays and players was always maintained. The finest artists in the American theater continued to appear on the Elitch stage. As new stars were born their services were secured. We find among the 1913 personnel such noted players as Jean Shelby, Ralph Morgan, Pedro De Cordoba, Ben Johnson, Alice Wilson, Justina Wayne, Eve Vincent, Dorothy Dalton, Bob Morris, and others of equal stature. In June, 1916, the Gardens silver jubilee was celebrated with Mayor Wolf Londoner officiating. "The Spendthrift" was the jubilee year play with Bruce McRae and Thais Magrane in the leading roles. Later in the season Jane Grey joined the company as Miss Magrane left to fill another engagement. Some of the supporting cast were Nina Gleason, Charles Miller, Charles Brokate, Albert Perry, Richard Barker, and Spring Byington. Plays of the season included "You Can Never Tell," "The Neighbor's Wife," "The Lottery Man," "Trial Marriage," "The Deserter," "The Master of the House" and "The Yellow Ticket."

In 1916 John M. Mulvihill assumed the direction of the Gardens and the theater. His regime was brilliant and constructive. Improvements were made in every department of the vast enterprise. He was an ardent lover of the arts, and the plays and players he selected followed the tradition long established.

At the time, he did not believe that the enterprise would require all his time. Having other business interests, he took the responsibility owing to his interest in the cultural advantages of the theater.

But he was soon to realize that the theater, the amusement park, and the greenhouses needed all his attention. In 1921 he severed all business connections and from that moment, all his energy and business acumen was used for but one purpose—, to carry on, and to hold the position the Gardens and theater had established in the affection of the people of Denver. An indefatigable worker and possessing boundless energy, his success was immediate. He engaged Rollo Lloyd as director for his first company, which included in its personnel Ann Mason, Helen Luttrelle, Charles Trowbridge, Richard Carlyle, Marion Ballou, Peggy Boland, Earl Mitchell, Albert Brown, George Pauncefort, Beach Cooke, and Hal Crane.

In the years that followed, glorious years in Elitch's history, Mr. Mulvihill brought to the famous boards of the theater such well known theatrical personages as Helen Menken, Edward G. Robinson, Violet Heming, Paul Gordon, Ernest

Glendenning, C. Henry Gordon, Sylvia Sydney, Isobel Elsom, Albert Hackett, Fredric March, Cora Witherspoon, Florence Eldridge, Tow Powers, Edna James, Douglas Dumbrille, Moffatt Johnson, Flora Sheffield, Madge Evans, George Brent, Lily Cahill, Florence Rittenhouse, Lea Penman, June Walker and Harold Lloyd.

In 1927 Mr. Mulvihill gave a garden party for the "Trelawney of The Wells" company who were playing an engagement at the Broadway Theater. Mary Elitch Long assisted Mr. Mulvihill and again met several former Elitch favorites who were in that all star aggregation. Effie Shannon and Henrietta Crosman were among them.

The death of Mr. Mulvihill in 1930 was a distinct shock to the entire community. The theater was flourishing and the vast enterprise was at the height of its success. His son-in-law, Arnold B. Gurtler, succeeded him as president of The Elitch Gardens Company and is, at present, its titular head.

Altho the theater in the East was having a terrific struggle to survive, Elitch's, under Mr. Gurtler's management, continued to give the people of Denver the best talent and plays procurable. Players of the stature of Roger Prior, Selena Royle, Millicent Hanley, Jessie Busley, Leonard Mudie, Elizabeth Love, and Orville Harris were brought to Denver by Mr. Gurtler. He was one of the first theatrical managers to recognize the potential talent of Don Woods when he engaged him in 1933. The success he has achieved is now well known to all theatrical minded folks.

It would be presumptuous on the part of any one to endeavor to recount the glories of Elitch's during the past decade. Its achievements are known to every theater lover in Denver. They are as proud of its history as any resident of London of "Old Vic." The old London playhouse may be a bit older in years, but its tradition is no richer than "The Glory That Is Elitch's." Each has achieved greatness. Each has given to the drama productions of rare scenic beauty, and players who have risen to the heights.

The writer, being "of the theater," has listened for two decades to stories of "Elitch productions" and "Elitch players." Wherever folks of the theater gather, the talk would ultimately turn to Denver and the theater in the beautiful gardens, the spectacular productions and the stature of its personnel.

He learned years ago that "Out Where The West Begins" was a rustic theater, a playhouse as rich in tradition as any theater in the World. He feels sure that Elitch's will continue to make theatrical history so long as it remains in the loving care of its present head, his heirs and assigns forever.

75. LAKEWOOD THEATRE
Skowhegan, Maine
Opened June 24, 1901

The oldest and one of the most influential summer theaters on the East Coast, the Lakewood Theatre in Skowhegan, Maine, was designated in 1967 as the official theater of the State of Maine. This playhouse in the woods has presented outstanding theatrical performances for residents and summer visitors since the summer of 1901 and throughout its history has maintained a very high quality of production.

The importance of this playhouse was recognized fairly early, when in June 1927 the following article appeared in the *American Magazine*:

75:1 The final curtain had fallen: and the audience, still laughing over the comedy which had just ended, was moving slowly toward the exits. It was the first night of a new play by Howard Lindsay and Bert

75:1. Allan Harding, "Broadway Comes to Lakewood," *American Magazine*, June 1927, pp. 144–51.

Robinson, familiar figures in the metropolitan world of the theatre.

The cast, headed by Arthur Byron, was a striking one. Even the "Voices Off Stage" were the voices of actors well known on Broadway. The settings were carefully built; the scenery excellently painted. The house was crowded and the audience enthusiastic.

In short, the whole atmosphere was that of a typical Broadway production in a first-class New York playhouse.

But—when the spectators reached the exits they did not step out into the blaze of the Great White Way! No clanging of street cars or hooting of taxicabs assailed their ears! And although it was early in August no wave of heat met them at the wide-open doors. Instead, they passed from the brightly lighted theatre straight into the velvety darkness of the Maine woods. Through the trees came a cool breath of wind from a lake, whose little waves could be heard swishing softly along the shore. The noise and heat and glare of New York seemed a million miles away.

It was an extraordinary experience. Imagine seeing first-class actors produce first-class plays in a well-appointed theatre away up in the Maine woods! And not for one night only, but six nights a week for a season of thirteen weeks! Some of the fish stories from those same Maine woods are easier to believe.

And here is something else which will tax your credulity. This theatre seats 750 persons.* Many nights the company plays to capacity houses! The weekly attendance averages 3,500; almost 600 a night. Yet the theatre is six miles from the nearest town.

"Then where do the audiences come from?" you demand.

"The answer is that they come from as far as seventy-five or even one hundred

*The theater was later renovated, and the seating capacity increased to 1070.

miles away; from the Canadian border on the north to Portland on the south; from Bangor on the east to the New Hampshire boundary on the west.

If you want to measure the appeal of this unique theatre, look at a map of the region from which it draws its audiences. Much of that region is wilderness. Other portions are sparsely settled. There are many towns and villages, to be sure; but, taken all together, they do not contain as many people as you will find within a mile or two of a Broadway theatre any night of the season.

When Governor Brewster came to this playhouse in the heart of the woods he declared that it ought to be called "The Mousetrap." He was thinking of the familiar saying, that if any man builds even a better mousetrap than other men have built, the world will make a pathway through the wilderness to his door.

People do come, some of them actually through the wilderness, to the door of this theatre. And they come because one man has had the vision, courage, and patience to create something that is worth the journey. The Lakewood Theatre is only one detail, although it is the most unusual one, in the vision he has been striving, for twenty-five years, to realize.

A man with less courage and less patience would long ago have lowered his aims. But Herbert Swett has stuck to his conviction that there are people everywhere, and a great many of them, who want the really fine things of life; the things which are fine, mentally, morally, and physically.

The story of the Lakewood Theatre begins with this man; but it does not end with him. Into it come other characters: the men and the women who, by their eagerness for the really fine things of life, have justified his faith in them.

The story begins about twenty-five years ago, with a chance meeting between two young men at Bowdoin College, in Brunswick, Maine. One of them, Mr.

Briggs, was already a graduate. The other, Herbert Swett, was just about to receive his diploma.

Briggs, who was a woolen manufacturer, had married the daughter of General Shepherd, one of the leading citizens of Skowhegan. Not long before the Commencement Week meeting between the two former college friends, General Shepherd had died. His son-in-law, Briggs, was temporarily managing the business interests of the general's widow.

It was a burden he could not carry indefinitely, and he was looking for someone to whom he could entrust it. Swett, in his management of various college activities, had proved himself able, energetic, and loyal. So Briggs asked him what he was going to do after graduation.

"Haven't decided," was the answer.

"Why don't you come to Skowhegan and take charge of Mrs. Shepherd's business affairs?" said Briggs.

They talked the matter over; and as a result of that chance meeting, the young Bowdoin graduate undertook the management of the Shepherd estate.

Among the interests involved was a street railway property owned by the Somerset Traction Company; and one of its assets was a small amusement park on the shore of Lake Wesserrunsett, then called Hayden's Pond, six miles from Skowhegan.

This car line served the country folk who lived near it. But its chief revenue in summer was the nickels paid by the townspeople for their outings at the park.

It hardly deserved to be called a "park" when Herbert Swett first saw it. The lake shore at that point was low and swampy. As one approached by the road, the only "view" was the ugly rear of a cheap hotel, decorated with ash heaps and garbage cans. The amusement devices were crude; the grounds littered and unkempt.

At one side stood a bare, barnlike theatre which would seat a few hundred people. Inside and outside, it was about as ugly as it possibly could be. But to the young man who, even then, had a firm faith in the finer instincts of human nature, this old barn of a building suggested far-reaching possibilities.

Admission to the theatre for people who rode on the electric cars was but a nickle, while those who lived in the Grove were admitted for ten cents.

At the time of Swett's advent, in 1901, a summer stock company had been engaged to present plays in this theatre, under the direction of James Durkin, an experienced stock actor.

You can imagine how much money, or, rather, how little, the players received when the admission was only a dime or less. Yet they put in the season there and did as good work as was then possible.

There are two groups of characters in this story who share the honors with Mr. Swett; and I am going to pay my respects to one of these groups right now.

This summer will be the tweny-seventh consecutive season of the Lakewood Players, which is believed to be the longest uninterrupted record of any stock company in the United States.

Now, I want to ask you to analyze your feeling about actors in general, to place beside this feeling the facts concerning the Lakewood Players, and to see whether they agree.

Isn't it true that actors seem rather artificial to you? Don't you think of them as caring only to be in the limelight of the stage, to breathe only the air of the theatre? Haven't you labeled them, in your own mind, as vain, jealous, self-seeking? Have you ever thought of them as sharing your own simple, wholesome tastes? You have dreamed, perhaps, of spending weeks in the Maine woods or some other haunt of nature lovers. But would you ever have dreamed of an actor as your ideal of a companion?

I doubt it. Yet, for more than a quarter of a century, there has been no dearth of actors at Lakewood. On the contrary, ten times as many as can be used there are eager to go.

Because of the money reward? Decidedly not! They go because they love just what you and I love!

I went to Lakewood myself last summer. I watched the members of the stock company rehearsing in the morning, playing in the afternoon, and play-acting in the evening. I never saw a happier set of people. And the secret of their happiness was that they were combining play and work! The work was just as necessary to their enjoyment as the play was.

Having been introduced to this group of figures in the story, let us go back to Herbert Swett, the leading character in it. Here, too, our traditional notions about people are likely to receive a stimulating jolt.

Mr. Swett, is a business man; a rather stout, rather bald gentleman, with the crisp, efficient manner of the typical office executive. He can think and talk in terms of dollars and cents.

But a surprising number of these unromantic-looking business men possess a certain unsuspected trait: They sincerely want their business to "show a profit" in something more than dollars and cents. They have their ideals; and they try to bring them into their business.

Herbert Swett is this kind of business man. When he found himself running a street-car line to an amusement park which was really a man-made scar "on the fair face of Nature," he began to work toward his ideal of what such a park might be.

Today, as you approach Lakewood by the road, you do not see a phalanx of garbage cans. You do not see even the rear of a cheap hotel. Instead, there is a vine-wreathed pergola, through whose white pillars come glimpses of blue water.

That pergola might be said to mark the site of a battle fought and won. When Mr. Swett proposed tearing down the hotel, the suggestion was received with consternation.

What! Tear down something that brought in money? Not much money, to be sure, but a little, nevertheless. Tear it down and put up a pergola, which wouldn't yield a nickel in revenue?

People thought he was crazy. They could not see, as he did, that order and cleanliness and beauty have an actual cash value.

As time went on, this battle for his ideals was fought again and again. After some years, Mrs. Shepherd, on whose sympathetic understanding he could always count, died. There were other changes in the personnel of his associates. Finally it came to a definite break. As he baldly described it, he was fired.

The situation was not one that would encourage a man to have faith in the ideal he had striven for. But Herbert Swett's faith remained unshaken. With a little backing from friends who shared his ideas, he acquired the traction company property, including the park.

During the previous twenty years, he had accomplished something toward its transformation. Now, with absolute control, he staked everything on his belief that peaple do want the finer things in life—beauty, simplicity, wholesome recreation, all that stimulates body and mind.

Other summer resorts have done some of the things which he is doing at Lakewood.

Other resorts have horses for riding, links for golfers, a country club for dancing, a tea-house, tennis courts, and dinners and bridge parties. They too, have canoeing and sailing and speed-boats. But Lakewood alone has the Lakewood Players! That institution is unique.

Two years ago, the old barn was enlarged and made into a real theatre. There wasn't any too much money with which to accomplish the transformation; not enough to spend on external show, if the interior was to be made comfortable and properly equipped. Outside, it is just a neat white building without architectural pretensions, although this will be changed in time.

But it is a real theatre; and in certain ways it is unlike any other theatre I have seen.

In the first place, it is always open! The doors are not closed, from early in the morning until after the audience has departed at night. All day long, people wander in and out.

The curtain is not down. There is the stage, set for the first act of the evening performance. On either side of the auditorium are groups of windows, with inside window boxes, filled with flowering plants. These windows, hung with gay cretonne curtains, open into the forest. But I watched the people, and they came and went; and it was not the forest outside that claimed their interest. Sometimes they would sit there for fifteen minutes without saying a word, or speaking only in hushed voices, almost as if they were in a church.

It may seen a little thing, this keeping the house open during the day; but it is an example of Herbert Swett's instinctive understanding of human nature.

To most of us the theatre, with its tremendous power to influence us, has been quite another world from the one in which we live. Not one person in a thousand ever sees the interior of a playhouse except during a performance.

If a city manager would leave his doors open, as some churches do, and let us go in and out at will, I believe there would come a subtle sense of mutual "belonging" which would bring our world and the world of the theatre much closer together.

To the people who go to Lakewood, this theatre is as accessible as your grocery store is to you. They have an everyday intimacy with it. If it wasn't a first-class playhouse they would resent the fact; just as you would resent having to buy your food at an unsanitary market.

It seems to me a fine thing that they should have that feeling. Yet this particular method of achieving the result never had occurred to me until I saw how Mr. Swett has done it at Lakewood.

In talking with me about the Lakewood playhouse, a good many people have spoken of it as a "unique theatrical venture." But if it were only that, I should not be writing about it. To me it seems an extraordinary human adventure.

Over and over again, Mr. Swett has had tempting offers from people who wanted to put in the "jazz" features common in most amusement parks. He refused these offers, even when he sorely needed money to develop his own plans.

He was called visionary and impractical. His ideals were laughed at. To give the best plays in the Maine woods, for instance! How would he foot the bills? Maine was a notoriously bad theatrical state, anyway. Even the town theatres, putting on cheap road shows, had hard sledding.

To all of which Mr. Swett replied: "Perhaps they have hard sledding because they put on cheap shows. Perhaps Maine is a bad theatrical state because its people want something better than they are offered. I was born and brought up in Maine. I know that I, for one, want the best, in the theatre and in everything else. I have enough faith in the people of my state to believe that they want it too."

We were in his office, which is in one corner of the theatre building, when he repeated this to me. We had been sitting there an hour, talking of his dreams and efforts at Lakewood. The conversation had been interrupted, every few minutes, by telephone calls. They came from Skowhegan, Madison, Augusta, Bangor, Jackman—almost at the Canadian border; from Solon, Bingham, Guilford; from villages too small to dream of supporting a theatre of any kind; even from farmhouses on lonely country roads.

These telephone calls were orders for seats: "bunches" of seats; three, four, five; even one for a theater party of twenty!

During the performance, the previous night, more than two hundred automobiles were parked under the trees which flank the roadway. After the play was over, it took these cars half an hour to pass, in a steady stream, up the road to the main highway.

There the stream divided and whirled away in three directions. Many of those cars would not reach their destination inside of an hour. Some of them would be two hours or more on the way. Lakewood plays begin promptly at eight and close at ten-thirty. But, even so, it would be early morning before some of the audience would get to bed. And in a region where early rising is more or less of a necessity this means decidedly more than it would in a city.

An audience at Lakewood is an interesting slice of life. In it you may see such men as Judge Pattengall, of the Supreme Court of Maine, one of the most brilliant lawyers in the state. He attends every play that is given during the season. Or you may see the head of a great corporation, with a party of guests—important business men from Boston or New York. You will find there "the best people" from the state capital, aristocratic Augusta.

But you will find, also, little groups from the villages "up-river;" people who are as hungry for entertainment. What kind of entertainment?

Well, how about "Outward Bound," a play which captivated the critics and other alleged high-brows? These Maine folks packed the Lakewood theatre every night of the week that "Outward Bound" was presented. They liked it so well that they asked to have it repeated. They crowded the house to see "The Green Goddess," "The Boomerang," "The Ghost Between," and other metropolitan successes. They are eager for the best in plays and in acting; and they appreciate the best when it is given them.

In some ways, the performances at this literally backwoods theatre are better than the New York ones. The company is called a "stock company;" but probably no other stock company can show so brilliant a list of members.

The director is Howard Lindsay, who directed the Broadway production of "The Poor Nut," "Dulcy," "To the Ladies," "The Haunted House," and other successful plays. Any city stock company would jump at the chance of getting Howard Lindsay. He goes to Lakewood instead; simply because he is happier there.

For the same reason, Arthur Byron heads the list of players. With his long and brilliant record on the stage, he is perhaps the star of the company. Stars are supposed to be decidedly "high hat"— jealous of their prestige, insistent on having all the "fat roles." Yet Arthur Byron, after playing the lead one week, will take a minor part, or even a small "bit" in the next week's production.

That is the spirit of the whole company. It is a splendid example of teamwork. No one tries to grab all the glory. In fact no one wants all the glory, because no one wants to do all the work! That is the understanding; divide the work so that everybody will get a chance to rest and to play.

The members of the company live in separate bungalows along the lake front; but they take their meals at a clubhouse which Mr. Swett has provided for their use. Here they eat at a common table.

If you could attend one of these plays, you would be amazed to learn that each one is put on after only five rehearsals. This would be impossible if the members of the cast were not experienced actors.

In one case, this was not true. Last summer, "The Old Soak" was given at Lakewood; and the leading role was played by its author, Don Marquis, the famous newspaper columnist and writer. It was Marquis's debut as an actor; but he gave a wonderful interpretation of the character which he had created.

There is another amazing thing about these Lakewood productions: A new play is put on each week—and the same scenery is never used twice!

If the theatre were in a city, there would be immense storehouses, crammed with scenery, stage settings, and properties, which could be rented. But these resources do not exist in the Maine woods! Yet, every single week of the season, the Lakewood stage blossoms out with newly painted scenery and newly-built settings. Where do they come from?

One morning, in search of the answer to this question, I went "backstage" to look around. I found myself in a lofty, open space, with a huge canvas leaning against the end wall. It was painted to represent a Spanish interior; and standing in front of it, was a man in paint-stained overalls.

This man's name is Charles F. Perkins, although it has been genially shortened to "Perk" by his Lakewood friends. I wish I could give Perk a story all by himself. He deserves it. For ten years he has been the scenic artist of this unique theatre; and as a scenic artist he, also, is unique.

Mr. Perkins lives "up at the corners," a group of three or four houses at a country crossroads. Originally, he was a house painter. During the spring and fall, house painting is still his occupation, but during the summer he becomes an artist, and by no means the least interesting of the unusual features of Lakewood life.

He has had no outside training for that job. He never has been backstage in a city theatre. He has taught himself the technique of his work. He must paint scenes from various countries and of various historical periods; but there are no art galleries or rich libraries to which he can go for ideas and for accuracy of detail.

When I asked him about this, he pointed to the iron-bound trunk on which I was sitting. His art galleries and libraries were in that trunk! It contained, so he told me, thousands of prints and photographs which he has been collecting for years; scenes from all over the world; streets and houses, exteriors and interiors; mountains and valleys; rivers and lakes and seas.

The day of my visit, he was preparing for the next week's production of "The Squall," a Spanish play by Madame Jean Bart. Incidentally, it was to be the first production of this drama in any theatre! The Maine "back country" was to see it before New York did. The author herself was there. Blanche Yurka and Pedro de Cordoba had come to Lakewood, to be guest stars in the production. A brilliant theatrical premiere in the heart of the wilderness!

I said before that taste and intelligence are not a matter of geography. I want to add that talent and ability are not a matter of social rank. If you doubt this theory, try it out in your own community. Try it in your civic activities, your school boards, your women's clubs. I have seen it done. And I have watched the general surprise when some hitherto humble citizen, or obscure housewife, turned out to be a shrewd counselor or to have some unexpected talent.

We talk glibly about "the best people" in our town. But we don't really know who the best people are, unless we give all of them a chance to show their value to the community.

That little sermon was preached to me, back-stage at the Lakewood Theatre, as I talked with Charles Perkins, gray-haired graduate from house painting.

Hanging on the walls were some of the small settings he had made for "The Green Goddess," a play whose scenes are laid in the Himalayan Mountains. I asked him how he, a Maine countryman, could paint these scenes.

"There's more than one way of traveling," he replied calmly. "Some people go al over the world, and see nothing. Some stay at home, and see pretty near everything. If you ain't got imagination there's no use traveling. And if you have got it you don't need to travel. I never was any nearer to the Orient than I am this minute. But I can feel what it's like because I have imagination.

"But you musn't think I depend entirely on that. I study a whole lot. I've got to be a good many things besides an artist. When I paint mountains, for instance, I got to be a geologist. I want to know how a stratum of rocks would run. I wouldn't want some scientist to look at my scenery, and say, "That ain't right! Them rocks wouldn't run that way!"

"When we put on 'The Bad Man,' I had to paint scenes out West in the desert, and folks said to me, 'How can you do that, when you ain't never been West?'

"But I could do it, because I know just how that dry burning heat would feel; and how the sunlight would make blue shadows on the sand. I got to know about air and climate and geography."

He picked up an illustrated magazine, and showed me a scene in Spain.

"For one act in this new play," he said, "I wanted to show, through an archway, a glimpse of distant mountains. I could have painted 'em in just any old way. But I dug up this picture of Spanish mountains. Then I figured out what season it was, the time of day, and what the air would be like, so I could get the right effect."

All this, for a mere detail of one scene, in a play that was to be given one week, in the Maine woods!

While we were talking, other "artists" were at work, each in his own way, to make this one-week production as perfect as possible.

In a separate building, the stage carpenter—another native product—was building the sets under the direction of James Bell, a well-known New York stage manager. Somewhere else, a native seamstress was making the costumes. On the stage itself, a brilliant cast was rehearsing the play. And, in the front office, the man whose vision and whose faith had brought all this about was reserving seats for people from many miles away.

It was an extraordinary bringing together of those who are eager to give the best and of those who crave to receive the best.

I asked one of the playwrights who summer at Lakewood how the audiences there compare with metropolitan ones.

"They are better!" he declared with emphasis. "Among theatrical folks there is a common saying that 'New York is the biggest bunch of rubes in the country.' Here at Lakewood we get the cream of the people for miles around; good old American stock shrewd and intelligent. It is a joy to play to them. I wish there were hundreds of theatres like this one. It would be a great thing for the American drama and a great thing for the American people.

"But that would mean having hundreds of men like Herbert Swett! Men who combine business sense with idealism— and who have the courage to build on that combination.

"Perhaps you haven't noticed one interesting thing about this place. Did you ever before see an amusement park without a policeman, or any kind of officer to preserve order? There is none here, and there is no need of one. The place has no pretensions to luxury or show. But everyone who comes here reacts instinctively to Mr. Swett's ideas of simplicity, quiet, order, and natural beauty. The spirit of jazz can't get in here. He won't let it in. And no one is more grateful to him than we stage folks are. I wish the season lasted six months instead of thirteen weeks.

"When Blanche Yurka arrived, the other day, it was raining; not the best conditions under which to see the place for the first time. But when someone asked her how long she could stay, she drew a deep breath and said, 'I don't know. But if I keep on feeling as I do now, I'll be here until Christmas!' It is that way with us all. We wish we could stay here, resting and playing and working indefinitely."

As for the Maine folks, they echo that wish. They know these actors as Broadway cannot know them. They see them off the stage; Arthur Byron and James Bell in corduroy trousers and flannel shirts, building a sailboat; Howard Lindsay and Robert Hudson and Pedro de Cordoba having afternoon tea at the well-named Arcadia Tea House,* while a dozen ladies from Skowhegan are enjoying a bridge party in the adjoining room.

Last summer they could see Don Marquis honeymooning there with his bride, Marguerite Vonnegut, the actress. Lakewood visitors learned to know the Kathryn Keyes of the stage as Mrs. Arthur Byron; and they saw the two young daughters of Mr. and Mrs. Byron make their debut in the Lakewood Theatre.

Nedda Harrigan, daughter of the once famous Harrigan of "Harrigan and Hart," was there with her husband, Walter Connolly, who acted last in "Applesauce." So were Albert Hackett, vacationing briefly from "The Cradle Snatchers;" Dorothy Stickney, Hortense Alden, Estelle Carter, Eric Dressler, Cornelius Van Voorhies, and Sam Wren.

The last-named gentleman performed the duties of publicity representative; and that reminds me of how this publicity has grown. Twenty years ago, the Lakewood

*The Arcadia Tea Room was torn down and the Lakewood Inn built on that site.

plays were advertised in only the two nearby towns, Skowhegan and Madison. Last season they were advertised in one hundred and twenty-five cities and towns!

"We are doing sixty per cent more business this year than last," Mr. Swett told me. "We are just striking our gait now—and it is a gait that goes by leaps and bounds. But the goal isn't going to be changed! It is the same one I had before me all through the years when I could only creep toward it, an inch at a time, as it seemed."

"And that goal?" I asked.

"Well," he said, "I guess I am trying to give people a chance to be healthy and happy; to give them surroundings which will be good for both mind and body. I have staked everything on my belief that people do want what is really fine. I have proved that the people of my own state want it. And although I, naturally, am prejudiced in favor of Maine," he smiled, "I don't suppose we have any monopoly of intelligence. I'd be willing to try this same experiment in any state of the Union."

The story of the Lakewood Theatre was updated in August 1969.

75:2   "Curtain going up" has been heard at the Lakewood Theatre for nearly 70 years—longer than in any other summer theater in the United States. Its story could almost make the plot for one of its plays—for in its 68 years of entertaining the people of Maine and her summer visitors, there has been excitement, discouragement, romance, tragedy, success and failure—coupled with the names and the influence of some of the outstanding stars of screen, television and the Great White Way.

At the turn of the century Lake Wes-

75:2. "Lakewood—America's Oldest Summer Theatre," *News and Views,* Aug. 1969. Reprinted courtesy Depositors Trust Company, Augusta, Maine.

serunsett's shores were popular in the summer as an amusement area. Here there were a theater, picnic area, bathing beach and rides for the children. Each day the *Marguerite B,* a 35-foot steamer, circled the lake bringing passengers to enjoy this picturesque site in Somerset County. Here, also, was the Somerset Traction Company which operated trolleys between Madison and Skowhegan— taking passengers from the boat to these towns to shop, or bringing picnickers to the amusement park for a day's outing.

In 1901, fresh from his graduation at Bowdoin College, Herbert Lindsey Swett assumed the management of the trolley line and amusement park for the widow of General R. B. Shepherd. He saw things to be done—he dreamed dreams and he had visions of what Lakewood could become—but his employer did not share his visions, and little could be done to change the swampy land, the tumbledown hotel, the modest restaurant, the bandstand, bowling alley and open-air lunch counter. There were also the children's playground and a few cages of monkeys and bears. One addition he made was the present pagoda near the tennis courts which he built to hide the view behind the "Arcadia Tea Room" of trash and garbage cans. His unwarranted expense was not appreciated.

Not until 1922 did the setting begin to change. The old inn was torn down and the first of the guest cottages was built. Two years later the *Marguerite B* was deliberately blown up in the middle of the lake as the highlight of the Fourth of July celebration. With the advent of the automobile, this means of transportation from the other side of the lake was no longer necessary—and only a few years later the trolley line fell to the progress of transportation.

In 1926 Herbert Swett realized his ambition, purchased the property, razed the bandstand and opened the new Country

Club. The next year the present inn was built and new cottages were added each year. A gift shop was added to the inn, and in 1937–38, the patio dining area was enclosed almost doubling the seating capacity of the restaurant.

The grounds underwent as drastic changes as the buildings. Low areas were drained, trees carefully selected for removal to make way for expansion yet maintain the natural beauty of the Lakewood setting with its evergreens and graceful white birches. Lawns, flower gardens, tennis courts and a nine-hole golf course have been added through the years.

Today there are 45 cottages with one to three rooms—each with an open fireplace and fully equipped with screens. The cottages and lodge can accommodate as many as 150 guests at a time. In addition, through the years many celebrities —directors, playwrights, actors and actresses alike—have found the scene so delightful they have built their own cottages to which they returned year after year. One of these was John B. Hymer, well-known writer of vaudeville skits, who later turned playwright. He came to Lakewood as a director in 1917 and was so charmed by its beauty and atmosphere, he arranged with Mr. Swett to build a large, attractive dwelling, known today as the Colony House. His son, Warren, later, became known as a movie star.

The visitor to Lakewood Theatre may anticipate one of the modern packaged shows shown each week from June to Labor Day—and he will not be disappointed—for the programs include top shows from Broadway with headlined stars of stage, screen or television. But as one walks through the lobby, walls lined with photos and programs from the seven decades of the theater's history bring nostalgic memories to many of the residents of Maine and the summer visitors who frequent the hallowed auditorium. Such magical names as Florence Reed, Ethel

Barrymore, Raymond Walburn, J. C. Nugent and Billie Burke join the ranks of more contemporary stars known to a younger generation—Mary Astor, Betsy Palmer, Cornelia Otis Skinner, Walter Pidgeon, Ginger Rogers, Van Johnson, Merv Griffin—and many, many others.

One of the photos is of Richard Dysart, who was one of last year's cast of *Little Foxes*. Son of Dr. Douglas Dysart of Augusta, he was born in Skowhegan, and when he came back to play opposite Geraldine Page in the all-star cast, he startled his friends by electing to camp out on the grounds rather than be housed with others in the cottages.

In the season of 1923 a young actress joined the Lakewood Players—then a resident group who produced and acted in the shows with a few invited guest stars. Her name was Dorothy Stickney. Two years later Howard Lindsay came to Lakewood as director, a capacity in which he served for five years. The couple fell in love and were quietly married in Madison, Maine during the 1927 season. A decade later a new play was tried out at Lakewood—*Life With Father*. Howard Lindsay wrote it in collaboration with Russel Crouse, and Lindsay and his lovely wife, Dorothy Stickney, portrayed Clarence and Vinnie Day. Five others of the Lakewood cast also went on to play it on Broadway—a show which set a continuous run record which still stands —3,224 performances. Eight years later Warner Brothers held the world premiere of the film version at Lakewood—another record production.

Life With Father was only one of many new shows which are either tried for the first time at Lakewood, or scheduled at the Lakewood Theatre for the "shakedown" tour during the summer season before opening on Broadway. This year's program also features a new comedy prior to Broadway—*The Chic Life* featuring James Whitmore from TV's *My Friend Tony* series, and Audra Lindley, who portrays Liz on TV's *Another World*. The show is scheduled for the week of August 4. Also included this summer was *I Do, I Do*—the musical version of *The Four Poster* which previewed at Lakewood in 1951, starring Hume Cronyn and his wife, Jessica Tandy.

The first show held in the Lakewood Theatre was *The Private Secretary* on June 24, 1901. The play was written by William Gillette and starred James Durkin, who was to both act and direct during a score of years. In those days vaudeville continued as an occasional part of the season's schedule, chairs were pushed back after the performance for dancing, and Friday nights fireworks were a regular attraction. On "bargain" nights, one could ride the trolleys, see the show and stay for dancing—all for 25 cents, plus assisting with the chairs.

In August 1935 the eyes of the world were focused on Lakewood. The play was *Ceiling Zero*—which was highlighted by an offstage plane crash. One of the members of the Lakewood Players was Mary Rogers, daughter of the great and much beloved Will Rogers. Her mother, Betty, was in the audience that day when news shocked the world that Will Rogers and his pilot, Wiley Post, had been killed in a plane crash in Alaska. Never has the switchboard been so busy as newsmen from around the world sought details of how the family had faced the tragedy and their plans. Hundreds of friends also called to offer assistance and sympathy. One long distance call from London quite stunned the operator as a voice said simply, "This is Charles Lindbergh."

In the cast of *Ceiling Zero* that night were Humphrey Bogart, Owen Davis, Jr., son of America's most prolific playwright and a native of Maine; Keenan Wynn, son of the famous Ed Wynn; and Grant Mills, now President of Lakewood Corporation.

Mr. Mills was a leading man for ten years, and he became president when Herbert Lindsey Swett died in 1946. Vice

President of the Corporation is Elizabeth Swett Mills, wife of the president and daughter of Lakewood's founder. She is one of the most devoted and hard-working members of the organization. Their son, Michael, is also part of the operation —one where everyone works. This summer he is working in the kitchen as an assistant cook.

Just as Lakewood has changed through the years, so also has the policy changed in keeping with the times. No longer can the Lakewood Players present plays using one or two guest stars. Under the regulations of Equity, today's cast must include ten players before non-professional extras can be used. This is not as simple as it might seem. Due to increasing production costs, few plays have more than five characters today. In addition, Equity requires that players be paid the same salary for rehearsal time as for their performances before an audience.

The natural outgrowth of these high production costs has been the formation of a Council of Stock Theaters. A group of the members of the council share rehearsal and production costs, thereby making summer theaters within the realm of practicality. Lakewood has been able to keep its ticket costs at a lower level than most summer theaters, and all are able to keep them well below the exorbitant prices on Broadway.

The Lakewood Theatre, remodeled three times through the years, has a seating capacity of 1085. The stage is 33 feet deep and has an opening of the same measurements. Acoustics and view of the stage are excellent from any seat in the house.

The regular staff includes Henry Richards, Production Director, who was our guide on the tour of the theater; Stuart Bloomberg, Public Relations Director; a scene designer, stage manager, lighting designer and technical director. Each has his assistant and there are ten technicians. All told, Lakewood employs about 100 during the summer. Very important to the work of the theater is the group of 10 or 11 learners—young people who are studying dramatics, stage management and other related subjects, and who find this work experience program invaluable in their chosen careers.

In 1967 the Lakewood Theatre was designated by the 103rd Maine State Legislature as the Official Theater of the State of Maine. Patrons come from all over the state as well as visitors from all over the country who find Maine the ideal Vacationland. A popular weekend plan—especially among our Canadian neighbors—is to arrive early enough to see the Friday or Saturday production, remain in one of the comfortable cottages for a weekend of golf, tennis, shuffleboard, swimming or just plain relaxing, and then see the new show on Monday evening before returning home.

Although the Inn is popular with those occupying the cottages or attending the theater, Maine residents from far and near come to enjoy the excellent cuisine and the atmosphere of the Inn. At the Shanty, light refreshments prove popular. . . .

76. WHARF THEATRE
Provincetown, Massachusetts
Summer, 1915

A converted fish house on a wharf in Provincetown, Massachusetts, became the birthplace of one of the most significant groups in modern American theater. It was during the summer of 1915 that George Cram Cook (who was called "Jig" by his wife and friends) and his wife, Susan Glaspell, met with friends in Provincetown and began to read and later to perform one-act plays together. A neighbor, Robert Edmond Jones, rigged various simple settings for them. By the end of the second summer in the Wharf Theatre, the Provincetown Players had been born and were ready to move to New York City for the winter season, returning to the Wharf Theatre each summer.

Susan Glaspell, in her autobiographical book *The Road to the Temple*, described the founding of the Wharf Theatre.

76:1 . . . Those were the early years of psychoanalysis in the Village. You could not go out to buy a bun without hearing of someone's complex. We thought it would be amusing in a play, so we had a good time writing "Suppressed Desires." Before the grate in Milligan Place we tossed the lines back and forth at one another, and wondered if anyone else would ever have as much fun with it as were having.

We wanted our play put on, as who doesn't, but even the little theatres thought "Suppressed Desires" "too special." Now it has been given by every little theatre, and almost every Methodist church; golf clubs in Honolulu, colleges in Constantinople; in Paris and China and every rural route in America. I wish I had the records of how many thousands of times Step-hen has been asked to be rooster. He has been far from special.

Well, if no one else was going to put on our play, we would put it on ourselves. Neith Boyce had a play—"Constancy." We gave the two in her house one evening. Bobby Jones was there and helped us with the sets. He liked doing it, because we had no lighting equipment, but just put a candle here and a lamp there.

A few minutes before it was time to give our play, Jig and I took a walk up the shore. We held each other's cold hands and said, "Never mind, it will be over soon."

But when it was over we were sorry. People liked it, and we liked doing it.

Neighbours who had not been asked were hurt, so we gave the plays again. Margaret Steele had taken for studio the old fish-house out at the end of the Mary Heaton Vorse wharf, across from our house. She let us have this, so more people could come. Jig became so interested

76:1. Susan Glaspell, *The Road to the Temple* (London: Ernest Benn Ltd., 1926), pp. 192–98.

264

74. Elitch's Gardens Theatre, Denver, ca. 1940. Courtesy of the Denver Public Library Western Collection.

74. Original drop curtain, Elitch's Gardens Theatre, Denver, ca. 1920. Courtesy of the Denver Public Library Western Collection.

75. Lakewood Theatre, Showhegan, Maine, ca. 1965. Courtesy of Lakewood Theatre.

76. Wharf Theatre, Province-town, Mass., ca. 1925. Courtesy of The Hoblitzelle Theatre Arts Library, The Humanities Research Center, The University of Texas at Austin.

he wrote another comedy, "Change your style," having to do with Provincetown art schools, a jolly little play. Wilbur Steele had written "Contemporaries," and those two we gave together. Thus ended the first season of the Provincetown Players, who closed without knowing they were Provincetown Players.

It might have ended there—people giving plays in the summer, if it hadn't been —Do you remember Jig's dream city, how there was to be a theatre, and "why not write out our own plays and put them on ourselves, giving writer, actor, designer, a chance to work together without the commercial thing imposed from without? A whole community working together, developing unsuspected talents. The city ought to furnish the kind of audience that will cause new plays to be written." "The Will to Form the Beloved Community of Life-Givers"—that is written through the papers of his years.

The summer people had gone. Jig would go out on the wharf and "step" the fish-house. Weren't there two feet more than he had thought? He would open the sliding door that was the back wall, through which fish, nets, oars, anchors, boats, used to be dragged, and stand looking across the harbour to the low Truro hills, hearing the waves lap the piles below him. He would walk back slowly, head a little bent, twisting his forelock.

"To write alone will not content me. The blood of backwoods statesmen is in my veins. I must act, organize, accomplish, embody my ideal in stubborn material things which must be shaped to it with energy, toil."

We were back early in the spring, after seeing more Broadway plays. Jack Reed came home from Mexico, where he saw a mediaeval miracle play which has survived in unbroken tradition among the natives of a certain village, as the poems of Homer existed for some centuries in the Ionian villages of Asia Minor.

Students of dreams tell us our dreams use the things of the moment as vehicle, pattern, symbol, for the deeply-lying thing. In our activities, as in our dreams, the accidental is seized to be shaped by our deep necessities.

"One man cannot produce drama. True drama is born only of one feeling animating all the members of a clan— a spirit shared by all and expressed by the few for the all. If there is nothing to take the place of the common religious purpose and passion of the primitive group, out of which the Dionysian dance was born, no new vital drama can arise in any people."

He and Neith Boyce said it together. He came home and wrote it down as an affirmation of faith.

The people who came back that next summer had little chance of escaping. Purpose had grown in him, he was going to take whom he wanted and use them for the creation of his Beloved Community.

We hauled out the old boat, took oars and nets and anchors to various owners, bought lumber at the second wharf "up-along," and Jig, Nordfeldt, Ballantine, Joe O'Brien, others helping, converted the fish-house into the Wharf Theatre, a place where ninety people could see a play, if they didn't mind sitting close together on wooden benches with no backs. The stage, ten feet by twelve, was in four sections, so we could have different levels, could run it through the big sliding-door at the back, a variety of sets surprising in quarters so small.

We gave a first bill, then met at our house to read plays for a second. Two Irishmen, one old and one young, had arrived and taken a shack just up the street. "Terry," I said to the one not young, "Haven't you a play to read to us?"

"No," said Terry Carlin, "I don't write, I just think, and sometimes talk. But Mr. O'Neill has got a whole trunk full of plays," he smiled.

That didn't sound too promising, but I said: "Well, tell Mr. O'Neill to come to our house at eight o'clock to-night, and bring some of his plays."

So Gene took "Bound East for Cardiff" from his trunk, and Freddie Burt read it to us, Gene staying out in the dining-room while the reading went on.

He was not left alone in the dining-room when the reading had finished.

Then we knew what we were for. We began in faith, and perhaps it is true when you do, that "all these things shall be added unto you."

I may see it through memories too emotional, but it seems to me I have never sat before a more moving production than our "Bound East for Cardiff," when Eugene O'Neill was produced for the first time on any stage. Jig was Yank. As he lay in his bunk dying, he talked of life as one who knew he must leave it.

The sea had been good to Eugene O'Neill. It had been there for his opening. There was a fog, just as the script demanded, fog bell in the harbour. The tide was in, and it washed under us and around, spraying through the holes in the floor, giving us the rhythm and the flavour of the sea while the big dying sailor talked to his friend Drisc of the life he had always wanted deep in the land, where you'd never see a ship or smell the sea.

It is not merely figurative language to say the old wharf shook with applause.

The people who had seen the plays, and the people who gave them, were adventurers together. The spectators were part of the Players, for how could it have been done without the feeling that came from them, without that sense of them there, waiting, ready to share, giving— finding the deep level where audience and writer and player are one. The last month of his life he wrote:

I am an audience insofar as the author is one with me,

And author insofar as the audience is one with me,
More than any person's name and fame
I will to hear
The music of the identity of me.

People sometimes said, "Jig is not a business man," when it seemed opportunities were passed by. But those opportunities were not things wanted from deep. He had a unique power to see just how the thing he wanted done could be done. He could finance for the spirit, and seldom confused, or betrayed, by extending the financing beyond the span he saw ahead, not weighing his adventure down with schemes that would become things in themselves.

He wrote a letter to the people who had seen the plays, asking if they cared to become associate members of the Provincetown Players. The purpose was to give American playwrights of sincere purpose a chance to work out their ideas in freedom, or give all who worked with the plays their opportunity as artists. Were they interested in this? One dollar for the three remaining bills.

The response paid for seats and stage, and for sets. A production need not cost a lot of money, Jig would say. The most expensive set at the Wharf Theatre cost thirteen dollars. There were sets at the Provincetown Playhouse which cost little more. He liked to remember "The Knight of the Burning Pestle" they gave at Leland Stanford, where a book could indicate one house and a bottle another. Sometimes the audience liked to make its own set.

"Now Susan," he said to me, briskly, "I have announced a play of yours for the next bill."

"But I have no play!"

"Then you will have to sit down tomorrow and begin one."

I protested. I did not know how to write a play. I had never "studied it."

"Nonsense," said Jig. "You've got a stage, haven't you?"

So I went out on the wharf, sat alone on one of our wooden benches without a back, and looked a long time at that bare little stage. After a time the stage became a kitchen,—a kitchen there all by itself. I saw just where the stove was, the table, and the steps going upstairs. Then the door at the back opened, and people all bundled up came in—two or three men, I wasn't sure which, but sure enough about the two women, who hung back, reluctant to enter that kitchen. When I was a newspaper reporter out in Iowa, I was sent down-state to do a murder trial, and I never forgot going into the kitchen of a woman locked up in town. I had meant to do it as a short story, but the stage took it for its own, so I hurried in from the wharf to write down what I had seen. Whenever I got stuck, I would run across the street to the old wharf, sit in that leaning little theatre under which the sea sounded, until the play was ready to continue. Sometimes things written in my room would not form on the stage, and I must go home and cross them out. "What playwrights need is a stage," said Jig, "their own stage."

Ten days after the director said he had announced my play there was a reading at Mary Heaton Vorse's. I was late to the meeting, revising the play. But when I got there the crowd liked "Trifles," and voted to put it in rehearsal the next day.

It was a great summer; we swam from the wharf as well as rehearsed there; we would lie on the beach and talk about plays—everyone writing, or acting, or producing. Life was all of a piece, work not separated from play.

I like to remember certain times late at night. The audience had gone home, the big door had been drawn shut; the last actor who wanted a drink had the last drop there was at our house, and Jig and I might stroll out on the wharf before going to bed. The sea had taken it all again—the wharf was the old wharf and the theatre the fish-house that had been there while so many tides came and went. Fishermen, people from deep in the land who wanted to write plays about both sea and land that—Why? At such times one wondered. It seemed now, on the wharf that jutted out from a sleeping town, as if we had not been at all; and before many more tides came in, it would indeed be as if we had not been at all. And yet, would it? Perhaps we wanted to write plays and put them on just because we knew, more intensely than the fishermen, that the tide comes, the tide goes. You cannot know that and leave things just as they were before.

One night I was lonely in the house, suspected where Jig was and went out to find him. The theatre a dark bulk behind him, he was sitting at the end of the wharf, feet hanging over. "Thinking about the theatre?" I asked after a little —things hadn't gone so well that night.

He shook ashes from his pipe. "No," he said. "I was thinking about raft boats on the Mississippi." . . .

77. CAPE PLAYHOUSE
Dennis, Massachusetts
Opened July 4, 1927

Since 1927 the outstanding professional playhouse on Cape Cod, the Cape Playhouse has provided entertainment to many thousands of summer vacationers. Together with the Cape Cinema and the Playhouse Restaurant, the Playhouse forms a complex of entertainment facilities. The Cape Cinema, with its mural decoration designed by Rockwell Kent and Jo Mielziner, is of interest to art lovers. The Playhouse itself might be considered one of the most historic theaters in America, for the founder bought the old 1790 Nobscusset Meeting House and had it converted to theatrical uses.

This brief history of the Playhouse is taken from the twentieth-anniversary booklet:

77:1   The 1946 season marks the twentieth year of our existence of the Cape Playhouse, "America's Most Famous Summer Theatre." It was in March, 1927 that the late Raymond Moore circulated a handsome four-page prospectus announcing his plan for a summer theatre easily accessible to all reaches of Cape Cod. The location he had chosen was Dennis and for his theatre building he selected the old Nobscusset Meeting House, which came into being about 1790 as a church. The Meeting House had been abandoned to more earthly purposes in the middle of the 19th Century, having become a school, a tin shop, a slaughter house and finally a garage, before serving as altar to the thespian muses. The building had been twice moved from its original location when Mr. Moore purchased it twenty seasons ago and took it for its third journey through the town of Dennis that year, this time to the present site on the King's highway just north of the Dennis Post Office. Here, in an attractive setting of three and a half acres of land, the Cape Playhouse was born.

Cleon Throckmorton, a theatre architect of prominence and scenic designer for the Theatre Guild, was assigned the chore to draw plans for adapting the century-old structure to its new use. In doing so, he retained the simple dignified lines of the Meeting House and at the same time met the problems of a theatre that was thoroughly practicable. Seating 500 persons, the Cape Playhouse includes a balcony and a group of boxes arranged in fours on either side of the auditorium.

After rounding up a company of professionals, Raymond Moore opened the Cape Playhouse on July 4th of that year, 1927, with Basil Rathbone and Violet Kemble Cooper starring in "The Guardsman."

The Cape Playhouse immediately caught the spirit of Cape Cod, bringing to the Massachusetts vacation spot a summer theatre that produced plays equal to the best Broadway could offer. From the start the Playhouse has been the hub of entertainment activity on the Cape.

As one of the first summer theatres on the boards, the Cape Playhouse has remained unique in many ways. Different from other theatres of the strawhat circuit, the Cape Playhouse is not a reconverted barn. Patrons find themselves sitting in seats as comfortable as those in a Manhattan movie palace. Further, the quality of performance and production that surrounds each play removes the Playhouse from the category of barnyard drama, with the care and skill that goes into the settings and costumes—as well as the direction and acting—comparing with the top in Broadway execution. When the late Raymond Moore founded the Playhouse, he told friends that he was not interested in establishing a little theatre movement in the country, but in bringing professional, legitimate theatre to the rustic environs of the country. The Cape Playhouse has adhered to his precepts and in the twenty years since Mr. Moore conceived his dream of building the Playhouse, it has earned and maintained the reputation of truly being "America's Most Famous Summer Theatre."

The Cape Playhouse was the first rural theatre to introduce the star system as we know it today. In the old days established stars would frown upon appearing at a summer theatre. It was below their dignity. A glance at the roster of Cape Playhouse plays and their players will attest to the success of the experiment; and the fact that other summer-month practitioners of the dramatic art have taken up the strawhat habit is further proof of its good theatre sense.

The famous names of stage and screen discovered many years ago that a lofty weekly stipend could be earned from

77:1. "America's Most Famous Summer Theatre," in Cape Theatre souvenir brochure (n.p., 1946).

appearing on the stages of the rural theatres. This pleasant dollar-sign plus the fact that a pleasant time is had by all—to say nothing of the healthy surroundings in which one works—have convinced everyone from Annabella to Zorina that acting on summer stages is the thing to do. In the beginning, the few stars who did appear performed at a modest sum just for the fun of it, but in the '30's when Raymond Moore commissioned Richard Aldrich, then serving as general manager for the Playhouse, to sign Jane Cowl at any cost ("Even pay her up to $500.00," Moore charged him), Aldrich set precedent by calmly signing Miss Cowl for the fee of one thousand dollars for the one week's engagement! Other managers were shocked, to say nothing of Raymond Moore. For such a summer theatre salary was then unheard of. But Richard Aldrich argued that a great star was worth the price, and his convictions were borne out by the gross receipts at the box-office. To employ the "Variety" vernacular, "Cowl proved boffo at the b.o.," and a good profit was had by all!

Breaking precedent in financial circles seems to stick to the Cape Playhouse. It was one of the first to follow the Actor's Equity Association's resolutions and to pay performers the Equity minimum salary which prevails on Broadway. Another policy that sets the Playhouse apart from other summer theatres is its arrangement with apprentices. As the ledgers will show, many a strawhat stage earns its profit by charging apprentices a good-sized fee for the privilege of working in the theatre for the summer, the charge being called tuition. The Cape Playhouse however, frowns on such custom. Instead, it neither pays nor is paid by its apprentices, who each week help build, paint and shift the scenery, along with professional designers and stage crews, ring up the curtain and occasionally play a walk-on or bit part with the regular professional company. The Playhouse manage-

ment feels that young people should be encouraged to work in the theatre but should not be charged for their own labors. Once again, the Playhouse has proved its good judgment when one considers that such famous stars of today as Bette Davis, Henry Fonda, Anne Baxter and Martha Scott served apprenticeship working as stage-managers, ushers, scenery-shifters, and extras in Cape Playhouse productions.

No account of the Cape Playhouse would be complete without a few of the backstage stories that make up the rich memories of past summers.

Tamara, the lovely singer who lost her life in the Lisbon Clipper crash while en route to entertain troops overseas, made one of her last appearances in America at the Cape Playhouse, in "The Duenna" in 1942. But her first appearance here was in "Marriage Royal" with Margaret Anglin in 1937. Regular patrons will remember that opening night when all the lights went out during an electrical storm; and while the Playhouse generator was being connected, Tamara with great poise and assurance found her way onto the stage and sang the song she made famous, "Smoke Gets in Your Eyes," holding a flashlight under her chin until the stage lights went on.

When Luise Rainer was playing "A Kiss For Cinderella," she returned to her dressing room one evening after the theatre was locked for the night. She tried to climb through the dressing room window and was greeted by a sinister "hands up!" accompanied by an outstretched pistol pointing into her face. The night watchman was on the job in the dark, and refused to believe she was the week's star. It took some fast talking for the shy Miss Rainer to keep from spending the night in a nearby Hoosegow.

The late Charles Butterworth had his share of toil and trouble. Flying to the Playhouse from Canada on the day of his opening, his plane stopped in Boston and couldn't continue. The plane company provided a local taxi which brought him to Dennis shortly before curtain time. But to add to the premiere's worries, his costumes had been shipped to New York!

Ethel Barrymore's arrival at the Playhouse was intended to be an auspicious one. Arrangements were made to provide a gala welcome. But somehow she arrived in the middle of the preceding night —by bus! If a couple of stay-ups had not noticed her on the theatre grounds, the great lady of the American theatre might have had to pitch her own tent on the grass for the entire night.

Tallulah Bankhead arrived with a small monkey one year. The next season she brought a lion cub.

Joe E. Brown's visit to the Playhouse so endeared him to Cape Codders that he was made an honorary member of the Dennis Fire Department.

Moss Hart's excursion into the realm of Thespis five years ago, as "Alexander Woollcott" in "The Man Who Came to Dinner" became such a pleasant experience for the playwright, he has played the role many times since.

When Jinx Falkenburg appeared here in 1941, the Brooklyn contingent of her fan club sent up several members to pay homage.

But of all the tales, the romantic one patrons like to recall is about the famous star who arrived on a rainy night several years ago. John Golden, the producer, had prepared Richard Aldrich by telling him that the actress would be arriving complete with maids, six trunks and twelve suitcases. Aldrich went to the station expecting to meet the stereotyped temperamental prima donna, and looking forward to a very unpleasant engagement, he nearly broke into immediate argument with his visiting star . . . P.S. Richard Aldrich and the star, Gertrude Lawrence, were married the following summer!

78. WESTPORT COUNTRY PLAYHOUSE
Westport, Connecticut
Opened Summer, 1931

The Westport Country Playhouse, because of its important ties with the Theatre Guild in its early days, has been one of the more important summer theatres in the United States. Started by Lawrence Langner and Armina Marshall in 1931 as a pre-Broadway tryout theater, the Westport playhouse became the springboard for a number of important Broadway productions. Langner and his wife continued as managers of the theater until 1958, when they leased it to James B. McKenzie.

The following brief history was provided by the management of the playhouse.

78:1   The Westport Country Playhouse has enjoyed an enviable reputation since its first summer in 1931.

The year before that Lawrence Langner and his wife Armina Marshall purchased an historic barn in what was then the edge of Westport ostensibly for the purpose of continuing its apple orchard. The Langners were, in those years, already approaching the status of a dynasty in the American Theatre. As the founders of the Theatre Guild, they were by far the most active producers in the United States. Their activities included a half dozen or more Broadway productions each season, and domination of the entire legitimate touring system in the country. As residents of Weston, Connecticut, they kept searching for ways to become further involved with the community. Mr. Langner laughingly claimed that when he found he didn't know how to grow apples he decided to convert the barn into a summer theatre, and thus began the Westport Country Playhouse.

The stage was designed to exactly the same size as the Times Square Theatre in New York City so that plays could be

---

78:1. "Wesport Country Playhouse," mimeographed (Westport, Conn.: The Playhouse, 1971).

270

tried out in Westport and moved easily to Broadway without restaging. The first show presented by the new Langner repertory company was "The Streets of New York." Members of the original cast included Armina Marshall, Dorothy Gish, Winifred Lenihan, Moffret Johnson, and Romney Brent. The first repertory season went well, and "The Streets of New York" opened in New York in the fall of 1931 to become Westport's first successful try-out.

The next summer the repertory company was headed by Osgood Perkins and June Walker, and included a new ingenue named Jane Wyatt. That year two of the try-outs made it to Broadway, including a rhymed version of Moliere's "School for Husbands" which Mr. Langner had translated and adapted for the American stage.

Each summer a succession of new plays were tried at the theatre, and many new actors began their theatrical careers in the little country playhouse. In 1933 "The Pursuit of Happiness" written by Lawrence Langner and Armina Marshall was tried out at the playhouse starring Peggy Conklin and Tonio Stewart and later went to New York to become a smash hit. The walls of the green room backstage are papered with legendary theatrical names such as Ilka Chase, Ruth Gordon, Laurette Taylor, Jane Cowl, Tallulah Bankhead, Tyrone Power, Olivia DeHavilland, Gene Kelly, Montgomery Clift, Jean Arthur, Lenore Ulrich, Ina Claire, Eva Le Gallienne, Helen Hayes, Shirley Booth, and dozens of others.

Every season one or two plays seemed to meet the approval of the Westport audience which automatically meant they were good enough for New York. Certainly among the most memorable was a try-out of "Green Grow the Lilacs" which became the Theatre Guild's "Oklahoma!"

In 1959 the theatre was leased as the Langners began to curtail their try-out activities. In that year the manager of the playhouse was James B. McKenzie, who is president of the Producing Managers Company, operators of the theatre at this time. Mr. McKenzie has been manager, co-producer or producer of the theatre for the past eleven years. During those eleven years the playhouse presented over 130 plays, and created quite a few wonderful and loyal Westport stars. Perhaps most liked by Westport audiences during the past decade have been Arlene Francis, Shelley Winters, Joan Fontaine, Shirley Booth, Betsy Palmer, Walter Pidgeon, Hans Conreid, Paul Ford, Carol Channing, Maureen O'Sullivan and Tom Ewell. Two or three pre-Broadway try-outs were produced each season, the latest of which is the current Broadway smash "Butterflies Are Free." In other seasons such try-outs as William Inge's "Family Things," J. P. Donleavy's "A Singular Man" and Arthur Sumner Long's "Never Too Late" were among the successful try-outs as well as "An Evening with Mike Nichols and Elaine May," and a review entitled "A Party with Betty Comden and Adolph Green."

In 1964 Mr. McKenzie joined with Spofford J. Beadle, Ralph Roseman and Kenneth Carroad to operate the playhouse under the banner of the Producing Managers Company. In addition to carrying on the summer season tradition, the new firm also presented an occasional off-season festival such as a spring season in 1966 featuring the American Conservatory Theatre in repertory, a spring season in 1965 consisting of three plays in repertory by George Bernard Shaw, and a fall season a [of] six new plays in sequence.

Today there are few actors on the legitimate stage who have not been associated with the Westport Theatre at some point in their careers. To date Westport has seen 373 of America's best plays in the country playhouse and has been host to more than 3000 professional actors.

In addition it has graduated some 400 apprentices to theatrical careers. The playhouse continues its extensive apprenticeship training program, which spawned such stars as Tammy Grimes, James Stewart, etc. It has helped develop the careers of many producers, directors, designers, and managers as well as actors.

The Westport Country Playhouse has become a landmark not only in southern Connecticut, but also the entire world of the legitimate theatre.

79. OREGON SHAKESPEARE FESTIVAL THEATRE
Ashland, Oregon
Opened July 4, 1935

The production history of the Oregon Shakespeare Festival Theatre in Ashland dates from 1935, when the founder, Angus Bowmer, began to present Shakespearean plays in an amphitheater left over from Chautauqua days. The idea took root and the project prospered, ultimately becoming two theaters: an outdoor Elizabethan-style playhouse modeled after the Fortune Theatre of 1599, and the Angus Bowmer Theatre, an indoor facility.

The opening of the new Elizabethan stage was previewed in the New York *Times*.

79:1 NEW STAGE FOR SHAKESPEARE IN OREGON
by Dorothy Nichols
Ashland, Ore.

The Oregon Shakespearean Festival here, dedicated to the production of the playwright in the form for which he wrote —swift, continuous action—will have a new Elizabethan stage this summer. In its nineteenth season the festival successfully faced a $275,000 fund-raising campaign. A grant of $10,000 from the Ford Foundation to Angus Bowmer, founder and director, has made it possible to bring back many of the festival's finest actors.

The opening play, "Twelfth Night," on Tuesday, will be preceded by an Elizabethan-style masque in honor of Oregon's centennial. A visitor can "stay four days, see four plays." With the other three, "King John," "Measure for Measure" and "Antony and Cleopatra" in rotation, the plays will run through Sept 5.

Good Audiences

Ashland is now one of the few places in the world where the complete Shakespeare canon of thirty-seven plays has been produced. The festival has maintained itself without subsidy, on admissions and private gifts. Last summer it attracted close to 30,000 spectators, yet the setting is a small town just over the border from northern California, a long day's drive each way from centers of population, Portland and San Francisco.

The festival has resisted the temptation of "big names"; its actors are young, drawn largely from college faculties and graduate students; some go on to careers in the theatre, or teach and direct, spreading the Ashland ideal.

The stage at Ashland, built to the specifications of the Fortune Theatre of 1599, with its many playing areas, upper inner, inner below, balcony and curtained center, permits the original rush of action when plot was the element that held the audience, and what we now revere, poetry and character were extras. On this stage there are no breaks in action; one scene begins as another ends. Everything falls into place: the abrupt shifts of mood, comedy relief, soliloquies, processions, battles.

The histories, in heraldic costuming, have been Ashland's most consistent artistic achievement. In these authentic productions the evolution of Shakespeare's form comes clear: from the juxtaposition of violent comedy with violent tragedy in Falstaff and Hotspur, to the emerging theme drama of the second "Henry IV." "King John" this season is the first of the chronicle plays to be repeated.

Except for the chronicle plays, Ashland permits a latitude in costuming only

79:1. New York *Times*, July 26, 1959.

272

77. Cape Playhouse, Dennis, Mass., 1946. Courtesy of the Cape Playhouse.

78. Westport Country Playhouse, Westport, Conn., 1966. Courtesy of Westport Country Playhouse.

79. Oregon Shakespeare Festival Theatre, Ashland, 1968. Watercolor. Courtesy of Oregon Shakespearean Festival Association.

79. Elizabethan Theatre, Oregon Shakespeare Festival, Ashland, 1963. Photograph by Dwaine Smith. Courtesy of Oregon Shakespearean Festival Association.

from Tudor to James. The stage is bare; the costumes make the color. But even in "A Midsummer Night's Dream" this becomes an advantage, for the focus was on the poetry, the true scene-painting in Shakespeare.

Festival Founder

The festival was founded in 1935 by Angus Bowmer of Southern Oregon College. On a bluff overlooking a canyon park which opens out of the town plaza, there was a walled oval left from Chautauqua days. Here the theatre was built and audiences sit under the stars—even through occasional thunderstorms. By day Ashland is any small town, though in Lithia Park visitors will be reading the evening's play by the pond with the Avon swans, and madrigals may float down from rehearsals in the theatre on the bluff above.

The actors, who have been unpaid except for fifteen scholarships, come recommended from every part of the United States. Nearly 500 applications were received this year from all over the world. Scholarship is taught from a theatre point of view in the affiliated Institute of Renaissance studies. Elizabethan dances and music are part of the spectacle and the dueling is expert.

With no tailoring to fit stars, without novelty angles of period or imposed interpretation, productions at Ashland, the less successful as well as the most impressive, have a way of lighting up some special value; each one illumines Shakespeare's form and intent.

The Festival published a brief outline history, reproduced here.

79:2   FESTIVAL HISTORY

1935 Founded by Angus L. Bowmer as part of a July 4th event.

1936 The Oregon Shakespearean Festi-

79:2. Oregon Shakespeare Festival publicity release (Ashland, 1970).

val Association was formed as a non-profit corporation. A third play was added.

1938 Originally a community event, with the actors and audience coming from the Rogue Valley, the Festival was by now attracting wider attention. Actors from other parts of the country wanted the experience of Shakespearean acting. Audience journeyed to Ashland to see the plays.

1939 The Festival was invited to appear at the San Francisco World's Fair. The Company played at the Federal Theatre on Treasure Island and also broadcast *The Taming of the Shrew*.

1940 A backstage fire destroyed all accumulated costumes. The Company finished the season in modern dress.

1941 Draft and war made it hard to get male actors. Production was abandoned for the duration and Festival funds were invested in war bonds.

1947 Production resumed. The damaged theatre had been torn down after the fire so a new one had to be built. This time a stage was constructed after the pattern of the Fortune Theatre of Shakespeare's time in London. Costumes were rented in 1947. In 1948 a costumer joined the Company and since that time all costumes have been designed and made by the Festival.

1941 The Festival began its chronological presentation of the history plays. A second director was added to the staff. The season was 16 performances, four of each play, six days a week.

1949 The season was extended to 20 days, and a fifth show was added. Two more directors were added to the staff.

1951　Sunday performances were added, and the season was extended to 25 nights. The first of the continuing series of nationwide NBC broadcasts were inaugurated from the Festival stage. The first of the room and board scholarships for deserving actors.

1952　The season was extended to 30 performances. Additional scholarships were given. A grant by Mr. Thomas D. Cooke of Los Angeles made possible the founding of the music program. Elizabethan concerts were given; the post of Music Director was created.

1953　The season was extended to embrace the full month of August. Scholarships for actresses, technical people and box office personnel were added. The Institute of Renaissance Studies was established.

1954　William Patton, the Festival's first full-time General Manager, was appointed. New stadium-type seats were installed.

1955　The 20th anniversary year of the Festival

1956　Plans for building a new theatre were announced.

1957　All of the Shakespeare chronicle plays, with the 1957 season, had been produced by the Festival.

1958　With the 1958 season, all of the Shakespeare canon had been produced by the Festival. A full performance-recorded library of tapes was completed. The season was extended over a six-week period, July 28 through September 4.

1959　The season opened in the newly constructed Shakespearean Theatre building. Another extension in season length saw productions running from July 28 through September 5. Productions of the history plays resumed.

1960　The first non-Shakespearean play from the Elizabethan era was produced—John Webster's *Duchess of Malfi*, for three special performances.

1961　The season was extended to 42 nights. A new lighting board was installed and the basement of the new wing was built.

1962　The season was extended to 44 nights.

1963　Another season extension brought performances to a total of 46 nights. Preparations began for celebration of the 400th anniversary of Shakespeare's birth.

1964　The 400th anniversary year Festival performed a total of 70 nights in two cities: 58 at Ashland and 12 at the first annual Stanford (University) Summer Festival of the Arts in Palo Alto. Planning began for observance of the Festival's 25th Anniversary season, in 1965.

1965　25th anniversary year for the oldest of the North American Shakespearean Festivals. Except for a lapse during World War II, the Oregon Shakespearean Festival has produced annually in Ashland a repertory of Shakespeare's plays on a stage patterned after those of his own era. Special honors for the original 1935 company.

1966　Launched $500,000 campaign to complete the 1956 Expansion plan —and prepared to start a second quarter century. Inaugurated ballad opera stagings with eight matinees of John Gay's *The Beggar's Opera*.

1967　The first phase of the Festival Building Fund Drive was completed as $300,000 was raised. Increased construction costs were faced and planning started for a final phase of fund raising, with an aggregate goal of $800,000 needed to begin construction; $1.2 million needed for the total facility.

1968 Seattle architectural firm of Kirk, Wallace, and McKinley A.I.A. completed schematics and siting of the indoor theatre.

1969 Early in April, 1969, the Economic Development Administration approved a matching grant of $896,000 for the City of Ashland——the bulk of which was earmarked to aid the Oregon Shakespearean Festival Association in completing a growth program which would allow an eventual move to year-round theatre in Ashland.

1970 The Festival experiences its greatest single jump in expansion. The opening of the Angus Bowmer Theatre and its formal dedication on March 21 through May 2. The summer season opens May 22 with a five week-end series and, on June 26, begins playing every afternoon and evening. The Bowmer Theatre houses daily matinees and the Elizabethan theatre is the setting for all evening performances. 160 performances comprise the season, which closes September 13.

The 30th anniversary year of the Festival. The 20th anniversary of the Festival's NBC radio show.

STAGE AND SETTING OF
THE ELIZABETHAN THEATRE

"America's First Elizabethan Theatre" is also the only theatrical organization of its kind in the Western Hemisphere. With the handsome stage, built for first use in 1959, the Oregon Shakespearean Festival furthered its international reputation as the home of true Elizabethan staging. Richard L. Hay, the Festival Stage Designer, created the design for the theatre and acted as theatrical consultant for Jack

Edson, the architect. The late Frank Fairweather was the builder. The design is closely patterned after the stages of Elizabethan England, and is built to such dimensions as stated in the Henslowe and Alleyn–Peter Street contract for the construction of the Fortune Theatre in 1599 London. With its multiple playing areas, its practical facade, its exciting uses of varying levels and areas, the stage is perfectly suited to the fluidity of continuous performance—the kind of rapid-fire, cascading action which Shakespeare conceived in the writing, that his audiences demanded, and that Ashland audiences applaud. On the Ashland stage, the plays are presented as originally, without any interruption of any kind, in one continuous flow of action, beginning to end. Only in Ashland can the theatre-goer find Shakespearean drama presented in its entirety, and in the same dramatic style that brought Shakespeare his original success as a playwright.

SEATING PLAN OF
THE ELIZABETHAN THEATRE

Comfortable stadium seats, installed in a continental manner (no aisles), are arranged in arcs around the forestage. The seats are tiered, with wide walkways between the rows, allowing ease and comfort in seating. Elevation of the outer tiers provides an excellent view of the stage from all seats. There are no visual obstructions and hearing is excellent in all parts of the house.

The Angus Bowmer Theatre opened March 21, 1970. A description of the playhouse and its background follows:

79:3   WHY A SECOND THEATRE
         FOR THE FESTIVAL

It had been common knowledge through recent years, that the Oregon Shakespearean Festival's increasingly larger audi-

79:3. Oregon Shakespeare Festival publicity release (Ashland, 1970).

ences had become a potent economic factor to Oregon tourism, but it took a panel of economists from the University of Oregon's Bureau of Business and Economic Research to put the actual figures into focus.

Completed in April, 1968, the report made the need for additional box office income very clear. "With operating expenditure increases of at least 10% annually, the Festival cannot stand still and hope to provide the annual repertory for very long. The Festival management knew there was even further potential for growth, particularly if a second, indoor theatre could be completed.

In Fall of 1968, word came of the possibility of Federal matching grant assistance through the Economic Development Administration of the Department of Commerce. E.D.A. was founded under the Public Works and Economic Development Act of 1965, and provides financial and technical assistance to communities and areas with lagging economies characterized by high unemployment. The Southern Oregon area had been officially designated such an area.

Because the Festival properties are located on park land, the City of Ashland undertook an application to E.D.A. in the Fall of 1968 for a $1,792,000 project, with the planned Angus Bowmer Theatre as a keystone. Also included in the project proposal were a major parking area, a remodeled administration building and box office, a scene shop and exhibit hall, landscaping and street realignment for easier access to the theatre complex.

Approval came from the Economic Development Administration in April, 1969. A total of $896,000 was approved, to match an equal amount raised through private donations during the past several years by the Festival Association.

The months of careful coordination and hard work which followed word of that grant approval, is a prime example of multi-agency cooperation. Regional E.D.A. staff, the Ashland City Council, Development Commission, City Development staff and Festival designers, architects and staff formed an effective planning unit in seeing Phase I of the project —the Bowmer Theatre—to completion in time for this Spring season. The remainder of the project is scheduled to be completed later this year.

Through this project, the Oregon Shakespearean Festival will be able to increase capacity between 1969 and 1970 by over 100%. This will be even greater as new seasons are planned for other times of the year, attracting more and more tourists to Southern Oregon.

(Detailed information on the 1968 study and the E.D.A. project is available on request.)

DESIGN OF THE BOWMER THEATRE
STAGE AND AUDITORIUM

"It's a natural extension of what has made this Festival something special for audiences for nearly thirty years. There is a certain quality . . . I suppose it has something to do with rapport and the importance we've always placed on the audience/actor relationship." It has been Richard Hay who, as much as any other single person, has helped to guarantee that this quality survive.

In establishing the overall direction and design for the Angus Bowmer Theatre, Hay, who serves as Festival Scenic and Theatre Designer, more than hit his mark. None of the 600 seats in the new theatre is more than 55 feet from the stage. During *Rosencrantz and Guildenstern Are Dead*, the set (also designed by Hay) reaches a scant three feet from the front row.

In most theatres, the audience is placed in one room, and the players in another. The proscenium arch forms a frame, through which the audience "views" the actors. In the Bowmer Theatre both audicence [audience] and actor are in the same room. Tunnels from within the seating area allow entrances directly to the stage.

The fore portion of the stage is on a hydraulic lift system, which allows a director to use the stage in any of a number of positions. The stage can emulate the outdoor thrust, move down to form a more conventional proscenium front, or it can move below auditorium floor level to form an orchestra pit. It can even drop a full two stories to assist in storage of equipment or scenery.

The walls of the auditorium, when they reach the stage, become movable, swinging in and out to close down the playing area onto the fore portion, or open it up to accommodate a larger production.

As in the outdoor theatre, seating is in the continental fashion, boasting wide spaces between rows and no aisles. Dark colors on the ceilings and walls resist reflection from stage lighting, and, at the same time, draw the patron's eyes to the stage from the moment he enters the auditorium.

In every way, the Angus Bowmer Theatre is a custom-designed theatre. Few repertory theatre organizations have this advantage. It is a house conceived with both actor and audience in mind.

BOWMER THEATRE ARCHITECTS, PLANNERS, CONSULTANTS, GENERAL CONTRACTORS, ARCHITECTS AND GENERAL CONTRACTOR

Architects
Kirk, Wallace, McKinley, AIA & Associates, Seattle, Washington
General Contractor
Robert D. Morrow, Inc., Salem, Oregon

CONSULTANTS

Theatre Design Consultant
Richard L. Hay, Ashland, Oregon
Supervising Architect
Jack Edson, AIA, Medford, Oregon
Structural Engineers
Skilling, Helle, Christiansen, Robertson; Seattle, Washington

Mechanical Engineers
Valentine, Fisher & Tomlinson, Seattle, Washington
Electrical Engineers
Sparling and Associates, Inc., Seattle, Washington
Landscape Architects
Royston, Hanamoto, Beck & Abey; San Francisco, California
Supervising Landscape Architect
C. E. Corry, Ashland, Oregon
Acoustical Consultants
Robin M. Towne & Associates, Inc., Seattle, Washington
Lighting Equipment Consultant
George Howard, Los Angeles, California
Stage Equipment and Audio Consultant
Paul Landry and Associates, Palo Alto, California
Interior Design Consultant
George M. Schwarz & Associates, Portland, Oregon
Graphics Design Consultant
Charles M. Politz, Portland, Oregon

FACTS AND STATISTICS
REGARDING THE BOWMER THEATRE:

Cost of Construction: $1.4 million as PHASE I of a project which will ultimately cost $1,792,000.

Type of Construction: Built of heavy timbers, to utilize Pacific Northwest materials. One of the first such uses for wood products in a public building of this size.

Seating Capacity: *600 when using tunnels*. 633 when seating plugs are used to fill in tunnels (not completed yet).

Heating, A/C: An all electric facility, heated and cooled by large electric furnace and air conditioner.

Total Square Footage: 31,534 square feet on all levels.
Lower Level = 12,083
Lobby Level = 5,018
Auditorium = 14,433

Seating: 600 seats arranged in the continental manner (no aisles), with generous leg room. The most distant seat is only 55 feet from stage. The front row is just a few feet from stage.

Vertical rise from auditorium floor to last seating row is 17.2½ feet.

Overall Phase I

Project Area: The Bowmer Theatre and all attendant walks and landscaped courtyard areas consume about a 200′ by 200′ area.

Height: The tallest point on the Bowmer Theatre is 38 feet . . . three feet shorter than the Festival's adjacent Elizabethan stagehouse.

Lobby: Over 5,000 square feet, enclosed in timbers and panes of plate glass as high as 13′ tall. The heavy glue-laminated beams overhead support the weight of the auditorium seating area and audience.

Stage: The minimum stage area is 36′ x 25′, and can be opened up to 36′ x 46′. The entire fore portion of the stage is on a hydraulic lift, which enables the stage to be lowered a total of two stories to accommodate various productions.

That fore portion can be lowered into seven positions, including auditorium level, orchestra pit level, and to a special storage room two stories below.

Lighting: Custom-made for the Bowmer Theatre by Kliegl Bros. at a cost of $150,000. Approximately 300 lighting positions are provided for. The lighting control board is located behind the glass walled control booth in the rear of the theatre, along with the stage manager's console and sound console.

EDUCATIONAL PROGRAMS

Few things are as capable of exciting young people's minds as theatre. What once was just a collection of anthologies in a classroom now comes to life under lights. New dimensions are added to earlier studies.

While the Ashland "experience" has excited many students of all ages in the past 30 years, an organized effort to appeal to the young has come only in comparatively recent years.

The Student Tour program was started in 1964, as one of several commemoratives for the 400th anniversary of Shakespeare's birth. The program's success with both instructors and students has been unparalleled. Participation has increased to the point where, today, thousands of high school and college students attend our summer repertory in classroom groups.

This trend held true this past Spring during "STAGE II," as schools bussed students from as far away as San Francisco and Seattle to attend plays. Special teacher's kits and after-play discussions were provided as incentives by the Festival. Completely unsubsidized by grants or foundations, this grass-roots effort clearly demonstrated the interest among schools in having quality theatre available to augment classroom studies.

The Shakespeare Apprentice program has for several years, provided a full schedule of concentrated workshop activity: lectures, demonstrations, reading projects, laboratory exercises and close observation of Festival rehearsals. Although not in session this summer, plans call for a resumption of this successful program with the cooperation of Southern Oregon College during the 1971 summer season.

New programs are now under consideration, and plans are being worked out by Festival staff members and local educators to explore new methods of making Festival artists available as classroom resources and as members of workshop teams which would help teachers develop new instructional techniques.

As the Oregon Shakespearean Festival continues to grow to meet new challenges, "students" of all ages and pursuits will

79. Stage, Elizabethan Theatre, Oregon Shakespeare Festival, Ashland, 1961. Courtesy of Oregon Shakespearean Festival Association.

80. Ogunquit Playhouse, Ogunquit, Maine. Photograph by Edward D. Hipple. Courtesy of Ogunquit Playhouse.

continue to be one of the keys to its success.

80. OGUNQUIT PLAYHOUSE
Ogunquit, Maine
Opened July 19, 1937

The Ogunquit Playhouse has long been noted as one of the most beautiful and important summer theaters in New England. This brief history is by Richard Schanke, one of the staff members of the playhouse.

80:1   What was to become the Ogunquit Playhouse, as we now know it, had its initial beginning in New Hampshire. In 1927 Walter Hartwig organized the Manhattan Theatre Colony in Peterboro, New Hampshire. After completing three seasons of summer theatre there he moved his company to Bristol, Connecticut, where he remained for another two seasons. Finally, in 1933 Mr. Hartwig moved to Ogunquit, Maine. Here he opened his Theatre Colony in an old garage in the center of the village. Two of the stars that performed in that first season were Leo G. Carroll and Ruth St. Denis.

Always an integral part of the Theatre Colony was the theatre training for apprentices. Designed to provide the experienced worker as well as the beginner with intensive training in the arts and crafts of the stage, courses were offered to supplement the actual work of production and were aimed at three areas: the actor's voice, his body, and his intelligence. They covered such subjects as stagecraft, makeup, radio, voice and diction, body control, business management, costuming, dramatic criticism, lighting and playwriting. Apprentices who demonstrated ability and talent were often invited to perform in the major shows.

The noted American actress Laurette Taylor said of this apprenticeship program,

80:1. "The Ogunquit Playhouse," mimeographed (Ogunquit, 1971).

"I think the work you do at the Colony with your apprenticeship is a most intelligent approach to the theatre. What surprised me in their performances was the amount of talent that you had there. Either you choose your apprentices very carefully or the scheme of training is very effective—probably some of both."

And Ruth Gordon claimed,

"I tell all the young people who ask me about schools of the one at Ogunquit. That and the one at the Old Vic in London are the only two that I could recommend."

The Colony apprenticeship which began in 1927 as one of the first schools of its kind in this country continued through the 1965 season when it became too unwieldy to maintain.

On July 19, 1937, Walter Hartwig opened the new Ogunquit Playhouse, located one mile south of the village. Designed by theatre artist Alexander Wyckoff in the New England architectural tradition, it boasted 700 seats with none of them obscured by posts, a plush lobby with a bar, running water, dressing rooms, prop rooms, offices, etc. For four years Mr. Hartwig continued as the general manager of the Ogunquit Playhouse and the Manhattan Theatre Colony. After he died in 1941, his wife Maude assumed the responsibility.

Some major changes were in store for the Playhouse. In 1950 John Lane purchased the theatre from Maude Hartwig. The previous winter the building had been severely damaged by a hurricane. Along with the necessary building repairs, Mr. Lane began beautifying the grounds by providing a larger parking lot, an abundance of flowers and shrubs, and planting trees. In more recent years, carpeting in the lobby, air conditioning and heating have been added to make the now 750 seat playhouse a truly comfortable and lovely building.

Through the years many great stars have performed on the main stage of the Playhouse. Their names read like a history book in American acting: Lillian Gish, Ethel Barrymore, Clifton Webb, Peggy Wood, Beatrice Lillie, Anthony Quinn, Tallulah Bankhead, Bette Davis, Sinclair Lewis, Cornelia Otis Skinner, Arthur Treacher, Fay Wray, Elsa Maxwell, Ethel Waters, Grace George. . . .

Mainly because of economics and changes in the styles of plays, the trend since the early fifties has been away from resident companies and from stars who perform with resident companies. The Playhouse now produces "packages." Producer John Lane selects the plays, auditions, hires the casts and the directors. But now, for the most part, the shows rehearse in New York City and travel to the Playhouse ready to perform. The Playhouse is still very involved in all the promotional and technical aspects of every production and employs a staff of nearly forty paid people to run the theatre each summer season.

81. AMERICAN SHAKESPEARE FESTIVAL THEATRE
Stratford, Connecticut
Opened July 12, 1955

By the early 1950s there were several Shakespeare festival theaters at various places in the United States. Two of the more famous were in San Diego, California, and Ashland, Oregon. Lawrence Langner of the Theatre Guild had a vision of a major Shakespearean theater, similar to that at Stratford-on-Avon in England, in which Shakespeare's plays would receive outstanding productions using the best actors, directors, and designers available, with an adjoining academy to train young actors in classical acting methods.

Stratford, Connecticut, seemed to be the logical location for such a theater. Not only was the name propitious, but the proximity to New York was particularly attractive. Lang-

ner already had had a great deal of experience with a summer theater in Westport, Connecticut, and knew that he could depend on a sizable audience from the New York metropolitan area in addition to thousands of people vacationing in New England.

A brief history of the American Shakespeare Festival Theatre tells something of the financing and building problems.

81:1 The American Shakespeare Festival in Stratford, (Conn.) first opened its doors to the public on July 12th, 1955. Five years of dreaming and planning, and plain hard work, preceeded that opening night.

Lawrence Langner was responsible for the dream: to build a theatre to house Shakespeare's plays and to train actors in the style of acting best suited to performing these works for an American audience.

In 1951, Edwin L. Howard, Westport architect was engaged to design the Festival Theatre. Offices and a fund-raising staff were established and a bill was presented to the Connecticut State Legislature granting the American Shakespeare Festival Theatre and Academy the status of a non-profit, educational corporation. The bill was signed by former actor, Governor John Lodge on June 9, 1951.

During the next three years, hundreds of volunteers worked tirelessly to bring the dream of the Shakespeare Festival into reality: Mary Hunter produced and Margaret Webster staged "An Evening with Will Shakespeare" which toured major Eastern cities for six weeks; Lewis W. Douglas, former Ambassador to Great Britain became National Chairman of the organization; the Rockefeller Foundation promised $300,000.00 a sum matched in 1954 by the Old Dominion Foundation; Joseph Verner Reed and Lincoln Kirstein became members of the Board of Direc-

81:1. "The American Shakespeare Festival Theatre," mimeographed (Stratford, 1971).

tors. During this time, a search was being conducted for a suitable site upon which to locate the Theatre and Academy. More than 50 locations in Connecticut were visited by Lawrence Langner, and finally a site was selected in Stratford, (Conn.). The American Shakespeare Festival acquired four pieces of land facing the Housatonic River for the sum of $60,000.00.

On October 24, 1954, several hundred guests gathered on the barren waste lots to witness the ground-breaking. Miss Katherine Cornell used a gilded shovel adorned with green ribbons to turn up the first spade-full of earth upon which was to rise the first professional playhouse to be built in the United States in a quarter of a century.

In March, 1955, the ASFTA announced its choice of plays: "Julius Caesar" and "The Tempest;" hired Denis Carey of the Old Vic to direct; and began assembling actors, designers and production crews. Rehearsals began, first in New York and later in a social hall in Stratford, while the building crews worked frantically to get the theatre ready for the 12th of July.

When the day arrived, the superintendant reported the following building trades still at work on the structure: carpentry, painting, cement work, roofing and sheet metal, electric, plumbing and excavation! Nevertheless "Julius Caesar" opened on time accompanied by speeches and congratulatory telegrams.

But a theatre is more than a building; a theatre is a small universe in which the stage, the auditorium, the artistic program and business policy, the actors, directors, technicians and the audience all combine to form a living and growing whole.

Serious artistic and structural problems plagued the first few years of the Festival's operation. A company of actors must be formed with some degree of cohesion and some hope of continuity, the stage must be adapted to provide a suitable platform upon which to present a diversity of Shakespearean productions—

a stage that must be all things to all plays.

These problems took time, patience and unstinting effort to solve. The company became the problem of Artistic Director, John Houseman, and his assistant, Jack Landau; the stage became the problem of numerous designers until, in 1964, the solution was found in a design by Will Steven Armstrong.

In 1962, Joseph Verner Reed, the Festival's present Executive Producer, was instrumental in securing a Ford Foundation grant for the purpose of "training actors in the classics" and the Festival's first Actors' Training Program was instituted. The grant has benefited both the Festival and theatre in the United States. Today there is a sizable and well-seasoned group of actors who received their training under this Ford grant. These actors are trained in speech, voice, fencing, modern dance and period dance. Due to the Ford Foundation program, the Festival has developed a company of performers so accomplished in these essentials that it has elevated itself to the top-most ranks of repertory theatre and has established a reputation for productions of the highest professional calibre. Its actors have developed a Festival "style" that is both vigorous and exciting, and following its lead, classical repertory companies have now sprung up all over the country.

No history of the American Shakespeare Festival can be considered complete without a discussion of the origin and growth of the Annual Student Audience Season, one of the first such programs in the United States. Begun in 1959 with a three week season playing to 39,000 students, this invigorating adjunct to the Festival has increased in size and length until, in 1966, the professional repertory company played 15 weeks for 150,000 students from 11 states. The students pay a greatly reduced price for their tickets; the Festival subsidizes this substantial loss through the fund-raising efforts of the American Shakespeare Guilds.

People from all over the United States have come to view each seasons productions, to visit the costume museum and Elizabethan art collection, and to picnic at outdoor tables on the lawns facing the Housatonic River. Lawrence Langner's vision has become a reality; to date, the American Shakespeare Festival Theatre and Academy has brought Shakespeare to over two million Americans.

In the souvenir program for the 1960 season was an explanation of the stage design concept for the festival theatre.

81:2   The Festival Theatre at Stratford, Connecticut, was designed by its architect, Edwin Howard, as an elegant and graciously anonymous frame within which Shakespeare's repertory might be performed according to the best contemporary interpretations of the essential intentions of its author. From the initial conception of our American house, the aim was to treat the poet as a contemporary who, if we were responsible in our analysis of his intent, would reward liberal imaginative treatment.

Our playing-area and acting-space has enjoyed three large mutations in a logical development of six years. The use of a proscenium-curtain and prescribed back-of-the-curtain-line restrictions were abandoned at the outset. The renderings of Horace Armistead's *Julius Caesar,* the first play produced, show architecture of the classic orders extending well into the auditorium. When Rouben Ter-Arutunian assumed visual direction, a new concept of the festival stage was created with capacities of fluidity, spatial variety and chances for rapidly shifting playing-areas, on many surfaces.

The central travelling platforms, with their flanking companions, raked imper-

ceptibly into the floor-surface, gave chances for projected intimacy comparable to close-ups developing from long-shots in films. The addition of two lower small platforms or "trays" further precipitated action into the domain of the audience, while maintaining a stylistic frame which is intensely theatrical. Our production concepts which aimed at a certain breadth of scale and festive generosity were now more easily realized.

Ter-Arutunian first hung high curtains of pierced wooden slats, similar to Venetian blinds. This gave many possibilities for high and low angels of raking, diffused or reflective light. The great height of the stage-opening, almost a fifty-foot square, permitted a grandeur on the human scale.

Now, for the 1960 Festival season, Ter-Arutunian has abandoned the slats, while retaining the fluid action of high proscenium moving wagons and trays. His first stage was powerfully, even puritanically, rectilinear. His second is a curving, plastic continuum. Essentially, it is a sliced-through invisible dome, suggesting a complete atmospheric surround, with neither beginning nor end, composed of neither beginning nor end, composed of innumerable graduated light plastic shells, hung in a mosaic of interlocking petals, translucent, transparent and reflective, capable of many variations of illumination. Ter-Arutunian's cyclorama offers itself as continuous air, but one can still pierce any portion of it, both for light, or for the intrusion of specific forms of moving scenery.

It may be some time before this subtle instrument can yield its full capacity. Its sensitivity to light, its imperceptible suggestions of changing palettes, not alone of color but of dynamics of action in lightness and darkness, and in shifts suggesting emotional mood or physical weather, will gratefully respond to the poetic, technical and dramatic analyses of stage-directors.

81:2. Lincoln Kirstein, "Development of the Stage," in American Shakespeare Festival Theatre souvenir program, 1960.

81. American Shakespeare Festival Theatre, Stratford, Conn. Courtesy of American Shakespeare Festival Theatre.

81. Interior, American Shakespeare Festival Theatre. Stratford, Conn. Photograph by Gottschio-Schleisner. Courtesy of American Shakespeare Festival Theatre.

Brooks Atkinson, drama critic for the New York *Times,* wrote a critique of the new project:

81:3 After five years of fanatical single-mindedness, Lawrence Langner has opened his Shakespeare Festival Theatre at Stratford, Conn.—the third Stratford now dedicated to the Elizabethan tradition.

Many people of good will have assisted him. Thousands have also contributed generously toward the cost, already $750,000, possibly a million before everything is finished. But it has been Mr. Langner who has pressed forward relentlessly year by year in the face of all kinds of obstacles. When the theatre opened on Tuesday evening with a performance of "Julius Caesar," the audience spontaneously rose when Mr. Langner appeared on the stage and saluted him for enterprise, industry and vision.

The building is not yet finished and the grounds have not yet been landscaped. But enough has been completed to indicate that the Shakespeare Festival on the banks of the Housatonic is going to be handsome, original and practicable. It is not a replica of what scholars today imagine the Globe Theatre was on the Bankside in London three and a half centuries ago. But it is in the same general style. It looks festive. It is comfortable and inviting. Shakespeare's wooden "O" has a modern successor that deserves a long enjoyable life.

It is this department's duty, however, not to praise theatre buildings but to discuss the performances on the stages inside. Nothing about a theatrical building is so vital as the production. For reasons with which everyone can sympathize, Mr. Langner preferred to open this year amid all the confusions attendant upon so great an undertaking, instead of next year when the plant would be ready to use, and a producing organization would be

81:3. New York *Times,* July 27, 1955.

ready to stage a performance without distractions.

FIRST PERFORMANCE

Denis Cary, the director imported from the Bristol Old Vic in England, has been preparing the current "Julius Caesar" for several months. But the company was not able to use the Stratford stage until quite recently, and it had only one full-dress rehearsal before the opening performance. No wonder that the performance is routine and uneven. Although the cast included several celebrated actors, they do not play together beautifully; most of them speak verse indifferently, and they never get inside the play to the core of ideas and feeling that distinguish it from spectacle.

In the circumstances a poor opening-night performance was almost inevitable. But that is not so disturbing as a suspicion that even if this "Julius Caesar" were done well it would not be comparable to the kind of vibrant Shakespeare that has been done at the Old Vic in London this year or to the dynamic Shakespeare that Tyrone Guthrie has developed in a large tent at Stratford, Ont.

The current "Julius Caesar" is comparable to the kind of Shakespeare that is being done this season at Stratford-on-Avon in England. For the stage at the Shakespeare Memorial Theatre there is similar to the new one in Stratford, Conn. It invites scenery, stage pictures and all the apparatus of the old-fashioned Shakespeare producing.

PRODUCING STYLES

After being in existence for many years England's Stratford has developed first-rate directors like Anthony Quayle and Glen Byram Shaw. This year Laurence Olivier and Vivian Leigh are the stars in one company; John Gielgud and Peggy Ashcroft are the stars in another. In time it is possible that the Connecticut enterprise will train actors and directors of equivalent skill.

But today's comments express the opinions of one theatregoer who wonders whether the style of producing at the English Stratford is worth imitating. Although it has an honorable past and a decent present, it may not have a flourishing future. Donald Seale's approach to the two parts of "Henry IV" at the Old Vic last month is much earthier, and therefore, sounder Spakespeare. Although Mr. Guthrie's productions in Ontario are not ideal in all respects, they are never dull. There is a keen mind at work behind everything he stages. None of his productions looks like the remnants of the nineteenth century.

On the contrary, they look like a modern adaptation of late sixteenth or early seventeenth century producing. For the Ontario productions use an authentic apron stage brilliantly designed by Tanya Moiseiwitsch. Her stage has made it possible for the directors to eliminate all the claptrap that has been accumulating in Shakespeare producing for years.

As it happens, "Julius Caesar" opened on the Ontario stage last month, directed by Michael Langham. It is deficient in character analysis—the Brutus and the Caesar being no more profound than their Connecticut counterparts. But it has a point of view. It presents "Julius Caesar" as a tragedy of political revolution. Good or bad, it contains interesting scenes that flow swiftly and feverishly across an open stage.

The "apron stage" in Connecticut is only a wide forestage in front of the curtain line. And the Connecticut "Julius Caesar" is a variation of the kind of Shakespeare that has not had much success on Broadway for years. Like Dryden, two and a half centuries ago, it assumes that Shakespeare has to be made palatable to a "refined age"—loaded with college graduates.

For the last five years the mind of the American Shakespeare Theatre and Academy has been absorbed in the gigantic labor of money-raising and building. It has succeeded with that mission. Now it will have to grapple with the problems of producing. Shakespeare has to be produced creatively. He was not a genteel writer. He had an intellect and spirit and an instinct for headlong theatre. There is a lot more to "Julius Caesar" than the Connecticut company has brought into a splendid new theatre.

Selected Bibliography of American Playhouses, 1900-1971

In addition to the repositories listed in volume 1, the Wisconsin Centre for Theatre Research should be noted as having extensive primary source materials for research in twentieth-century theater. The Museum of the City of New York, the Library of Congress, the Research Library of the Performing Arts of the New York Public Library, and the Library of the University of California at Los Angeles all should be consulted by anyone doing research on American Playhouses from 1900 to 1972.

Newspapers that proved of great assistance are Atlanta: *Journal* and *Constitution*; Boston: *Christian Science Monitor*; Cincinnati: *Enquirer*; Houston: *Chronicle*; Iowa City: *Register*; Los Angeles: *Times* and *Citizen-News*; Minneapolis: *Tribune*; New Haven: *Evening Register*; New Orleans: *Item*; New York: *Dramatic Mirror, Herald-Tribune, Times*, and *Tribune*; Oklahoma City: *Daily Oklahoman*; Waco, Tex.: *News-Tribune*; Washington, D.C.: *Washington Post*.

Magazines with articles on specific playhouses were: *American Architect, American Magazine, Architectural Forum, Architectural Record, Arts and Decoration, Birmingham, Commonweal, Life, Nation, New Republic, Newsweek, Progressive Architecture, Saturday Review, Scientific American, Survey, Theatre Arts Monthly, Theatre Crafts, Time, Virginia Cavalcade.*

For a list of general works see the Selected Bibliography in volume 1. In addition to those books, the following works contain valuable information about twentieth-century American playhouses:

Beeson, William. *Thresholds; The Story of Nina Vance's Alley Theatre*. Houston: Alley Theatre, 1963.

Block, Anita. *The Changing World in Plays and Theatre*. Boston: Little, 1939.

Boyle, Walden. *Central and Flexible Staging*. Berkeley: Univ. of California Pr., 1955.

Burris-Meyer, Harold, and Cole, Edward C. *Theatres and Auditoriums*. New York: Reinhold, 1949.

Cheney, Sheldon. *The Arts Theatre*. New York: Knopf, 1925.

————. *New Movement in the Theatre*. New York: Kennerley Co., 1914.

————. *The Open Air Theatre*. New York: Kennerley Co., 1918.

Crowley, Alice Lewisohn. *The Neighborhood Playhouse: Leaves from a Theatre Scrapbook*. New York: Theatre Arts Books, 1959.

Deutsch, Helen, and Hanau, Stella. *The Provincetown: A Story of the Theatre*. New York: Farrar & Rinehart, 1931.

Eaton, Walter Prichard. *The American Stage of Today*. Boston: Small, Maynard, 1908.

———. *At the New Theatre and Others*. Boston: Small, Maynard, 1910.

Felheim, Marvin. *The Theatre of Augustin Daly*. Cambridge: Harvard Univ. Pr., 1956.

Geddes, Clarence. *Literature and Theatre of the States and Regions of the U.S.A.* Chapel Hill: Duke Univ. Pr., 1967.

Glaspell, Susan. *The Road to the Temple*. London: Ernest Benn Ltd., 1926.

Gorelik, Mordecai. *New Theatres for Old*. New York: French, 1940.

Grau, Robert. *The Stage in the Twentieth Century*. New York: Broadway Publishing Co., 1912.

Hughes, Glenn. *The Penthouse Theatre*. Seattle: Univ. of Washington Pr., 1950.

Isaacs, Edith J. R. *Architecture for the New Theatre*. New York: Theatre Arts Books, 1935.

Jones, Margo. *Theatre-in-the-Round*. New York: Rinehart & Co., 1951.

Joseph, Stephen. *New Theatre Forms*. New York: Theatre Arts Books, 1968.

———. *Theatre in the Round*. London: Barrie & Rockcliff, 1967.

Lewis, Emory. *Stages: The Fifty-Year Childhood of the American Theatre*. Englewood Cliffs: Prentice-Hall, 1969.

Lewisohn, Ludwig. *The Drama and the Stage*. New York: Harcourt, Brace, 1922.

McCleery, Albert, and Glick, Carl. *Curtains Going Up!* New York: Pitman, 1939.

Macgowan, Kenneth. *Footlights Across America*. New York: Harcourt, Brace, 1929.

———. *The Theatre of Tomorrow*. New York: Liveright, 1921.

MacKaye, Percy. *The Civic Theatre*. New York: Kennerley Co., 1912.

Morosco, Helen, and Dugger, Leonard Paul. *The Oracle of Broadway*. Caldwell, Idaho: Caxton, 1944.

Morris, Lloyd. *Curtain Time*. New York: Random, 1951.

Mullin, Donald C. *Development of the Playhouse: A Survey of Theatre Architecture from the Renaissance to the Present*. Berkeley: Univ. of California Pr., 1970.

Sexton, R. W. *American Theatres of Today*. 2 vols. New York: Architectural Book Publishing Co., 1930.

Sheean, Vincent. *Oscar Hammerstein I: The Life and Exploits of an Impresario*. New York: Simon & Schuster, 1956.

Simonson, Lee. *The Stage Is Set*. New York: Harcourt, Brace, 1932.

Skinner, Richard Dana. *Our Changing Theatre*. New York: Dial, 1931.

Stagg, Jerry. *The Brothers Shubert*. New York: Random, 1968.

Index of Theaters
Arranged Alphabetically

References are to entry, not page, numbers.

Index of Theaters
Arranged Geographically

References are to entry, not page, numbers.

ALABAMA. *Birmingham*: Birmingham-Southern College, 72.

CALIFORNIA. *Los Angeles*: Music Center of Los Angeles County, 55; University of California, L.A., 68; *Pasadena*: Pasadena Playhouse, 46; *San Diego*: Old Globe Theatre, 49.

COLORADO. *Denver*: Elitch's Gardens Theatre, 74.

CONNECTICUT. *New Haven*: Yale University, 63; *Stratford*: American Shakespeare Festival Theatre, 81; *Westport*: Westport Country Playhouse, 78.

DISTRICT OF COLUMBIA (*Washington*). Arena Stage, 52; John F. Kennedy Center for the Performing Arts, 60.

GEORGIA. *Atlanta*: Atlanta Memorial Arts Center, 58; Theatre Atlanta, 54.

ILLINOIS. *Chicago*: Goodman Memorial Theatre, 45; *Urbana*: Krannert Center for the Performing Arts, University of Illinois, 73.

IOWA. *Grinnell*: Grinnell College, 67; *Iowa City*: University of Iowa, 64.

LOUISIANA. *New Orleans*: Le Petit Théâtre du Vieux Carré, 44.

MAINE. *Ogunquit*: Ogunquit Playhouse, 80; *Skowhegan*: Lakewood Theatre, 75.

MASSACHUSETTS. *Cambridge*: Harvard University, 66; *Dennis*: Cape Playhouse, 77; *Provincetown*: Wharf Theatre, 76.

MINNESOTA. *Minneapolis*: Guthrie Theater, 53; *St. Paul*: Macalester College, 70.

MISSOURI. *St. Louis*: Loretto-Hilton Center, Webster College, 69.

NEW YORK. *New York*: Adelphi Theatre, 41; Adolph Phillipps Theatre, 17; Alvin Theatre, 39; Ambassador Theatre, 26; A.N.T.A. Playhouse, 30; Bandbox Theatre, 17; Belasco Theatre, 6; Bijou Theatre, 21; Billy Rose Theatre, 24; Biltmore Theatre, 32; Booth Theatre, 16; Brooks Atkinson Theatre, 33; Century Theatre, 8; Coronet Theatre, 31; Cort Theatre, 14; Craig Theatre, 41, Earl Carroll Theatre, 27; Erlanger Theatre, 38; Eugene O'Neill Theatre, 31; Folies Bergere, 12; Forrest Theatre, 31; Fulton Theatre, 12; Globe Theatre, 9; Guild Theatre, 30; Hammerstein Theatre, 40; Helen Hayes Theatre, 12; Henry Miller Theatre, 23; Hippodrome, 5; Hudson Theatre, 3; Imperial Theatre, 28; John Golden Theatre, 36; Lincoln Center for the Performing Arts, 43; Little Theatre, 13; Lunt-Fontanne Theatre, 9; Lyceum Theatre, 4; Majestic Theatre, 37; Mansfield Theatre, 33; Martin Beck Theatre, 29; Maxine Elliott Theatre, 7; Morosco Theatre, 20; Music Box Theatre, 25; National Theatre, 24; Neighborhood Playhouse, 18; New Amsterdam Theatre, 2; New Lyceum Theatre, 4; New Theatre, 8; Playhouse, 11;

Index of Personal Names and Theatrical Specialties

References are to entry, not page, numbers.